D0759005

"This wonderful addition to the field of leadership studies is scholarly without being pedantic. It is biblically based, yet relevant. It is replete with practical help for organizations of many kinds and sizes. Utilizing a variety of scholars, it is a book that brings together various visions into a common thread of helping good leaders become better, while helping solid organizations become even more effective. I recommend David Dockery's book *Christian Leadership Essentials* without hesitation."

Frank S. Page
President, Executive Committee of the Southern Baptist Convention

"*Christian Leadership Essentials* will be an invaluable tool for those who need to provide leadership with biblical conviction and creative vision. Rarely does one book on leadership combine such a variety of authors and collection of wealth from experience across diverse disciplines of leadership. This book should remain within arm's reach for all of us who serve by leading."

Mark L. Bailey
President, Dallas Theological Seminary

"I recommend *Christian Leadership Essetials* to anyone who is privileged to lead in ministry. The book's authors are dynamic Christian leaders and educators who have thought deeply and carefully about how to provide Christlike leadership for Christ-centered organizations. Their practical counsel is grounded in biblical truth, theological reflection, and spiritual discipline, and thus it will help anyone who wants to learn how to cultivate the gift of administration and manage for the glory of God."

Philip G. Ryken
President, Wheaton College

"Every leader of a Christian organization, including presidents of Christ-centered colleges and universities, knows that there is a deep well, somewhere, full of knowledge and wisdom to aid and enable the effective leadership, management, and stewardship of the institutions we serve so passionately. For many leaders, that important wisdom well is often frustratingly elusive and difficult to locate, much less to draw from. What David Dockery has done in this wonderful volume is not only to generously provide the well itself, easily accessible for all those who seek it, but also to find an unequalled collection of Christian leaders who masterfully draw out of the well the most quenching drinks of sage and salient experience and advice. Thirst no more!"

Beck A. Taylor
President, Whitworth University

David S. Dockery is the author or editor of 30 books. For the past 15 years he has served as president of Union University in Jackson, Tennessee.

CHRISTIAN LEADERSHIP ESSENTIALS

A HANDBOOK FOR MANAGING CHRISTIAN ORGANIZATIONS

DAVID S. DOCKERY

EDITOR

ACADEMIC
NASHVILLE, TENNESSEE

Christian Leadership Essentials:
A Handbook for Managing Christian Organizations

Copyright © 2011 by David S. Dockery

All rights reserved.

ISBN: 978-0-8054-6477-1

Published by B&H Publishing Group
Nashville, Tennessee

Dewey Decimal Classification: 303.3
Subject Heading: LEADERSHIP\MANAGEMENT

Printed in the United States of America
1 2 3 4 5 6 7 8 9 10 11 12 • 17 16 15 14 13 12 11
SB

CONTENTS

In Piam Memoriam

WITH GRATITUDE TO GOD
FOR THE LIFE, INFLUENCE, AND LEGACY
OF

Ted W. "Dr. Ted" Engstrom
(1916–2006)

LEADER OF LEADERS,
LEADER AMONG LEADERS,
AND
A FRIEND AND MENTOR TO MANY

PREFACE

*C*hristian Leadership Essentials is designed as a resource volume for leaders at various levels within Christian organizations of all types. While many of the contributors to this volume have invested the largest part of their leadership years in academic settings, they have also served churches, publishing houses, missions organizations, and other types of parachurch ministries. The contributors have served in senior leadership roles for a combined total of more than 350 years. The chapters reflect their thorough knowledge of the subject as well as their vast experiences. The contributors reflect many differences, including denominational diversity represented by Reformed, Wesleyan, Baptist, Pietistic, and nondenominational Evangelical backgrounds. They share in common a commitment to the importance of Christ-centered and church-focused ministry, whether represented in institutions, organizations, publishing houses, or other parachurch agencies.

I am often asked what a leader of a Christian organization does. The responsibilities are manifold, but I have attempted to identify the primary things one would need to understand to carry out a key leadership role in Christian organizations. It is impossible to put together a comprehensive volume that would still be manageable. We hope our focus has allowed us to approximate comprehensiveness while remaining reader friendly.

We hope the volume will serve current leaders, future leaders, and board members. Each of the contributors has been asked to focus on a key area that would help current and future leaders. While each chapter has a specified focus, inevitable overlap occurs from time to time. We have chosen to allow the overlap because we recognize that many people will choose not to read the book from beginning to end but to use the volume as a reference for reviewing various topics or for addressing particular issues.

I want to thank all of the contributors for their collaboration in this cooperative venture. I count it a genuine privilege to participate with them in this effort. I also want to thank Brad Waggoner, Jim Baird, Terry Wilder, and Dean Richardson at B&H for their invitation to put together such a volume and for their enthusiasm for the project.

I am genuinely thankful for the capable support provided for this volume by Melanie Rickman and Cindy Meredith. I also want to express my deep appreciation to and love for Lanese, who has joyfully provided encouragement through the processes of yet one more project. For 35 years she has been a blessing beyond description in and for my life.

This volume is dedicated to the life, legacy, and memory of Ted W. Engstrom (1916–2006). Many of the contributors to this volume were blessed to know and learn from "Dr. Ted." Engstrom served as president of World Vision and Youth for Christ. He was one of the most influential leaders in American Christianity for more than six decades. His books and articles on leadership and organization have shaped many who serve in leadership roles today. In addition to many of the contributors to this volume, Billy Graham, James Dobson, Chuck Colson, Leighton Ford, Bill Bright, and Jay Kesler, among others, have pointed to "Dr. Ted" as a significant mentor. I am privileged to have books and letters with his life verse, Psalm 32:8, accompanying his signature.

His influence through his writings, his service on dozens of boards, and his direct and indirect mentoring roles with many gave him a seemingly ubiquitous influence within American Christianity.

"Dr. Ted" was a leader of leaders and a leader among leaders. We offer this volume with gratitude for his vast influence and in doing so we say, "Thanks be to God." We also offer this book in loving memory of his years of service with the prayer that this volume might, in God's good providence, be used to shape a new generation of leaders who will be used of God to advance the gospel message and extend the work of God's kingdom.

Soli Deo Gloria
David S. Dockery

INTRODUCTION

David S. Dockery
President, Union University

C hristian organizations have a distinct identity and mission. They desire to evidence faithfulness to the Christ-centered message of the gospel. Faithfulness to the gospel and to institutional or organizational mission will not happen apart from the renewing power of God's Spirit and the development of godly and well-equipped leaders. From a human perspective the need of the hour is leadership, Spirit-enabled leadership. This book is about leadership, Christian leadership. It is also about organizations and the challenges involved in providing the leadership needed to guide these organizations.

W. Bennis says:

> Leadership is a word on everyone's lips. The young attack it and the old grow wistful for it. Parents have lost it and police seek it. Experts claim it and artists spurn it, while scholars want it. Philosophers reconcile it (as authority) with liberty and theologians demonstrate its compatibility with conscience. If bureaucrats pretend they have it, politicians wish they did. Everyone agrees that there is less of it than there used to be.[1]

The contributors to this volume are people who have significant experience in key administrative roles in Christian organizations and institutions. With over 350 years of combined experience with parachurch ministries, mission boards, publishing houses, Christian colleges and seminaries, these authors have joined together to share insights, observations, personal stories, and biblical principles regarding all aspects of organizational leadership.

Influence

Leadership provides significant opportunity for influencing organizations toward greater missional faithfulness and effectiveness. Leaders live with the motivation of William Carey, the father of modern missions, who in 1792 urged his fellow British Baptists to "expect great things from God; attempt great things for God." Christian leadership is founded upon the deep realities of the Great Commandment (Matt 22:37–39) and the Great Commission (Matt 28:18–20), with a focus on people more than programs. While most leaders tend to be driven people, genuine leadership operates more out of a sense of calling than drivenness.

Leaders take the lead, initiate ideas and plans, and move people to follow by showing them consideration and affirmation. Leaders seek to articulate a compelling vision with clarity. They know how to build teams that have a shared vision, shared life, shared goals, shared partnership, shared risks, and a shared future. Team members will follow leaders who identify with them, who give them responsibility and empower them to carry it out. Leaders learn to magnify their strengths and complement their weaknesses by the leadership team members who are invited to serve with them.

Grounded in the Truth; Marked by Vision

Leadership is not value neutral; it is grounded in the truth of God's revelation to us in Christ. While founded on the truth of God's Word, effective leadership recognizes the need to be culturally sensitive and contextually relevant. Leaders are marked by vision. Vision makes the difference between leadership and misleadership. Vision includes goals and strategies developed with team members. Vision dreams the most possible dream, not the impossible dream. Leaders recognize that vision gives direction while mission provides purpose. Vision should result in consensus but does not always develop by consensus. Leaders learn from the past, live in the present, and plan for the future.

Leaders are marked by loyalty, truth, fidelity, constancy, expectancy, and humility. They seek to exercise compassionate authority with emotional wisdom. In doing so, those in leadership work to accept people as they are and not necessarily as they would like them to be.

Though no leader reaches full maturity in any of these areas, they do make every effort to approach relationships and problems in terms of the present rather than the past. In doing so, they desire to trust others without being naïve, even when the risk seems great. While all leaders are encouraged by affirmation, they nevertheless seek to serve faithfully without constant approval and recognition from others. Future-directed leaders are always looking for ways to build better conditions for tomorrow.

Past, Present, and Future

Those who have the privilege and responsibility to lead recognize the need to be open to change as long as the changes help advance the overall mission and purpose of the organization. While learning from past failures, leaders remain open to taking well-informed risks as they envision the future. Leaders carefully strategize how to respond to an unexpected crisis or challenge. They respond and implement change through various means of communication, for they recognize that perceptions regarding change matter.

Different types of leaders are needed at various stages of an organization's history. At whatever stage that might be, leaders attempt to bring the best of the past and present together while exploring new opportunities for the future. In communicating opportunities for change and course correction, leaders recognize that what people hear is as important as what is said. A close connection exists between clarity of communication and clarity of purpose. Knowing *when* to communicate information in this regard is often as important as the content that is being communicated.

Leadership in the Context of Community

Leaders of small institutions, larger organizations, or global ministries recognize that the people they lead are a part of a community where people have a sense of belonging together and being linked together through emotional ties. The concept of family or community captures well the picture of these organizations. In such a place people believe they share purposeful work that promotes a shared "life together," if we may borrow a phrase from Dietrich Bonhoeffer. Leaders recognize that a calling to provide guidance for a Christian organization grounded in a Christ-centered mission is a distinctive type of leadership. The quest for the experience of community, family, and belonging needs to be the overarching vision. In this context a leader is characterized by skills and traits commonly associated with a team leader, pastor, coach, or teacher. The idea of covenant shapes these relationships. Leaders who fail to recognize the need for belonging among those who serve in a Christian institution or organization will likely face fragmentation among the constituency.

Challenges and times of controversy are inevitable in leadership roles. Understanding that these times of challenge are taking place within the context impacts the way leaders deal with controversies, finances, other constituencies, and particularly the governing board. Serving in the context of covenantal community influences not only how leaders relate to personnel but also how leaders manage their schedules and their personal and family responsibilities on a day-to-day basis. The recognition of the importance of serving in a context characterized by a sense of belonging will shape the expectation of a leader and will influence the leader's expectations of others.

Leaders as Educators and Mentors

Leaders are role models, examples to others, and teachers. Leaders have numerous responsibilities as indicated by the various chapters in this book. Leaders must focus on administration, fund-raising, and relationships with various constituencies, but finding ways even in these contexts to remind others of the importance of Christ's call on one's life, of serving others, and of advancing the Christ-centered mission of the organization must remain paramount. The pressures of leadership force one to deal with other things besides the main thing.

Leaders understand that teaching or mentoring can take place when bringing reports to boards about issues facing the organization. It can take place when communicating with personnel regarding issues impacting the constituency, the denomination with whom the organization is affiliated, or when dealing with local or regional matters.

Leaders must maintain at least an overview-type understanding of social and cultural issues. Engaging with these important issues of our day requires habits of reading and learning. Someone has well said that "leaders are readers and readers are leaders."

The role of the leader involves shaping the ethos of the organization through one's vision about the nature, purpose, identity, and mission of the organization. The pattern for most leaders in the twenty-first century, or so it seems to most, is to spend more time with matters of administration and external constituencies. If that is the case, leaders must be intentional about recognizing that the articulation of the vision and the shaping of ethos for the organization rank among the most important tasks of leaders and ones to which they must give high priority.

Leaders as Administrators

The attempts to create efficiency and order, following the patterns of corporate America, have greatly influenced the role of leaders in Christian organizations. More and more the leadership literature reflects these realities. Yet, while the corporate administrative model is vitally important, it is insufficient as a stand-alone leadership model. In addition to team leader, pastor, coach, mentor, and educator, leaders must function as entrepreneurs, mediators, managers, catalysts, politicians, final arbiter, and judge.

While the community/family model takes priority in the leadership of Christian organizations, these organizations also have legal and ethical responsibilities as well as contractual obligations. Leaders, therefore, function with administrative authority and must assume the unending responsibilities related to these twenty-first century realities.

Leaders must live with the realities of competing demands and expectations, learning to serve faithfully in the tension that characterizes these different worlds. Such an acknowledgment requires leaders to embrace an organizational and structural approach that will enable the ministry to be effectively managed. Governing boards expect administrative competence from leaders while organizational staff and personnel are most often looking for someone to envision a preferred future for the organization while sensitively serving in a people-focused way each and every day.

Leaders as Servants

These tensions can only be carried out and held together as leaders recognize that their calling to lead is a calling to serve. Leaders are called to define vision, set priorities, and accept responsibility. They are called to make decisions based on both qualitative information (insights regarding the thoughts and actions of people, the intensity of feelings, the breadth of understanding, and depth of importance) and quantitative information (numbers/statistics/data for careful planning). Decision making based alone on quantitative information is inadequate. Servant leaders seek to make decisions that are also informed by people's thoughts and feelings. Ultimately leadership is carried out in behalf of people for the glory of God. Christian leaders will seek to emulate Jesus Christ Himself who came "not to be served but to serve, and to give his life as a ransom for many" (Mark 10:45 ESV).

Contributors to this book carry out their leadership roles and responsibilities differently. They have served in a variety of contexts. They have distinctive gifts and strengths. The chapters reflect these differences while evidencing core commitments to Christ-centered servant leadership. We offer this volume as a team of leaders who pray that God will use our work to influence the next generation for good. We dream of a new generation of leaders committed to the Great Commandment and the Great Commission, who hope to extend the kingdom of God through God-glorifying Christian organizations. We pray that this work, *Christian Leadership Essentials*, will be an instrument of grace and a tool for good in the lives of many for years and years to come.

Resources for Further Study

Barton, Ruth Hailey. *Strengthening the Soul of Your Leadership.* Downers Grove: InterVarsity, 2000.
Bennis, Warren, and Burt Nanus. *Leaders.* New York: Harper and Row, 1985.
Blanchard, Ken. *Leading at a Higher Level.* Upper Saddle River, NJ: Prentice Hall, 2007.
Blanchard, Ken, and Phil Hodges. *Lead like Jesus.* Nashville: Thomas Nelson, 2005.
_____. *The Servant Leader.* Nashville: Thomas Nelson, 2003.
Cordeiro, Wayne. *Leading on Empty.* Minneapolis: Bethany, 2009.
De Pree, Max. *Called to Serve.* Grand Rapids: Eerdmans, 2001.
Dyer, Charles. *Character Counts.* Chicago: Moody, 2010.
Emis, Leroy. *Be the Leader You Were Meant to Be.* Wheaton: Victor, 1975.
Engstrom, Ted. *The Making of a Christian Leader.* Grand Rapids: Zondervan, 1976.
Ford, Leighton, *Transforming Leadership.* Downers Grove: InterVarsity, 1991.
George, Bill. *Authentic Leadership.* San Francisco: Jossey-Bass, 2003.
Iorg, Jeff. *The Character of Leadership.* Nashville: B&H, 2007.
Marcuson, Margaret J. *Leaders Who Last.* New York: Seaburg, 2009.
Munger, Robert. *Leading from the Heart.* Downers Grove: InterVarsity, 1995.
Pollard, William. *The Soul of the Firm.* New York: Harper, 1996.
Stott, John. *Basic Christian Leadership.* Downers Grove: InterVarsity, 2002.
Zigarelli, Michael. *Ordinary People. Extraordinary People.* Gainesville, FL: Synergy, 2002.

Questions for Further Reflection

1. What is leadership? What does it mean to actually lead an institution or organization?

2. Since leaders must function in a variety of roles, how can they increase their capacity to influence both their vision and execution in areas where they are weak *and* where they are strong?

3. Is leading a Christian organization different than leading another type of institution or organization? If so, why? How?

Endnote

[1] W. Bennis and B. Nanus, *Leaders* (New York: Harper and Row, 1985), 1.

Chapter 1

A BIBLICAL MODEL
OF LEADERSHIP

Robert B. Sloan
President, Houston Baptist University

This chapter would better be entitled *"Toward a Biblical Model of Leadership"*; that is, I want to suggest what I believe to be the most important elements and *considerations* of a biblical model of leadership, but I do not claim either to be exhaustive in my presentation or to have correlated theologically all of the ramifications of these proposals. In fact, it is probably impossible to set forth *in writing* a comprehensive biblical model of leadership since by its nature, and as indicated by Scripture's use of the idea of *wisdom*, biblical leadership is something that not only is read about but also is learned through experience. Nonetheless, ideas about leadership are important, and therefore I will suggest some of the most important of these for a biblical model.

First we must be clear about what we mean by *leadership*. Leadership is the art and practice of exerting an influence on the behavior and beliefs of others. Leaders shape and influence people, institutions, and events. Leaders and leadership are determined not by the number of followers but by the changes effected over time for the good of God's world. Clearly we are talking about changes for the good. Some leaders whose ideas and deeds were decidedly on the side of evil have effected enormous change in

8

human history; Hitler and Stalin in the last century come immediately to mind. They attracted followers, but the evidence is clear that their motives, ways, and ends were evil.

With reference to leaders and leadership, we must not shy away from the word *power*. By definition leaders exert various kinds of power, or else they would have no influence on others or lack the ability to effect change in the world. Though the word *power* often has a negative connotation, the *stewardship* of power and influence—a softer form of power—marks the nature of leadership. Like money and fire, power is capable of producing change, but it is the *nature* of that change—here change involves the full spectrum of motives, means, and ends—that determines the good use of power. Power may come from the sheer force of one's position, from physical strength and/or the ability to marshal the strength of others, and also from ideas, persuasion, and example. Those with power by virtue of the force of their position are often in political or corporate jobs where money, executive authority, and military might are at their disposal. The power of ideas, persuasion, and example is often associated with individuals like Rosa Parks, Mother Teresa, or Saint Augustine. All of these means of power—whether from position, example, or ideas—can be good or evil. Again, the *ways* they are used, the animating motivations and the nature and limits applied to each means, and the *ends* to which these ways are used determine the moral character, whether good or evil, of such uses of power. Christian leaders, and all leaders who follow biblical patterns, exercise their power to the greatest extent possible in ways and for ends consistent with all things good, honorable, and according to the will of God.

We must therefore begin with the ways and character of God. The ultimate leader is, of course, the living God, since His power, will, and character ultimately create, shape, hold together, and influence all things. A biblical view of leadership must begin with God. Human leadership, if it is good leadership, is analogous to the ways and motivations of God's ultimate acts of influence.

God has, however, created human beings as His agents in the world. We are made in the image of God, and at each place in Genesis 1 where the image of God is referenced, the idea of dominion or responsibility for human creatures is close at hand (1:26–28). There are many debates about what the image of God in Scripture may consist of, but at the very least it relates to the *responsibilities* that God has given men and women, the highest creatures in the creation—Adam was, after all, given the responsibility for naming the animals—in caring for, superintending, cultivating, and thus managing His creation. Humans have been given the greatest role of leadership with respect to the created order, and it is a functional responsibility directly connected to their being made in God's image.

The importance of the image of God (*imago dei*) for a biblical model of leadership goes even deeper than the fact that the human creatures, men and women, have been made *in* God's image. Scripture goes on to say that Christ is the image of God (Col 1:15). Put another way, Christ is not *made* in the image of God as Adam and Eve were. Rather, He *is* the image of God. Thus, in the fullness of New Testament theology, the first humans were made according to Christ, the Son of God. Christ, who is God's agent in creation, who is the one who sustains creation, and is the one to whom all of the created order and all of human history are directed (John 1:1–4; Eph 1:3–10; Col 1:15–20; cf. also Hebrews 1:1–3), is the one after whose likeness men and women are made. Thus, the responsibility for stewarding and managing God's creation—the significant leadership role that we as humans have been given—is accentuated because of the centrality and lordship of Jesus Christ in all things, whether we think of creation or whether we think of His distinctive role, by His death and resurrection, in salvation.

A biblical model of leadership that begins with God must therefore find its behavioral and convictional patterns in Christ the Lord. He is the distinctive, supreme presence and revelation of God in human history. Again, the one true Creator God, the God who has spoken through Israel and the prophets, the God who reveals Himself in Scripture and in history, has definitively spoken and revealed Himself through Jesus, who, as the image of God and the superintending Lord of the universe, is the clearest model and declaration for how God acts and how He uses His power.

As Lord He acts with purpose, including ends; and for His desired ends He is constrained by His nature (for example, God cannot lie: Num 23:19; 1 Sam 15:29; Ps 89:35; Ezek 24:14; 2 Tim 2:13; Titus 1:2; Heb 6:17–18). With Him there is thus no moral fragmentation between ends and means. To act as He acts is to lead, to use power, as He uses it. To be sure, we are not God, but we have been given by God—again, we are made in the image of God—responsibilities over His created order. We cannot, as He did, create from nothing; but we are put in charge of that which He has created; and we are to tend it, cultivate it, manage it, and shape it in ways that reflect and honor His original purposes for creation. To understand the responsibility, therefore, that we, as creatures made in His image, have been given, we must look to the one who *is* that very image and see what He has done to fulfill the will of His Father. The Son Himself has been given great responsibilities by the Father, and one day the Son Himself will bow before His Father when the tasks given to Him have been fully completed (1 Cor 15:28). To God's Son we turn.

Looking at Christ

Leadership theory is accustomed to thinking of mission, vision, and strategies. The New Testament does not organize itself or the life of Christ around such categories, but it is nonetheless not difficult to see that Jesus clearly understood Himself to have an assigned mission from His Father. We can, therefore—knowing that Jesus acted to perform the overarching work given Him by His Father—also look at the behavior of Jesus as indicating, though perhaps with different orders of magnitude, the various tactics and strategies He employed for accomplishing the will of His Father.

Before looking at the habits and teachings of Jesus, we must note that, first of all, it is clear from the Gospels that Jesus understood and presented Himself as having a mission. In John, He repeatedly uses phrases like "I am come . . ." (cf. 5:43; 6:38; 7:28; 8:14,42; 12:46–47; 13:3; 15:22; 16:28; 18:37). These passages, and many others, point to the larger mission of Jesus as received from His Father. In John, He also says that He does what the Father does or wills (cf. 4:34; 5:19,30; 5:36; 8:28–29; 10:25,37–38), or He speaks what the Father wills Him to speak (cf. 7:17; 8:26,28,38; 12:49–50; 14:10). The Gospel of Luke, as well, points to the larger mission of Jesus. In Luke 4:16–30, Jesus is the long-awaited Servant of the Lord predicted in Isaiah 61 who announces "the favorable year of the LORD" (v. 19 NASB), fulfills the long-awaited promises of God, and inaugurates the end of the world. In the conclusion to that Gospel, when speaking to the two on the road to Emmaus and also shortly thereafter to His gathered disciples in the upper room, Jesus uses Scripture to tell them of the divinely ordained purpose of His mission, that everything He did was in fulfillment of the scriptural plan of God, and that it was not accidental but in fact *necessary* "that the Christ would suffer" (24:25–27,44–47) and that as a consequence "repentance for forgiveness of sins would be proclaimed in His name to all the nations" (24:47 NASB).

The narrative presentation and theological comments of the Gospel authors likewise frame the mission of Jesus as being according to the intention of God. The Gospel of Matthew, for example, points to the comprehensive plan of God for human history through Jesus. The genealogy, which goes from Abraham to David, from David to the deportation, and from the deportation to Jesus, has three series of 14 generations (1:17). The point for Matthew is that God is in control of human history and that Jesus is the fulfillment of Jewish history, a history that ultimately involves not just Jews but also Gentiles (28:19–20). The birth of Jesus in Luke 2:10 causes the angels to sing of the good news which shall be for *all people.* The Gospels—though they include many particular incidents, scenes, and sayings of Jesus—never lose sight of their overarching message: specifically, that Jesus, according to the eternal plan of God, is the Son of God who has come from heaven for our salvation. He is mysteriously and supernaturally conceived; His story is the fulfillment of all of Jewish history; and beyond that, His genealogy (see Luke 3:23–38) extends all the way to Adam, the father of us all. But beyond Adam, we are reminded, Jesus was the Word of God present at creation. He is the one through whom all things were created, and this Word ultimately became flesh and dwelt among us (John 1:14), so that we might have now the life of the age to come (John 5:24–25; 10:10; 11:25–27).

It is not just in the Gospels that Jesus as the fulfillment of God's larger plan for human history is seen. In Romans 5, Jesus is the one who reverses the dismal story of Adam and by His obedience initiates in the midst of the old and fallen creation the new creation for which He is the second Adam. Colossians 1:15–20 refers to Him as Lord of both the old and the new orders. He is preeminent for both the original creation and for the new creation that has now begun. In Heb 10:1–10, Jewish Scripture is used to point to the work of Jesus, and the life and work of Jesus are summarized by the single phrase, "I have come . . . to do your will, O God" (Heb 10:7–9 NASB). Similarly, in Revelation, Jesus is described as both the beginning and the end, the ultimate steward of life and death and the firstborn of God's creation (1:5,17).

Whether in the sayings of Jesus, in the narrative and editorial comments of the Gospel writers, or embedded within the letters and other literature of the New Testament, the overarching thesis is clear: Jesus was sent by God to restore, reconcile, and recreate God's original creation. He did so by being obedient to the will of the Father in all things, an obedience that led inexorably and predictably to His death (Phil 2:8). The New Testament thus also contemplates a conclusion to Jesus' cosmic mission, a deep and final mystery, that after the return of Jesus, in His final work of raising all the dead who are loyal to Him, transforming all the living who embrace Him, judging all those who have rejected Him, and inaugurating the new heaven and the new earth, He will finally Himself bow before the Father, having completed all the purposes given Him by the Father, in full and complete obedience (1 Cor 15:22–28). Since, therefore, the convictions and behaviors of Jesus reflect His obedience to the will of God and His devotion to the mission His Father gave Him, we must now look at the *actions* and *words* of Jesus in broad categories to see how, whether strategically or tactically, they reflect His intention to implement the overarching mission of God.

The Behaviors and Attributes of the Lord Christ

Our goal in this section is to provide brief summary statements of the kinds of things Jesus taught and did, supplying scriptural references. The goal is not to work out the managerial implications of these various summary statements but to provide a series of brief statements that reflect on Jesus' typical actions and thus to hint at those implications. Leadership and even managerial theories that derive from these can best be constructed when all of these are seen together. For now we are interested in considerations *toward* a biblical model of leadership.

Jesus Spoke Knowledgeably

From the beginning of His ministry, the crowds were amazed at Jesus' theological assertions. In the Nazareth sermon (Mark 6:1–6; Luke 4:16–30), His hearers were amazed that one from their own hometown could speak with such authority and boldness as an interpreter of Scripture. The same is true in the Gospel of Matthew at the conclusion of the Sermon on the Mount (7:28–29). The crowds were amazed that He spoke to them as one possessing authority, not as their scribes and teachers. These statements are reflections of Jesus' repeated actions and declarations to have either fulfilled the Scriptures (cf. Matt 5:17–18; 11:5; 21:1–11; 21:33–46; Luke 4:21) or of His public pronouncements whereby He starkly reinterpreted the Scriptures. The Sermon on the Mount has several of these where Jesus, after citing an Old Testament text and the traditional interpretations applied to it by Jewish rabbis, said, "You have heard that it was said of old, but I say to you . . ." (Matt 5:21,27,33,38). Such assertions—to have fulfilled the Scriptures or to have reinterpreted virtually the whole of Jewish cultic law (Matt 9:10–19; 12:1–8; 15:1–20; John 2:19–22)—show Jesus to have been a knowledgeable thinker. Christian circles rightly refer to the *events* of Jesus' life, especially His death and resurrection, as the center of the gospel message and the events that deliver the accursed creation and its peoples from the consequences of sin. Nonetheless, it must not be forgotten that Jesus was a thoroughgoing *interpreter of Scripture* who first criticized and then reformulated Israel's role and mission, its cultic system, and its understanding of the temple and the role of the Messiah.

Jesus knew, based on His reading of the Law, the Prophets, and the Psalms (Luke 24:25–32,44–47), that the Scriptures had been profoundly misunderstood by Israel and that it was of paramount importance for His followers to understand not only how rightly to interpret the Scriptures but also how *He* interpreted the Scriptures, especially as they found their fulfillment in Him. All of subsequent Christian thinking with regard to the sacrificial system, the temple, the nature of the Messiah, the character of God, the work of the Holy Spirit, the nature and mission of the church, the judgment of the end times, the resurrection of the dead, the coming of the Son of Man in glory, and God's final purposes for Israel, the nations, and creation found its corrective formulation and theologically foundational reinterpretation in the thinking and teaching of Jesus, *both* in His words and in His actions, not omitting, of course, His death and resurrection. Jesus the theologian, Jesus the preacher, Jesus the teacher and interpreter of Scripture radically altered the established Jewish understandings of religious life and formed the underpinnings of later New Testament and Christian theology.

There is no substitute for leaders whose *knowledge* of life, reality, their business, work, and the facts related thereto drives their behavior and decisions.

Jesus Was a Teacher Who Gathered around Himself Concentric Circles of Learners

Whether it was (1) Peter and John (cf. Acts 3:1), or (2) Peter, James, and John (Matt 17:1), or (3) Peter and Andrew, James and John (Matt 4:18–22; cf. 10:2), or (4) the Twelve (Luke 6:12–16), (5) the 120 (Acts 1:15), (6) the 500 (1 Cor 15:6), or (7) the multitudes (Matt 5:1), Jesus had different levels of audiences with whom He could share His thinking and convictions. The Twelve, of course, were in most instances His most intimate circle, but He also had various groups around Him, as, for example, on the Mount of Transfiguration, He had with Him Peter, James, and John (Matt 17:1), and on other occasions He had with Him a group of financial supporters called the "women from Galilee" (Luke 8:1).

Jesus taught regularly, had different circles of hearers and constituents, and used the opportunities available to Him to teach and to instruct. Leaders know their various audiences and can appropriately relate to them.

Jesus Corrected Clearly, Quickly, and Impartially

Coming down from the Mountain of Transfiguration, Jesus spoke with great frustration to the disciples there who could not heal a boy of his falling sickness (Matt 17:17). On other occasions Jesus showed surprise and sometimes an amazed irritation at the dullness of the disciples in their inability to understand His metaphors and His ways of speaking (Matt 16:5–12; John 11:11–14). Jesus honored sincere seeking (Matt 8:5–11; Mark 9:24) but was not reluctant to criticize dullness (Mark 9:19) and to correct either bad thinking, as in Peter's completely erroneous view of Jesus' messiahship and mission (Matt 16: 21–23), or petty jealousies (Mark 10:41; Luke 22:24–27).

Jesus was not afraid to offer *public* critiques of *public* figures. The woes by Jesus in the marketplace and in the temple area upon the scribes and Pharisees are remarkable for their biting quality and for the accuracy of their prophetic critique. The religious leaders who should have nurtured and fed Israel with the Word of God were publicly blistered by Jesus both in tone and in rhetoric for their hypocrisies and failures as leaders (Matt 15:12; 21:44; 23; Luke 11:45–46). But not only religious leaders felt the sting of Jesus' verbal attacks: His earthly sovereign, Herod, was also the object of a sharp critique. When Jesus detected Herod's hypocritical motives for seeking Him, He sent a message back to "that fox" that He (Jesus) would do the will of God how and when He discerned *God's* purposes in doing it (Luke 13:31–35 NASB).

Jesus, unlike many leaders in public life today, was not afraid to criticize either His friends or His enemies and to do so in a way that made clear that He neither sought their approval nor feared their reprisal. His remarks give no evidence of being politically diplomatic merely for the sake of sparing others' feelings. Jesus had a wide range of religious, economic, and political associates, and He had a reputation of deferring to no one (Mark 12:14). Though it is commonly thought that Jesus spent time only with the poor and the outcast, which He certainly did and for which He was roundly criticized by the elite, He nonetheless also numbered both wealthy and prominent people among His friends and associates (Nicodemus, John 3:1; Lazarus, John 11; the women from Galilee, Luke 8:1–3; and Joseph of Arimathea, Luke 23:50). His blessings and His instructions were for all, and He was not above scolding even His closest friends when they chose trivial priorities over the priority of listening to Him (Luke 10:38–42).

Jesus the Teacher Used Both Public and Common Settings for His Teachings

The Gospel of John orients the activities and teachings of Jesus around the great festivals in Jerusalem. There we see that Jesus was present for the Feast of Booths and especially the Passover. On these occasions the ceremonies involving light and water became great opportunities for His public teachings (John 7–8). He frequented the marketplaces and the great porches of the temple for opportunities to teach; and He amazed the crowds, criticized the powerful and hypocritical, expelled the business leaders from the temple while upsetting their money-changing tables, and took on all questions, whether of good faith (Mark 12:28–34) or bad (Matt 22:15–33).

Jesus also particularly used everyday settings, especially meals, as a format for teaching. He enjoyed eating and drinking with friends as well as with religious outcasts (Matt 4:24; 9:9–11; Luke 19:1–10). At a meal He could forgive the downcast (Luke 7:36–50) as well as stifle the religious exuberance of His shallow supporters (Luke 14:15–24). For the biblical leader every circumstance and setting, large or small, constitutes a teachable moment and should be so seized and understood.

Jesus Had a Strong Devotional Life

His public experiences of stress and controversy in the temple, the marketplace, and at the great festivals did not prevent Him from a rich life of private prayer. Though we do not have biblical narratives that refer explicitly to Jesus' study of the Scriptures, from the time of His youth, when at the age of 12 He was discussing with the theologians in the temple the "concerns of his Father" (Luke 2:46–49), to the times in His public ministry when He profoundly and repeatedly expounded and reinterpreted the Scriptures (Matt 7:28–29; 13:54; Luke 4:16–30), Jesus had a rich life of prayer and study. We know that He often went off by Himself to pray (Luke 5:16; 6:12; 9:18,28) and that He commended prayer to His disciples (Matt 6:5–13). So touched were they by His life of prayer that they asked Him to teach them to pray (Luke 11:1). He warned against showy public prayer (Matt 6:5–6), but He did in fact pray in public (Matt 11:25–27; John 12:27–30). His life of devotion is referenced throughout the Gospels (recall especially His 40-day period in the wilderness and the temptations by Satan, Matt 4:1–11), but it is most profoundly expressed in His pervasive conviction that all of life must be lived according to the will of God (Matt 6:32–33) and that nothing is so trivial as to be unnoticed by

God (Matt 10:29) or so obscure as to be unimportant for God's purposes (Matt 6:32; 10:30).

His tortured dying on the cross gives every evidence that His instinctive vocabulary and frame of mind were directed toward the things of God. He prayed the words of Scripture, "My God, my God, why have you forsaken me?" (Ps 22). He prayed for forgiveness for His torturers (Luke 23:34), and He cared for His mother by committing her to the care of the beloved disciple (John 19:26–27). He paid attention to the agony of the penitent thief by promising him that he would soon be in paradise (Luke 23:39–44), and He interpreted all of His life and particularly His obedient dying as a fulfillment of the mission given him by God ("It is finished!" John 19:30 NASB) and prayed from the hymnbook of Israel with His final breaths (Luke 23:46). Such prayers and spontaneous uses of Scripture indicate a life saturated with prayerful, reflective, and intentional interactions with God as revealed in Holy Writ.

Jesus Had a Shrewdness that He Practiced and Commended

The Jesus of the older Hollywood films, the Jesus who walked about almost passively, staring into the mid-heavens, was not the Jesus of the Gospels. In the Gospels, He told His disciples to be as shrewd as serpents but as harmless as doves (Matt 10:16), and He followed His own advice. When taunted by His brothers, who thought Him insane, to go to Jerusalem and "show Yourself to the world," Jesus refused. Nonetheless, He did go up secretly, though not for the purposes they intended (John 7:1–10 NASB). He commended in one of His parables a shrewd steward and told His disciples that they, too, should "make friends . . . by means of the wealth of unrighteousness" (Luke 16:1–9 NASB). He showed shrewdness in *timing*, in the strategic unfolding of His heavenly identity. Jesus repeatedly evidenced His awareness of the importance of "the hour" of His disclosure as Messiah, thereby wisely and strategically doing the will of God (cf. John 2:4; 7:6,8,30; 8:20; 12:23; 13:1,31). When the crowds or even individuals misunderstood the kind of Messiah He was and thus wanted to speak quickly of His messiahship, He severely warned them to hold their tongues (Matt 8:1–4; 9:27–31; 12:15–21). After commending Peter for the Caesarea Philippi confession that He is "the Christ, the Son of the living God," Jesus told His disciples that His messiahship necessitated His rejection, suffering, and resurrection; but He severely warned them to tell no one (Matt 16:16,20–21 NASB). His disciples did not understand, and Peter even chided Jesus for speaking of a suffering messiahship, but the rebuke was turned back on Peter, whose voice was described, rather undiplomatically, as that of Satan (Matt 16:21–23). The timing of His ministry and particularly of His death was critical. He had work to do, teaching to spread, and a gathering of His disciples to accomplish before His mission could be consummated in His death and resurrection, and so He lived with shrewdness. He never spoke for the purpose of deception, but neither did He always tell everything He knew (recall the story of Nicodemus, who could not understand heavenly things, John 3:1–12).

An honest shrewdness is a gift to be sought and cultivated by today's leaders.

Jesus Commended God-Honoring Risk Taking

In the cause of His Father's kingdom, the Parable of the Talents continued a well-known teaching by Jesus that His followers were expected to live with a sense of urgency in light of a coming day of reckoning and that they must accept the responsibilities given them and, unlike the "worthless servant," be faithful for the cause of Christ (Luke 19:11–27). Jesus Himself knew that obedience to the Father would require His own suffering and death. He had to reject the temptations of Satan to take the path of plenty, fame, or self-protection (Matt 4:1–11; Luke 4:1–13) and instead, as He told His disciples, drink the cup He was chosen to drink, undergo the baptism He was sent to endure (Mark 10:35–45), and thus precipitate the beginning of the world's end as He "cast fire upon the earth" (Luke 12:49–53 NASB).

Jesus's all-consuming commitment to the will of His Father (Luke 2:49; John 2:13–17) was borne irrespective of the consequences for Himself. Such faithfulness meant that He was willing to put everything on the line to accomplish what the Father sent Him to do. This faithfulness is seen also in the lives of some of His greatest New Testament followers who, like Paul, counted all things to be loss in view of the unsurpassed gain of knowing Jesus, the Lord (Phil 3:8). As Paul wrote, Jesus' obedience to the will of the Father was accomplished at a great cost, not only death but a tortured death by Roman crucifixion (Phil 2:8). Such self-sacrificing behavior by Jesus was also what He expected of His followers, to whom He said that they must be willing to give up all—money, family, homes, and possessions—to follow Him (Matt 19:21–30). They, as He, had to take up the cross (Matt 10:38; 16:24–26).

Leadership must always be willing to take a path of resistance, rejecting the plaudits of the cultural elites and accepting the slurs of the majority for the sake of doing what is right, whether popular or not. A leader does not have the luxury of refusing to choose or testing the winds. The leader leads in spite of the whims and fickle chants of the crowd.

Jesus Had an Uncompromising View of the Provisional Nature of Possessions

The Sermon on the Mount represents much of the teaching of Jesus that His disciples were to learn, teach, and live out. The treasures of earth can be eaten by moths and rust or stolen by thieves (Matt 6:19). The only ultimate values are those that have an honorable motivation and ultimately a heavenly destination. For Jesus there is a continuity between this life and the life to come, and that continuity is seen in those ultimate goods and good things that have their roots in this life but are laid up in heaven (Matt 6:19–34). Paul, too, believed that all things committed to Christ and done in faith are things that are not "in vain" and thus have an ongoing power and value (1 Cor 15:58 NASB). The world is good—it was made by God—but it is now, because of the great rebellion and universal human complicity in that rebellion, deeply flawed. Even the good things of this world—food, shelter, and ornate clothing—are secondary (Matt 6:25–34) and can have a perverting tendency on those who hold them as being too dear. Whether family, fortune, goods, or power, Jesus understood and taught and lived the true view of these things—that is, the provisional and qualified nature of them. Quarterly earnings and the rush to give the kind of guidance that protects stock values and bonuses are a short-term substitute for the long-term stewardship of a business or a life that belongs to God. Decisions whose sole criterion is financial gain or self-promotion are likely to be gravely flawed.

Jesus Had a Strong View of Family and Marriage, Based on Genesis 1–2

Jesus was known for His rejection not only of adultery, which every honorable Jew would have rejected, but also for His critique of the commonplace practice, even among Pharisees, of divorce. Jesus regarded adultery as something that started in the heart (Matt 5:27–28) but was also expressed in the behavior of serial marriages and divorces. Those who divorce except for the cause of impurity and marry another not only commit adultery but also cause those who marry them to commit adultery, according to Jesus (Matt 5:31–32; 19:3–6). So startled were the Pharisees at such teaching that they defensively pointed to the command of Moses that they should put away their foreign wives (Matt 19:7), to which Jesus responded sharply, "It was not so from the beginning, but Moses permitted you to put away your wives because of your hardness of heart" (Matt 19:8). Jesus's appeal to the time *"from the beginning"* indicates that God's original plans were revealed in Scripture in the story of Adam and Eve (see Gen 1:27; 2:24) as involving one man and one woman.

His strict teachings on the sanctity of marriage were preserved, reiterated, and also applied in the new circumstances of the church, where Christian and non-Christian were married and had children (1 Cor 7:12–16). Though the natural bonds of family could never take precedence over the claims of the kingdom of God, where the two come in conflict, the foundational nature of Genesis 1–2 for Jesus' understanding of marriage, remarriage, divorce, and adultery is clear: one man and one woman is the basis of marriage. There is to be no divorce except where sexual infidelity has already broken the bonds of marriage (Matt 5:32) or where an *unbelieving* spouse voluntarily leaves (1 Cor 7:15). Remarriage is permitted only when the unbelieving spouse has left or death takes the husband or the wife. If two Christians separate, they must either be reconciled or remain unmarried (1 Cor 7:10–11).

Jesus honored marriage and the family by His presence at the wedding feast in Cana of Galilee, the site of His first miracle (John 2:1–11), by His promise that in the kingdom of God the blessings of family would be multiplied (Matt 12:46–50; Mark 10:28–31), by His care for His mother from the cross (John 19:26–27), and by His and the early church's continued use of the language of family to describe the relationship between Jesus and the God of Israel (He is, as the disciples learned from Jesus, "Abba," Father; Matt 26:39,42: Rom 8:15). The early Christians continued the verbal and conceptual habits of Jesus by describing the whole complex of relations between and among Christians as that of children, brothers, and sisters (Gal 4:21–31). Christian leaders, by example, policy, and practice, affirm marriage as between one man and one woman and support the family as a natural and spiritual unit established by God.

Jesus Profoundly Honored the Truth Both in Living and in Speaking

Jesus' description of Satan as the father of lies (John 8:44) and of Himself as the true and faithful expression of the will of the Father (John 8:38, 46–4) places enormous premium for the followers of Jesus on the truth, whether in speaking or in learning. The gospel in the New Testament is referred to as the word of truth (Col 1:5; cf. Rom 2:8; 1 Pet 1:23–25), and such a description not only points to the faithfulness of God in keeping His word by fulfilling His promises but also honors the words of God as spoken and fulfilled by Jesus. Jesus severely criticized those who misrepresented the words and ways of God as hypocrites and deceivers (Matthew 23). His entire life and ministry were built around the conviction that His understanding of God was true and that the God who revealed Himself in Scripture was deserving of obedience. Such obedience is justified only on the basis of the truthfulness of those assumptions and convictions.

Leaders today, especially in times of stress and conflict, must always seek to know the truth. They cannot be like those whom Jesus criticized as following the currently popular political whims. Referring to His kinsman, the prophet John the Baptist, Jesus, with a weary humor, mocked the hypocritical rejection of John as a crazy ascetic by the same people who disingenuously opposed Jesus for being a glutton and a drunkard (Matt 11:1–19, especially 16–19). The inability to apprehend the truth goes far beyond an objective appraisal of the facts, according to Jesus. There can be an *unwillingness* to see the truth (Matt 12:24–37; 13:14–15), recognize the truth, and obey the truth that reflects a deeply spiritual moral flaw, a scornful pride that wills not to know the truth and be set free by it (John 8:31–32). Leaders humbly submit to all the truths they encounter and order their lives, and the processes and goods under their influence, accordingly.

Conclusion

The study of leadership began as a cottage industry several decades ago and today has exploded into a flood of pamphlets, books, and case histories on the topic of leaders and leadership. Many of these works are excellent and can be used to great benefit. In fact, it is interesting to note how many of the best books on leaders and leadership reflect old and traditional Christian truths. But if leadership theory and practice is to be truly Christian, it must be grounded in a biblical model that begins with Christ. Though I have in this chapter pointed to the convictions and behaviors of Jesus that must go *toward* a biblical model of leadership, I conclude by observing, based on the elements I have mentioned above, the following central features of a biblical model of leadership.

First, in beginning with Christ, Christian leaders do not merely, as some clichés indicate, "see the future" but in fact, like Jesus, study the ancient sources of the past in order to establish a foundational depth from which to lead. We have seen the profundity of Jesus' understanding of the Scriptures and with it His knowledge of the character of God, the mission and role of Israel and Israel's law, and the mission and work of the people of God in the world as God's agents in building a new creation. His theological brilliance must not be dismissed as merely a reflection of the divine omniscience, but—to be true to Luke's depiction of the 12-year-old Jesus in the temple—understood to be the result of a willing heart and a disciplined mind immersed for thousands of hours in the words of Scripture.[1]

Second, to follow Jesus, and to follow the ways of Jesus, leaders must steel themselves with the knowledge that their decisions will not always lead to popularity or to success, *as popularly understood.* Christian leaders, based upon all that we bring to bear from Scripture and Christian tradition, seek to affect the present and the future in ways that shape people, institutions, and events along the lines of *God's* ultimate values. We do so at the risk of being misunderstood. We do so without fear of being either traditional *or* different. We lead without regard for whom we offend (Gal 1:10) or how others label us (1 Cor 4:9–13). We seek to know the will of God, the facts of the world around us—especially the flawed nature and brokenness of human beings and the world we inhabit—and the desire of God to shape us into Christ's likeness as He marshals us, His people, to live faithfully and courageously.

Finally, leaders have a strong sense of purpose that is adaptable to the facts of reality. Jesus called and used humble, broken, arrogant, petulant, selfish, impetuous, and sometimes even traitorous followers. He worked through institutions whose leaders were often power hungry, deceitful, murderous, hypocritical, greedy, and abusive to the poor. But He did the will of His Father and, at the very moment of apparent defeat, entrusted Himself in obedient abandonment to His Father (Luke 23:46; Heb 5:7) and, in the end, experienced a vindication that only His Father could bestow. What others meant for evil, God meant for good (Acts 2:23–24: cf. Gen 50:20).

Knowing God's will and having the courage—amid the frustrations of a broken world—to live it out, with a humility born of the wisdom He gives to those who persevere (Jas 1:2–5), are the attributes and practices that evidence the leadership of Jesus.

Resources for Further Study

Blomberg, Craig L. *Jesus and the Gospels: An Introduction and Survey.* 2nd ed. Nashville: B&H, 2009.

Bock, Darrell L. *Breaking the Da Vinci Code: Answers to the Questions Everyone's Asking*. Nashville: Thomas Nelson, 2004.

Bruce, F. F. *Jesus: Lord and Savior*. Downers Grove: InterVarsity Press, 1986.

Köstenberger, Andreas J., L. Scott Kellum, and Charles L. Quarles. *The Cradle, the Cross, and the Crown: An Introduction to the New Testament*. Nashville: B&H, 2009.

Ladd, George Eldon. *Jesus Christ and History*. Chicago: InterVarsity Press, 1963.

Marshall, I. Howard. *I Believe in the Historical Jesus*. Grand Rapids: William B. Eerdmans, 1977.

Meyer, Ben F. *The Aims of Jesus*. With a new introduction by N. T. Wright. Princeton Theological Monograph Series, ed. Dikran Y. Hadidian. Eugene, OR: Wipf and Stock, Pickwick Publications, 2002.

Moule, C. F. D. *The Origin of Christology*. Cambridge: Cambridge University Press, 1977.

Reicke, Bo. *The New Testament Era: The World of the Bible from 500 B.C. to A.D. 100*. Trans. David E. Green. London: Adam & Charles Black, 1978. Originally published as *Neutestamentliche Zeitgeschichte* (Berlin: Alfred Töpelmann, 1964).

Wright, N. T. *Who Was Jesus?* First North American edition. Grand Rapids: William B. Eerdmans, 1993.

Questions for Further Reflection

1. What characteristics of Jesus' behavior and personality most surprise you?

2. Why is it important to recognize Jesus as *the very image* of God?

3. Jesus voluntarily laid down His life for us. But why did the Jewish leaders of His day want to kill him? What aspects of His behavior or teaching were offensive and threatening?

4. What patterns of behavior in Jesus' life are most *unlike* the stereotypical descriptions of Jesus?

5. Leaders are sometimes described as authoritarians, visionaries, coaches, autocrats, teachers, etc. Is there another way to think of Jesus' leadership style? Does He fit several or none of these patterns?

6. If you had to pick one characteristic of Jesus' behavior that is key to His fulfillment of God's plan for Him, what would it be? Why?

Endnote

[1] B. Reicke, *Outliers: The Story of Success* (New York: Little, Brown, 2008), 35–68. A brilliant New Testament scholar and my doctoral advisor at the University of Basel, Switzerland, once told me that he was persuaded that the mind of Jesus was saturated with the Scriptures, especially the Psalms. I am intrigued by Malcolm Gladwell's reference to "ten thousand hours" as an important threshold of practice and learning for anyone who would achieve expertise in any discipline or craft.

Chapter 2

CHRISTIAN LEADERSHIP AND THE IDENTITY AND MISSION OF AN ORGANIZATION

David J. Gyertson
Distinguished Professor of Leadership, Regent University

At every level of society we seem to be living in an era of unprecedented change. Few systems, structures, and organizations are able to remain unaffected by the massive shifts in context and culture occurring in almost every corner of our globe. Instantaneous communications, the rising influence of the two-thirds world, population migrations due to diminishing resources and increasing governmental instability, the move to a knowledge-based economy as well as the constant threat of terrorism as the primary multifront approach for resolving conflicts, all make doing business as usual an impossibility.

Among the most significant societal trends is the deterioration of confidence in institutions in general and their leadership in particular. The level of trust in organizations, systems, and leaders may be at one of the lowest points in modern history. Underpinning all of this is the deterioration of moral certitudes that have formed the basis for much of Western business, government, and interpersonal relationships. The Golden Rule of doing unto others as you would have them do to you can no longer be counted on as the prime directive for much of business, government, or interpersonal relationships.

Despite this vacuum created by the neglect of historic moral absolutes, something within the fiber of humanity still longs to identify with causes, and those who lead them, that call us to live beyond and not just for ourselves. Significance, as well as success, remain as driving motivators of the uniquely human quest for meaningfulness. When a natural disaster or a major social crisis occurs, this instinct to be our brothers' and sisters' keepers reawakens. Institutions, which cultivate an identity through a record of integrity and servant leadership that speak to such longings, are finding new opportunities to shape culture and appropriate the God image of sacrificial service for the betterment of others.

What factors shape institutional and organizational identity inspiring the best in humanity? How do leaders influence the development and maintain the integrity of that identity? Is being intentionally and responsibly Christian in precept, motivation, and action the answer to the longings of those who seek, as the prophet Micah described, a mission that seeks "to act justly, to love faithfulness, and to walk humbly with your God" (Mic 6:8 HCSB).

Christian Leadership and Institutional Identity

For faith-based organizations the link between leadership and the mission and identity of the organization is self-evident. The vast majority of Christian entities are the offspring of dynamic founders whose personalities, passions, and dedication focus energy and enlist followers. Their compelling presentation of vision and call to sacrifice in order to achieve it are the driving forces God uses to address the selected needs of society. Organizations usually prosper in addressing their specific missions as their leaders remain active, effective, and focused. By contrast, when these leaders leave, die, retire, or most significantly fail, the organization's ability to sustain its mission can falter. The management metaphors that *streams rise no higher than their sources* and *fish rot from the head first* are true anecdotally for many secular as well as faith-based entities.

Even as organizations mature, their significant dependence on leaders to create, project, and maintain identity, particularly in faith-informed organizations, remains strategic. The quality, passion, and character of leadership casts vision, creates structure, and drives the staffing of mission, as well as the effective marketing and successful fund-raising required to fulfill the mission. While without a vision the people perish (Prov 29:18), without the visionary, the people needed to perform and fulfill the vision soon lose sight of and commitment to the mission. And as leadership goes so go funding, service impact, and the effective performance needed to deliver on the organization's promise.

However, faith-based organizations have an amazing resiliency—a factor that should not be surprising to those who understand the nature of God's sovereign call on, provision for, and protection of these entities conceived to incarnate His love for a needy world. As an organizational and leadership consultant, I regularly am challenged by the fact that many of these entities—though aerodynamically unsound in terms of systems, structures, operations, and even leadership—are like the bumblebee that flies despite the inherent limitations. Something is at work that moves beyond reason, science, and systems that can only be attributed to a loving Heavenly Father who likes to remind us that our thoughts, as well as our ways, are not always His (Isa 57:8–9).

One of the mysteries of faith-based leadership is that God often chooses champions who illustrate that it is "not by strength or by might, but by My Spirit" (Zech 4:6 HCSB) that His work ultimately is accomplished. I remember well the counsel I received from a senior leader in an international ministry who served as the right hand to the organization's founder. Painfully aware of the limitations, as well as being in awe of the talents and capabilities of the founder, he reminded me that all leaders are human with feet of clay. He went on to illustrate and celebrate God's wisdom in deploying leaders who hold the treasure of their calling in "clay jars" (2 Cor 4:7 HCSB) so that in the end it is clear that the excellence and the power belong more to God than to them. Those insights informed my own attempts to lead, as well as follow, through the past four decades of service to intentionally Christ-centered organizations.

Understanding Leadership Impact on Mission and Identity

Before exploring the implications and impact of Christian leadership on organizational mission and identity, we need to review some of the foundational research on this topic to provide working constructs and contexts. The concept of corporate identity was popularized in the early 1950s with an initial focus on organizational image and its relationship to marketing effectiveness. Brand development, and the protection and enhancement of brand image as it impacted corporate profits, drove much of the early research on institutional identity. The focus in these early stages was on shaping an institutional or product presence that would be distinctive and thus dominate the market for that organization in a specific industry niche.

However, for image and identity to have integrity, to ring true for the consumer and thus positively influence the bottom line, it must be an accurate expression of the values, commitments, and work product of those within the corporate structure. For "quality to be job one," a highly effective marketing tag line for the Ford Motor Company, for example, such a priority needed to infuse the quality culture from the boardroom to the assembly line and out the door to the sales floors and service shops of dealerships. It became clear that to *say it* but not actually *do or be it* would do more harm than good. While there is continuing research and application of the concept of organizational identity, two primary resources are important for reference here.

L. Ackerman, in his groundbreaking book *Identity Is Destiny,* notes that with the rise of the disciplines of industrial psychology and the emphasis on the importance of the human factors in business success, research on institutional identity began to ask questions such as: "Who are we? What do we stand for? What business are we in? And where do I fit in?"[1] These core questions shape the identity and validate integrity as promised by stated mission and vision. And faith-based organizations and entities should regularly ask these significantly relevant questions.

While answering these questions is the responsibility of all who work within the organization, Ackerman asserts that leaders in particular must recognize identity as "a significant force that shapes the futures and fortunes of organizations and all the lives these entities touch." He states that if leadership demands anything, it first demands insight—into people, organizations, circumstances, and situations. Without the knowledge that comes with insight, all the courage in the world will amount to nothing. He suggests that this view of leadership stands in contrast to the popular depictions of leaders that place priority on those who "demonstrate courage under fire, boldness in the face of uncertainty and determination against all odds."[2] While these qualities are important for heroic leadership, without the benefit of insight their exercise is only temporarily beneficial at best and potentially destructive at worst.

Ackerman sees organizations as living systems—as organisms more than organizations—that are shaped by the forces and influences of the people who catch the vision, embrace the mission, and deliver the product. He proposes a set of eight laws that leaders should embrace if organizational

culture and institutional identity are to achieve their highest levels of
health, integrity, and integration. Space does not permit a full explanation
and application of these here. The following summary, however, should
encourage you to explore further these dynamics that have relevance to our
Christian worldview of organizations and their leadership.

1. **The Law of Being**—Organizations, because they are made up
   of people, are alive in their own right (organisms more than
   organizations) and as a result have distinct characteristics that
   derive from but also transcend the individuals who make up the
   entity.
2. **The Law of Individuality**—The weaving of the individuals who
   make up the organization produces a distinctive tapestry in terms
   of the entity's image and identity.
3. **The Law of Constancy**—While basic identity is primarily fixed
   in the core DNA of an organization, transcending time and place,
   its manifestations are constantly changing and evolving.
4. **The Law of Will**—Every organization is compelled to create
   value in keeping with its core identity.
5. **The Law of Possibility**—Identity implies the potential to make
   contributions of significance and lasting value.
6. **The Law of Relationship**—Identity is anchored to and
   dependent upon the nature and quality of interpersonal
   relationships within and beyond the organization.
7. **The Law of Comprehension**—The capacity of the organization
   to create value is dependent on the perceived value of the
   organization as a whole.
8. **The Law of Cycle**—Identity development is a continuous
   process because identity governs value, which produces wealth,
   which in turn fuels identity.[3]

Throughout Ackerman's research, the critical role of the leadership in
understanding and applying these eight laws of identity-based management is emphasized. When followed, these help leaders develop efficient,
enduring organizations of reliable and predictable integrity. Ackerman
suggests that these qualities converge to produce a higher state of being
characterized by *power* and *grace*. By power he means the resources to
do good, to operate in a constructive rather than destructive fashion for
the ultimate benefit of all touched by the organization. And by grace he
means the ability to respond and adapt to success and defeat, opportunity

and challenge, in a seamless and effortless way that demonstrates health and robustness.

And what are the results of such a leader-led commitment to shaping identity? Ackerman summarizes, "Companies and individuals operating in such a state of health are very likely to realize their potential through productivity, through creation and through distinctive contributions to customers, markets, industries, society and no less to families and friends." He concludes that the most predictable outcomes from achieving this level of identity management are "relationships that are deeply rooted in trust."[4] For those who lead Christian organizations, the outcomes of Ackerman's model for identity development and management are consistent with the value propositions and missional intentions at the heart of our Lord's Great Commission mission as well as His Great Commandment mandate.

A second important foundation undergirding the research on leadership impact on identity and mission is E. Schein's *Organizational Culture and Leadership*.[5] His work is among the most helpful for considering how leaders influence, for good or ill, the corporate cultures of their organizations. The effectiveness of vision, mission, and identity is the result of how leaders shape corporate culture through a variety of value propositions, business strategies, and reward systems that are anchored within the character and commitments of the individual leader whose humility creates the context for continuous learning.

Schein asserts that leaders must be learning and growing constantly in self-understanding, as well as professional and business acumen, in order to shape the vision, create the identity, and deploy the resources needed to accomplish the mission of their organizations. These *learning leaders* of the future will need to demonstrate six core qualities in order to address the major changes on the horizon.

1. New levels of insight into the realities of the world and themselves
2. Extraordinary motivation to endure the pain that necessary change will produce
3. Emotional strength to manage their own and others' anxiety as change occurs
4. New skills in analyzing and changing cultural assumptions
5. Willingness and ability to involve others and encourage their participation

6. Ability to learn the assumptions of rapidly changing
   organizational cultures

He concludes his assessment of learning leadership and its impact on
organizational vision, mission, and identity by saying:

> Learning and change cannot be imposed on people. Their involve-
> ment and participation are needed for diagnosing what is going
> on, figuring out what to do and actually doing it. The more turbu-
> lent, out of control and ambiguous the world becomes, the more
> the learning process will have to be shared by all members of the
> learning unit. If the leaders of today want to create organizational
> cultures that will themselves be more amenable to learning they
> will have to set the example by becoming learners themselves
> and involving others in the learning process. . . . Ultimately, we
> cannot achieve the humility required to live in a turbulent cultur-
> ally diverse world unless we can see cultural assumptions within
> ourselves. In the end, cultural understanding and cultural learning
> start with self-insight.[6]

The research on the significant impact of culture, values, and leadership
on organizational identity provides an excellent foundation for considering how a truly Christian approach to leading can influence organizational
effectiveness. The findings show a decided shift from just the *what, when,
where,* and *how* of organizational systems and structures to the *who* and
why of character, attitude, and motivation that ultimately determine mission and influence identity.

Using the baseline insights from Ackerman and Schein, we turn next to
a set of leadership motifs in an attempt to understand and apply these and
other constructs of shaping institutional mission and identity.

Leadership Motifs—Impact on Mission and Identity

It is helpful in my goal to understand the impact of Christian leadership on organizational mission and identity to explore four basic models,
or what I characterize here as *motifs*, of leadership style and motivation.
Models are almost always artificial and as a result incomplete. No leader
fits fully into any one of these characterizations due to the raw materials of personality, experiences, motivations, and skill sets each individual
brings to the specific situation. Current institutional needs and emerging

opportunities also influence the tailoring of these off-the-rack suits to fit the person with the place.

Effective leaders understand their preferred motif of leadership and work from these positions of experience and disposition. However, the most effective leaders willingly adapt their leadership preferences to changing conditions as required. With those caveats we consider four biblically based models of leadership—prophets, priests, kings, and apostles—in an attempt to better understand leadership predispositions and their impact on institutional identity. We can only provide here a cursory overview with an emphasis on those qualities and characteristics of the motif as it influences mission and identity.

The **prophet motif** is the one most characteristic of founder leaders. The prophets of the Old Testament stood as emissaries on behalf of God, declaring in compelling, and often convicting as well as correcting, tones His plans for His people. The missions of organizations led by such prophets tend to be focused, specific, and targeted in their ministry objectives. The fingerprints of the leader are evident, with the organization taking on the personality and characteristics of the leader. These leaders have an urgency to their vision, believing that time is short, needs are great, and this cause is worth both living and sacrificing for in terms of commitment and resources. Often their mission takes on a militaristic, confrontational tone—a culture wars characterization—that positions them in the forefront of the battle between good and evil, right and wrong in apocalyptic proportions. For such leaders their mission has world-changing, culture-shaping implications; and their identity is driven by a conviction that they have a unique and distinctive call from God to be His John the Baptist voice to and for this generation. Theologically there is often an emphasis on God's power and presence, with a particular focus on the authority of God's Word and/or the infilling power and gifts of the Holy Spirit.

Where the prophet motif speaks to the people on behalf of God, the **priest motif** speaks to God on behalf of the people. Here the mission is one more of comforting the afflicted in contrast to the prophetic motif of afflicting the comfortable. Peace, grace, compassion, mercy, reconciliation, and caring are the *foci* of institutional mission. Pastoral tones and perspectives shape the identity of the organization where care for the least, the left, and the lost dominates the nature and, as a result, the identity of the organization. As with the prophetic motif, the organization reflects the style, dispositions, and character of the leader, usually with an emphasis on God's love, forgiveness, mercy, and compassion.

The **king motif** distinguishes itself from prophet and priest primarily in its approach to getting God's work done. While prophets cajole and reveal and priests comfort and revive, kings tend to create structures and issue the commands necessary for the implementation of the vision. In this motif measurable evidences of success drive the leader. Growth and expansion are highly valued rubrics for determining God's blessing. Loyalty to the leader and the mission are expected; there is little tolerance for those who do not embrace the mission as identified and projected by the leader. In these organizational cultures followers implement mission as directed by the leader and are rewarded for their effectiveness in fulfilling the CEO's expectations. This is a top-down culture very dependent on the leader for mission interpretation and communication.

As we move to the **apostolic motif** of leadership, there is a decided shift from the earlier models where the focus primarily is on the leader to create identity and determine mission to a cooperative, collaborative, and facilitating leadership disposition. Prophets cajole, priests comfort, and kings command, but apostles coordinate and facilitate, as well as course-correct and nurture the vision and mission at the heart of institutional identity. The first three motifs operate in an independent fashion assuming the final authority for decisions and direction. Even if they have boards, these function more as ratifying and advisory councils than as governing, accountability-based entities.

While elements of the prophet, priest, and king can be present in the apostle's calling, much of the functions are building, as Paul described the mission of the church, into the body of Christ with each part functioning in mutual support and submission under the headship of Jesus as its Lord (1 Corinthians 12). Mission and identity emerge out of the collected and cooperative collaboration of those called to serve the vision of the organization. The leader facilitates the crafting of the organization's identity rather than creating or primarily controlling it. And in this motif the leader has a clear sense of responsibility to some governing and guiding force such as a board. Paul, for example, submitted his teachings and plans to the Jerusalem Council for advice, validation, and direction.

In my service at Asbury Seminary, and later Asbury College, I became aware of the quilting bees so characteristic of the creative work of Appalachian women. Each would come with the knowledge that the goal was to make a quilt. Together they discussed and decided on the overall design— double wedding rings, pomegranate, double propellers, and several other historic patterns were among the many options. Quilters brought scraps of fabric they could afford or had available. And under the coordinating eye of the *queen* of the quilting bee, they decided together where their scraps best fit. Each woman's contributions of fabric, as well as skill sets, were valued and then employed to create a *whole* that was always greater than the sum of its parts. While usually there is a recognizable pattern, depending on design choice, each quilt is distinct due to the fabric contributed and stitching techniques of its individual participants.

In a similar fashion the apostolic approach to leadership involves and invites the key stakeholders into the process of identity formulation. While the leader remains the primary catalyst for developing, communicating, and resourcing the vision, those who implement and support it are elevated to a higher level of involvement and responsibility. In this motif, followers are cocreators with leadership rather than just tools of leadership. Given the increasing rate of turnover in senior leadership positions, institutional memory and stability are enhanced by spreading the responsibilities of organizational culture and identity to those who carry the day-to-day workload of the mission. Leaders then serve as *quilting bee conveners,* encouraging and making room for the specifics of the vision to be revealed through the contributions of those God calls to serve.

Paul, as you might expect, is the New Testament example for the apostolic motif. However, he was an interesting blend of all four motifs as he addressed the various start-up and course correction needs of his churches. Nehemiah is an Old Testament illustration of the apostolic motif working to serve under authority while involving and facilitating participation across the various categories of key stakeholders needed to achieve the objective of rebuilding the walls. I find C. Barber's *Nehemiah and the Dynamics of Effective Leadership* an insightful study of leadership that reflects much of what this particular motif brings to organizational mission and identity.[7]

Paul, in Philippians 2, provides an excellent insight into the Jesus model of leadership that I continue to explore in my own search for effectiveness. He suggests that the ultimate characteristic of Christlike leadership adapts the chosen or preferred leadership style to the *needs of the led* rather than to the *needs or preferences of the leader*. This orientation stands in stark contrast with much of the strengths-based, shape-the-leadership-opportunity-around-the-leader theories present in both secular and Christian literature.

While it should be obvious that my predisposition is toward the apostolic motif, there are times and circumstances when what is needed for the good of the mission is one of the other leadership styles. The needs of the led dictate the style of leadership chosen. Any of the four motifs can be appropriate and effective when driven by this simple but profound insight. With such a servant leadership priority, each of the four styles has the potential to sharpen mission and project an identity that is consistent with our understandings of the Jesus model of leadership we long to appropriate.

Board Governance Influences on Institutional Mission and Identity

We need to take an aside here to consider one of the most significant and frequently overlooked influences on mission and identity, the role and function of the group charged with the legal oversight of the organization. One of the most important needs of effective leadership, as suggested above, is a context of accountability. When mission and/or identity crises occur, it is not unusual to find the root causes in the relationship between the governing board and the CEO.

For federally recognized, tax-exempt, nonprofit entities, the board of trustees, board of directors, board of visitors, board of elders, the official board, or a variety of other names identifies the group that is legally, morally, and functionally responsible for the supervising of the organization's stated mission and objectives. Robert Andringa's "Governance and Board Relations" chapter in this book provides an excellent overview of how effective boards work so those specifics are not addressed here. What is considered are those factors of board culture, process, and function that directly impact how the organization's mission and identity are shaped by the governance process.

We live in an era of expanded scrutiny and, as a result, increased responsibilities of governing boards in general and nonprofit boards in particular. The failures of industry and financial systems, and the resulting calls for better oversight triggered by the Sarbanes-Oxley legislation, make it necessary for governing boards to be proactive legally, morally, ethically, and operationally. Boards must increase their roles in monitoring, evaluating, and guiding the mission of these institutions. While administrative leadership (presidents/CEOs and their executive teams) carry the primary responsibilities for implementing the mission of the organization, boards must enhance the skills and commitments to their explicit duties—as defined by accrediting, certifying, best practices, and governmental requirements—as well as their implicit obligations, holding in trust the mission and integrity of the organization on behalf of its stakeholders.

In addition to the implicit and explicit responsibilities of nonprofit boardsmanship, two other recent factors demand enhanced board governance. The first is the current financial reality facing most of these organizations. The majority of faith-based nonprofit organizations operate on thin margins with limited reserves. Underperforming endowments, reductions in corporate and charitable foundation support, increasing deferred maintenance, rising levels of capital debt, and competition for gift dollars along with declines in major donor giving capacity mean that boards need more assistance in managing the critical components that impact identity and mission. Being both efficient in the use of resources and measurably effective in deploying them to fulfill the promises of mission impact the identity of the organization.

A second reality demanding improved oversight is the approaching retirement of the majority of senior leaders in many nonprofit organizations. In the next few years an estimated 60 percent of the current administrative and board leadership in these organizations will leave office. In addition, leaders at the chief executive level are serving for shorter terms—down from the average 10–15 years to between five and seven years. Boards are now required to assume a greater responsibility for continuity and stability due to these leadership trends and transitions. This turnover in leadership impacts institutional memory and history, putting at risk the continuity of vision and mission needed to anchor the next generation of service.

Using Andringa's adaptations of the Carver model for developing governance policies and procedures, boards need to pay special attention to those elements of their oversight that speak specifically to mission, organizational core values, and executive limitations—all of which impact mission and identity.

Andringa's policy manual template suggests the organizational essentials foundational to clarifying, projecting, enhancing, and protecting institutional identity. These elements usually include:

- Clear, compelling statements of *organizational vision* and *institutional mission*
- A description of the *core values* that will guide the organization in fulfillment of its mission

- An articulation of the *moral owners* to whom the organization feels accountable and responsible along with a description of the organization's *beneficiaries*
- An overview of the *major functions* as well as the *primary strategies* the organization uses to serve its beneficiaries, keep faith with its moral owners, and fulfill the promises implied in its declaration of mission
- A statement of both short- and long-term goals to achieve its stated objectives, along with the *monitoring and validating strategies* to measure success and validate results

Also important to the board's tasks of giving leadership to institutional identity is its clear definition of executive leadership expectations, limitations, and operating parameters. Most identity crises occur as a result of a lack of clarity and common understanding between the governing board and its CEO over institutional goals, values, performance expectations, and accountability measures.

Leadership Transitions, Influences, and Implications

One of the most significant influences on and shapers of institutional mission and identity occurs during times of leadership transition. Why leaders leave, and how that transition is handled, may either disrupt or support the continuity and clarity of organizational identity. Tommy Thomas provides an excellent chapter in this book on managing leadership transitions particularly related to the search process. Here we will look more at the various styles of leadership in transition and consider the implications for organizational mission and identity.

One of the more helpful books for addressing the challenges of leadership transitions is J. Sonnenfeld's *The Hero's Farewell: What Happens When CEOs Retire*. Connecting to the theme of heroic stature, Sonnenfeld researches a wide range of senior leadership departures. Out of his findings, he developed a typology categorizing the exit styles of corporate executive officers. Sonnenfeld uncovered the existence of a unique nature among departing CEOs that included "a heroic self-concept . . . a feeling that one has a unique role to fill and that only the hero is capable of carrying out the responsibilities of the job. He also concluded that this attitude often serves as a barrier to the hero's exit.[8]

Four categories emerged in Sonnenfeld's work that he uses to describe CEOs' departures from their organizations. They include: monarchs, generals, ambassadors, and governors. You are encouraged to explore these more fully than we treat them here to better understand the implications and impact of these observations for Christian organizations. All transitions are influenced by three tensions: internal tensions, tensions between generations, and tension with the organization. Leaders, and boards in particular, need to use the insights to help ensure that momentum and mission are not lost in managing these tensions during seasons of leadership transition.

Monarchs, Sonnenfeld posits, are CEOs who do not leave voluntarily but either die in office or leave under duress. Faith-based leaders whose predominant motif is the king often exhibit similar behaviors when exiting. While this predisposition is seen most often in founders, it also is present in those who have reengineered the organization through a significant crisis or season of change. Monarchs can create a serious identity crisis for themselves and their organizations as they depart. I have seen cases where monarchs, usually unwittingly, do things to disrupt the mission and, as a result, diminish the organization's as well as their own reputations. Questioning of the next generation's leadership integrity and or motivations, undermining relationships with significant donors and board members, and using their influence with primary stakeholders, monarchs raise doubts about the future by creating an us-against-the-interlopers climate of conflict. In these attempts to preserve their legacy and protect what they believe to be the nonnegotiables of the organization's mission, they end up hobbling and, in some cases, seriously crippling, the identity of the organization they gave their lives to advance.

Managing well the transition of a monarch is critical to the ongoing success of the organization, at least in the short term. Wise successors who understand that they cannot *replace* but can only *follow* monarchs will do all they can to celebrate and honor the legacy of those who preceded them. Misunderstandings should be addressed privately between the monarch and successor. Keeping the monarch informed about upcoming changes and providing the rationale, as well as opportunity to comment on such changes, can minimize public conflict. Wise boards will encourage a time of transition where appropriate so that monarchs feel their work and contributions are valued, appreciated, and respected. King David's example in following Saul provides a rich resource of insight on honor and self-control that can help the successor better manage the inherent conflicts in a monarch's transition and minimize the disruptive impact on organizational identity and mission.

Generals represent those who leave only with great reluctance, often plotting ways to return. They exhibit similar disruptive behaviors and tactics to the monarch but with their underlying motivation driven by the belief that when the organization comes to its senses the general will be invited back to salvage the ministry. Generals carry a sense that their work was not completed. Frequently they leave because of weariness, health issues, or burnout. Out of office for a season, they recalibrate and realize that their lives are empty, that they have not developed an identity and life purpose outside of their previous leadership role.

Boards need to work with generals well in advance of retirement when possible to help leaders prepare financially, emotionally, and spiritually for the next chapter in their life's callings. Like monarchs, generals need the assurance that their contributions are valued and legacy honored. Similar strategies of engagement to those noted for monarchs work well with generals. Usually generals exhibit prophet or priest motifs in their leadership roles. Understanding the underlying motif can help boards and successors facilitate a continuation of that style in other settings. Providing periodic opportunities, when appropriate, for the general to return for ceremonial duties can help with the transition. Since they played such important roles in shaping the direction of the organization, wherever their contributions to institutional identity can be celebrated and emphasized will help both them and the organization manage the leadership transition positively.

Ambassadors represent those who exit gracefully, retaining amicable relationships with the organizations they leave. The apostolic and priest motifs of leadership often fall into this Sonnenfeld category of transition. Many organizations create emeritus positions for ambassadors, providing opportunities for these leaders to assist with the successful transition of the new leader. Helping introduce the new CEO to the various stakeholder constituencies, being available for counsel, and particularly helping transition the message and resources can be helpful. This proactive passing of the mantle of leadership can be most beneficial when organizational continuity is preferred and important. This requires unusual grace and significant wisdom on the part of the incoming leader as well as the board. Such transitional roles need to be clearly defined, limited in scope, and predetermined in terms of tenure.

The best of these ambassador transitions places the former leader on the staff of the new CEO, taking direction from the new leader. However, this type of relationship is often awkward for employees, board members, and significant contributors. The ambassador must facilitate the required transition of power and, most significantly, the transfer of loyalties by supporting the new leadership fully. I enjoyed an unusually positive relationship with my predecessor Dr. Jay Kesler during my tenure as president of Taylor University because of his integrity in always respecting my calling as the president for a new season. Another example was the president emeritus relationship of Ted Engstrom who served with grace a series of presidential successors at World Vision. I regret to say, however, that these are notable exceptions. In many faith-based organizations, the ambassador role is often a mixed blessing, frequently creating too long a good-bye unnecessarily delaying transitions to new paradigms required to address emerging challenges and opportunities.

Governors are those who enter a given organization, stay for a time, but then leave when their tour of duty is completed, maintaining few relationships or other ties. Prophets often fit this category, appearing on scene for a specific purpose and then departing once their mission is completed. The navy military model of leadership transition is a helpful illustration. Ship captains are assigned for a specific tour of duty focused on a particular mission consistent with their experiences and skill sets. When the assignment is completed, they are piped ashore and move on to a new position, rarely returning to the previous billet. These leaders usually do not stay for long periods of time, often less than five years. They are assignment focused, hired to help the organization through a transition. They usually are either crisis management or opportunity management specialists. They are motivated by the need for change and challenge, often becoming restless when systems are fixed and running smoothly.

The numbers of governors present in faith-based organizations are increasing for a wide variety of reasons. One of the biggest is the increased use of interims to help organizations assess current conditions, understand future leadership needs, and provide breathing space after the service of monarchs in particular so that the next generation of leadership can focus energies on new directions. Governors may reshape mission and identity if there has been a major crisis of integrity, but more often they help clarify existing mission and determine current strengths, opportunities, weaknesses, and threats so that the governing boards have an accurate picture of the institution and its leadership needs. My own path has been primarily that of the governor stepping in to help start new entities or more often transition existing missions. Governors usually depart quickly, which can be unsettling to stakeholders if their leadership mission was not clear from the beginning or the reasons for transition not well communicated.

Governors, while desiring to have their contributions and legacies valued, most often are satisfied by completing the necessary tasks on their *watch*. They leave with few regrets, anticipating the next duty station and retain limited connections to their previous assignments.

We spent significant time here on the matter of leadership transitions because how these are managed can have significant influence on mission continuity and organizational identity. While who takes up the leadership mantle next has the greatest impact on the emerging mission and identity of the organization, how the transition occurs and particularly the way previous leadership handled, and was handled, in the transition also impacts the organization's ability to move forward smoothly. Faith-based organizations produce leaders of *heroic stature*. Understanding, celebrating, and guiding such a disposition well, particularly during transitions, is an important key to preserving the integrity of organizational mission and identity.

I find D. McKenna's book *The Leader's Legacy*[9] an insightful resource for understanding and navigating the various challenges of transitions from the CEO's perspective. Another helpful book is G. Edwards' *A Tale of Three Kings: A Study in Brokenness*,[10] a sobering examination of leadership motivations and their impact on organizations and followers. Perhaps the most helpful reality therapy for my own journey is Luke's commentary on the leadership calling of King David in Acts 13:36: "For David, after serving his own generation in God's plan, fell asleep, was buried with his fathers, and decayed" (HCSB).

Sooner or later our leadership calling will end, our contributions hopefully having served our generation well; but they soon decay, making way for the birth of new leadership better suited for the times and opportunities their generation brings.

Spiritual Formation in Mission and Identity

As we bring this chapter to a close, some spiritual formation insights can help us focus the identities of the sacred missions entrusted to us. The reality about mission is that it must be alive in us in order for it to be vital and compelling for those we lead. Keeping the vision and mission burning in the bones of leaders requires an unquenchable awareness, a revelation, of the divine mandates required to lead the work entrusted to us.

P. Greenslade, in his book *Leadership, Greatness and Servanthood*, provides helpful insight on where effective mission and clear identity originates. He exhorts:

> *Revelation* is vital to leadership. God's view of things and not man's has been the starting point for all great movements. We need to know who God is and where He wants to take His people. . . . When God's chosen instrument (the leader) has seen God's plan and purpose he can stir and motivate the people of God, keeping them on course when the going gets rough—as it usually does.[11]

Anchoring his exhortations to the familiar "without a vision" passage in Prov 29:18, Greenslade offers another rendition of this benchmark challenge. He suggests that "where there is no prophetic vision (among the leaders), the people whom they lead become confused, disorganized and rebellious." The point of his focus is that leaders must seek a spiritual understanding, a *revelation*, of the unique work that God calls them to that is more than just the appropriation of best practices or success models of others whose ministries we admire or too often envy. Many leaders are so consumed with their business for the ministry that little time is devoted to understanding and embracing God's business for that ministry. Making the time to "seek first the kingdom of God and His righteousness" (Matt 6:33 HCSB) for our organizations through the inner vision that comes only from the Holy Spirit requires an appropriation of spiritual disciplines and an attitude of teachable humility that is inherently difficult for the typical Type A personalities usually drawn to leadership roles. Being still and knowing who and what is of God (Ps 46:10) requires the cultivation of the disciplines of divine revelation.

Various theological traditions emphasize differing means for awakening and sustaining God's revelation of calling and purpose. Some primarily use the disciplined study of the Scriptures as the pathway for understanding God's revelation. Others find periodic retreats of prayer, reflection, and meditation the most helpful for sensitizing the heart and mind to God's Holy Spirit. Some find divine leading clearer in places and experiences of worship and praise. And still others believe that God's direction is best determined in the context of the wise counsel of those who demonstrate track records of spiritual wisdom and insight. In my own journey all of these, in varying degrees and at different times, become important means of grace for seeking and finding God's revelation of His plans and purposes for my calling. Whatever disciplines awaken your spirit to the divine voice need to be employed regularly in order to keep our minds clear and hearts focused.

Greenslade's insights in his chapter "The Vision and the Dream" help guide my own disciplines for practicing the presence of God in order to understand His person and purposes for my leadership call. In the intimate connections that come from seeking to be with, and as a result understand both the heart and the mind of Christ, many of the conflicts and confusion about my personal identity are resolved. My sense of personal inadequacies and limited abilities become means by which I allow God's power and purposes to take center stage. In this intimate connection to the One whom I serve, I receive the clear vision needed to give His people a sense of purpose and destiny to fulfill our ministry's calling. This clarity provides the source of endurance and persistence, the long obedience in the same direction, that God's work inevitably requires. It reminds those who do both the business and the ministry of our ministry that our continuity rests not in temporal leaders but in the eternal God who has planned our mission from the foundation of time and is faithful to bring it to fruition and completion (1 Thess 5:23–24). Such revelation compels me to *serve* with the sacrifice needed to achieve His kingdom purposes. It also makes me only satisfied with the work of my hands when I know that what has been done has been for His glory because it comes from a circumcised heart so that His will might "be done on earth as it is in heaven" (Matt 6:10 HCSB).

The challenge we are given as leaders to cast vision and shape identity is nurtured and protected in the revealed presence of the One who has called us. No Christian leader will perform this calling without the exercise of the spiritual disciplines necessary to keep in touch with and submissive to the Master on whose behalf we serve until He returns.

Benedictions and Exhortations

Several in my generation who stepped up to the challenges of leading Christian organizations were influenced deeply by the character and commitments of the late Ted Engstrom. As CEO of World Vision, and through his pioneering efforts to improve Christian organizational and leadership effectiveness, he demonstrated what it meant to cast vision and create identity that seeks "first the kingdom of God and His righteousness" (Matt 6:33 HCSB). I still have every copy of his monthly *Leadership Letter* through which he consistently challenged and informed my own journey. In the closing years of his life, I was honed in my leadership by his unique ministry of mentoring encouragement. Despite our brief personal encounters, whether by handwritten note or one-on-one visits, "Dr. Ted," as he was known to many of today's Christian leaders, always reminded me of the high calling I had received in Christ Jesus.

In T. Beals' *The Essential Engstrom: Proven Principles of Leadership,* a summary of Ted's lifelong principles of Christ-centered mentoring are recorded. My reflections on his *Keys to Leadership in the Future* are used here to conclude this discussion of Christian leadership and the identity and mission of the Christian organization.

1. Commit yourself to God. He wants to share the privilege and the joy of carrying His Word.
2. Set your goal on the next runner. Miraculously we bear not one but untold thousands of torches; the more we hand out the more we have to share.
3. Be motivated by the things that motivate God.
4. Open your heart to God, and He will fill it with genuine enthusiasm.
5. Live in honesty. Those who receive the torch from you must be willing to believe you when you speak of its importance.
6. Be strong and of good courage. Though the night is dark, you will always walk in light when bearing His torch.
7. Decide to decide. Indecision is inaction, and inaction leads to failure.
8. Act responsibly.
9. Keep first things first.
10. Respect the future. He who inhabits eternity invites you to share His home there with Him.[12]

In my last meeting with Ted before he died, I asked him about the master key to effective Christian leadership. Without hesitation he looked across the table and declared, "Integrity!" As we exercise our leadership, shaping the mission and identity of the sacred trusts God permits us to steward, let us demonstrate the integrity that comes from the revelation that God has called and equipped us. Barclay translates Eph 1:18 as a benediction for all of us called to lead: "I pray that your inner vision may be flooded with light, to enable you to see what hope the fact that He has called you gives you. And, I add, through you to others."[13]

Out of such hope we who are called to Christ-centered leadership shape the mission and identity of God's work for such important times as these. May we demonstrate integrity in the carrying out of our heavenly vision by doing justly, loving mercy, and walking humbly with our God (Mic 6:8).

And when our final transition comes, like King David, may we be laid to rest with our fathers having served the purposes of God in our generation (Acts 13:36).

Resources for Further Study

Ackerman, Laurence D. *Identity Is Destiny: Leadership and the Roots of Value Creation.* San Francisco: Berrett-Koehler, 2000.

Barber, Cyril. *Nehemiah and the Dynamics of Effective Leadership.* Old Tappan, NJ: Loizeaux Brothers, 1999.

Barclay, William. *The Letters to the Galatians and Ephesians.* The New Daily Study Bible. Louisville: Westminster John Knox, 1976, 2002.

Edwards, Gene. *A Tale of Three Kings: A Study in Brokenness.* Wheaton: Tyndale House, 1992.

Engstrom, Ted W. *The Essential Engstrom: Proven Principles of Leadership.* Compiled by Timothy J. Beals. Fort Worth: Authentic, 2007.

Greenslade, Philip. *Leadership, Greatness and Servanthood.* Minneapolis: Bethany House, 1984.

McKenna, David L. *The Leaders Legacy: Preparing for Greater Things.* Newburg, OR: Barclay, 2006.

Schein, Edgar H. *Organizational Culture and Leadership.* San Francisco: Jossey-Bass, 1992.

Sonnenfeld, Jerry. *The Hero's Farewell: What Happens When CEOs Retire.* New York: Oxford University Press, 1988.

Questions for Further Reflection

1. Of the four motifs of leaders (prophet, priest, king, and apostle), which best describes your leadership and/or that of your organization? What are the strengths and weaknesses of that leadership style as you cast vision and create identity?

2. Do you have a leadership transition strategy in place that takes into account the significant impact a transition will have on the leaders (leaving and coming) as well as on the current mission and identity of your organization?

3. Are governance policies and practices in place to guide the leading of vision and mission for your organization?

4. What personal disciplines do you exercise to keep the revealed vision burning in your bones so that you in turn can perform your calling to lead with integrity, effectiveness, and humility?

5. Do the implementation of the mission and the projections of its identity truly glorify God and serve those whom Jesus would serve were He leading your organization today?

Endnotes

[1] See L. Ackerman, *Identity Is Destiny* (San Francisco: Berrett-Koehler, 2000).

[2] Ibid., 2.

[3] Ibid., 11.

[4] Ibid., 206.

[5] See E. Schein, *Organizational Culture and Leadership* (San Francisco: Jossey-Bass, 1997).

[6] Ibid., 392.

[7] See C. Barber, *Nehemiah and the Dynamics of Effective Leadership* (Old Tappan, NJ: Loizeaux Brothers, 199).

[8] See J. Sonnenfeld, *The Hero's Farewell: What Happens When CEOs Retire* (New York: Oxford University Press, 1988), 3, 62.

[9] See D. McKenna, *The Leader's Legacy* (Newberg, OR: Barclay, 2006).

[10] See G. Edwards. *A Tale of Three Kings: A Study in Brokenness* (Wheaton: Tyndale, 1980).

[11] P. Greenslade, *Leadership, Greatness and Servanthood* (Minneapolis: Bethany, 1984), 41.

[12] See T. Engstrom, *The Essential Engstrom: Proven Principles of Leadership*, comp. T. Beals (Fort Worth: Authentic, 2009), 293.

[13] See W. Barclay, *The Letters to the Galatians and Ephesians*, New Daily Study Bible (1976; repr. Louisville: Westminster John Knox, 2002).

Chapter 3

LEADERSHIP, VISION, AND STRATEGIC PLANNING

Bob R. Agee
President Emeritus, Oklahoma Baptist University

Introduction

In the summer of 1999 I taught a course on leadership at the International Baptist Lay Academy in Budapest, Hungary. My students were young lay leaders ranging in age from 20 to 35 from Baptist churches throughout Eastern Europe. Among them were students from Hungary, Romania, Latvia, Yugoslavia, Bosnia, Serbia, Albania, and Macedonia. They were office workers, doctors, nurses, teachers, pastors, youth ministers, mechanics, and a variety of other occupations. They were only a decade removed from the time when their countries were under Soviet domination and their churches had suffered decades of oppression. As we worked on defining what leadership is and tried to help them understand that the invitation to be a child of God includes a call to influence others to want to be His child and follow Him, it occurred to me that in many ways we have often missed the critical importance of helping our students here in the U.S. to understand that very thing.

These young adults brought to the class a passion to make a difference in their part of the world. They had an abundance of bad leaders to look at in their homelands, and they wanted to learn how to be good leaders, ones who could be effective in the process of developing strong churches in alien cultures. They also wanted to understand how to take a different approach to leading their families, their communities, and their workplaces to be more effective representatives of Christ. They were faced with a horrendous array of obstacles. Their countries were in economic shambles, their churches were struggling with near poverty conditions, and they had few Christian institutions or organizations to encourage them or provide training for them. Sometimes their family members were scattered in refugee camps, the destiny of their homelands was uncertain, and they had watched bombs drop and seen blood shed while they tried to figure out how to apply the words and spirit of Jesus where they lived. The entire purpose of the class was to help these young leaders shape a vision for the future of their churches, their families, and their workplaces which would effectively represent the gospel in their part of the world.

Leaders emerge when there are needs to be met or a task to be done and someone cares enough to want to make a difference in whatever context and under any conditions. An organization or institution never rises above the strength and capability of its leaders. When you see a college or university, academy, or any other Christian organization marked by growth, progress, and achievement, you can be assured that people in various roles have caught a vision of what that institution ought to be and accomplish. Without fail a person in the primary leadership role has been captured by a vision and possesses the instincts and skills to help others catch that vision.

Within a Christian organization (college, university, academy, or other nonprofit enterprise) the ultimate responsibility for providing leadership rests with a board of trustees or board of directors who have been empowered by a corporate charter and/or a covenant relationship with a sponsoring church body to oversee the work of that organization. The first and foremost responsibility of a board is to elect a president (or some other CEO designation) who will be entrusted with the task of leading the organization/institution to carry out its mission and purpose. Boards elect and hold accountable the person they select for that executive role. Being selected for that chief leadership role is indeed a weighty task, which one should accept only with a keen sense of spiritual stewardship for the life and work of the organization.

The president/CEO then faces the task of assembling a team of people to help him carry out the mission and purpose of the organization. The old adage: "The key to greatness is not being able to do the work of 12 people but is found in getting 12 people to work" proves true in any organizational effort. The task of team building will be discussed later in this chapter.

Necessary Ingredients for Being Effective in Influencing People, Groups, or Organizations

We can safely assume that every person who accepts a leadership role wants to be effective in that role. Some may accept a position because they are enamored with the title and believe that everyone within the organization will simply fall in line and follow whatever the leader commands. Experience and observation have taught me that leadership does not work that way. The leader who wants to be truly effective must possess certain necessary ingredients.

A Clear Sense of Mission and Purpose

A Christian institution or organization has been brought into being to accomplish a mission that will help to advance the larger cause of the kingdom of God in the world. Every person in a leadership role must have a strong, clear understanding of that mission and be committed to doing whatever they can to make the institution strong and effective.

Vision

The King James Version of the Bible translates Prov 29:18 as, "Where there is no vision, the people perish." Research into organizational and leadership behavior has verified that this phrase carries a timeless truth. What a difference is made when a leader is willing to dream dreams for an improved future of the organization, prays for a sense of direction, and develops a passion for that dream. An institution's future has no more critical element than visionary leadership.

Spirit

Dynamic growing institutions are normally marked by an atmosphere that causes even the casual observer to know that something significant is going on at that place. For a Christian institution that spiritual dynamic flows from three very important sources:

A sense of divine compulsion. It occurred to me a long time ago that the Christian institutions I served were not born merely of human imagination. Somewhere along the line, some founder(s) felt a call from God that He wanted that institution to come into existence to carry out a mission in the world. Leaders will experience times in life when they stay involved in the work because they believe God's purpose drives the mission.

A burning conviction about the importance of the work and mission of that organization. A CEO who lacks that burning conviction will have a difficult time remaining in the arena of hard work if that passion does not exist deep within.

A spirit of excitement and enthusiasm about the mission, the people, and the place. Enthusiasm is caught, not taught. Organizations/institutions are made up of people—those serving and those being served. If the leader does not generate an enthusiasm for the work and the possibilities for the future, the rest of the campus family will have a difficult time manifesting much excitement and enthusiasm.

Sound Informed Methodology

Every organizational arena has standards of best practice. The effective leader is a student of best practices within the profession and thinks strategically about ways to lead the institution/organization to embody those best practices. An important aspect of the witness of a Christian institution to the larger world is to set standards of excellence and become a model for the way to carry out mission. Leading your organization to strive to become a leader in the larger world of your professional arena speaks volumes about the nature and purpose of the institution.

Action

The role of leader is hard work. A good friend who was a prominent U.S. senator accepted the invitation to become president of a major state university. After six months in the job, he called me and said: "Agee, why didn't you tell me that being a university president is such hard work?" My response was, "You wouldn't have believed me if I had told you. You have to experience that for yourself." The role of organizational/institutional leader at whatever level involves countless hours of effort and a willingness to do what needs to be done however long it takes. The bottom line is that leadership calls for action.

Without doubt the most important ingredient of effective leadership is vision. Mission and vision are not the same thing. An institution's mission defines its purpose. A vision for the institution's future describes the sense of direction and a compelling dream for the future. Nothing will transform an organization like a powerful and transforming vision.

Why Is Vision Important?

A meaningful vision for any organization flows out of gathered information, a clear sense of values, and a compelling sense of the importance of the nature and purpose of the institution. B. Nanus has aptly stated: "While vision is in a very real sense a dream, it is a special kind of dream built upon information and knowledge. The art of developing an effective vision starts with asking the right questions—and asking lots of them. . . . Values are the principles or standards that help decide what is worthwhile or desirable."[1]

A difference-making vision really cannot be shaped until the leader dares to gather information about the past and present of the institution. Gathering information about the history of the organization and appreciating its past accomplishments, its heroes, its good times, and its bad times will help a leader begin to see what ought to be. Taking the time to gather knowledge and input from a variety of sources into the strengths and weaknesses of an institution and then exploring the needs around you (internally and externally) that the institution should address begin to shape the dream for the future. Both vision and goals for the organization grow out of defined strengths, weaknesses, needs (internal and external), and opportunities.

What Are the Characteristics of a Powerful and Transforming Vision?

1. Effective visions lift the sights of the people within the institution to focus on standards of excellence and high ideals.
2. Effective visions clarify an institution's mission and set a sense of direction.
3. Effective visions inspire enthusiasm among people who work for the institution and all those who have a stake in its outcome.
4. Effective visions are defined in a way that encourages commitment on the part of stakeholders.
5. Effective visions are clearly stated and readily understood. A useful guideline is: Make it clear. Keep it simple. Say it often. Make it burn.
6. Effective visions are ambitious. They stretch the imagination and understanding of the nature and purpose of the organization and challenge people to think beyond the status quo.

7. Effective visions demand thoughtful planning designed to make visions become reality.

What Do Effective Visionary Leaders Do?

Organizations and institutions today are facing a changing landscape that calls for strong, proactive, interactive leaders. The demands of complex service organizations call for a leadership style that can best be defined as a *catalytic leader*. A *catalyst* is a chemistry term used to describe a substance that initiates or accelerates a chemical reaction without losing its own identity. It is often used to describe something that causes an important event to happen or stimulates an organization/institution to move toward a meaningful change in direction. *Catalytic leaders* possess a vision and a dream, commit themselves to the mission and purpose of the organization, value the people around them, foster a team spirit, enlist the insights and passions of others, empower people to lead their part of the dream, set high standards of performance, and monitor progress carefully. This approach to leadership tends to build strong institutions and nurtures potential leaders who know how to dream dreams, see visions, and work toward making dreams become reality.

Perhaps the best biblical example of the *catalytic leader* is found in the Old Testament book of Nehemiah, which describes his pilgrimage and work. Nehemiah was captivated by a vision of a work to be done, prayed diligently for strength and guidance, developed a deep burden for the task that needed to be done, planned carefully, gathered needed resources, enlisted others to help him, assigned responsibility carefully, monitored the work regularly, made contingency plans for dealing with obstacles, and inspired the people to work hard. The book of Nehemiah is an excellent textbook on how to accomplish great things in the face of great difficulty. It is also a great example of what effective visionary leaders do.

The effective visionary leader understands what he or she is expected to lead. Accepting the role of leader of or within a Christian institution or organization forces a person to recognize the difference between position and task. The title of president does not guarantee that the person understands the work of being a president. The title of vice president or director or dean does not mean the person holding the title understands that he or she is expected to assume a leadership role to influence the attitudes, atmosphere, and actions of that part of the organization or group of people. People who rely on the position they hold or the title bestowed upon that position to get people to do what they want them to do will accomplish little.

The effective visionary leader has a clear understanding of mission and has a dream of what the group or organization ought to be and do to be better and do better. When a person assumes a leadership role either as chief executive of the institution or organization or an administrative leader within that organization, he or she must at some point come to grips with and buy into the nature and mission of the institution and what it takes to lead that organization to be and do what God brought it into being to be and do.

Effective leaders look for ways to challenge the status quo and capture the imagination of others regarding mission and purpose. Over a period of time institutions or organizations can stagnate and become content with the way things are or with the way things have been. They exist to survive or survive to exist, and they lose sight of the mission and purpose entrusted to them. They need to rediscover their God-given mission and realize that they exist to make a difference and to lead that organization to be a stronger contributing part of the larger work of the kingdom of God in the world.

Leaders earn the right to lead over time as they build relationships and demonstrate that they can be trusted to make good decisions and help people shape an appropriate and compelling vision and sense of mission. In order to lead a college, university, academy, or parachurch organization effectively, leaders must understand the nature and mission of that organization.

Effective visionary leaders envision goals for the future and involve others in sharing the sense of direction in which the organization should be headed. A study of leaders in the Bible like Moses, Joshua, David, Nehemiah, Jesus, Paul, and others reveals that there was always a future toward which they pushed themselves and led others. Moses knew what the goals were before he went back to Egypt. Joshua's goal orientation was nurtured over many years of mentoring by Moses, and he knew what the task was from the moment God and Moses told him the leadership job was his when Moses died. Nehemiah left the king's court with a set of goals that drove him until the task was finished. I am convinced that the apostle Paul understood not only his mission but also the goals that were part of that mission. Jesus certainly understood His mission and the purpose for which He had come to earth. Effective presidents and department leaders who take their areas of responsibilities to new levels of growth, development, and achievement are people who are goal-oriented and have some sense of how the future of the institution/organization ought to look.

An effective leader enlists people to commit to a common mission, values, purposes, and goals. They are able to catch people up with them in a shared sense of destiny about what ought to be. A president or other leaders within the organization will do well to work at involving others in thinking about the vision for the future and in talking about what they would like to accomplish.

The effective visionary leader takes the initiative to try to motivate others to dream the dreams, see the visions, and work toward the goals that have been set. The principal difference between the servant leader and other kinds of leaders is found in the way they motivate others to dream the dreams.

Effective leaders tend to be more participative and interactive in their approach and work to involve others in dreaming the dreams, seeing the visions, and setting the goals that will move the group or organization forward. They are sensitive to the history and culture of the institution/ organization and treat that history and culture with respect. They take the time to learn about the good things the organization has done in the past, identify the high points in the institution's history and affirm those, identify the heroes in the organization's past and brag on them and their accomplishments, take the time to understand the way the institution has made decisions and transacted business and treat that with respect even as necessary changes are made, and identify the people with influence among the stakeholders and build a positive working relationship with them. The effective leader understands the leader's role as teacher, coach, and mentor whose task is to guide the organization while equipping others to help carry out the mission and purpose of the institution. The most effective leaders tend to be people builders as part of their approach to leadership. They walk and work alongside those who work with them, seeking to build a sense of shared mission and shared vision. This approach may take a little longer, but the work that is done tends to be more lasting.

Effective visionary leaders strive to achieve workable unity. They value people and recognize that the college/university or any organization will achieve more by people working together than by everyone doing his or her own thing. They work at building trust between the leader and those being led and make the effort to build teamwork between president, staff, faculty, and students. People matter but so does the task to be done, and the leader searches for an effective balance between task orientation and people orientation.

When leaders are overly task oriented they will tend to do whatever it takes to achieve what they want to get done. People are not very important and sometimes are more of a hindrance than a help. Leaders who are overly people oriented will tend to focus so much on taking care of individuals and their problems with the goal of keeping everyone happy that the organization gets little done and accomplishes little toward fulfilling its mission. Leaders must develop a healthy balance between task orientation and people orientation in order to enlist people to follow their leadership.

The effective visionary leader is a teacher—working at explaining the mission, the vision, the values, the goals, the methods, and the content so that people understand what is being done, why it is being done, and when it should happen. Leaders want people to understand the task and the rationale for the effort and the cost. They work hard to motivate people to buy into the work to be done.

The effective leader watches for every opportunity possible to tell people about the institution's mission and vision and works at convincing the listeners that the organization is distinctive and valuable to society. As president of a Baptist university for 16 years, my sense of mission and goal was repeated hundreds of times: "We will be academically strong, unapologetically Christian and unapologetically Baptist." Whether speaking to faculty, students, alumni, churches, or other constituent groups, it was my responsibility as a leader to teach and cast the vision.

The effective visionary leader takes the time to listen to people and tries to understand their perspective. An amazing dynamic flows within an institution where the leadership respects the collective thinking process and the leader chooses to give up the mantle of omniscience. The demands of leadership call for more knowledge and insight than any one person can possess. Surrounding yourself with knowledgeable, capable people and creating a culture where people can think, envision, and create will result in exceptional growth and progress. When leaders assume a know-it-all attitude, they cut off a valuable flow of insight and possibilities.

The effective visionary leader embodies the best of what the mission and the vision represent. We owe the people we are trying to lead at least three things: love, best effort, and a good example. Regardless of the popular notions about leadership style, there is a strong correlation between character and competence. A leader who expects hard work of people needs to be noted for working hard at the task. A leader who expects sacrificial service and giving from people needs to be serving and giving sacrificially. A leader who expects a gracious, courteous, considerate spirit from others needs to model a gracious, courteous, considerate spirit. If we expect passion for the mission and the vision for the institution's future from those we lead, we need to model passion for the mission and the vision of the organization. If we expect absolute professionalism and integrity from those who work around us, they need to be following our example of high standards of professionalism and integrity. The effective leader symbolizes what the organization is about and what it represents to the larger world.

The effective leader gives attention to the work of the organization and provides sound management for the work being done throughout the institution. While effective leaders learn to assign and delegate the work to be done within the institution, they must be informed and alert to those dynamics that will result in institutional growth, development, and progress. Effective management of an enterprise is comprised of these essential ingredients:

- Put a strong emphasis on planning and setting priorities.
- Give attention to organizing people for action and institution building.
- Work at keeping the system functioning.
- Set the agenda and provide a good example of sound decision making.
- Work at exercising sound political judgment.

These tasks cannot be ignored or neglected by leaders at any level within the organization.

In the final analysis, effective visionary leaders recognize and accept four critical roles:

1. They set the direction for the organization. The leader has a conviction about what ought to happen and works at guiding the thinking and planning toward the desired goals and outcomes.
2. They function as "change agents." When a leader fails to recognize that the organization has not yet accomplished all it needs to accomplish and fails to recognize that the best way to do things has not been found yet, stagnation sets in. More than one person holding a leadership position has presided over decline and demise because they do not grasp the importance of building on the accomplishments and achievements of the past

to become better and more effective at carrying out the mission of the institution. When the person filling the position or holding the title of leader merely manages the status quo, the organization quickly enters a period of decline.

3. The effective leader is expected to be the spokesperson who keeps all constituencies aware of the importance of the mission, purpose, values, and goals of the organization. If leaders lack the ability to present the mission and vision with passion on their own, they must find someone to work alongside them who is effective at telling the story and stirring others to buy into the dream.

4. The effective leader functions as a coach, guiding the planning and sense of direction. An effective coach works at developing a game plan and makes sure every member of the team understands the strategies that will be employed to play the game. The coach works at seeing that every player makes preparation to carry out the game plan. Coaches recognize that when even one player fails to carry out his/her assignment, the team usually loses.

Key Ingredients for Building Strong Teams

Effective leaders know the wisdom of surrounding themselves with capable people who will work alongside them to dream dreams and see visions of greater possibilities for the institution/organization. To try to carry the entire burden of an enterprise on the leader's shoulders alone is foolish indeed. That limits the possibilities for the organization to just the thoughts and interests of the person in the leadership role. There is tremendous power in a strong functioning team that will share a common sense of mission and common vision for the future of the institution. An effective collective thinking and planning process will infuse an organization's future with exciting possibilities for growth, progress, and achievement.

Having worked as part of an executive leadership team, sitting in the chair of chief executive, and working close enough with more than 100 institutions of higher education, I have observed leaders who understood the value of an effective team, enlisted capable people for the team, empowered them to do their jobs, and created a climate where the team could function. Inevitably the institutions led by team builders and team leaders were successful in their endeavors.

Guidelines for Building Strong Teams

1. Develop a clear understanding of what needs to be done in every administrative area of responsibility. Every organization's mission calls for specific tasks to be performed in a number of areas. When the chief executive understands those functions, he or she can be more effective in enlisting team members to see that things get done.

2. Develop an organizational structure that assigns responsibilities for every vital and strategic function of the institution. A chart can aid the chief executive and the board in being sure that essential tasks are being addressed. Flow charts portray lines of accountability and responsibility and provide a mechanism for performance review and evaluation.

3. Recruit the most capable and best qualified people you can find to whom the essential tasks can be assigned. Some leaders limit their recruiting to "yes" people, those who will allow the chief executive to command and the recruit will seek to carry out the demands. Others look for people who have the abilities and potential eventually to become chief executives themselves.

4. Treat everyone with respect. The most effective presidents of universities I have known view themselves as holding the rank of "first among equals." Every employee has value to the institution. All team members hold their positions because they have been deemed to have the knowledge and ability to carry out their responsibilities. An effective leader works at creating a corporate culture that reflects a deep and abiding mutual respect.

5. Involve people in developing mission, vision, goal-setting, action strategies, evaluation, and renewal efforts. The planning model that will be discussed later in this chapter calls for a high level of collaboration and collective thinking. Effective leaders foster and nurture collaboration. The president is the spokesperson for the mission, vision, and core values and insists that all thinking and planning are guided by those components.

6. Empower people around you to do their jobs. If team members must ask the chief executive for permission to do everything, the team member will not be an effective contributing part of efforts to grow, progress, and achieve. The following steps can be taken to be effective at empowering people:

- Be specific about desired results (work together to define outcomes in terms of both quantity and quality).

- Be sure team members understand the boundaries within which they will carry out their responsibilities.
- Discuss and understand available resources to get things done (financial, human, technical, organizational).
- Define lines, systems, and processes of accountability. Be sure the team member understands who answers to whom.
- Involve team members in setting goals and objectives for their areas of responsibility.
- Work toward self-management. Once team members have been enlisted and assigned an area of responsibility, expect them to get things done. A chief executive who tries to micromanage every administrative area is usually ineffective.

7. Establish a network and pattern for ongoing communication within the organization. Every employee of an institution needs to be kept informed about what is happening within the life of the organization. The purpose of a formal and systematic effort at institutional communication is to create a sense of community. People function best when they are informed and enlisted to be involved.

8. Be with the people. Years ago as a university president I learned the value of MBWA (management by wandering around). Periodically walking through key gathering places of employees, offices, or students and speaking to people allows team members to put a face and voice to leadership. Sheer presence is essential for effective leadership.

9. Develop a pattern and process for recognizing people for their work. A good leader makes heroes out of a lot of people.

10. Develop others. Effective leaders are people builders. They recognize the importance of developing the human resources that make up the overall team. Challenging those who work with you to raise their ambitions to prepare better and achieve ever higher standards of professionalism will enrich the organization.

11. Love the people and the institution/organization you seek to lead. The people around leaders can detect when they truly care about those who work with them and have a passion for the success and advancement of the institution. When people believe the leader really cares, they will work harder to make institutional dreams come true.

Effective Visionary Leaders Plan Their Work and Work Their Plan

Planning is much like the proverbial weather: everyone talks about it, but few actually do it with the depth and comprehensiveness that will make a difference in the life and performance of an institution. Effective planning is a formal, systematic, comprehensive, participative, flexible, and futuristic approach to shaping an institution's sense of direction. When an institution commits itself to developing a thoughtful, in-depth definition of mission and pursues a strong clear sense of direction, good things happen. The more comprehensive the plan, the better the chance that the institution/organization will move forward. The more participative the process, the better the chance of people who are expected to carry out the plan being committed to the plan.

We are indebted to the worlds of business and education for much of the research and experimentation that has helped shape effective models that can be followed to guide an organization's planning process. Excellent resources are readily available to help leaders understand what ought to be incorporated into the model that will be used. Within higher education, most of the models are described in journal articles, research documents, and reports that provide details in ways institutions plan their work. The most comprehensive resource is the *Education Resources Information Center* (ERIC), which contains more than 800 articles and papers on planning (Web site: www.eric.edu.gov). Over the years doctoral dissertations have been researched and written comparing and proposing planning processes, and these can be researched with the help of most public or university librarians. Major publishers such as Jossey-Bass, Eerdmans, and others, which focus on educational administration/leadership materials, provide access to books that focus on planning. Organizations such as the National Association of College and University Business Officers (NACUBO) www.nacubo.org, the National Center for Higher Education Management Systems (NCHEMS) www.nchems.org, the Society for College and University Planning (SCUP) www.scup.org, also provide helpful material to design an approach to planning.

The model described in the following paragraphs embodies a logic stream that if followed will enhance an organization's ability to be marked by growth, progress, and achievement. It incorporates the best elements of approaches used by colleges and universities supported by evidence gathered in a major research project conducted by the author. It has been adapted for use by colleges, universities, seminaries, denominational agencies, private academies, major charitable not-for-profit organizations, chambers of commerce, and churches small and large. A partial list of institutions that have used the logic string represented in the following model can be found on the Web site: www.asadevelopmentservices.com.

Steps in an Effective Planning Process

The steps defined below are designed specifically for an educational institution. The process can be adapted for uses in other organizational settings by identifying the strategic categories that are appropriate for the nature of the organization.

1. Decide to undertake comprehensive strategic planning. At some point the president and the board of trustees make the decision to launch a formal, comprehensive, systematic approach to long-range strategic planning. It is advisable to project the timeframe to be addressed in the planning at the beginning of the process. The leadership of the organization must recognize that planning must become a priority and will focus the best energies and thought on shaping a sense of direction for the future of the institution. The greater the extent to which the organization commits to *priority* and *focus*, the more successful will be the planning process.

2. Develop an organization for planning. The president, in collaboration with the chairman of the board and key members of the executive cabinet, identifies a representative group who will work with the president in developing the plan. The president appoints the committee (has been referred to as a task force, planning team, etc.) comprised of 12 to 15 people who are key leaders within the institution or organization and who have demonstrated a commitment to the growth, development, and well-being of the university. The committee should represent the various constituencies of the organization.

3. Adopt a planning model and develop a calendar for the planning process. Use a specific planning model as a road map for keeping track of progress. Be sure the planning model is appropriate for the type of institution and identifies the vital and important steps toward an effective plan. The term "long-range strategic planning" can be adapted to however long into the future the leadership wishes to attempt. Experience has taught us that the most workable projection for a master plan is about five years. The process for developing the plan for an educational institution is not a quick and easy task. The priority given and the willingness to devote blocks of time to the process will determine how long it will take to develop a comprehensive five-year plan. It is not unusual for institutions and organizations to engage a consultant to provide guidance to the endeavor and to move the process along toward completion. If you choose to employ a consultant, be sure he/she has led an institution in planning and has led an institution to carry out the plan.

4. *Orientation and training of the planning committee.* A formal orientation experience for the planning committee is beneficial. The planning committee must understand the model to be followed and agree to follow that road map. If a consultant is employed, that person will come to the campus to orient the planning committee to make sure the group understands and is willing to follow the planning model. The consultant will explain the various steps and stages that will be followed.

5. *Develop or clarify the statement of mission and purpose.* The first step in planning should be devoted to the development of a strong, clear statement of mission for the institution. If the institution already has a board-approved mission statement, the committee should devote a period of time to careful review of the published statement. In reviewing the mission statement, the following questions should be raised: (1) Does the statement reflect the current reality of the program and work of the institution? (2) Does the statement represent the vision and commitment of the board and the leadership of the institution? (3) Does the statement allow for visionary, creative, and futuristic thinking on the part of the administration, board, and various constituencies?

6. *Identify core values.* What are the guiding principles or values to which the institution is willing to commit itself? The planning committee will devote time to discuss and list the core values of the institution as a way of understanding the essential character and nature of the institution and the way it wants to be known. Those core values will be reflected in defining goals for the future and will be used to help various constituencies understand the basic commitment of the institution.

7. *Conduct an assessment of organizational needs.* The planning committee will attempt to determine both internal and external needs that ought to be addressed by the board and the administration as the institution plans for the future. The assessment of internal needs will focus on issues such as compensation, equipment, educational resources, facilities, personnel, professional development, what is needed to upgrade performance and reputation, and other internal considerations. Surveys of the faculty and staff to help identify internal needs will be useful. The assessment of external needs will focus on issues such as needs within the community, the workplace, the denomination, the state, region, and nation that the institution ought to be addressing. The external needs will suggest possibilities for programs and services the institution can provide.

8. Develop a set of current planning assumptions. The planning committee will conduct a SWOTs analysis of the institution. Using as much research as possible, the committee will seek to identify key strengths, weaknesses, opportunities, and threats (SWOTS). Soliciting from the faculty and staff their opinion of the strengths, weaknesses, and opportunities will help them feel a part of the planning process. Asking board members and alumni to offer their opinions provides valuable insights as well.

9. Formulate a statement that defines the vision for the future. Based on the information gathered and guided by the institution's mission and purpose, the leader will guide the committee in formulating a clear, brief, easily articulated vision which projects the direction and hoped-for destination of the institution.

10. Formulate general institutional goals for five years. Goals that will guide the institution's efforts into the future flow out of the defined strengths, weaknesses, opportunities, and needs (internal and external) which have been identified. The planning committee will develop general institutional goals in seven strategic areas: (1) educational outcomes, (2) campus environment, (3) enrollment, (4) programs, (5) facilities, (6) finances, and (7) management.

Developing goals by categories will help institutional leaders think about the full scope of the work of the institution. Defining the educational outcomes desired and setting goals for the campus environment will do much to shape the identity of the organization. Different types of organizations will call for goal categories that are appropriate to the nature and purpose of the particular entity. Goals are an attempt to address issues raised by mission, values, needs, weaknesses, and opportunities.

11. Circulate foundational documents for review and action by the board of trustees. Once the general institutional goals have been developed, they should be shared with the faculty/staff for review and discussion, with the effort made to help the faculty/staff understand the goals being recommended. The materials developed should then be mailed to the trustees at least two weeks in advance of the board meeting, and the primary focus of the meeting should be to review and vote on the mission statement, core values, and general institutional goals. Review of needs and SWOTs will help clarify the context for the goals being recommended.

12. *Engage the various administrative and academic units in developing their own plan as their way of helping the institution carry out the board-adopted five-year plan.* Once the board adopts the plan, it becomes the road map for the next five years. Every vice president, director, and program director should study the board-approved plan thoroughly (normally they have been involved in developing the plan). All unit heads then develop a mission statement for their areas of work, project goals for their departments, and develop objectives (action strategies) for each year (often three years in advance).

13. *Develop a calendar for annual review and planning.* A formal process for reviewing what has taken place enables the president and board to track the progress being made in carrying out the board-approved plan. Unit/department heads should be expected to present a written report on the objectives developed for the year and opportunity provided for the accomplishments to be shared with others on the administrative team. The unit heads should then be expected to present a list of objectives for the coming year. A digest of administrative unit objectives will then be presented to the board to let them know what steps are being taken to move the institution forward.

The steps taken above help to shape and give substance to a vision for the future of the institution. A compelling sense of mission, a strong commitment to core values, an in-depth awareness of needs, and a challenging set of goals are essential elements of a vision for the future.

Good planning is flexible and should never close the door to fresh thinking and possible new initiatives. Annual review provides opportunity for new insights and new initiatives to be injected into the institutional master plan. Goals and objectives are developed that will stretch the imagination and stir fresh ideas. Effective goal setting will always push the institution to think beyond where it is right now and to dream the kind of dreams that may seem impossible to achieve.

The effective leader is one who builds a management culture around insistence on thoughtful, systematic planning. Educational accrediting agencies insist that institutions demonstrate that they are serious and comprehensive about their approach to thinking about the future.

It is not unusual for an in-depth planning process to give birth to the need for a capital campaign. Over the 16 years of my tenure as president of a Baptist university, we developed three five-year plans that gave birth to three major capital campaigns. The result was significant growth in enrollment, construction of 11 new buildings, and renovation of 12 buildings.

Advances in areas such as academic reputation, retention rates, financial health, faculty preparation and credentials, improvement of technology, and a formal approach to the faith and learning dialogue grew out of thoughtful, systematic, comprehensive planning efforts.

Resources for Further Study

Belasco, James A. *Teaching the Elephant to Dance.* New York: Crown Publishers, 1990.
Bradford, David L., and Allan R. Cohen. *Managing for Excellence.* San Francisco: John Wiley, 1984.
Collins, Jim, and Jerry Porras. *Built to Last.* New York: Harper Business, 1994.
_____. *From Good to Great.* New York: Harper Business, 2001.
Covey, Stephen. *Principle-Centered Leadership.* New York: Summit Books, 1991.
_____. *Seven Habits of Highly Effective People.* New York: Simon & Schuster, 1989.
Deal, Terrence, and Allen Kennedy. *Corporate Cultures.* Reading, MN: Addison-Wesley, 1982.
Dressel, Paul. *Administrative Leadership.* San Francisco: Jossey-Bass, 1981.
Gardner, John W. *On Leadership.* New York: The Free Press, 1990.
Hesselbein, Frances, et al. *The Leader of the Future.* San Francisco: Jossey-Bass, 1996.
Jones, Gareth R., and Jennifer M. George. *Contemporary Management*, 4th ed. New York: McGraw-Hill, 2006.
Kouzes, James, and Barry Posner. *The Leadership Challenge.* San Francisco: Jossey-Bass, 1995.
Maxwell, John. *Developing the Leader Within You.* Nashville: Thomas Nelson, 1993.
Nanus, Burt. *Visionary Leadership.* San Francisco: Jossey-Bass, 1992.
Weems, Lovett H. *Church Leadership: Vision, Team, Culture and Integrity.* Nashville: Abingdon, 1993.

Questions for Further Reflection

1. Explain the difference between vision and mission. How are these critical components complementary and yet different?
2. Is there a difference between leadership and management. Can a person be a good leader without being a good manager. If so, how?
3. How can the chief executive (or the leader of any team) both position and empower team members to function collaboratively all the while carefully defining boundaries and processes of accountability?
4. When beginning the process of strategic planning, how can a planning model be effectively used to guide the process from beginning to end?

Endnote

[1]B. Nanus, *Visionary Leadership* (San Francisco: Jossey-Bass, 1992), 1.

Chapter 4

GOVERNANCE AND
BOARD RELATIONS

Robert Andringa
President Emeritus, Council for Christian Colleges and Universities

B oards are the most underdeveloped and least leveraged
asset of most nonprofit organizations. Few boards step up
to the level of ownership and leadership that moves organizations from
average to extraordinary.

Why is this? In part, chief executive officers are reluctant to cede control
to their lay, volunteer boards and so keep them at arm's length from the
central issues of mission accomplishment. CEOs can view their boards
as competition rather than partners, taking more of their time than it's
worth, or they have not developed the respect for the board required for
transparency and trust. Then, at least as important, boards often lack the
leadership to clarify their roles, recruit only the best board members, agree
on a reasonable structure and process, and build a culture conducive to
good governance. This chapter is about moving beyond these obstacles so
ministry can thrive.

Should Christians Be Better at Governance?

Believers should have an edge in leadership and in the act of governing.
We understand the order of creation, have access to godly wisdom, know
hundreds of precepts that prove true over and over again, and experience
grace and the power of forgiveness. We believe in putting others first, or

at least thinking of others more highly than ourselves. The indwelling of the Holy Spirit guides our path, bears the fruit outlined in Galatians 5, helps us resist temptation, and helps us do that which is true and good. We have more guidance in the use of time, talent, and financial resources than any other belief system. Indeed, I have witnessed all of these wonderful attributes of the Christ-follower while assisting more than 500 faith-based, nonprofit organizations.

Yet we must be honest with ourselves. We also can be blown away by how fellow Christians gossip, undermine, and inflict pain on one another while working with ministries. Some invoke the Bible as the basis for personal vindictiveness, arbitrary actions that are not supported by those around them, making unwise and even hurtful decisions "because God told me to."

I love the governance process because it requires consensus in decision making. Boards should be self-correcting when one or a few behave in ungodly ways. Hopefully several members know how to speak the truth in love. Hopefully board members can forgive when one of their own, or their CEO, acknowledges fault and seeks reinstatement according to biblical principles. Hopefully most board members recognize wisdom when it is spoken and reject false teaching that can lead the organization down the wrong path. Yes, *hopefully*. And thankfully, that is more often the case than not.

Do We Know What Works in Governance?

Too many boards lack good models of governance and do not take the time to learn principles that work. Globally, more than six million nonprofits (almost two million in the U.S.) and research and experience have uncovered principles that work in the vast majority of situations. The need is great to take seriously what is known to work and merge these principles with the advantages Christ-followers bring to the boardroom so that worthy missions can be accomplished in extraordinary ways.

With the space allotted for this chapter, we can look briefly at the most important principles of governance about which almost all who focus on this area can agree. When I observe an approach to governance that seems to work over and over and in at least 90 percent of all nonprofits, I call it a principle. While every board is unique, often because of personalities currently leading within a culture shaped over many years, we want to expand in this chapter on the core principles of successful, Christian, nonprofit organizations.

These principles can be implemented differently but within a fairly narrow range of options. The goal should be mission accomplishment in God-honoring ways. All boards do a few things well. Great boards do most of these things well. (Note: Throughout the text that follows, I will reference by a letter many of my most used training tools that relate to the issue being discussed. All of these are in one pdf document that can be downloaded at no cost at www.TheAndringaGroup.com and used for training as you see fit. Click on Bob Andringa, then look for "A Handbook for Christian Leadership—Governance.")

Principle 1—Boards and their CEOs must work in partnership, with the chair managing the board and the CEO running the organization as the "one agent" of the board.

Many board chairs view their roles as almost honorary, asking the CEO just before meetings what to do, then assuming there is little to be concerned about until the next meeting. Wrong! A board should elect a chair that is ready and willing to "manage" the board. CEOs have their hands full managing the organization and run into relational land mines when they try to manage people who hired them.

1.1 What Is the Role of the Chair?

With the average U.S. board at 16 (the range is from three to as many as 60!), it takes a good leader to help the board function well (A). It is always best to have a volunteer board member elected by peers assume the chair's leadership role. Yes, this role requires easily twice the number of hours as others on the board. Yes, this means helping to plan the meetings, recommend committee assignments, stay in regular communication with the chief executive, see that good policies about board structure and process are adopted and monitored, represent the board to various outside constituencies, correct individual board members when they behave inappropriately, maintain the integrity of the board's decisions about itself and the organization, and much more.

Choosing the chair is one of the most important moments in the life of the board. It should be a democratic process resulting in the election of the one most trusted by the majority to function as their leader. To choose a person based mainly on one's level of giving, length of service, or even pleasing personality is not good enough. Great boards have great chairs.

1.2 What Is the Role of the CEO in Governance?

The chief executive has a delicate role. On the one hand, she or he is an employee of the board. The CEO runs the organization on a day-by-day basis. Selecting CEOs who respect the legal and moral authority of the board—and help the board succeed—is a fundamental challenge for all boards. While my perspective on good governance emphasizes active boards, no governing process works well without the full support and participation of the CEO (B). The CEO also involves direct reports in the work of governance. Helping those people understand the partnership role between the board and staff is critical. Together, senior staff can make a huge difference in moving governance from good to great (C).

1.3 What Does a Board-Oriented CEO Do?

By observation of many, fewer than 50 percent of CEOs are truly board-oriented. That is, most put their best foot forward in preparing for and participating in board meetings, then give a sigh of relief and focus on other things until a few weeks before the next board meeting. Be honest, CEOs! What every board needs is a chief executive who believes a strong board is an advantage, not a problem. A board-oriented CEO thinks "good governance" every day, literally. Board-oriented CEOs can think like board members and actually enter into strategic thinking with board members that may challenge the status quo. These CEOs really listen to the board and adjust to how the board wants more time for discussion in meetings, how written reports should be more focused, and how the stated values are carried out.

Board-oriented CEOs go out of their way to know each board member and his or her family. They send handwritten notes, cards, and personal e-mails. They have a schedule to be sure they talk personally with each board member between meetings. (Are you seeing the value of smaller boards?)

These smart leaders have little mental or written notes about how to engage each board member beyond their role in governance. Successful CEOs spend as much as 10–15 percent of their time on board-related matters, including helping to nurture future board candidates.

1.4 Should the CEO Be a Board Member?

It is easier for a CEO to be board-oriented if he is a member of the board. I prefer that he be *ex officio* without vote. Why without vote? Because that allows him to be viewed as a peer during governance activities, fully able to engage in board dialogue, and to think as a board member (when not consumed with the tasks of management). But when the board has spoken in its one voice, the job of the CEO shifts to saluting the board decisions and implementing them faithfully. Why force a CEO to vote one way or the other, risking disappointing some fellow board members? Besides, most CEOs can influence far more than one vote during board discussion.

There is an important intangible at work when a CEO is board-oriented and is perceived as a board colleague. How one thinks is important. When a CEO is invited to think like a board member, there is less defensiveness, more long-term thinking and openness to change. And that helps the CEO prepare the staff to serve the board. It's a different view, and it takes both the governance view and the staff view working in partnership to move a board from good to great.

Principle 2—Boards must take ownership of written policies to be used in electing, orienting, developing, evaluating and even terminating board members.

2.1 What Are the Keys to Electing Good Board Members?

Jim Collins (author of *Good to Great*) got it right when he suggested that getting the right people on the bus and in the right seats is half the battle. Most boards are too casual about finding, electing, orienting, and training board members. No NFL team can win the Super Bowl unless every position has the best possible player. Good boards, no matter what size, think through and define in writing the specific qualifications for board membership. This "profile" guides the board's search for candidates so that, in time, each board member contributes to the makeup of the dream team (D).

To prevent any misfires ("If I had known X before I said I would serve on this board, I would have said no"), it is best to provide a good orientation to board candidates *before* they are asked to serve (E). This "truth in advertising" step allows a person to read the bylaws, latest Form 990, the audit, and strategic plan in advance of becoming a nominee. It makes for more satisfied and loyal board members. And should a candidate go through this first step of orientation only to decline the nomination, both the candidate and the organization are better off.

2.2 Should the CEO Have a Role in Electing Board Members?

A board governance committee (often called the board development committee or something similar) should take the lead in drafting the board profile for full board approval. All board members, including the CEO, should then recommend people who fit the profile. The CEO or another staff person can help maintain the database of prospects, do some of the due diligence on those determined to be potential candidates, provide the preelection orientation materials, and be one of those who meets with candidates prior to election. Realistically, if there is any reason for a CEO to express strong doubts about a candidate prior to elections, the board should take that seriously.

2.3 What Are the Pros and Cons of Term Limits?

If there is a trend, it is toward term limits. Boards discover they need "new blood" on the board as the times change. Even a casual observer of ministries knows that it has taken years to find room for women and minorities on boards whose members stay on and on and on. More recently, boards need expertise in the applications of technology, understanding how to be more global, or relating to the younger generation. Either the board grows unreasonably large to accommodate these needs, or it determines that some strategy of rotating board members in and out makes sense (F).

Key decisions include the length of individual terms. The most common terms are three years, but two or four could make sense. The number of consecutive terms also varies, but seldom is it more than three. Whatever the combination, asking someone to serve for more than nine years without a year off is asking a lot. Good people are busy people, and good busy people usually are more willing to serve if they see an end in sight. While term limits make good sense in most organizations, finding other good busy people is a constant challenge.

2.4 How Can We Mitigate the Downsides to Forcing Great Board Members Off the Board with Term Limits?

Most great board members understand the need for turnover in any organization that wants to stay vital, relevant, and successful. They generally support term limits. From the organization's perspective, however, you never want to lose the 20–30 percent "really great ones." So put them to work after their terms are up. Ask those individuals to serve on an advisory group, head up a special task force, become an advisor to the CEO, or even serve as the board coach. After the mandatory year off, many would accept the invitation to start over with a fresh new term.

Some organizations have wonderful people on the board whose loyalty and maybe generous giving make them "keepers" even when they reach an age too old to serve on the board. I like the idea of creating a "board alumni hall of fame" or some such designation for lifelong membership once a person has served "X" years. This allows the CEO to communicate and interact with these folks who want to stay connected with the ministry. Yes, some of them will end up including the ministry in their estate plans.

2.5 Who Is Responsible for Board Training?

Great boards know that ongoing board training is essential for good governance. And they assume responsibility for that task, usually through the guidance of the governance committee. Some boards opt for short training periods as part of every meeting. Others prefer to be immersed in governance training for a weekend. Every board has a few who actually love issues surrounding the governance challenge. They should be invited to attend a governance conference, read appropriate resources from Board-Source, and probably serve on the governance committee. Again, it works best when the board does not depend on the CEO to fulfill this training responsibility for them. However, it is good for the CEO and any senior managers who help staff board committees to participate in the training.

Because most boards have members who have served on other boards, there are lots of assumptions about governance sitting around any board table. Until your board agrees on how you want to function, many individuals leave board meetings frustrated because things were not done according to their own paradigm.

2.6 Should Individual Board Members Be Evaluated?

Assuming the culture of the organization encourages periodic performance reviews of all paid and volunteer staff, why should a board exempt itself from positive ways of improving its own members? Of course no one wants to be judged based on unknown expectations or arbitrary criteria. So it is important that the entire board approve some form of a "report card" and the process for using it (G).

Normally, a board development committee is tasked with evaluating individuals whose term will end soon and who are eligible for renomination. The report card of expectations could be given to the members whose term is up for them to do a self-evaluation. The committee could ask all board members to evaluate their peers using that tool. Or the committee could use it only among themselves. Subjective factors also weigh in during the process of renominating board members, but sticking to agreed-upon variables reduces finger pointing and hard feelings.

Another tool many boards adopt is called an annual affirmation statement (H). Often combined with the annual signing of its conflict of interest policy, this annual ritual allows every board member, even after the first year, to read again all the expectations the board has of its members and affirm that everyone is willing and able to honor them. Some of these items could include behavior such as "supportive of the organization's leadership" and "honors the confidentiality of board deliberations." No one is being picked on. This tool simply recognizes that life changes for people within even a year and it is best to allow board members to reassess the level of commitment they are comfortable with or use this annual "no fault" process to indicate it is best to resign voluntarily.

2.7 Should a Board Ever Terminate One of Its Members?

It is difficult for a board of volunteers to meet only periodically and do the work of governance well. When one or two members are constant problems—or simply never show up—it is up to the board to take action. The first step is to put in writing what the expectations are for board membership. The chair, as manager of the board, then uses that position quietly and respectfully to provide feedback to any who stray too far.

The bylaws should make clear that the board has the right, without cause, to terminate one of its own members by vote. But most boards find this difficult to do. That is why I like the annual affirmation statement so board members thoughtfully and prayerfully review the common expectations and are provided a "safe" way to exit on their own. Most of us know when we are not beginning to meet the group's expectations. We should be honest with the group and bow out.

Principle 3—Boards must evaluate regularly the right size, structure, and procedures of the board to be most effective.

3.1 What Is a Good Size for a Nonprofit Board?

Unfortunately (my opinion), most boards are too large. Why is it that multibillion-dollar global corporations can be governed by 10 or fewer, while the average nonprofit organization needs 16? And private colleges, symphonies, and theater groups often average more than 30! The primary reason is that some believe loading up the board with real or perceived major donors is the way to financial success. And, indeed, that may work for some.

Be careful, though, in making assumptions. Major donors often say they would prefer being on some blue-ribbon advisory council rather than the governing board. They do enjoy being with peers and supporting the organization but often are too stretched with other commitments to be good board members. And, let's be frank, some entrepreneurs with high net worth got there by exercising their gifts of independent thinking and quick decision making, not the slower, deliberative culture of nonprofit boards. So the challenge is to engage major donors in ways that fit their interests and needs.

If I had to pick "the best" size for most nonprofit boards, I would say 11–13 people who are all fully engaged and carefully selected to fill specific areas of expertise. Eleven or 12 people can easily fit around a table, allow for everyone to be engaged in dialogue, build good relationships of trust, and more easily stay informed. With a small board, few if any committees would be necessary.

3.2 Which Committees Make Sense?

Here is the key: committees help the board in the work of governance, not oversee or help staff in the work of administration.

Boards of 15 or more usually decide a few committees are important. The basic committees, although often with more creative names, are these:

- Finance (budget, asset management, risk management, audits and compliance)
- Programs (all activities the organization uses to achieve its mission)
- Advancement (fund-raising, public relations, communications, etc.)
- Governance (nominations, orientation, training, evaluation, bylaw review, etc.)

More complex organizations might have a separate audit committee. Or they may have more than one committee overseeing and proposing policies regarding programs. The tendency is to have too many committees whose membership and jurisdictions overlap, causing confusion or delay. Each committee should have a clear definition of its role. The challenge is to make wise use of committees, and that task has many parts (I).

3.3 What About Executive Committees?

The committees listed above "speak to the board, not for the board." That is why nonboard members could be used to beef up the expertise on an important committee. The committee is only doing good homework for the board. Its decisions are tentative until its recommendations are made to and approved by the full board.

The exception to this rule is an executive committee (J). This committee, often comprised of the officers and chairs of the standing committees, is expected to "act for the board" between full board meetings. It is a way for large boards to get done certain things required of boards when it is inconvenient or costly to convene the full board. With a smaller group of fully engaged board members, dialogue is more productive, and decisions get made expeditiously.

The risk in having an active executive committee is that over the years the "real meat" of governance can gravitate to this more efficient group and the full board becomes more a rubber stamp board. Or nonexecutive committee members feel left out, even second-class. One way to prevent this evolution toward a too active executive committee is to specify in the bylaws that the executive committee can act on behalf of the board *except* it may not . . . (hire or fire the CEO, buy or sell property, amend the bylaws, etc.).

3.4 How Can We Tap Expertise beyond the Board?

No board of whatever size has all the expertise to deal with complex issues, especially those coming as a surprise. A good process strategy is to ask, "What three to five people could give us the best advice within X days?" Often board members know people whose position and expertise could benefit the board far quicker and better than referring a tough issue to a standing committee. These busy people are often honored to serve on a board-created ad hoc task force. The group of experts may need to meet only once. Or even provide what the board needs following one conference call.

Other reasons to convene short-term, ad hoc task forces include opportunities to engage people who could be future board candidates or keep involved great board members who are in their mandatory year off because of term limits.

Another way to tap outside expertise is to retain a board mentor, someone uniquely equipped to coach the chair, CEO, and chair of the governance committee. This person is often able to observe and see problems others do not see and offer solutions as an independent third party that the official players may be reluctant to suggest.

Principle 4—Board meetings must be both memorable and effective to retain the best board members and do the work of governance well.

Most board members who become frustrated or disillusioned do so because of poor board meetings. It is so easy to get into a rut and follow the same boring format meeting after meeting.

4.1 How Many Meetings a Year Make Sense?

The simple answer to this question is "as many as are required to do governance well." Two per year is usually the minimum. Every month is way too many. Generally, boards find that fewer board meetings of longer duration make sense. Especially for boards whose members have long distances to travel, coming for an overnight or two makes sense and helps build relationships that contribute to board trust and unity.

Every year or two, the board should schedule a board retreat away from headquarters. No ties! Time over meals and between meetings, often including spouses, builds good board and staff relationships. The extra hours allow for long-term envisioning, participating in board training, and generally getting ahead of the curve in good governance.

4.2 Who Should Plan Board and Committee Meetings?

Staff drive way too much of board and committee agendas. Board members love the help, but they must take ownership of how those precious hours each year are spent. When staff drive the agenda, it is too easy for them simply to put the biggest management issues on the docket rather than think as a board member thinks. What must the board know? Can we give them that in advance over our board Web site, on a CD, or even in a printed advance board book? Which new policies must be developed? What old policies no longer work? Which committees need to meet in advance of the full board meeting? Are there new board members to elect? Should we have a rotating cycle of topics so the big topics get more focus every third or fourth board meetings? These are among the questions board members should work on together with the CEO and the leadership team.

4.3 What Makes for Great Meetings?

Great meetings? Yes, the goal should be that every meeting is memorable. Sure, there is similar work to be done at every meeting, but be creative! Great meetings include some or all of these things:

- Committee meetings focused on information that leads to board policies
- President's report (CEOs, be creative)
- Time for fellowship, often a meal with staff, students, donors
- Educational input from an expert that contributes to wiser policies
- Show and tell time so the board hears and sees results of the programs
- Visit to some facility or program that informs or allows the board to celebrate
- Plenary sessions to hear and act on committee reports
- Time for sharing and prayer
- Possibly some special events for board spouses

Of course the lodging, food, meeting rooms, PowerPoints, displays, and handouts need careful attention. Small gifts to board members are always a hit. The setup should be around a table or U-shaped tables with only board members seated there. I like the chair and CEO sitting next to each other. Senior staff should sit at a side table where they can observe and be "on call" should the CEO (the "one agent" of the board) need to call upon them. Someone has to take notes for the minutes; others may need to help board members with travel or other last-minute needs; still others are needed to make sure the food and snacks are also memorable. Great meetings are never taken for granted (K).

4.4 Why Two Executive Sessions?

Apart from the open meeting sessions, most boards now have one executive session without any staff. A few years ago I observed an even better format. Early in the board meeting, the chair convenes a "board members only" session *without* the CEO. The main question is, How are we doing with our CEO? The session might take less than 10 minutes.

During a break the chair gives the CEO a heads-up and suggests that when the board and CEO meet later in executive session the CEO should address topics A and B. As you can see, most board members would not bring up A and B when the CEO was present. Thus, important relational or policy issues don't get raised in a timely manner. When the second executive session comes at the end of the meeting, the CEO addresses A and B (having the benefit of some time to think about them), then often says, "Before we meet again, I am thinking of doing X and want to give you a confidential advance notice so you understand my thinking." These two short sessions can prevent small issues from growing to intractable problems.

Principle 5—Boards must clarify their roles *vis á vis* staff and speak with one voice, ideally cataloging all policies legitimately in the domain of board leadership in one evolving board policy manual.

5.1 What Is a Simple Way to Distinguish the Role of the Board *vis á vis* Staff?

Boards set policies around their own and the organization's mission. Both board members and staff *formulate* board policies (generally, whatever the board decides to "own" by voting on it becomes board policy). Only the board, of course, *determines* board policy. Usually, only staff *implement* board policy. And—here is where most boards break down— the board must determine how it wants to *monitor* board policies. Even though staff do the tracking and research necessary for monitoring board policies, the board should document what it wants and when.

Board members wear two, and often three, different hats (L). The *governance hat* is worn only when the board or a committee is properly convened with a quorum present. The CEO reports to the board when members are wearing their governance hats. Governance is always a group process, not something an individual does alone. When the meetings are over, most board members should figuratively put on their *volunteer hat*. When wearing this hat, they help the organization in various ways that make sense to each one individually. And with this hat on, they are usually working for the CEO or staff. Once in awhile, the board actually delegates a task to a board member, who would then put on an *implementer hat*. Both board members and staff are helped by remembering which hat is being worn!

5.2 Is There a Hierarchy of Policies in an Organization?

Hey, someone is asking good questions! Yes, understanding the hierarchy of policies can eliminate a lot of confusion and help the board stick to its own business, not micromanage or function simply as a rubber stamp. As you look at this hierarchy, think about *authority* flowing down and *accountability* flowing up.

1. Federal and State Laws
2. Applicable Denominational or Parent Organization Documents
3. Articles of Incorporation
4. Bylaws
5. Board Policy Manual (BPM)
6. Institution-Wide Policies, e.g., Strategic Plans, Employee Manuals, Faculty Handbooks, etc.
7. Department/Unit Policies

From the board's perspective, the CEO is expected to alert the board to issues flowing from box 1. The boards that need to address box 2 usually have representatives of the denomination or parent organization on the board. The full board needs to take ownership of boxes 3, 4, and 5 (more later), allowing the CEO considerable flexibility and noninterference on boxes 6 and 7 (M).

5.3 What Is a BPM?

Some boards leave it to old minutes to document all their policies. But who remembers, let alone is motivated to read, minutes from 10 or 20 years ago? Other boards ask staff to cut and paste important policies in one document. But these are usually ad hoc policies that often contradict one another and leave big gaps in the topics of governance that should be addressed. The best answer to giving a board a "governance management system" is what is called a board policy manual (BPM)—all policies about all topics a board is expected to speak to with one voice (N). It is the single most important tool of governance in my opinion. I joined my colleague Fred Laughlin in writing *Good Governance for Nonprofits* (American Management Association, 2007) that provides a BPM template and walks the reader through the decisions in each section. Using this template has saved boards hundreds of hours in finally addressing issues that are governance in ways that honor the legitimate role of management.

While boards make decisions through votes that are not necessary to document in the BPM (O), the main outcome of a board meeting should be wiser, clearer policies that guide the board and CEO until good monitoring shows the need to change them. In fact, boards using a BPM make several changes during every meeting! And all this can be done in fewer than 20 pages of straightforward language!

Principle 6—Boards must adopt powerful missions with important outcomes and goals and identify the values and strategies most important to success.

6.1 Are You Driven by Your Mission?

Many mission statements are simply short descriptions (or not so short!) of what the organization does. Few inspire. A good mission statement points to the outcomes (some would say ends) one should observe as the mission is accomplished. In the nonprofit world we are about changed lives. Leave the programs (some would say means) to other foundational statements. Sometimes a tagline following the organization's name can add zip and zest. Many organizations also craft a vision statement, often pointing to the highest aspirations (e.g., eliminate poverty in our country) that require collaboration with others. A vision points to a desired future. It is important for the board and staff to focus considerable energy every few years on reviewing the mission statement: What will result from our work? Once agreement is reached, a mission statement should drive policy, prevent the ministry from "mission drift," and guide everyone in making the tough financial decisions every organization faces these days.

6.2 Do You Have Meaningful Written Values?

Christian ministries are rightly guided by biblical precepts. But there should be other "values to guide us" that are important for a board to state in its BPM. Here are a couple of examples: "We seek collaborative partnerships" and "We are transparent with our constituencies." A handful of these, carefully determined, provide a means for evaluating the "how" of mission accomplishment. Crafting these values is especially important when a board decides that it needs to change how things are done in the near future.

6.3 How Do Goals Guide Strategic Planning, and Who Does That?

I often say board policies are written from the "10,000 feet perspective." Too many boards get consumed by the work in the trenches—a ground-level view that few have the time, energy, or knowledge to handle. Flying at 10,000 feet allows the board to use its knowledge of history, trends, and issues in society, what other organizations are doing, etc., to craft a few big goals that point the direction, guide management, and stimulate all constituencies. These goals, crafted with the full involvement of the CEO and stated so some level of measurement is possible, then drive the development by the staff of the more comprehensive strategic plan (P).

Some boards think they should write or at least approve a multiyear strategic plan. I disagree. A strategic plan that will mean anything has to be crafted with heavy investment from those who will carry it out. Planning needs to take into consideration current staff talent, funding needs, timing, technology, laws and regulations, other obligations, and much more. A smart CEO will often invite a couple board members whose expertise is in planning to help in the process (wearing which hat?), and the board will resist "approving" every sentence in the strategic plan because that would make it a board document (box 5), making it more difficult to amend as the environment, funding, or staffing requires to keep it current. Yes, the board should definitely review the strategic plan, but if there is consensus about something that needs changing, the appropriate response for the board is to amend its BPM so the CEO is required to make changes in the plan (authority flows down and accountability flows up). Does this make sense for your organization?

Principle 7—Boards must define the information and schedule of reports they need for good governance.

7.1 How Should Boards Monitor Board Policy?

Too often boards get reports on what management is doing. Financial reports, especially, often are at a level that only the CFO fully understands—data relative to process rather than results. And most board members receive more reports than they want to read. What is the answer? The board itself must define for management what reports it wants and when.

Keying off the mission statement, most boards can dialogue with management and come up with a schedule of reports that focus on achievement, overall financial condition, and other key indicators of the condition of the ministry. Measuring nonprofit missions is more difficult than for most businesses where the bottom line is the ultimate measure. But trying to gather the best qualitative information is an effort worth doing. Some reports should be monthly, others quarterly, and others annually. A few comprehensive reports might even be scheduled for every two or three years.

Other ways to improve on board reports include using private board Web sites to place the reports for easy access way in advance (and long after) board meetings. Or giving more detailed reports only to committees as part of their focused education. All reports from key executives who report to the CEO and help staffing board committees should be provided in advance, in writing, and in just a few pages. Few, if any, oral reports from the CEOs direct reports should be necessary in full board meetings.

7.2 Why Are Dashboard Reports So Popular?

In recent years, "dashboard" reports (most drivers depend on what they see on the dashboard to understand what is going on under the hood) have found popularity among boards. Why? Because most board members are frustrated with reams of unconnected, too-detailed reports written by staff from a staff perspective.

Boards like *historical* data (How does this compare with where we were one, three, and five years ago?). They like data put into *context* (How does this compare with five similar organizations?). And they like graphs and other *visuals*. Some dashboards lay out the key goals and simply show colors to keep the board informed, using green (We are on target!), yellow (We are watching this carefully to see what changes are required), or red (We are way behind on this and may need the board to reconsider it as a goal). Which colored items do you think the board would spend time on?

In a time of unprecedented amounts of information, great boards learn how to instruct their CEOs on what they want and when. Using a format that becomes familiar over time is one good way to solve this information-overload problem.

Principle 8—Boards must evaluate themselves and their chief executive officer annually so that the organization constantly is improving based on agreed-upon standards.

8.1 What Is the Purpose of the Board's Evaluating Itself?

To stand still is to atrophy. Living things grow and change. What doesn't get measured doesn't improve. Do you agree with these statements? The purpose of evaluation is to improve, encourage, affirm, correct, and adjust. Good boards understand their own need to model good evaluation by regularly assessing board size, structure, process, effectiveness. This is usually carried out by a plan presented by the board's governance committee and approved by the full board. When the board evaluates itself in thoughtful ways, it is easier to expect the whole organization to assess its different people and parts in ways that lead to improved performance.

Evaluations of the board as a whole usually involve a survey, created internally or purchased from a few vendors who have created generic surveys. Or it might involve a board consultant who observes, surveys, reviews documents, interviews board leaders, and makes a report with recommendations. Some boards evaluate every meeting, either with a few minutes before board members depart or use a survey sent through the mail a week or so later. The important thing is to evaluate and improve!

8.2 How Should a Board Evaluate Staff?

This is a trick question! The board should evaluate only its one agent, the chief executive. That person is expected to evaluate the staff, directly or through internal policies that guide the process in a large organization. In its BPM, the board might lay out the expectation for staff training and evaluation, as well as broad guidelines on staff compensation.

There are good books on varying ways to evaluate a CEO, but here is a common approach that can be started at any step in the annual cycle:

- Subgroup (often an executive committee) negotiates personal and professional goals for the CEO to focus on for the year. Sometimes others see our strengths and weaknesses better than we do and can help keep us working in our sweet spot.
- The CEO uses these goals as reference points in written and oral reports to the board during the year.
- The CEO is asked to write a self-evaluation based on the previously negotiated personal and professional goals (often, but not always, linked to the board's goals for the whole organization).
- This self-evaluation (perhaps five to seven pages) is circulated to the entire board for comment by individual board members to the chair of the evaluation committee.
- The evaluation committee meets to discuss the self-evaluation and all comments from board members. They agree on the key points and discuss possible personal and professional goals the board would like to see the CEO pursue in the coming year. This committee often is tasked with adjusting the compensation of the CEO.

- The committee meets with the CEO to discuss the self-evaluation, the general feedback from board members, and to agree on personal and organizational goals and performance indicators related to the CEO for the year ahead.
- The committee chair prepares a written letter to the CEO with the committee's summary of the year past, compensation adjustments, and documenting the agreed-upon performance goals for the year ahead. Some boards want only a report from the committee, while others may want to give formal approval to such a letter prior to its going to the CEO.

Principle 9—Both board and staff must contribute to a God-honoring culture in which a clear and meaningful mission can be set, monitored, and updated.

9.1 How Can We Identify Our Culture?

Over the past 24 years, I have had the opportunity to get up close and personal with more than 250 faith-based, nonprofit boards and their CEOs. Working with them has been a great joy and brought much of the significance I desire in life. Amazingly, each board culture is quite different! I wish I were smart enough to write a book on organizational culture. Let me suggest several ways you might get a grip on your own culture:

- Ask a nonboard member to interview each new board member after six months.
- Ask the same person to interview each departing board member.
- Invite an observer to board and committee meetings for one year; then take seriously any observations and recommendations.
- Engage a board mentor who has worked with many boards to coach the chair and CEO toward good practices.
- Encourage board members to discuss "what I liked about other boards on which I served" and "what I wish our board and staff could do better."
- Do a Web-based survey after every meeting to evaluate what people liked and what they think could be improved.
- The annual CEO performance review is a good time for transparency about the interpersonal dynamics around governance.

The point is that some boards' cultures could be described in any of these ways: unified, forward looking, driven toward excellence, welcoming of diverse views, nurturing of staff, engaged; or the description could be: complacent, divisive, risk adverse, totally dependent on staff, confrontational, self-aggrandizing, competitive with staff, ignorant of the field we are in. You get the point. Some cultures are more conducive to mission achievement than others. And when a board engages in its key roles from a scriptural perspective, it should have the advantage (O).

9.2 How Can We Change Our Culture?

Leadership. Leadership. Leadership. First, agree and hold everyone accountable to honor God in all you do, even when that sparks debates about what that means. These commitments might be stated as values. Second, take seriously who is elected to the board and who is appointed to each key staff position. Seek competence, spiritual maturity, character, commitment, and good chemistry. Third, everyone needs to be trained. Send leaders to the best workshops, purchase good books to pass around, use speakers and consultants. Fourth, cultivate and reward a spirit of learning and a culture of evidence. Change is inevitable, so welcome it and try to manage that change in these ways.

Organizational culture is difficult to change, but good leadership is willing to speak the truth in love, admit mistakes, seek forgiveness, apply grace, direct people to the Word, cover all things in prayer . . . you get it! Hopefully this book will encourage you along this way.

Resources for Further Study

Web sites will take you to helpful information on board governance. Here are four useful sites:

BoardSource, located in Washington, DC, is a membership organization worth joining, and it has outstanding resources on every topic: http://www .boardsource.org/.

For institutions of higher education, consider joining the Association of Governing Boards (AGB), also located in Washington, DC, and a source of quality resources: http://agb.org/.

Ministries, many of whom pay dues to belong to the Evangelical Council for Financial Accountability, located in Virginia, will find good practices at this site: http://www.ecfa.org/HomePage.aspx.

Likewise, ministries of all types will find useful materials on leadership, management, and governance at the Engstrom Institute, managed by the Christian Leadership Alliance and found here: http://www.engstrom-institute.com/.

Questions for Further Reflection

1. If you used these nine principles as an evaluation checklist with all your board members, each rating your organization on each principle using a scale of 1 (low) to 100 (highest possible), would your average score on each principle be higher than 75 percent? If not, try discussing the low-scoring principles and related questions at a future meeting.

2. Do you have at least three board members who are motivated to become students of governance by reading the good books, attending good board development programs, and learning from other good boards? If so, join one of the organizations previously mentioned and budget a few hundred dollars to start a board library.

3. Do you need a board mentor or coach to help facilitate a good board evaluation effort and help the board be accountable for change? Consider a former chair, another organization's leader in your city, or someone who specializes in helping boards in this way. (A list of 16 Christians who have successfully trained ministry boards can be found at this link: http://www.theandringagroup.com.)

Chapter 5

MANAGING THE ORGANIZATION

R. Judson Carlberg
President, Gordon College

Walking across campus on a warm, bright June morning in 2007, I felt relaxed and well prepared for my first task of the day, which was to review the agenda and reports for a trustee executive committee meeting scheduled for late that afternoon. I was fully expecting a benign, comfortable meeting since I had already sent the trustees my positive assessment of our performance against our goals for the year just ending.

My assessment had been strong because our applications for fall admission were the highest in our history; our annual fund giving was on target; and our budget projections indicated a slight surplus for June 30, the end of the fiscal year. Strolling across campus in the sunshine, I had no inkling that, over the next five hours, some harsh realities would come to light, realities ensuring that our board meeting would be high stress rather than routine.

The drama began at about midday, when my chief financial officer asked to see me. In his hands he held our business office's latest year-end financial report. After briskly reviewing the numbers, he flipped to the last page and showed me the bottom line: We were suddenly projecting a $360,000 deficit! Stunned, I listened incredulously as he tried to explain how this had happened. He said the projected shortfall was due in small measure to unmonitored end-of-year overspending within a few departments but was mostly attributable to mandatory accounting adjustments just uncovered.

My mind was racing. How, I wondered, was I going to explain this development to the trustees in just a few hours? Why hadn't I known of it sooner? How were we going to meet our bank ratios on our long-term residence hall construction debt? These and other acutely uncomfortable questions were replaying over and over in my mind.

Later, as I drove up Route 128 from Boston's North Shore and on to Waltham to the office park where we hold our executive committee meetings, I felt sick. There's really no other word for it. I had been at Gordon College as chief academic officer and then president for over 30 years, and in my experience nothing like this had ever happened, and certainly not in the 15 years of my presidency. As the trustees gathered, I grew increasingly anxious about what lay ahead. After a few moments given to routine business matters, I pulled out the budget report and laid it before the executive committee. They were as shocked by what they saw as I had been, and they had every reason to be.

The meeting was to have focused on my personal performance, a topic which had suddenly become anything but benign! Ignoring the meeting's agenda, the trustees immediately shifted to trying to understand the startling numbers before them and to exploring the best way to address the shortfall. In the midst of that meeting, as we concentrated on the financial challenges ahead, I was keenly aware I had broken some of the most basic rules of administration-board relationships:

- Pay sufficient attention to management details, so that danger signals are recognized early.
- Address minor issues before a crisis erupts.
- Most of all, never surprise the board leadership.

By early evening the trustees had determined that our 30-year string of balanced budgets must remain unbroken, and they insisted we find a way to balance the budget by June 30, 2007. A date only 19 days away!

To make matters worse, several days after the executive committee meeting, I learned that not only did we have a budget deficit; we also had a potential admissions problem. It was becoming increasingly apparent that our record number of admission applicants was not necessarily going to translate into a record number of new student deposits. As we now know, the national trend that spring was for students to apply to more colleges in an attempt to enhance their prospects of getting into at least one. So, even as we were frantically trying to achieve a balanced budget for the fiscal year just ending, we were also facing revised admissions projections for the year just ahead of us requiring us simultaneously to redraft the next year's budget.

In June 2007, as we scrambled to meet those challenges, we were still a year away from the shockwaves crashing through the world economy. But we recognized that after years of wonderful growth in student enrollment, in the number of faculty and staff positions, and in the size of our physical plant, we were suddenly managing in a climate of scarcity. We searched for the best response, asking ourselves many hard questions, including: "Was this a management problem? A leadership crisis? Or both?" I had some sleepless nights followed by desperate early morning prayers. And I didn't have much time to ponder alternatives. Action was needed FAST!

I immediately turned my attention to the task at hand, which, in a nutshell, was increasing income and minimizing the risk of financial failure. Soon after calling my administrative team together to respond to our financial crisis and pray, plan, and prepare for the 2007–2008 school year, we saw that we had to cut our adjunct faculty and full-time staff before the fall semester, a morale buster at the worst possible time.

Moreover, these unforeseen events were an overlay on an already crowded agenda. Presidents are often shocked by the sheer quantity and variety of stuff clamoring for their attention. And, since time is a finite commodity, it cannot expand to fill the tasks assigned to it. Presidents are expected to be both managers and leaders on call 24 hours, seven days a week; ready to step into any crisis with direction or decisions *now*; ready to offer an appropriate word of admonition or encouragement *now*; ready to visit a major donor *now*; ready to articulate the vision of the institution in ways that will be attractive and compelling *now*; ready to write a blog entry, column, or report *now*; ready to be transparent, even about the details of their personal life, *now*; ready to open the door of their homes to students, staff, or strangers right *now*; and ready to solve a budget crisis *NOW.* Given that college presidents and other leaders cannot deal adequately with every item that comes their way, they need great wisdom to recognize what is essential and what is peripheral. They will live and die with the choices they make between the two.

Fallout from that June executive committee meeting was soon evident. The finance committee of the board went into high gear, requiring more budget details than ever before, including specific end-of-the-month reports on overspending. They also asked the treasurer of the board to meet with the administrative team before every meeting of the full board and every meeting of the executive committee to examine the books and review any budget aberrations. The disturbing possibility of failing to meet bank covenants on our long-term residence hall debt had triggered deep interest among our trustees in how those bank covenants were being administered; concern exacerbated when banks began to fail and loan markets tightened.

As we entered into full crisis management mode in the year following June 2007, I found our processes slow and cumbersome. We were double-checking, overanalyzing, overreporting, and creating unnecessarily redundant systems. The harder and more obsessively we tried to compensate for the mistakes made in our budget process, the more the board's confidence in our leadership began to erode. We found ourselves in serious danger of losing the large deposit of trust that had been built up between the trustees and the college over decades.

The Trust Factor

In short, our board's finance committee felt they could no longer trust the financial reports I was giving them. I, in turn, felt I could no longer trust our internal budget reporting process. But the trust factor went well beyond me and my administrative leaders and the board. When I held an all-campus meeting to tell the faculty and staff of our tight financial situation, they, too, lost a measure of trust in me, my leadership team, *and* the trustees.

In the midst of the chaos, I read a book that helped put events on our campus into perspective. Pondering the conclusions of *The Speed of Trust: The One Thing That Changes Everything* by Stephen M. R. Covey, I knew I had to move especially quickly on one front, and that was in redoubling my efforts to restore trust. As Covey says, "Simply put, trust means confidence. The opposite of trust is suspicion. When you trust people you have confidence in them, in their integrity, and in their abilities. When you distrust people you are suspicious of them, of their integrity, their agendas, their capabilities or their track records. It's that simple."[1]

When trust abounds, processes tend to move more quickly, decisions are made and implemented more fluidly, and goals are met more rapidly. Again, as Covey puts it, "Trust is a function of two things: character and competence. Character includes your integrity, your motive, and your intent with people. Competence includes your capabilities, your skills, your results, and your track record."[2] No one within the board of trustees or the faculty was questioning my character, but our sudden financial crisis gave them reason to question my management and perhaps my leadership.

To restore trust, I knew I had to behave in ways that would engender it, to send the right signals by promptly exerting strong leadership and addressing failures in management. So, after that fateful afternoon in June, I returned to my office and spent the rest of the week with my staff analyzing the erroneous reports we had been unwittingly submitting to the trustees for months. I spent many hours working with my team, comparing faulty financial statements and shaky admissions projections with the accurate information that surfaced later. Only then was I able to sketch out for the trustees the origin of the problems and the steps we would take to resolve them and regain their trust.

I knew we had to act quickly and consistently, demonstrating our competence as a leadership team. As Covey says, "The first job of a leader is to inspire trust. The ability to do so in fact is a prime differentiator between a manager and a leader. To inspire trust is to create the foundation upon which all truly successful enterprises and relationships stand."[3]

Showing Loyalty and Righting Wrongs

I began rebuilding trust by taking several decisive steps and making some subtle changes. First, I made a concerted effort to reach out to others in the college community who were competent leaders and managers. Realizing I could not turn the campus around alone, I had to bring our best people into the process, apprising them of the problems and seeking their involvement. These were people with years of strong performance behind them; respected, even loved, and dedicated to the mission of the college. Their informed participation would be necessary if we were to emerge as a stronger Christian college. Recognizing their hard work through the years and their considerable investment in Gordon College, I had to demonstrate loyalty to them by being open with them about our failures.

In addition, I had to address some specific failures in management. Sometimes Christian managers tolerate incompetence or lack of performance because of the mistaken assumption that the love of Christ and His compassion require unqualified support for all employees regardless of performance. In my years of leadership in higher education, I have even had some disciplined or terminated employees (or their friends) tell me I was acting in an unchristian way for releasing them for failure to meet high performance standards. Such criticism is usually expressed in such phrases as, "I thought this was a Christian place. I thought Christians were supposed to treat everyone equally with love! Where is the second-chance principle? How can you let X, Y, or Z employee go and still sleep at night?"

In response, I would say that a careful evaluation of an employee's performance must be conducted, and honest and candid feedback must be offered. But if an employee's subsequent performance shows little or no improvement as measured by agreed upon standards, the leader who wants to be trusted *must* take action. Others usually know when colleagues are not doing their jobs well. They expect corrective action; and, if it is not taken, they begin to see leadership as complacent and untrustworthy. Yes, letting employees go does lead to sleepless nights for both the employer and the former employee. I struggle with knowing that my decisions might mean that families are uprooted, children's college educations put on hold, or friendships severed. But, when justified by a good and fair performance-evaluation system, appropriate terminations accelerate trust within a community. By contrast, mistrust resulting from tolerating poor work contributes to diminished productivity and, on a Christian college campus, substantially increases the cost of delivering education. This is simply not good stewardship.

One of our responses to the 2007 crisis was enacting a much more refined and comprehensive system of performance reviews for staff members. (Faculty reviews are conducted separately and according to long-established criteria.) I, along with the leadership team and the trustees, now develop five to eight major priorities for the entire college each year. We manage those priorities, reporting to the board every few months on whether we are achieving them. Those priorities also form the basis of the annual performance review of every staff member, as I invite every employee in the community to participate with me in this process of evaluation and assessment based on our agreed-upon priorities. Staff members take the priorities relevant to their areas and develop individual goals flowing from them. At the end of each academic year, supervisors sit with their employees to evaluate how well they accomplished their goals and whether they contributed to the achievement of the overall institutional priorities set by the president and the senior leadership team. One of the strengths of this system is that it is much easier to hold employees to their own goals than to make them accountable for those imposed upon them by superiors.

Demonstrate Transparency by Talking Straight

Our predicament also reinforced something I knew instinctively but did not always practice faithfully. Leaders serve best when they are transparent, telling the truth and leaving the right impression. If the proverbial elephant is in the room and looming large, leaders need to talk about it. Leaders who are consistent, practicing maximum transparency behind the scenes and in public, have no fear of contradiction or being viewed as manipulative. And, in a time of crisis and uncertainty, leaders must be visible and available. If they cannot be found up front during a crisis, leaders are not fulfilling their calling. The communities we serve both deserve and embrace leaders who are candid and who offer a clear vision for the future.

My leadership style is usually characterized by straightforwardness in interpersonal interaction coupled with an inclination toward introversion when faced with addressing thorny issues in public. I would have rather written an explanatory letter conveying our financial challenges than call an all-campus meeting to lay out our difficulties in an open forum. But in the cloudy, uncertain days following the perfect storm that blew through Gordon in the summer of 2007, I overcame my inclinations and talked straight in a series of faculty and staff meetings. Seeking to be transparent, I shared the reasons for the financial shortfall along with the hard options we were facing. I also invited questions and comments from the floor. Where it was appropriate, I used humor, some of it self-deprecating, to diffuse tense moments without belittling the issue or other people. These sessions, which I have continued on a more occasional basis, are recorded and made available to anyone unable to attend. In between the open forums, I sent out written updates to the campus community as circumstances changed or new information became available.

The open forums made an immediate impact. Faculty and staff thanked me for being candid, assured me of their prayers, and offered good, and often tough, follow-up questions for me or the administrative team. When I announced that we had no alternative but to suspend temporarily both salary increases and the generous payments the college makes to our employee retirement program, I expected cries of dismay. Instead, to a person, the campus community offered support, and many asked me how we could work together to make these tough measures temporary.

Encourage Respect by Listening First

On campuses committed to shared governance, faculty, staff, and students expect presidents to collaborate with them in shaping the contours of the college's vision for the future. This sounds simple, but it is preached much more often than it is practiced: Leaders must also be listeners! Sometimes listening can be the best thing a president does. As a wise person once said, "Use the ear rather than the mouth."

Leaders have little chance of succeeding if they ignore those who are following. The stereotypical evangelical Christian leader is all too ready to pronounce final decisions with absolute certainty. But truly Christlike leaders are reasonable, approachable people. Listening says: "I respect your opinion. I appreciate your taking the time to think through these matters and offer your ideas. I value your contributions to the organization and will weigh your perspectives as I work with my team and the trustees to chart our direction." If leaders demonstrate an ability to listen to many voices and to fashion a coherent vision reflecting various perspectives, the chances of rallying support in difficult times increase dramatically. Moreover, leaders who listen come across as confident rather than defensive, which, in turn, inspires confidence in others.

Leadership transpires in a context of converging currents of thought and action, sometimes swirling, sometimes meandering. The personality of the leader, the history and ethos of the college, and the needs of the moment converge to shape the appropriate response. Leaders cannot afford to be passive, nor can they be dogmatic and controlling, trying to impose their views on the community. Sometimes leadership means protecting the right of the minority to have "a place at the table" or in the classroom.

Several years ago we sponsored a campus forum involving a faculty guest from another Christian campus, one of our science professors, and an alumnus and donor who is a research scientist in the business sector. The panel addressed developing a Christian position on stem-cell research, an undisputedly controversial topic. The discussion was spirited, and the contrasts between positions were sharp and contentious. In short, the forum did not go well. Not only did the scientist challenge the faculty members' interpretations of the biblical and scientific evidence, but the faculty members were at odds with each other on whether stem-cell research using human embryos was ever permissible. Afterward, I knew that I would be asked such questions as, "Why did you let these people express such views in a public forum with students present? Do you allow this sort of thing in classrooms and labs at Gordon, too?" I knew I would face these questions even though none of the panelists had contradicted the statement of faith which all of our faculty sign; no one had advocated an antitheistic view; and no one had violated our community behavior standards.

While I wished some things had not been said as they were by the forum's participants, my support of academic freedom meant I had to defend their right to explore the controversial subject of stem-cell research while coming to different conclusions. Gordon College is a place dedicated to understanding God's creation and our obligations within it in light of biblical sources and scientific evidence. The two cannot be in contradiction if God is the author of all truth, as was eloquently argued by philosopher Arthur Holmes of Wheaton College three decades ago in his book *All Truth Is God's Truth*. Before God we need not fear academic freedom, even in such thorny areas.

By listening and then responding as I did, I respected the presenters' right to hold their positions, as controversial or wrong as they might seem to outsiders. I upheld the integrity of the Gordon educational process, which says that students and faculty have the right to explore truth wherever it might lead. Though I had no basis for censoring the faculty members involved in that forum, I paid a high price for my refusal to do so. My friend, the donor and scientific entrepreneur, turned away from Gordon and threw his wealth and endorsement behind causes more in line with his positions.

This incident, which occurred several years before our financial crisis, is an example of showing respect for others and our cherished values, whatever the cost. Although I lost a donor, I won greater trust from a number of faculty. Subsequently, when the financial adversity of 2007 eroded trust, such deposits from prior years helped restore equilibrium and bring our accounts back into balance more quickly.

Openness and respect can also be extended to students, who are both disarmed and reassured by a president and administration secure enough to risk transparency. Here at Gordon, our students were recently invited to participate in "Gordon's Green $ Gold: Where Does All the Money Go?" an open forum sponsored by the campus stewardship committee. Students submitted questions to our chief financial officer, the executive vice president, and me. At the end of this event, students responded with surprising affirmation for our presentation which helped them understand the budget drivers and the challenges of projecting income in uncertain times, not usually the stuff of exciting late afternoon student conversation.

Get Better Quickly by Taking Action

When faced with adversity, a leader must act quickly not only to build trust but also to offer hope and a way out. When Nehemiah, a key advisor to the king of Babylon and one of my Old Testament heroes, learned of the turmoil and deterioration of his home city, Jerusalem, he prayed, fasted, and mourned the news. Then he went into action. Even though he could have been killed for his boldness, he went before the king with a sad countenance. King Artaxerxes responded with compassion and asked a question every leader wants to hear: "How can I help you?" Nehemiah responded by outlining an action plan for restoring Jerusalem. Management and leadership principles jump off every page; and prayer, thoughtful reflection, and careful planning undergird each decisive action taken by the young leader. The rest of this success story is told in great detail in Nehemiah's memoirs.

While Gordon College, unlike Jerusalem, was not facing annihilation, the flood of negative news which swept over us in 2007 and 2008 had to be countered. To restore confidence and hope along with trust, we took several simultaneous steps that had an immediate positive impact.

First, we determined what areas of the operating budget might be reduced. In quick succession, we eliminated positions through attrition and early retirement, curtailed discretionary college travel, took steps to be better stewards of God's creation by intensifying recycling efforts and exploring the latest means for generating our own electricity through wind power, and eliminated unnecessary events which were nice to have but did not contribute directly to our students' educational experience. For example, we replaced our annual Christmas gala for faculty and staff with its gourmet menu and elaborate program with a simple but elegant Advent reception. The response was immediate and positive. Several longtime faculty said, "This is a much better way for our community to celebrate Christ's birth. At the gala dinner we sat with our close friends, ate too much, and met no one new. Now we spend a couple of hours celebrating old friends and making new ones while munching on healthy, light refreshments." While some might say this change is only symbolic, greater good resulted for our community, and we saved several thousand dollars.

Second, we sought to stabilize our long-term residence hall debt. As many higher education institutions learned in the fall of 2008, variable interest rates originally pegged to low benchmarks suddenly skyrocketed, creating shock waves on many campuses. Banks around the world became overextended, and chaos ensued. One of our international banks suddenly withdrew from all U.S. operations and retreated to the United Kingdom, leaving their U.S. banking partner and our prime bond underwriter stranded. Not only were interest rates soaring out of sight, but letters of credit were withdrawn, causing cash reserves to become a major necessity overnight. As our trustees warned us: "We have entered into a new era of doing business in the financial markets. We need to act quickly and get well before the next shoe drops and it is too late." We did just that, and in the process I got a crash course in banking relationships and the intricacies of international financing!

We entered the volatile financial markets to refinance our bonds, solidify our relationship with our prime U.S. banking partner, and find another investment bank willing to work with us. Also, we quickly built a substantial cash reserve to help us get through the lean times in each budget year, negotiated a favorable fixed interest rate for five years, and explained to anyone interested why we took those actions.

Third, after two key cabinet level managers left, we urgently mounted two national searches to find a new vice president for finance and a new vice president for recruitment and marketing. Within a few months new leaders were on board and taking appropriate action in their respective areas to strengthen our financial management and student recruitment efforts. Confidence was returning in both of these areas, confidence badly shaken by the events of the prior year.

Though it takes a considerable investment of time, the good leader and manager will identify the best people for crucial roles and prepare them for their tasks by:

- Helping them mold a coherent approach toward attaining their goals.
- Giving them the resources and training necessary to reach their objectives.
- Requiring them to evaluate whether they have accomplished their goals.

At the same time a wise president will address weak performance and move nonproductive persons out of the organization. As I noted above, this is difficult in a Christian setting where individuals sometimes feel protected by a soft Christian ethos, not recognizing that to be good stewards of resources also requires accountability for excellence in performance.

Fourth, to look toward the future while simultaneously addressing issues raised by the past, we launched a strategic planning process across the entire campus. Our last planning effort was completed in 2001–2002, when enrollments and optimism were at their highest. Most goals in that plan were achieved. Now we needed to reset the context for planning and action for the next five to seven years in light of new realities. Not only had the foundation of the financial world shifted beneath us, but educational delivery systems had changed. For-profit institutions, promising immediate jobs and paychecks, had become the biggest competition to private higher education. Though for-profits have become formidable competitors, they stand in stark contrast to Christian colleges like Gordon, which take a longer route and a more nuanced approach toward education. In the context of a deep respect for traditional Christian teaching and diverse cultural heritages, the Christian college is geared toward nurturing the life of the spirit, developing character, and fostering intellectual maturity along with inculcating a desire to serve the church and larger society. As part of our planning, Christian colleges such as Gordon *must* take greater pains to articulate their message and goals to our increasingly shallow, anti-intellectual and materialistic society.

Finally, we addressed a management issue that faces most organizations: ineffective meetings. In higher education we often embrace the concept of shared governance. This is most often expressed in meetings of one kind or another, where, as one would put it, sometimes everything has been said but not everyone has had a chance to say it! Patrick Lencioni, a management consultant who focuses on improving how organizations function, maintains that meetings are vital to college management but adds that they are often boring because they lack drama and ineffectual because they lack context.[4]

For most of my life, I have been a manager of meetings, setting agendas, guiding discussions, and listening to various points of view. I think I do this fairly effectively, but I have added another ingredient to ensure that meetings are no longer boring. I now not only more clearly define the purpose of each meeting, but I also look for conflict, story, or drama, which has the potential to keep everyone at the table engaged in the conversation. I no longer avoid tension; in fact, I actively create it. Our recent financial challenges helped uncover constructive ideological conflict among us, and I believe that engaging everyone around the table in passionate discussion is helping us toward better decisions.

To guard against ineffective meetings, I have also created a different context and definition for our cabinet. Until my direct reports were reduced to only three in the interest of greater efficiency, the cabinet was the primary managing entity of the college. To help augment the leadership of my direct reports, our college cabinet was recently restructured to take on the responsibility of guiding the strategic planning effort.

To ensure having a wide range of voices at the table, I appointed two faculty members and two staff members, as well as our scholar in residence, who has a significant lifetime of teaching and leadership positions in several higher education institutions. These new members now join me at cabinet meetings along with the three senior administrators (my direct reports) and all the other vice presidents. This means we have a large group of 16 people at the table. To ensure that everyone remains focused on the specific challenges of the day, I asked the dean of college planning to work with me in establishing our semester-long agenda. At each of our biweekly meetings, we focus on a key planning issue. Often inherent conflicts are built into the topics we are addressing. For example, as we plan the next capital campaign, we must ask: "Which buildings should be built and in what priority? What noncapital lines should be funded (endowed chairs, endowed scholarships, new and innovative programs, or the latest technology)?" Such questions and tensions give clear context and purpose to every meeting; and, if there is no controversy, I actively seek to create it.

Greater attention to effective meetings has also been extended to meetings with our board of trustees. As our trustees were asking for more accountability from us, we were asking for more engagement from them. The high purpose of a college and the higher purpose of a Christian college demands the best from every member of the Gordon community, including each member of the board. Thus, we must aspire to the quality of conduct and accomplishment demonstrated in many of the leading boards in higher education. Since the issues before our board are large and weighty—from curriculum to finance, from mission to enrollment, from physical plant to personnel performance—we have defined some best practices to be considered in pursuit of effectiveness and comity.

Involve the Board in Building Trust

To build more trust with our administrative team, our board of trustees recently committed to a much more powerful and engaged approach to our regular meetings and board retreats. Since each trustee's preparation for board meetings is a sign of his or her respect for Gordon's mission, care for the community, and the seriousness of our work, trustees agreed to accept several duties:

- To read the agenda and other documents posted on the board's Web page before each meeting.
- To demonstrate working knowledge of the life of the college and the principal issues in higher education and society influencing the college.
- To examine, support, and participate in a wide range of campus activities in order to experience firsthand the life and spirit which keep us engaged and excited about our callings.
- To ensure that all items on our agenda are considered fairly and to make decisions in ways that respect our commitment to community.
- To engage *all* board members in important, and perhaps controversial, matters rather than perpetuating the perception that the most important topics are handled in certain board committees, such as the executive and finance committees.
- To examine ourselves in light of goals and benchmarks to improve continually our service by means of a formal evaluation tool or other means of constructive reflection after every meeting.

As a group of faithful trustees and college leaders aligned in support of the college, we owe one another a respectful hearing and thoughtful response. In an educational setting like this, we have much to learn from one another. Open hearts and sensitive minds go a long way toward good board decisions and sustainable relationships in Christ. Thus, we must be free to debate and deliberate freely as peers committed to Gordon's best interests, without the fear that a word spoken in discussion might be cast in stone without collegial agreement. Moreover, our conclusions are surer when we all adhere to rules of order with their promise that all are heard and respected. In keeping with this, the bigger the issue, the fuller the board discussion must be. And committee recommendations on strategic or even tactical issues merit full board consideration if board members wish it. In this spirit we are working to reach agreements verified by a majority vote of the board.

Seek Spiritual and Physical Rejuvenation

Even after taking the measures outlined above, I still had more to do. Our crisis had demanded swift, decisive action. But sometimes leadership also requires withdrawal, reflection, and rejuvenation for the challenges ahead. For me that opportunity came during a discussion with other Christian college presidents gathered for a meeting of the Christian College Consortium. There, Messiah College President Kim Phipps urged us to focus on Eccl 5:18–20:

> Here is what I have seen to be good: it is appropriate to eat, drink, and experience good in all the labor one does under the sun during the few days of his life God has given him, because that is his reward. God has also given riches and wealth to every man, and He has allowed him to enjoy them, take his reward, and rejoice in his labor. This is a gift of God, for he does not often consider the days of his life because God keeps him occupied with the joy of his heart. (HCSB)

God encourages us to find ourselves dancing from the bottom of our hearts. Work should not be viewed as drudgery, but instead we should find joy in it. We must take pleasure in our calling, recognizing that our identity is in Christ, not in our role, title, or the affirmation (or defamation) that goes along with it.

Particularly in the midst of crisis or in its immediate aftermath, when our energies are most drained, leaders must nourish the soul side of their lives, looking for ways to build close friendships, to nourish their spiritual selves, and, thus, to be ready when new challenges come. The gathering of Consortium presidents reminded me that we care about one another because of our relationship in Christ. Our reason for being is a higher spiritual value than simply keeping an organization going. And if we are not joyful in our callings, how can we reasonably expect our colleagues to be? One of the ways my wife and I ensure time for withdrawal from all the activity and demands of the college presidency is to plan at least two weeklong vacations during the academic year rather than during the summer, perhaps during the Christmas holidays or at spring break. Occasionally we've even tried to get away when school is in session. This has the added advantage of giving other leaders on campus a confidence boost. They find that, "Hey, we can lead this campus too!" And, with instant communication possible from almost anywhere in the world, I can always be reached if necessary.

Leaders or Managers: What Is Our Calling?

When things are orderly, predictable, and going well, people want managers, not leaders. In times of crisis, people want leaders who take bold action. In such times leaders can't afford to be indecisive and weak since this increases feelings of anxiety, powerlessness, and insecurity within the organization. Not all good managers make good leaders, but all good leaders understand the importance of competent management. Under stress good leaders emerge, sometimes from the management ranks. They define the mission of the organizations they are leading; they create strategies and goals the organization's members can commit to. They communicate frequently and persuasively to those in the organization, providing the pieces of information people really need and clarifying what the organization must focus on to get through the crisis. In a crisis good leaders will behave with integrity, communicate in person, and be open to dialogue.

In his forward to *The Leader of the Future,* Peter Drucker says there is no such thing as a leadership personality, leadership style, or leadership gene. "The one and only personality trait that effective leaders I have encountered did have in common is something they did not have: they had little or no charisma and little use for the term or what it signifies."[5]

Drucker suggests that effective leaders ask: "What needs to be done? What should I do to make a difference? What are my organization's mission and goals? What constitutes performance and results?" Strong leaders are tolerant of diversity in managers. They do not want or need to create carbon copies of themselves. But they are intolerant of substandard performance against standards and values. Andrew Carnegie said he wanted the following to be written on his tombstone, "Here lies a man who attracted better people into his service than he was himself."

The best leaders need not be charismatic, but they must submit themselves to the "mirror test," making sure the person they see in the mirror in the morning is the kind of person they want to be, respect, and believe in. Not only are they people of integrity, but they are also committed to action. As Drucker concludes, "Effective leaders delegate a good many things; they have to or they drown in trivia, but they do not delegate the one thing that only they can do with excellence, the one thing that will make the difference, the one thing that will set standards, and the one thing they want to be remembered for. They do it."[6]

In short, effective leaders must bring vision and implementation together. That is why Gordon College not only has a clear mission statement but why we are serious about performance management assessment. It is also why we define five to eight key priorities to manage from each year—priorities embraced not only by the trustees, president, and key leaders but also by those across college ranks. Lastly, it is why we are ready to meet the crisis we in higher education face today.

Conclusion

It has been over three years since that fateful June afternoon, but the ideas explored in this chapter are still being implemented. The process of building trust is ongoing and, by its nature, will never be complete. But the trust tank level is nearer the top than it was three years ago. And, by the way, we did not end the 2007 budget year with a deficit. Our trustees, God bless them, agreed to write the checks necessary to ensure that, come June 30 and the end of the fiscal year, we were in the black. What a way to build trust!

Resources for Further Study

Covey, Stephen M. R. *The Speed of Trust: The One Thing that Changes Everything*. New York: Free Press, 2006.

Hesselbein, Frances, Marshall Goldsmith, Richard Beckhard, eds. *The Leader of the Future: Management and Leadership*. Claremont, CA: The Drucker Foundation, 1996.

Lencioni, Patrick. *Death by Meeting: A Leadership Fable*. San Francisco: Jossey-Bass, 2004.

Questions for Further Reflection

1. What if someone at your college wrote a series on the presidents of your organization or institution? What are the main contributions other presidents have made to the life of the institution? How will historians assess your contributions or legacy?

2. Are you a leader, a manager, or both? How do you know? What do others tell you? Can you be one without the other?

3. Are leaders born or made? If the latter, what goes into the making of a leader? What are the essential qualities?

4. How do you effectively build trust in your administrative team?

5. When you have disruptions in your relationship with your board, how do you go about rebuilding trust?

6. Apart from financial compensation, which is of course difficult or impossible to increase in times of scarcity, what can leaders do to affirm their employees and encourage continued commitment to their organizations?

7. If you are a committed Christian, how does your faith inform how you think and act in times of failure or stress? In what ways does it give you the strength to make tough decisions, even when they are viewed by others as unfair or not in an individual's best interest?

8. What biblical principles should guide tough personnel decisions? When is it appropriate to terminate an employee in a Christian organization?

Endnotes

[1] S. M. R. Covey, *The Speed of Trust: The One Thing That Changes Everything* (New York: Free Press, 2006), 5.

[2] Ibid., 30.

[3] Ibid., 286.

[4] P. Lencioni, *Death by Meeting* (San Francisco: Jossey-Bass, 2004), 224.

[5] P. Drucker, *The Leader of the Future*, ed. Frances Hesselbein, Marshall Goldsmith, and Richard Beckhard (Claremont, CA: The Drucker Foundation, 1996), xii.

[6] Ibid., xiv.

Chapter 6

FINANCIAL OVERSIGHT
AND BUDGET PLANNING

Jon Wallace
President, Azusa Pacific University
with Jim Canning
Former CFO of World Vision International

I n framing this chapter on organizational finance and budgeting, I recalled my own journey through Christian nonprofit organizations. Following my graduation from college, I served as a custodian supervising a team of six others. My undergraduate business degree assisted me in compiling accurate information for my supervisor regarding supplies used and jobs accomplished. However, I quickly learned that allocating janitorial supplies to a half-dozen custodial closets is really an act of vision casting and motivation. Receiving critical supplies that supported their daily work assignment absolutely motivated my team. Connecting the stewardship of valuable cleaning supplies and their 40-hour workweek to the Christ-centered mission and vision of the university proved to be a remarkably easy next step. Thus began the seed of my conviction that the leadership opportunity of every CEO/president leading a faith-based institution is to motivate and excite a community through a compelling vision while simultaneously navigating the challenge of limited resources.

I realize that many Christian nonprofits feel the tension between limited resources and a kingdom-sized mission. As leaders of these organizations, we shoulder the responsibility to bridge the gap between the reality of our budget and the ideal of fully accomplishing our mission. In this place of wonderful tension, I encourage every leader to see the financial parameters and budget process as an opportunity to fulfill the institution's core mission.

It All Starts with the Vision

A friend, who served for many years as CFO of a large Christian organization, reminded me that the budget process and the financial goals associated with it start with a clear and compelling vision. A previous chapter in this volume touches on the importance of crafting and executing a great vision, but nowhere is this more important than in the decision-making process of creating and managing the income and expense of your organization. Proverbs 29:18 states, "Where there is no vision, the people perish" (KJV). A compelling vision impacts every area of planning and implementation by empowering God-honoring leaders to move forward with clear stewardship goals. To lead an organization that promotes effectiveness, measured results, and excellence in budget execution, the leader needs to articulate a clear and compelling vision.

Few tools lie at the leader's disposal that touch as many areas of the organization with the same transformational potential as the allocation of financial resources. The leader's ability to create a persuasive vision, change course when necessary, and build critical momentum will be strengthened, or conversely weakened, based on one's commitment to effective and God-honoring stewardship policies, procedures, and leadership. Specifically, I believe the leader's primary responsibilities in the area of financial oversight can be identified as follows:

- Convey and articulate a compelling vision for the organization.
- Strive to protect and strengthen the fiscal integrity of the Christian nonprofit by regularly providing benchmark fiscal measurements to the board of trustees. These measurements must give clear and understandable information regarding financial performance for the board's review and approval.
- Inform the board regularly of the organization's status of compliance with all applicable policies, rules, laws, and regulations governing institutional financial accountability.

- Provide the board with results and assessments of the institutional budget in light of the organization's mission, strategic plan, and core values.

Financial oversight involves the process of overseeing the handling of an organization's finances. As the president or leader of a school or other ministry, your role is to ensure that the finances are properly managed but not be too involved in the details; that is the job of the CFO or financial manager. The budget process stands as one important planning aspect of managing and allocating an organization's finances.

Good financial oversight includes formal processes, procedures, and structures that ensure the organization has the necessary qualified financial staff to handle its finances, that funds are handled properly, that an effective annual budget process unfolds, and that income and expenses are monitored on a regular basis.

Many aspects comprise budgeting, but at its core a budget is a plan of expected income and expenses needed to carry out specific activities and goals within a set period of time. Budgets are projections and plans expressed in numbers. The budget assists the leader(s) in the planning and wise use of financial resources so that the organization has the resources necessary to accomplish its purposes. Core financial and stewardship values modeled by the organization and its employees might include the following:

- An organizational commitment to God-honoring excellence evidenced in every area, including financial planning and budgeting oversight.
- Commitment to a budget that supports a strategic vision and ensures results oriented with measurable outcomes.
- Policies and procedures that unite the institution in "forward-looking" actions. The evidence being a community with high values of stewardship and sustainability.
- A budget that focuses on mission-critical efforts and initiatives. Management should not be distracted by nonmission-critical or periphery programs and underperforming programs. This may result in decisions to increase funding to strengthen struggling but critical programs or to reduce and eliminate funding for underperforming programs.

While the word *budget* does not appear in Scripture, the Bible does have a lot to say about money and how we handle it. Proverbs 16:9 says, "We should make plans—counting on God to guide us" (TLB). It also tells us that "any enterprise is built by wise planning, becomes strong through common sense, and profits wonderfully by keeping abreast of the facts" (Prov 24:3–4, TLB). And Luke 14:28 (ESV) advises us to "sit down and count the cost" before beginning to build a tower to make sure we have enough money to complete the job. (Note: In today's world this also applies to the building of new buildings and the launching of new programs.) A proper budget reflects all these scriptural principles.

For a church, school, or other ministry, budgeting feels like an act of faith; but it is faith coupled with judgment and discernment. Using the best judgment and insights God gives us, we then trust Him to do the rest. Many leaders of Christian nonprofits find help and encouragement in specific scriptural passages. A few additional passages that may be helpful as you consider your organization's budget and planning process are found in Addendum B at the end of this chapter.

Types of Budgets

Most people are familiar with an annual operating budget, but many organizations, particularly larger ones, often find it helpful to use more than one budget. The three most common types of budgets used in colleges and other nonprofit organizations are:

- General or operating budget—Shows the projected income and expenses for the general operating activities of the organization for the year.
- Capital budget—Shows income and expenses related to special capital projects such as the acquisition of land, new buildings or improvements, and major equipment purchases.
- Special purpose budgets—Shows income and expenses for a specific project or activity outside of normal operating activities such as a special missions program, a onetime donor-funded project, or a similar special endeavor outside your normal operating budget.

A word of caution: When planning a capital or special-purpose budget, beware of the *substitutionary effect* of giving on your general or operating budget. People who normally support your regular activities may feel led to give to a capital or special purpose appeal but then reduce their giving to your normal operating budget, thereby decreasing the amount you have to meet regular operating expenses.

Mission Creep

The effect of mission creep on valuable resources keeps me awake some nights. Have I allowed the allure of a new program to displace or slightly move the center of the organization's mission? As senior leaders know, there is never a shortage of dynamic new ideas that people would like for the organization to undertake. Over the years I have stood in awe to see God move through an unexpected gift and passionate donor to expand the size and impact of our mission. I happen to lead a pretty nimble organization, and our strengths include innovation and entrepreneurial decision making by our leadership. This organizational appetite to see "what God is up to and align ourselves with it" has served us well. There have also been a few misses—times when we jumped before full consideration of how a significant new endeavor would impact the center of our mission and purpose. When a donor approaches you with funding to support a new program or idea, saying no can be difficult. The momentum any organization gains from such a gift, however, must be measured against the cost and long-term impact it could have on the organization.

Mission Accomplished

With a strong vision in place, you should determine what needs to be measured and evaluated as you spend time, energy, and resources to accomplish the organization's mission. In other words, before, during, and after a budget process, how will you know if the investment of human and financial resources has accomplished the vision and mission that binds it all together? Before beginning the budget process, ask some of the following questions:

1. How will success be measured?
2. Is growth important? If so, how will it be measured against the resource allocation to accomplish that growth?
3. Would it be helpful to measure your organization against others? This might apply to:

   • *Comparing salary and compensation, especially those of senior leaders, against similar organizations and associations.*

- *Fund-raising income and expense as a percent of total budget.* This is especially important in determining the percent of every dollar raised that goes to overhead.
- *Mission effectiveness.* In higher education, we look at graduation rates. In other not-for-profits, it might be number of clients served per full-time employee or long-term impact of programs and initiatives for those served.
- *Comparing income and expense budgets to industry and association norms.* Specifically compare expense categories such as salaries and benefits, insurance, office and equipment, and other defined parameters.
- *Market share.* If possible, can you determine what the total need is that your organization seeks to address; and, if so, what percent of that total need are you meeting? For example, how many orphans are in a specific country, and of those how many does your ministry impact?

4. Most nonprofit organizations have a well-developed catalog of programs and services that have grown up around the vision and mission. Does your budget and resource allocation support only those vital and mission-centered programs? Do the various programs and initiatives complement each other with a multiplier of synergy, or are they "stand alone"?
5. What is the two- to five-year plan for current and envisioned new programs? Do these programs directly support the vision and values of the organization?

Effective financial management must include rigorous and ongoing examination of where and how you spend the valuable resources of your organization.

Faith or Presumption: How Do You Bridge the Gap?

Perhaps like me you find yourself at the center of an important budget process for a faith-based organization. Organizational leaders gather around a compelling kingdom mission to plan for the next fiscal year. The history of the organization offers powerful examples of God's faithful provision, perhaps even miraculous deliverance during difficult times. As the senior leader of a group of Christ-centered men and women, you must create the financial plan that will carry the organization forward. Sometimes the financial stewards of Christian organizations wrestle with a final budget dependent on some uncertain income streams.

One of the most important income streams to a Christian nonprofit is the year-to-year financial generosity of key donors and constituents. This annual giving often increases or decreases by decisions beyond our control. How then does a responsible Christian leader balance his/her faith in God's ability to provide with the responsibility of allocating limited resources to mission-critical programs? Most of us have sat in a church budget meeting and listened to a compelling argument supporting a "stretch budget." We have also listened as the "doom and gloom" folks point to the downward trend in attendance and giving to support their position for crafting a downsized and more reasonable budget. While I do not have the space here to unpack fully the depth and breadth of the faith or presumption leadership dilemma, my own journey would suggest, at least, the following:

- Every Christian organization dependent on donations should enter the budget season prayerfully asking God for these resources. In fact, Christian institutions and organizations must approach every budget line item and every program expenditure as a gift from God and evidence of His provision.
- Christian institutions and organizations should strive to be the best examples of decision making that supports the budget process, financial management, and wise stewardship. I believe this means building appropriate reserves and contingences into every budget. This gives both the leader and the organization a margin of financial protection against uncertain future outcomes. One of the best examples of this forward thinking perspective comes from Genesis 41. You remember that Joseph interprets Pharaoh's dream and helps the nation of Egypt prepare for seven years of drought. Key to this plan was the country's forward-looking decision to stockpile valuable resources during the seven years with more than enough resources. Christian organizations should do the same. Every budget and forward-looking financial plan should contain some measure of savings to grow your reserves to remain healthy against an uncertain future.

Seeking Counsel and Advice

The book of Proverbs (11:14) affirms the safety found in a multitude of counselors. Fortunately, the board of trustees fills this role in providing wise counsel to the organization. Today's increasingly complex world makes this even more important. It is impossible for the leader or any one person to stay abreast of what is happening in all the areas under his/her span of care. Because of this, good financial oversight includes some board members experienced in finance who are able to provide counsel and advice in this area.

Building the financial strength of your board drives your organization forward. Boards with a strong commitment to excellence constantly seek to improve their financial decision making and oversight abilities.

When considering a financial expert for the board, however, keep in mind that while businesses, schools, and other organizations have many similarities, differences abound. Seek board members who understand those important nuances. Nonprofit organizations are subject to certain accounting rules and requirements that differ from for-profit businesses. All to say, while an individual may be a good accountant with strong business experience, that individual may not be the right candidate for service on your board.

It is also helpful to include someone seasoned in the management of a nonprofit organization. In addition to that experience, someone who has served on the board of a nonprofit organization can bring added understanding of how such organizations function. As the leader, your goal is to build a board composed of individuals with the right mix of skills and backgrounds to ensure proper oversight of the organization. To support your board, consider the following:

- Provide regular and ongoing development for the board.
- Include individuals with specific financial leadership gifts.
- If your organization requires an audit committee, recruit a practicing CPA to serve as a member.
- Use the expertise and recommendations of your auditors to address areas for improvement.
- Regularly express appreciation by affirming those who serve and lead as board members.

In addition to building the financial acumen of your board, wise leaders should include among their friends or acquaintances at least one individual with experience in finance who can be a sounding board or advisor when needed. This relationship provides the opportunity to ask dumb questions and receive valuable financial mentoring. As this relationship grows and develops over the years, there can be a significant payoff in having a trusted financial expert to provide valuable advice needed to navigate the occasional financial storm.

Role of the Financial Officer/Manager

Depending on the size of the organization, you may have a few or many individuals involved in the financial area. Normally someone with the title of chief financial officer (CFO), finance manager, controller, or something similar leads this area. In larger organizations a separate budget manager or budget department may exist. Make sure sufficient and properly trained staff are employed to handle the task.

Once the vision and other guidelines have been set, the finance department gathers the appropriate income and expense projections by department area and program to put the budget together. This can take from a few weeks to several months depending on the size of the organization and complexity of the budget. During this time the leader should consult periodically with those responsible for the budget preparation to ascertain that they have all necessary information and are advised of any changes in projects, projections, or other matters that might affect the end result. This also helps verify that the leader stays informed and avoids last-minute surprises. Once the budget is approved, it is the job of the finance department to monitor actual income and expenditures against the budget and keep the leader informed.

Lessons Learned

The past 10 years of presidential leadership have taught me several important lessons with regard to financial oversight. As a leader you probably would agree that your most valuable insights have come from challenging moments. Allow me to share several from my tenure as CEO/president.

Experience and time revealed that various constituents inside and outside an organization often have different perspectives of the annual budget. This chart depicts some of the diverse perspectives and concerns that may be present within each group.

Stakeholder	Perspective/Responsibility	Questions/Concerns
Board /elders (external perspective)	Uphold organizational integrity and sustainability	Does the budget accomplish the mission?
President (external/internal perspective)	Accomplish the mission within the budget and determine how to raise the necessary resources	Where will the funding come from, and can we raise it?

Stakeholder	Perspective/Responsibility	Questions/Concerns
VP/CFO (internal perspective)	Maintain the fiscal integrity and solvency of the organization	Is the budget sufficient, or will adjustments be necessary?
Managers (internal perspective)	Manage resources entrusted to them	Can I operate within this budget?
Staff (internal perspective)	Accomplish tasks given available resources	Can I finish my assignment?

The president/CEO should intentionally look for and attempt to understand these viewpoints and the needs/concerns shared by various stakeholders. These perspectives support a common vision when understood and valued as an important part of the whole.

Over the years I have also learned the importance of a fair and insightful evaluation of the CFO or chief budget officer. This can be challenging for the senior leader who may lack experience and training in finance. Frequently the audit firm, who works closely with your organization's financial office, will have key insight regarding the CFO's strengths and weaknesses that might be included in a performance review. Financial advisors sitting on your board or serving on your volunteer committees may also be helpful in accessing strengths and weaknesses. A thorough review every two to three years that includes these important people will propel your financial leadership team in the right direction.

Delaying hard budget decisions can cost your organization opportunities for improvement and perpetuate mediocrity. Difficult decisions to reduce expenditures or eliminate underperforming nonmission-centered programs should not be avoided. Some of my biggest mistakes around these kinds of painful decisions had little to do with the outcomes but everything to do with how the decision was communicated. Every effort should be made to overcommunicate to stakeholders anytime an organizational decision is made that impacts the budget. The work to undo nervous rumors or misunderstanding is infinitely more challenging than strong communication on the front end.

Nonprofit organizations often feel the tension between an urgent need and a long-term, strategic direction. There have been times when I wished I could undo a quick fix because later it became an unnecessary, long-term expense. On other occasions strengthening the short-term financial health of the organization is critical to long-term sustainability. In my own organization I have noticed that the tyranny of the urgent often displaces the opportunity for a well-executed plan. Avoid this quagmire by fully engaging those men and women gifted with financial ability and wisdom despite a pressing time frame.

Building strong relationships with leaders of organizations similar to the one I lead has proved useful too. Time and again I have been encouraged with their insight and counsel regarding important issues I currently face that they have confronted and discovered innovative, insightful, and excellent results. Because few understand the complexities of leadership in a position similar to yours, these peer relationships can be a significant support.

Some of the best advice I received as a new president was to embrace a transparent accountability for myself and those that make up the senior leadership team. Three principles that support this mutual accountability include:

1. Bad news first
2. Full disclosure
3. No surprises

If a president honors the leadership team with this kind of mutual transparency, then all areas of the organization can move strongly toward excellence, including finance.

Wrap Up

The institution you lead will move in the direction shaped by your financial processes and budget decisions. Having a compelling vision offers clear direction for all areas of your organization, including the budget. Organizational mission remains critical, but careful resource planning through a budget is imperative to carry your vision and values into every corner of the organization. Any lack of formal financial training should not deter you from building an organizational ethos of financial excellence. The right people in the right roles with appropriate authority and accountability are key to successful financial leadership.

Appointing an exceptional CFO or chief budget officer and finding and recruiting financially gifted men and women to your board and volunteer committees will help determine the difference between missional success and failure. Commit yourself to finding a coach who will walk with you over time, advising you on important fiscal issues, and one who will be at your side during seasons of financial challenge. Hold fast to fiscal principles and values that will build financial strength and sustainability within your organization. Create a legacy of a strong, robust, and financially sustainable organization for the next generation of leadership.

Resources for Further Study

Many great organizations and resource materials exist to help leaders in their task. Almost all professional organizations, including those listed below, have newsletters, papers, sample forms, and other resources, often downloadable at no charge. The following are just a few of these resources with which you may want to be familiar.

Organizations

Council for Christian Colleges & Universities (CCCU)—A voluntary membership organization whose mission is to advance the cause of Christ-centered higher education and to help its member institutions transform lives by faithfully relating scholarship and service to biblical truth.

Christian Leadership Alliance (CLA)—An association of more than 9,000 members in more than 4,500 organizations worldwide. CLA seeks to build the body of Christ by helping organizations move toward organizational excellence in governance, leadership, stewardship, and management through seminars, publications, and other resources.

Evangelical Council for Financial Accountability (ECFA)—An accreditation agency dedicated to helping Christian ministries earn the public's trust through adherence to seven standards of responsible stewardship. Established in 1979, the ECFA provides accreditation to leading Christian nonprofit organizations that faithfully demonstrate compliance with established standards for financial accountability, fund-raising, and board governance.

National Association of College & University Business Officers (NACUBO)—An institutionally based membership organization designed to help those involved in higher education through various resources and professional development programs.

Books and Articles

Breitenberg, Matt, and Art Caccese. "Ensuring Mission Impact: How to Move from Strategy to Results." *Christian Management Report*. December 2003.

Collins, Jim. *Good to Great*. New York: HarperCollins, 2001.

Dropkin, Murray, Jim Halpin, and Bill La Touche. *The Budget Building Book for Nonprofits: A Step-by-Step Guide for Managers and Boards*. San Francisco: Jossey-Bass, 2007.

Drucker, Peter F. *Managing the Nonprofit Organization.* New York: HarperCollins, 1990.

Engstrom, Ted W., and Bobb Biehl. *Increasing Your Boardroom Confidence.* Phoenix: Questar, 1988.

Gardner, John W. *On Leadership.* New York: Free Press, 1990.

Hignite, Karla. "Diagnosing Fiscal Fitness [in Colleges]," *Business Officer.* April 2009.

Jeavons, Thomas H. *When the Bottom Line Is Faithfulness.* Bloomington: Indiana University Press, 1994.

Watts, Steve. "Your Budget: A Living Document." *Christian Management Report.* November/December, 2000.

ADDENDUM A

Guiding Questions

You may find reviewing and responding to the following questions to be helpful.

		Yes	No	Unsure
1.	Does the organization have a clear vision translated into goals that are clearly understood and supported by employees, friends, and donors?	—	—	—
2.	Does the organization have adequate policies and procedures to ensure the proper handling and accountability of the organization's funds?	—	—	—
3.	Does the organization have skilled financial managers on key committees and in key leadership positions committed to fiscal excellence?	—	—	—
4.	Is the organization's budget clear and understandable to those responsible for its implementation and oversight?	—	—	—
5.	Do you have indicators for course correction as you spend down the budget?	—	—	—
6.	Are appropriate reserves built into the annual budget as a hedge against unexpected emergencies?	—	—	—

	Yes	No	Unsure
7. Do you have a financial coach who provides you with a safe place to ask important financial questions and who is willing to help you navigate rough seas?	—	—	—
8. Do you provide regular and ongoing financial reports for your board?	—	—	—
9. Does your organization have an independent audit committee with at least one member holding a CPA license?	—	—	—
10. Do you have processes in place to review the organization's financial decision making and fiscal policies? This should include periodic performance reviews of the CFO and auditors.	—	—	—

ADDENDUM B

Biblical Guidelines

1. **Make plans.** "We should make plans—counting on God to direct us" (Prov 16:9 TLB).

2. **Count the cost before starting.** "But don't begin until you count the cost" (Luke 14:28–30 TLB).

3. **Faith is rewarded and multiplied.** "Here is a boy with five small barley loaves and two small fish, but how far will they go among so many?"(John 6:8–9 NIV).

4. **Seek wise counsel.** "Plans fail for lack of counsel, but with many advisers they succeed" (Prov 15:22 NIV).

5. **Gain wisdom.** "Have two goals: wisdom—that is, knowing and doing right—and common sense" (Prov 3:21 TLB).

6. **Anticipate problems.** "A prudent man foresees the difficulties ahead and prepares for them" (Prov 22:3 TLB).

7. **Monitor carefully.** "Any enterprise is built by wise planning, becomes strong through common sense, and profits wonderfully by keeping abreast of the facts" (Prov 24:3–4 TLB).

Chapter 7

DEVELOPMENT, CAMPAIGNS, AND BUILDING PROJECTS

Evans P. Whitaker
President, Anderson University

The first priority of any organization is to survive. But leaders of Christian organizations desire more than survival for their organizations. They want their causes to flourish. Donor contributions are essential for charitable organizations to survive *and* thrive.

A new leader of an organization is much like an heir to an estate. Whether you enter into an organization with a long history or you intend to build the organization from the ground up, you come into your leadership position having inherited something of value. For those who initiate new organizations, your inheritance is simply the vision and opportunity God gives you. For those taking up the mantle of leadership from a predecessor, you inherit the work and contributions of those who have gone before you in addition to the door God has opened for you to join in the work of the cause.

Leadership as Stewardship

My friend, Robert "Bob" Fisher, president of Belmont University, shares a wonderful image of a good stewardship perspective for leaders. Bob says that when you inherit something, you do not want simply to maintain it, and you certainly do not want to preside over its decline. Rather, you want to invest yourself into it so that by the time you pass the mantle of leadership to your successor, the organization is significantly more valuable than the day you joined it.

Thus, leadership is much the same as stewardship; or, at the very least, stewardship is a key function of leadership. Good causes must thrive so they can touch the lives of more and more people, and to do that, leaders must persuade others to join them in their causes and give for the never-ending advancement of their organizations.

Biblical Perspectives on Giving and Asking

While the Bible does not offer a comprehensive guide on the proper motivations for giving and the right circumstances under which to ask for support, it does provide several descriptions dispersed throughout both the Old and New Testaments.

One of the better books dealing with theological perspectives on giving and asking is T. Jeavons and R. Basinger's *Growing Givers' Hearts: Treating Fundraising as Ministry.*[1] The material under this heading is essentially a brief summary of their chapter on what the Bible says about giving and asking.

The Bible says more about giving than it does about asking for support. Asking for support is overwhelmingly a New Testament theme. It is interesting to compare the two testaments for differences between motivations for giving.

Old Testament giving was motivated primarily out of a sense of obligation to God and/or to the community of faith. The most notable purposes for giving were: (1) to support the maintenance of a place of worship and the practice of religious services (Exod 30:11–16); (2) the obligation of each member of "the people of God" to give for the common good of their covenanted community; and (3) the obligation of each member of the community to "act justly and to love mercy" (Mic 6:8 NIV), not only among themselves but also for others. A secondary motivation for giving during this time was an expectation that the act of giving would cause positive actions that accrued back to the community, not in the contemporary perverted sense that giving will return income or other consideration to the donor but in the sense that the act of giving creates a faithful and healthy community in which all members will be blessed.

By comparison the New Testament says little about giving out of obligation, an expectation of reciprocity, or a need to honor a community or tradition. As Jesus did with so many themes, He challenged the old notions about giving and reframed them. He brought forward the Old Testament expectation that people give out of a sense of justice and a more general sense of reciprocity in the precept, "Do to others as you would have them do to you" (Luke 6:31 NIV). Moreover, He extends justice further by asking His disciples to "love [their] enemies, and do good, and lend, expecting nothing in return" (Luke 6:32–36 NASB). These exhortations move giving principles beyond reciprocity (see also Matt 5:40–42) and shift the motivation for giving from obligation to opportunity.

Jesus teaches His disciples to do good not because they have an obligation to give back or to receive something in return but to give as an expression of their gratitude for God's blessings and absolute trust in God's love for them and all people. Nothing in Jesus' teachings suggests that fear or guilt are good or healthy motivations for giving or service.

Finally, in Matt 6:2–3, Jesus is specific in teaching against giving for self-aggrandizement. As for asking for support, Jesus instructs His disciples to depend totally on God to meet their needs. In fact, His instructions (Matt 10:5–15; Mark 6:8–11; Luke 9:3–5) suggest that He discourages asking for money. However, in giving these instructions, Jesus seems to assume that the voluntary support of others is the primary way God will provide for the disciples' needs, as donors are receptive to the gospel and give out of their appreciation for God's grace.

Moving forward to Paul's ministry, we find much of the New Testament justification for what we would now refer to as fund-raising. While Paul seems to have made no apology for asking for support, he was careful to be just as concerned that both his motives for asking and the donors' motivations were pure. Thus, Paul writes to the Corinthians, "If I give all I possess to the poor . . . but have not love, I gain nothing" (1 Cor 13:3 NIV). Paul argues that he has the right to support—that all apostles do—and that church members should be pleased to provide support out of appreciation for the ministry and the spiritual growth in them it has encouraged (1 Cor 9:1–12). Paul makes clear that he does not expect such support for himself but for the cause of Christ (1 Cor 9:15–18). Anything less than that approach to asking could, in Paul's eyes, be an impediment to people hearing the gospel.

Practically speaking, Paul uses a tried-and-true method of fund-raising, and his example offers something of a model for asking. The first component of his method is to tell about the generosity of others, suggesting that others' giving should be a source of encouragement to those who are being asked to give. For example, in 2 Corinthians 8–9 he tells the

Corinthians how much the Macedonians gave to encourage their generosity. He is careful not to focus on the specific size of the Macedonians' gifts but says the Macedonians gave a generous gift, "even beyond their ability" (2 Cor 8:3 NIV). He then goes on to tell the Corinthians that he hopes they will "excel in this grace" (2 Cor 8:7 NIV) of giving. In this way Paul sets forth the notion that they are all to be partners in God's work. Paul wanted people to see that giving could be an act of deep joy and thanksgiving, without recognition or notoriety. Throughout Paul's work, his notion of reciprocity matches that of Jesus. Giving was a joyful response to God's prior generosity. The benefit donors receive from giving is an experience of abundance that comes when giving is motivated by obedience to the Great Commandment, loving God and loving others.

Development Defined

The term *development* is simply a synonym of *fund-raising*. It is a term most often used to refer to an organization's program of activities that lead to gaining donor support for daily operations, special projects, and capital improvements.

Today we are so bombarded with fund-raising appeals that development has taken on a negative connotation, and in some cases it may be deserved. The fund-raising field, even fund raising for Christian causes, has certainly had its share of scams and carpetbaggers. But on the whole most Christian causes are more than worthy of support. As a leader you should never view fund-raising as anything more than a noble undertaking.

Today churches have elaborate stewardship programs. Educational institutions, ministry organizations, and nonprofit organizations have formal development programs. Fund-raising consultants abound to assist organizations of all types design and implement stewardship and development programs and plan and conduct campaigns. Through development efforts, billions of dollars are raised each year for countless causes, all of which depend on contributions to make their work possible.

Development programs take many forms. They are most often a collection of functions that involve the cultivation and solicitation of donors. In organizations that are well staffed, the development office may include individuals who are responsible for annual gifts, major or special gifts, planned gifts, foundation and corporate grant seeking, stewardship, gift records, prospect research, campaigns, and staff support.

Many organizations also have a number of complementary functions that are essential for a successful development program. These include communications and marketing for many. For colleges and universities, the functions of alumni relations, church relations, parent relations, and community relations are also essential. When these complementary functions are linked together with development functions in educational institutions, they form a broad category of activities sometimes referred to as *institutional advancement.* This term is used because the functions work together to advance the organization's mission.

Not every organization has the ability to staff all the development functions, and not all functions are essential for every organization. The mission, vision, strategic plan, and goals of the organization together with its size, scope, resources, and complexity should determine the extent to which a development function is staffed and implemented.

Fund-Raising Functions

Prospect Research. Fund-raising begins with the identification of individuals who would most likely be interested in giving to your organization. They are *suspected* to be potential donors but not technically considered *prospects* until they have been researched to confirm their interests, giving history, giving capacity, and giving inclination.

Annual Giving. Most organizations rely on a regular stream of financial support to fund their operations from day to day, month to month, and year to year. Annual or *sustaining* gifts form the foundation of any organization's development efforts. Universities, seminaries, hospitals, children's homes, ministry organizations, and churches have sustaining gift programs. Sustaining gifts are given with regularity. They typically do not require a personal solicitation; and oftentimes a specific solicitation letter, brochure, or friendly reminder is all that is needed to generate a sustaining gift.

Major or Special Giving. Major gifts are generally sought and given for organizational priorities that *advance* the organization's work as opposed to sustaining the work. Each organization decides what it considers a major gift, but in any case it is larger than the high range of what the organization considers a sustaining gift. Accordingly, major gifts are given less frequently than sustaining gifts. Regardless of the organization's definition, donors define what a major gift is to them based on their resources.

Grant Seeking. This specialty area within the development field involves seeking grants from private foundations and government organizations. Most foundations have specific causes their charters specify, and they typically limit their giving to those causes or to certain geographic boundaries. Most foundations require official proposals or written requests for funding, and they will typically indicate on their Web site or published materials the guidelines they expect grant seekers to follow. Government grants are available to Christian organizations that qualify and are willing to accept conditions placed on the grant. Strong writing skills are needed for grant seeking.

Planned Giving. This is a specialty area within development that requires special knowledge and skill. Donors sometimes use planned gifts through vehicles such as wills, trusts, and other estate plans to accomplish charitable goals. This is a complex area, as knowledge of the tax implications of various giving options are needed in order to provide donors with reliable information to move them to create a planned gift. Often the cultivation and closure of such a gift will ultimately require the involvement of the donor's personal tax and legal advisors, making it important for those who represent the organization to be able to relate well with these special players in the planned gift process. Two excellent sources of information, training, and computer software involved in planned giving are:

Crescendo Total Planned Giving Solutions of Camarillo, California
Web site: www.crescendosoft.com

Pentera, Inc. of Indianapolis, Indiana
Web site: www.pentera.com

Campaigns. A campaign is a fund-raising effort for a specific cause and typically with a deadline, usually taking place over one or more years. While organizations may call their annual sustaining gift program an "annual campaign," the word is more often associated with an effort to secure funds for construction or some other capital improvement. Sometimes campaigns are modified by the adjective *comprehensive.* Comprehensive campaigns typically involve fund-raising efforts for several purposes that are "packaged" together in one effort. For example, the typical comprehensive campaign in higher education will include capital giving, endowment giving, and sustaining giving components and goals with a projected completion deadline. Capital giving campaigns require an intense, organized effort to secure gifts for projects critical to the organization's advancement.

Gift Records. Organizations that raise money must keep proper records of gifts received, and they must promptly receipt and thank donors for every single gift they make. A well-documented donor file will not only provide records for the current tax year but will describe a donor's relationship with the organization for future generations of leaders. In most organizations at least one individual has the responsibility for gift records.

The CEO's Role in Development

A successful fund-raising effort is a result of strong leadership. The CEO is the organization's chief fund-raiser, but that does not mean he or she does the work of the chief development officer and the staff. It simply means that the CEO sees the development function as teamwork and that he or she plays a specific and significant role in setting the stage for successful fund-raising and participating in cultivating and soliciting the organization's most generous donors.

The great risk of any CEO is that he or she becomes disproportionately involved in or disproportionately detached from the development effort. The goal is to strike an appropriate balance of involvement, working with a framework of internal development systems and staff, and spending his or her time where it is most needed and most effective.

N. Francis suggests that there are several things a CEO must do to provide effective top leadership for fund-raising, among them:

1. The CEO must take the lead in crafting or updating the organization's mission and vision statements. Vision is especially important to setting the tone for the future and inspiring prospective donors to help.

2. The CEO must view fund-raising as an integral part of the organization as opposed to an ancillary function. I know of no charitable organization, regardless of whether it generates income, that can survive—much less thrive—without philanthropic dollars. Fund-raising in most of these organizations is ongoing as opposed to episodic. Thus, the CEO must think about fund-raising with only slightly less attention than he or she gives the organization's core "business."

3. The CEO must make the necessary budgetary provisions to fund the development staff and activities adequately.

4. The CEO must spend his or her time where it most counts. Cultivating and soliciting the organization's top 1–3 percent of

donors and prospects is typically where an effective CEO can be found spending the majority of his or her time in development work.

5. The CEO must expect accountability from the chief development officer and all development staff. A development officer can appear busy doing various things but not producing much fruit. The CEO must hold the development staff accountable for measurable results.[2]

Finally, a leader of a Christian organization needs to remember that people are constantly watching to see how he or she acknowledges God in the life of the organization. All too many CEOs allow their egos to expand to the extent that to varying degrees they behave as if the organization's success depends on them alone. At Anderson University in South Carolina where I have served as president since 2002, I began my tenure with a proclamation that if anything good was accomplished while I serve as president, we would publicly attribute it to God's blessing and thank Him for it. The faculty, staff, and administrators have worked hard over the years as if everything depends on us but with the constant underlying awareness that in reality our success depends on God alone. I tell people that when I pray in the morning, I always conclude with the acknowledgment and petition, "Lord, things are going pretty well around here. Don't let me mess up anything today."

A CEO of a Christian organization must acknowledge that he or she does not own the organization served. As stated earlier, leadership is a matter of stewardship. The organization belongs to God. Ask God to make the organization you serve all He wants it to be, and pray that He will make you a humble, willing servant through which He accomplishes His plans.

The Importance of Mission and Vision

The purpose of fund-raising is to fuel and advance the mission and vision of the organization. Donors must understand the organization's mission and vision in order to know if they want to support it. It is the leader's responsibility to develop mission and vision statements and keep those statements up-to-date with contemporary, relevant language.

Mission is simply the response to the question, Why does this organization exist? All organizations, for-profit and not-for-profit, exist for a fundamental reason.

Vision is the response to the question, Where does this organization seek to go in terms of the proportions of its impact and its reputation? It can be understood as a picture of your organization in the future, and it becomes your organizational inspiration. It is a direction in which your organization is continuously headed.

Mission and vision statements express how the organization is going to be the kind of cause Paul suggests is worthy of God's people's support—how the organization is sharing the Christian message, impacting people's lives for Christ, and putting hands and feet to the gospel. They form the foundation of the case for support you will build. They give donors and potential donors a clear sense of what the organization is trying to accomplish, what it is trying to become, and how it is trying to change people's lives and even the world.

The Five I's of Development: Cultivating Productive Donor Relationships

Martin Luther once remarked, "There are three conversions necessary [for the Christian life]: the conversion of the heart, the mind, and the purse."

Luther was no doubt referring to the conversion that takes place by God's Spirit, but we are aware that God regularly uses His servants to inspire one another. Hence, the conversion of the purse is often times a thoughtful, intentional process on the part of God's servants in fund-raising.

Donor relationships are like any other relationship: they require an investment of time and energy. The goal of donor cultivation is to create a lifelong, mutually beneficial relationship between the donor and the organization. Both receive something valuable out of a continuously maturing relationship. The organization receives ongoing, ever-increasing support that fuels its mission and vision. The donor receives multiple benefits, the most important being the chance to express gratitude to God for His love, mercy, and goodness. Other benefits include the joy of knowing that they are helping make the work of a worthy cause possible and the joy of knowing and supporting the people who work in the organization and embody its mission and ethos. Finally, while it is typically the least important motivator in giving, tax benefits are also received.

G. T. Smith codified several stages in building a donor relationship. They are called the Five I's.

1.   *Identification.* Potential donors must be identified by the
     organization seeking support. Sometimes the way to identify
     prospects is obvious. For instance, a church's most likely donors
     are its own members. A university's most likely donors are its
     own alumni. But others might be interested in supporting the
     work of your organization, and they must be identified.
2.   *Information.* Potential donors must be informed about the
     organization. They must first understand the organization's
     mission and be familiar with its good works. They must
     understand its vision. They must trust the organization's
     leadership and be familiar with the leadership's ability and
     integrity. The organization must inform the prospect of all these
     things by a combination of communication, marketing, and
     personal cultivation strategies.
3.   *Interest.* For the relationship to go forward, the prospect has
     to develop a genuine interest in the organization's work. The
     organization must constantly look for clues that indicate a
     prospect has moved from being informed to being interested.
4.   *Involvement.* People typically give to those organizations in
     which they are involved. The organization must offer ways for
     those interested in its work to become involved. Events and
     activities, committees, teams, and boards are typical leadership
     involvement mechanisms.
5.   *Investment.* At this stage the prospect converts to a donor,
     investing in the organization's work.

The last four stages form something of a cycle whereby the donor must
continuously be kept informed, interested, and involved to one degree or
another to increase the probability that repeat investments will be made.

This is a good place to mention that there is a significant difference in
the attention an organization devotes to the development of a sustaining
donor relationship as opposed to a major donor relationship. Major gift
relationships require far more time, thought, and energy than sustaining
gift relationships, and organizations must depend on the prospect research
functions as well as clues their leaders pick up from sustaining donors to
know when it is time to pursue a major gift relationship.

The Pyramid of Giving illustrates the various levels of giving, the
progression of the Five I's as the giving levels increase, and the types of
contact appropriate for each level.

The Pyramid of Giving

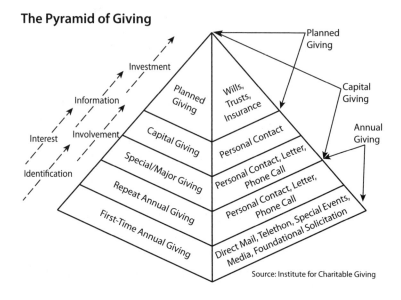

Source: Institute for Charitable Giving

Leadership for Major Gifts

Leaders should understand some basic concepts about how major gifts are cultivated, solicited, asked for, and how major gift decisions are made. Each organization must define what it considers a major gift and that donors themselves make decisions about what a major gift is for them. When cultivating and soliciting a major gift, the decision-making role of the donor is superlative. The best test for determining whether the prospective donor will consider the amount of the gift you are soliciting is what W. Sturtevant calls the "stop and think" test.[3]

To illustrate, if you were to ask a donor for a gift of $50 to support your cause, she would likely be able that instant to tell you whether she will make the gift. She does not have to think about it, pray about it, or consult her husband about it. At that moment, she knows in her heart whether she cares enough about your work and whether she has enough money on hand to write the check. She does not have to think much about that decision. However, if you ask the same woman for a gift of $100,000, she would likely not be able to give you an instant response. She might need to think about how much she cares about your ministry, discuss it with her husband, check with her accountant, pray about what she will or will not do, etc. She has to "stop and think" about whether she will do as you have asked. No matter the size of the gift for which you ask, any "stop and think" gift is a major gift to the person being asked, and those who ask for major gifts will need to cultivate the donor to the extent that they are ready to be asked, be patient as the donor decides, and not give up if the donor says no.

Sturtevant explains that when a donor says no to a request, it does not always mean "absolutely no." It may mean no to the amount asked for, but the prospect may say yes to a lesser amount. It may mean no right now but yes a year from now. It may mean no for the purpose but yes to another purpose. Thus, it is important for anyone asking for a major gift to probe as much as the prospect will allow into the reasons behind a negative response. Informed by the prospect's rationale, a good major gifts solicitor will revise his or her plans and, when the time is right, ask donors to consider something to which they are more likely to respond with a yes.

Whether an organization is in a campaign or not, it should have at least three levels of leaders involved in its major gift program, including the chief executive officer, the chief development officer, and volunteer member-leaders of a major gifts committee or board. The chief executive is essential because he or she will often be involved in cultivating and soliciting major donors. The chief development officer is needed because he or she is the coordinator of all cultivation and solicitation activity, much like the conductor of an orchestra. Leader-volunteers are needed because they often have the primary relationships with prospective donors and are able to play a significant role in cultivation and solicitation.

Leader-volunteers on the major gift committee should be carefully selected. These individuals will often include governing board members, current major gift donors, and other people of influence who are "sold out" to the organization's mission and vision. In every case these are individuals who have significant wealth and have significant influence with other people of wealth. Their previous major gifts to your cause give them the credibility they need to ask others for support.

The work of the major gifts committee is highly confidential. Members will meet regularly to engage in the ongoing development of donor profiles and plans for approaching prospective major donors for support. Information like the prospect's biography, people who influence the prospect's giving decisions, history of giving to other organizations, and financial information is documented in the prospect's file and safely guarded by the staff. Once the committee feels it has enough information about the prospect to develop a cultivation and solicitation plan, it makes decisions about how to structure cultivation activities, who should be involved in those activities, who should conduct the solicitation, what to ask for, and how much.

The premier systematic process of developing plans for cultivation and solicitation is called Moves Management©, pioneered by G. T. "Buck" Smith and D. Dunlop when they were on the development staff at Cornell University. The concept is now copyrighted by the Institute for Charitable Giving. W. Sturtevant calls it a "fail-safe tool of nurturing fund-raising." The scope of this chapter and the complexity of the Moves Management system does not permit a full discussion, but any organization that is serious about major gift fund-raising should further investigate and consider implementing this proven system for cultivating and soliciting major gifts. Moves Management is discussed in detail in Sturtevant's *The Artful Journey: Cultivating and Soliciting the Major Gift,* and seminars are offered that address this system through the Institute for Charitable Giving in Chicago (www.instituteforgiving.org).[4]

In concluding this section, I would like to make a personal recommendation for those interested in becoming skilled at major gift fund-raising. As a 27-year veteran of fund-raising seminars, articles, and books, I have learned the most about fund-raising from J. Panas and his associates at the Institute for Charitable Giving. Panas has written several books on the subject. I suggest you obtain and read them all and attend one or more of the Institute's seminars.

Leadership for Campaigns and Building Projects

Whether you are involved in a *capital* campaign for a specific purpose like a new building or a *comprehensive* campaign that has multiple goals for buildings, endowment, and sustaining gifts, the leadership principles and campaign structures are essentially the same. The success of any campaign depends on the ability of the organization to secure the commitment of a strong, example-setting leadership team.

The typical structure for a campaign is to have a campaign leadership committee or team, complemented and supported by various other committees or teams of volunteers appropriate to the size, scope, and priorities of the campaign. It is both likely and desirable that some members of your major gifts committee will also be members of the campaign leadership team. The chief executive officer and chief development officer will work with the campaign leadership team. The chief development officer and other development staff members will work with the supporting committees.

Generally, members of campaign committees will have the same characteristics as members of your major gift committee. All campaign leaders must be donors themselves, be influential with others who have the capability to give, and be people of such integrity and character that their involvement with your cause would not be questioned.

There are several stages of activity leading up to launching a campaign.

Setting the Stage for Campaign Success

Needs Assessment. This applies primarily to a comprehensive campaign or a capital campaign with more than one building project. The needs assessment is simply a listing of the needs the campaign is to address. The assessment may need to be adjusted if it is later discovered in the feasibility study that the amount needed to address all needs exceeds the organization's ability to raise the funds required.

Case Statement. A case statement is a narrative that describes the institution's rationale or *case* for support. J. Panas says that the case statement should address four main questions:

1. How is the organization positioned in the community, and what is its heritage?
2. Why is a campaign necessary?
3. Is the organization fiscally sound?
4. Does the institution have strong leadership?

In his book *Making the Case*, Panas presents a no-nonsense guide for writing case statements and elaborates on the questions above, including a fail-proof checklist for all the elements of a strong case statement.[5] The statement will have a listing of all the campaign priorities, dollar goals, and naming opportunities. Once it is written, the case statement is used first in the feasibility study as a draft by which leadership seeks to test the statement's effectiveness on likely major donors. After the feasibility study the case statement is often published with a professional appearance and becomes the centerpiece communication item of the campaign.

Recruiting the Campaign Committee. Volunteers are essential to the success of the campaign, especially the overall campaign steering committee. Other volunteers on the campaign committee include the chairs for the organization's various segmented constituencies.

Campaign Chair. The campaign chair is often the first volunteer recruited by the chief executive officer, assisted by the chair of the board and the chief development officer if needed. The chair must be an individual of financial means, sterling reputation, and proven and well-known generosity to the organization. This individual must be able to command the attention and respect of the organization's entire campaign audience. Ideally it will be the most powerful, widely known, influential, articulate, winsome, and assertive friend the organization has. The chair will preside at all campaign committee meetings, make personal solicitations with the CEO, and generally set the leadership tone for all other volunteers. Organizations sometimes designate two individuals as cochairpersons, but a single chair is often more successful.

Major Gifts Chair. Recent fund-raising experience demonstrates that as much as 90 percent of the fund-raising goal will come from the top 10 percent of all donors to a campaign. Thus, the same characteristics of the campaign chair are required of the major gifts chair. The campaign's success will rest on major gifts, and this individual will often be involved in cultivating and soliciting the gifts along with the campaign chairman and CEO.

Board Chair. Every trustee must make a significant gift to the effort. An organization will be doomed for failure for lack of credibility if it cannot say that all the members of its governing board made sacrificial gifts. Typically, the chair of the organization's board of trustees will be a member of the campaign committee and will be responsible for assisting the campaign chair and CEO in trustee solicitation.

Corporate Gifts Chair. While most gifts come from individuals as opposed to corporations and businesses, depending on the organization's proximity and appeal to thriving business and industry, a corporate gifts chairperson is often appropriate. This individual should be a well-positioned CEO or other significant executive as he or she will also participate in solicitation calls on other business leaders.

Foundation Gifts Chair. If the organization will seek grants, a chairperson for this constituency will be needed. Ideally, this individual will be the board chair or CEO of a foundation that will make a significant gift to the campaign. This individual will be required to make personal contacts with other foundation decision makers in setting the stage for securing grants.

Annual Giving Chair. If the campaign is a comprehensive campaign that includes annual giving, a chair for this effort will be needed. This component of the campaign will have the most donors and the smallest average gift. Nevertheless, this chair should be a winsome, well-known personality to the organization's broad constituency.

Honorary Chair. Sometimes it is helpful to have an honorary chair of the campaign. This is often a significant figure in the life of the organization that is for some reason not readily available to chair the campaign and/or attend campaign meetings but may be essential in securing a few key major gifts in the campaign. This individual is often a larger-than-life person and will lend extraordinary credibility and influence to the effort by his or her endorsement.

Members-at-Large. Organizations often have individuals that are perhaps not larger-than-life figures in the organization but are nevertheless key major donors and need to be involved in the campaign effort either for the work they will perform during the effort or the added credibility they will bring. Two to three at-large members are adequate, but there is no limit on these individuals as long as the size of the committee stays manageable enough to make timely decisions.

Campaign Communications Chair. It is often helpful to have a well-connected media or public relations executive to serve as chair of the effort to publish and distribute communications and advertisements about the campaign.

Chief Executive Officer. The organization's chief executive officer should obviously be a member of the campaign committee.

Chief Development Officer. The organization's chief development officer should be a member of the committee as he or she will be known not only by his or her organizational title but also as the campaign director, even if paid campaign counsel is employed.

Optional Members. Depending on the nature and complexity of the organization's broad audience, chairpersons for various constituencies may be in order.

Campaign Counsel. Organizations often employ fund-raising consultants to provide overall direction to the campaign effort, even if the organization has a chief development officer. Services range from ongoing advice on a periodic basis to the assignment of an experienced fundraising professional to the organization. Campaign counsel should provide all training for volunteers. He or she will suggest, confer, and advise but cannot do the work for you. A fund-raising consultant is a wise investment.

Feasibility Study. The organization will typically employ a fund-raising consultant to conduct a feasibility study to test the case statement, the campaign priorities and dollar goals, and gauge whether the campaign will succeed as planned. The feasibility study process is an excellent way to inform the organization's key major gift constituents of its needs and give them an opportunity to be involved in shaping the final case statement and the campaign components. A paid fund-raising consultant is used for this stage to ensure maximum objectivity of the feasibility study results.

Prepare the Fund-Raising Plan. The CEO, campaign director, and paid consultant will work with the campaign committee to develop a written plan for how the campaign will be carried out, including fund-raising and communications strategies, deadlines, staffing needs, etc.

Church Campaigns. Basic fund-raising principles are as relevant to church campaigns as they are to other organizations. There are a few differences, however. The first obvious difference is that most of the gifts will come from regularly involved members who are well informed of the church's mission, vision, plans, and needs. They are a captive audience and easily accessible.

Second, fund-raising firms specialize in church campaigns and approach campaigning from their own fund-raising philosophy yet one that, more often than nonchurch campaigns, place a great deal of emphasis on spiritual growth through giving. The consultant you choose must be a committed Christian with appropriate experience in assisting churches in capital giving, and he or she must understand and appreciate the special context of your church. Congregational emphases on prayer and stewardship are appropriate to central activities leading up to the campaign kickoff. P. Gage of The Gage Group (www.thegagegroup.com) says that a church campaign must be based on three biblical principles: the stewardship principle, the sacrifice principle, and the voluntary principle:

- *The Stewardship Principle*. Stewardship is the recognition that God owns all we possess. It is an acknowledgment that God will provide all of our needs and the resources we need to do God's work in the church. We are simply managers of what God provides for our lives, and we are accountable for all that He has given us. Our giving must always be an act of love and gratitude.
- *The Sacrifice Principle*. What sacrifice is to one person is not always the same to another person. Sacrificial giving is an act of setting aside our financial resources for God. Jesus chose as models for giving those who gave sacrificially: the widow who gave two mites, the boy who gave his lunch, and the woman who gave her alabaster box of perfume.

- *The Voluntary Principle.* A church campaign, or any campaign for that matter, must not resort to pressure tactics or coercion. It is not biblical, and it will damage the credibility and effectiveness of the campaign.

Church campaign committees and structures often differ from the typical capital campaign. Campaign counsel will assist church leaders in developing the proper structure and voluntary leadership roles.

Conducting the Campaign

Belmont University trustee chair L. T. Thrailkill, speaking to fellow trustees during the launching of the $170 million Keeping the Promise Campaign, said: "God has all the resources He needs to make this campaign successful. The challenge is . . . much of it is in your pockets." All the preparation for the campaign up to this point is essential, but it will not guarantee the success of the campaign unless someone asks someone for a gift.

With some minor exceptions in church campaigns, people rarely make major gift commitments without being asked by another individual. Thus, gift solicitation involves one or more people asking other people to make a gift commitment. The choice of the solicitor should be carefully considered as it should be the individual to whom the prospect will most likely respond positively. While gift solicitation improves with experience, the most important thing to remember is to do it.

Often a solicitor's success will be greatly enhanced if he or she has been trained in gift solicitation by campaign counsel or the organization's development staff. Familiarity with the various ways to make a gift will be a key part of the training. Many individuals who make major gifts do so in the form of a pledge they pay over a period of time, often years. Some may choose to give noncash property such as real estate, stock, or valuable personal property such as art. Others use planned gift vehicles such as trusts or an estate plan that includes a gift. The solicitor is not required to be an expert in these fields, but he or she should be familiar enough with the various methods of giving to discuss the basic concept with the prospect and get professional assistance involved.

Conclusion

It is impossible to grasp fully all the considerations and details of leading fund-raising efforts from this brief chapter. As with anything, personal experience is the best way to learn in addition to observing the experience and wisdom of others.

Leadership is essential to fund-raising. Without it not much would be accomplished. Few funds are given without someone's communicating a vision and a need followed by an "ask." The responsibility for fund-raising begins with the head of the organization or CEO, who sets the stage, inspires and motivates the governing board, key volunteers, and the donor base. Everyone involved in the effort has an opportunity to respond to God's grace and blessing by using their talents and giving their resources to support the Lord's work however it manifests itself in churches, parachurch ministries, mission work, hospitals, children's homes, retirement homes, schools, universities, seminaries, relief organizations, and on and on.

Those who give freely and cheerfully are a delight to God as they acknowledge that everything they are and everything they have are free gifts to be opened, celebrated, and shared for the cause of Christ. They are stewards who carefully manage their assets so they can give in both life and death. They leave behind them assets for the Lord's work that touch lives and spread the gospel to a lost world that groans for redemption.

Resources for Further Study

Axelrod, T. *Raising More Money: A Step-by-Step Guide to Building Lifelong Donors*. Seattle: Raising More Money Publications, 2001.

Fisher, J. L., and G. H. Quehl. *The President and Fund Raising*. New York: Macmillan Publishing Company, 1989.

Francis, Norman C. *The President's Management Role in Development*. Washington, DC: Association of American Colleges, 1975.

Gage, P. *Brentwood Baptist Church Campaign Notebook*. Colleyville, TX: The Gage Group, 2000.

Jeavons, T. H., and R. B. Basinger, *Growing Givers' Hearts: Treating Fundraising as Ministry*. San Francisco: Jossey-Bass, 2000.

Lawson, D. M. *Give to Live: How Giving Can Change Your Life*. La Jolla, CA: ALTI Publishing, 1991.

Matheny, R. *Major Gifts: Solicitation Strategies*, 2nd ed. Washington: Council for Advancement and Support of Education, 1999.

Muir, R., and J. May, eds. *Developing a Major Gift Program: From Managing Staff to Soliciting Gifts*. Washington: Council for Advancement and Support of Education, 1993.

Panas, J. *Boardroom Verities: A Celebration of Trusteeship with Some Guides and Techniques to Govern By*. Chicago: Precept Press, 1991.

_____. *Born to Raise: What Makes a Great Fundraiser: What Makes a Fundraiser Great*. Chicago: Pluribus Press, 1988.

_____. *Finders Keepers: Lessons I've Learned About Dynamic Fundraising.* Chicago: Bonus Books, 1999.

_____. *Making the Case: The No-Nonsense Guide to Writing the Perfect Case Statement.* Chicago: Institutions Press, 2003.

_____. *Wit, Wisdom & Moxie: A Fundraiser's Compendium of Wrinkles, Strategies, and Admonitions That Really Work.* Chicago: Bonus Books, 2002.

Pocock, J. W. *Fund-Raising Leadership: A Guide for College and University Boards.* Washington: Association of Governing Boards, 1989.

Smith, G. T. *Developing Private Support: Three Issues.* Washington, DC: Association of American Colleges, 1975.

Sturtevant, William T. *The Artful Journey: Cultivating and Soliciting the Major Gift.* Chicago: Bonus Books, 1997.

Questions for Further Reflection

1. Over the last half century, the predominant American mind-set has shifted from a Judeo-Christian perspective to a postmodern perspective. In what ways might this affect peoples' willingness to give for reasons consistent with Scripture, and what can we do to address any negative consequences of this shift in perspective?

2. Cultural norms and practice reflect that the focus of estate planning (and the estate-planning profession) is to pass on assets to family, often at the total exclusion of charity, yet the best opportunity most of us have to leave the ultimate gift of a lifetime is in our estates. What can be done in our churches to inform members about the great opportunity they have to extend their Christian witness beyond their lifetime by making provisions for Christian causes in their estate plans? At the end of our lifetime, what message do we send to the family members we leave behind when we remember the Lord's work in our estate plans?

3. Transparency is of utmost importance in building a relationship based on trust. What role does stewardship play in the ability for Christian causes to build lifelong relationships with donors and attract future support?

Endnotes

[1] T. H. Jeavons and R. B. Basinger, *Growing Givers' Hearts: Treating Fundraising as Ministry* (San Francisco: Jossey-Bass, 2000).

[2] N. C. Francis, *The President's Management Role in Development* (Washington, DC: Association of American Colleges, 1975).

[3] W. T. Sturtevant, *The Artful Journey: Cultivating and Soliciting the Major Gift* (Chicago: Bonus Books, 1997).

[4] Ibid.

[5] J. Panas, *Making the Case: The No-Nonsense Guide to Writing the Perfect Case Statement* (Chicago: Institutions Press, 2003).

Chapter 8

INSTITUTIONS, ORGANIZATIONS, AND FOUNDATION RELATIONS

Alvin O. Austin
President Emeritus, LeTourneau University

For the idolaters eagerly seek all these things, and your heavenly Father knows that you need them. But seek first the kingdom of God and His righteousness, and all these things will be provided for you.
—Matthew 6:32–33 HCSB

B efore exploring the issue of approaching a foundation to accomplish a mission, it is often advisable to consider all possibilities. Some foundations might even require the exhaustion of all other resources before funding the effort of an organization, institution, or ministry.

Finding Resources to Accomplish the Mission of an Organization or Ministry

Whether a person is contemplating an initial move into a position of leadership in a Christian ministry or organization, embarking on a fresh new challenge, or is firmly established as a seasoned veteran, a key ingredient in moving a project forward from initial point of vision to full implementation is the possession of adequate resources. Resources come in many forms. Leaders should not immediately fall prey to the idea that any good thing requires new money, especially up-front money, before the effort can be launched. Resources for the support of effective leadership include such things as fresh ideas; available people and their time, talents, and energy; space to function, which might include buildings or property; and prayer support, an ever-present need for the Christian leader.

Fresh Ideas as a Resource

Most of us who have had what we deem to be successful careers, providing leadership over an organization or an institution, know that many of the things that worked best for our ministries were not ideas born in our own minds. A good leader is always on the lookout for new ideas that, when incorporated into one's own structure, will bring new outreach, energy, focus, or success to our work. It costs nothing to be a good observer and listener. It takes little money to attend conferences, read appropriate journals or publications, or gather together a focus group of individuals to pursue "blue sky" ideas for accomplishing our vision or mission.

People as a Resource

Volunteers are a great resource. Leaders don't have to look far and wide to see great ministries that are substantively enhanced by volunteers. Given the right impetus, people are prepared to give of themselves to worthy causes ranging from disaster relief, drug intervention, community support, and evangelistic programs to more ongoing enterprises such as hospitals, colleges and universities, and churches. The university where I was privileged to be president regularly encouraged our students, many of whom came from some distance, to give back to the local community through work projects and volunteering in local organizations that provide care for those in need. In recent years these students have given between 40,000 and 70,000 volunteer hours a year. Even if one measures this by minimum wage equivalents, it amounts to many hundreds of thousands of dollars of resources provided at no cost to the community or to the ministry.

Donated or Free Space as a Resource

While buildings and space are often needed to house a ministry, it isn't always necessary to buy or build to obtain such facilities. I have served on the board of a sizable broadcast ministry that has existed for years in space donated or made available at rock-bottom prices by a benevolent donor. Churches are among our nation's most underused spaces. An institution might work out a relationship with a local church to use some of their space in off hours in return for some service provided to their congregation. The use of public facilities, parks, and even woodlands often comes at little or no cost.

Gifts-in-Kind as a Resource

People regularly donate to charitable causes materials and equipment that they no longer want or need. Vehicles, machinery and tools, travel trailers, airplanes, office equipment and supplies, vacant land, or equity in ownership of an organization are examples I have observed. One should be careful in accepting gifts-in-kind, as the donor might have an inflated sense of the worth of the item and seek to take a tax deduction that cannot be supported by a fair market appraisal. While the IRS deems it the responsibility of the donor to substantiate the value of the gift, the recipient is sometimes caught in the trap of trying to help donors defend their declared value when the value is challenged by the IRS.

In addition to the problem of establishing a fair market value, organizations should act with care when accepting a gift-in-kind as the gift might be a "white elephant," one the donor offers to your ministry because he was unable to find another means of disposal. The impulsive decision to take any outright gift might later make it necessary to dispose of that gift at a loss to the organization. When I first came to the presidency, we had in our possession an old hotel in downtown Longview, Texas. Though it was actually the second hotel ever built by Conrad Hilton, it was long outdated and had been shuttered. It came as a take-it-or-leave-it late year-end gift offer. The university accepted it without having time to research the property or its value. The donor booked the gift at a value of $500,000, and the university recorded it on its books at that amount. The university used it for a year or two as a satellite student housing site but soon shut it down. Boarded up, it was a constant magnet for breakins and vandalism. When I arrived, we made the decision to sell it but to no avail. In the end we had to write down the booked value to zero, hurting our audit statements, and then spend several hundred thousand dollars to remove the asbestos and demolish it before convincing the city to take the property off our hands and convert it to a downtown park.

Redistribute Existing Resources

Too often we think we must have new money in order to accomplish a new project or a new focus of our work. While sometimes that is true, often we fail to look internally at our budgets and programs to see where some resources, which could be used to accomplish the desired task, might be hidden. This might include the reduction of funds in some areas or elimination of a program that is no longer viable or has lost its priority.

Prayer as a Powerful Resource

Prayer support costs nothing, but we too often fail to ask for it. As I spoke to hundreds of alumni, parent groups, community forums, and friends of the university over the almost 40 years I spent in a leadership role in higher education, I would often end by asking the audience a rhetorical question, "How can you help?" The answer to my own question was frequently, "By sending us your students, by providing financial resources to support our work, and by praying for our efforts." I was always amazed when someone would come up after my presentation and say, "At a previous meeting you asked me to pray, and I have prayed for you since that time." At a retirement ceremony, as I was leaving my role as president of LeTourneau University, a person came up to me and said, "I have prayed for you every day for the 21 years you have served as president." What a powerful resource this is when a leader has godly people upholding him or her and the work of the organization in prayer!

Money as a Necessary Ingredient

While I have tried to lay the foundation for this chapter on working with foundations with the challenge to look beyond the need for money as the only resource for supporting the work, I have to admit that financial resources—yes money—are an important ingredient in supporting a ministry and enhancing leadership initiatives. As management and leadership guru P. Drucker is quoted as saying, "Napoleon said that there were three things needed to fight a war. The first is money. The second is money. And the third is money."[1] Possibly this is why Napoleon, finding his empire stretched thin and under duress, agreed to sell the vast Louisiana Territory to President Thomas Jefferson for just pennies an acre. Money is an important resource to which a leader must gain access in order to undergird the work in an institution or organization.

Foundations as a Resource

Where does an organization turn in looking for financial resources? In this chapter we will provide specific focus on an area of fund-raising that deals with a group of grant-making entities called foundations. In the

United States alone are more than 50,000 such organizations ranging from the extremely large ones like the Bill and Melinda Gates Foundation, Pew Charitable Trusts, Lilly Endowment, and the Kresge Foundation, to name just a few, to the many mom-and-pop family foundations. In total these foundations grant more than $41 billion a year or 13 percent of the more than $308 billion of charitable donations given in a recent year. Some of the foundations resources represent "old money," left by earlier donors who wanted their financial legacy to be the support of worthy causes. Other foundations are funded by young entrepreneurs who have been successful in their careers and want to use the foundation model as a means of giving back some of what they have earned. Some foundations are national in scope in terms of whom they will support, and many others are regional or even local in their outreach.

Types of Foundations

Private Foundation

The Foundation Center describes a private foundation as "a nongovernmental, non-profit organization with funds (usually from a single source, such as an individual, family or corporation) and program managed by its own trustees or directors. Private foundations are established to maintain or aid social, educational, religious, or other charitable activities serving the common welfare, primarily through the making of grants."[2] The private foundations, also referred to as independent foundations, vary in size and assets from over a billion dollars to some with just a few thousand dollars.

Family Foundation

Many of the private foundations are actually family foundations. Some are large such as the Bill and Melinda Gates Foundation, W. M. Keck Foundation, the Lilly Endowment, and the Pew Charitable Trusts, to name only a few. These have large holdings and large professional staffs, have printed annual reports, and often have complex written guidelines for making application for grants. About two-thirds of all private foundations are actually family foundations, which provide about one-third of all awards made by private foundations.

Many smaller family foundations have limited resources and often have no full-time professional staff. Members of the donor family, children or grandchildren of the initial donor, and perhaps an attorney make up the board of smaller family foundations. They might have guidelines or primary interest areas to which they will make grants, but they often have no printed materials or application forms. These foundations often have a group of preselected organizations to which they will provide support.

Community Foundation

Community foundations are established as a means of consolidating the charitable resources within a community or within a limited geographical area. Usually the funds donated on their own would not warrant the expense of an organizational structure to oversee and administer the grants to be made. By providing the medium of a community foundation, more persons within the community are encouraged to donate funds. This provision of staff and structure makes for a more stable and professional grant-or-grantee environment and can also offer a means for donors to remain anonymous, avoiding the personal appeals that can become burdensome if overseeing their own grants.

While a donor must give up legal claim to the funds being donated to a community foundation, the process has several benefits for the donor. First, donors can contribute all of their funds in a given tax year, receiving the tax benefits from that timely gift, but then designate the funds to be distributed by the community foundation over a longer period of time. Second, the foundation might allow the donor to provide counsel over how or to whom the funds will be distributed. These are called donor-advised funds. Community foundations might also have endowments restricted for the benefit of the community where they are established and managed by a community-based foundation board. If the grant seeker fits the profile established by the community foundation, this can be a convenient source for financial support.

Corporate Foundation

Some for-profit corporations use a foundation as a means of distributing grants to causes they choose to support. Some corporations have a policy of dedicating a certain percentage of corporate profit to charitable causes or, if their boards or leadership desires, for business or public relations purposes, to establish a charitable presence in the marketplace. Corporations often use their foundations to make contributions to organizations, community welfare groups, and the like, within their service or business areas. This gives the local office or store manager the opportunity to make selective grants within their communities.

We have all seen businesses make public donations to various chari-table entities and publicize their gifts locally, a practice that enhances their image as a good community citizen while benefiting local organizations. Typically the corporate foundation does not have an endowment from which to draw but gets funding from corporate earnings. One of the most broadly used corporate foundation-giving mechanisms is the matching gift program wherein the corporate foundation encourages employees to make donations to acceptable agencies, after which the corporation will match, sometimes as high as three to one, the donation given by the employee. If one can identify the employees of matching gift companies, and there are online lists of such companies available, an organization can often moti-vate the employee to make contributions with the added satisfaction that their gift will be leveraged by that of their employer.

Other Foundation Distinctives

In addition to the types of foundations we have identified, foundations have some specific distinctives you should know before making a grant request.

Regional or Geographic Limitations

Some foundations provide grants on a national or even international basis with no geographic limitations. However, many limit their grants to specific regions or locales, either by formal policy or by actual grant-making practice. For example, the M. J. Murdock Foundation of Oregon makes grants only within five Northwestern states. The Reynolds Founda-tion makes grants only in three states where the originating corporation had holdings. While not limited by absolute policy, the Lilly Endow-ment provides a bulk of its grants to institutions and organizations within Indiana. The Houston Endowment grants much of its funding within the immediate Houston area. While one might have cause to make a proposal to a regional foundation, even if you are outside the area of their focus, in most cases that will be a waste of time for both parties.

Special Interests of the Foundation

Many foundations limit their grants to areas of selected special interests. Some favor health care while others give almost exclusively to higher edu-cation or lower-level education. Some limit their giving to nonsectarian causes. Some intentionally give only to sectarian causes, even subcatego-ries such as evangelism or missions.

One large Midwest foundation will not give to any entity that receives any federal government support. Because our university received federal support from the National Institute for Health and the National Science Foundation benefiting some engineering projects in our quest to develop low-cost prosthetic limbs for Third-World countries, we could not seek grants from that particular foundation. It is important to know the limitations of the respective foundation before making a grant proposal.

Proactive, Reactive, or Interactive

N. O. Thorpe has described these distinctives based on how the foundation interacts with the grantee.[3] Some foundations have established a process whereby they identify a problem they would like to see addressed and proactively seek parties that can help them find a solution, making that party a partner in the effort by granting them resources. The foundation, in that case, initiates the process. Other foundations await the proposal from parties seeking funding for their own projects, review the proposals, and, if in agreement, react to the proposal by funding it. A blended method is one in which the foundation develops, over time, relationships with various entities and, by interacting with them those organizations develop mutually beneficial projects.

Seeking Foundation Support for Your Organization

If the three most important elements in buying real estate are location, location, location, the three most important qualities of successful fundraising are relationship, relationship, relationship. Whether asking a member of the church to contribute to the organ fund, requesting a gift from a local banker, or submitting a proposal to a foundation, large or small, relationship building is a fundamental precursor to being a successful grant recipient. How are relationships built?

Know the Donor

The leader of a larger organization or institution will have someone in the development or advancement office that will have primary responsibility for building foundation relationships. This person might be the chief development officer or a foundation and grants director. If the ministry is small, this task may fall directly on the shoulders of the organization's leader.

Research

The first place to begin in knowing a donor is to perform background research. If an organization is interested in a particular foundation, that organization should seek all the information available. If they have an annual report, a copy should be requested. A foundation's Web site is a great source for reviewing their guidelines. The foundation will often provide listings of other entities they have funded. *The Foundation Directory*; *Guide to U.S. Foundations, Their Trustees, Officers and Donors*; and *The Directory of Corporate and Foundation Givers* are valuable resources. A valuable, fee-based, electronic source is foundationresource.org. Study the foundation's pattern of giving, the size of gifts, the timing of their receipt of proposals, and the schedule of making awards. These same resources can assist you in identifying other foundations that provide gifts to similar organizations, in your region, for the same types of projects.

Referrals

Identify other entities that have had relationships with the particular foundation or its officers or board members. If approached professionally and with sensitivity, most organizations who have been successful in gaining funding from a foundation will share some of their firsthand knowledge about the foundation and the best means of approach. I have even had entities provide a copy of their successful proposal once they knew we would not be competing head-to-head with them on a similar project. Organization leaders who are brand-new in the field and have no professional relationships should attend some meetings of fund-raising professionals in the field and make their acquaintance. Groups such as the National Society of Fundraising Executives, Christian Stewardship Council, and Christian Management Institute have local, regional, or national meetings that are invaluable in developing relationships. They also have workshops and seminars to help train you in the various fundamentals of fund-raising.

It is possible that a member of your institution or organization might know a board member or officer of the foundation and can meet with them. Better yet, the assistance of that person might be sought in making a presentation to the foundation. If there is a mutual acquaintance, known to the organization and to the foundation, who might agree to assist in gaining an appointment, that relationship will often make the difference in getting the desired audience.

Preproposal Contact

If at all possible, prior to presenting a proposal, a personal visit to the foundation office is wise. A meeting with their executive or one of their review officers and a simple introduction to your leadership as well as your organization, sharing with them some of the organization's accomplishments, builds credibility for your request. Specific questions to be asked include: "What current areas of interest of the foundation align with our organization or activities? Do you see anything from what I have presented to you that would preclude the foundation's interest in funding my organization?" The foundation staff will often provide good insight and maybe even some insider clues as to how to approach the foundation.

Unfortunately, there is a trend among foundations to deny personal visits and to request a brief, written preproposal, often delivered electronically. They will assess the preproposal to determine what follow-up involvement they will allow.

Any visit should be followed by a thank-you letter. Additional information should be enclosed with the letter, such as an up-to-date news clippings or a new brochure. Correspondence should be done periodically so that your organization maintains a face in the foundation office. As a part of this initial visit, it is helpful to get to know the gatekeeper for making future appointments. If it is the receptionist, time spent getting to know that person is worthwhile as he or she will often be the one who will take a call and make the appointment. That person's name should be noted and used in a personal greeting with each call. If the gatekeeper has a favorable recollection of the caller, that knowledge can often help in obtaining a follow-up appointment and can tip the scales allowing you entry into the foundation's schedule. Remember relationships, relationships, relationships!

Presentation

When making a presentation, the presenter should be as professional and personable as possible. Many foundations will want the proposals or applications to be mailed. With increasing frequency electronic delivery is preferred. However, if at all possible, the delivery should be made in person, with the highest level of leadership from your organization making the presentation. The foundation prefers to see those in high leadership roles involved in the process. They want to see how important their funding is to the leader and to the organization and might judge this by the level of leadership who participates in the proposal. One should be succinct in the presentation, but let the foundation officer dictate the pace. The important points should be covered at the outset of the meeting, as the length of the meeting usually is not known ahead of time. Flexibility is important, as the foundation staff might ask questions or choose to engage in dialogue with the presenters.

The presentation team should include one or two persons who will reinforce your organization's commitment to the foundation's values. If the foundation is eager for grantee organizations to include women and minorities in leadership roles, and if examples of that commitment exist within your organization, a couple of those capable individuals should be included in this meeting.

Putting the Best Foot Forward

Funding sources, foundations or otherwise, have far more requests than they have resources to meet the requests. How can the organization be prepared to succeed in a grant request? Here are some fundamental attributes that will help achieve success, the five P's to building credibility: purpose, plan, people, product, and promotion.

A Clear Purpose Statement

Make certain the leadership, the board, and all constituents of your organization know what the organization you represent is committed to accomplish. In former times the simple commitment to provide higher educational opportunities for young people sold many donors. Not anymore. With more than 4,000 accredited colleges plus many other special interest schools, a college must have a stronger, more defined purpose if it is going to capture the interest of donors. That same specificity should be applied to your organization, be it health care, child and family ministry, evangelism, missions, environmental preservation, or any other worthy cause.

A Clear Plan of Action

Whether the plan is called a strategic plan or a long-range plan, it should be clear, with identifiable goals, objectives, implementation strategies, and measurable outcomes. Donors want to see results, and they will want to hold the organization accountable for its stated intentions.

The Right People in Place

The key to the successful organizational accomplishment of goals is having the right people in the right place. People make the difference! Having the right institutional leadership and subleadership in place should be evident to others. Having the right people on a governance board, who will not only hold the leadership accountable but will also bring credibility to the organization, is important. If a foundation can identify by name or by experience that quality people are involved with the organization to take it through to project completion, they are more likely to grant the needed support. People give to people!

A Good Product

The product or program being offered and for which support is being requested should measure well against its competition. If this means having the Good Housekeeping Seal of Approval, accreditation by a professional entity which oversees this kind of organization, the personal endorsement of those who receive benefit from the services of the organization, or other groups that are considered partners in an endeavor or ministry, one should make certain to have the highest possible level of endorsement.

In my field of higher education, some Christian schools have felt that outside professional accreditations are not important, or they gain those endorsements from agencies who endorse only Christian schools. While staying consistent to our Christian mission, we should seek to provide the best programs and offerings that will withstand the scrutiny of the same agencies that accredit or judge all institutions of higher education. This applies to most areas of ministry. In making grant proposals, it is always beneficial to give evidence of the endorsement of those agencies that carry credibility to all parties. Concrete examples of the success of your organization's efforts should be provided, with references to these successes, such as articles or news releases by the news media and other leadership groups.

Promoting the Organization

If you have the right purpose, plan, people, and product, those facts should be broadly and enthusiastically promoted. It is always best when others from without the organization do the promotion, but in today's marketplace, where many groups are trying to accomplish similar objectives, the leadership of an organization must position it favorably. Good promotional pieces are essential to any ministry. This can be done in print form, on the Internet, using public forums or the media.

Submitting a Proposal to a Foundation

No single template exists for a successful grant proposal. One size does not fit all foundations. A boiler-plate proposal, mailed in mass to a number of foundations hoping it will hit a target, is not effective. It will be obvious to the foundation that the proposal has not been personalized to its guidelines. A good proposal is based on researching the foundation of choice and then carefully following their guidelines. If you have participated in a preproposal interview with a foundation staff member, don't ignore what was conveyed. If your institution needs help funding a new building but the foundation says it is not funding brick-and-mortar projects, submitting a proposal for brick and mortar is not wise. The initial relationship with the foundation should not be damaged by such an endeavor. It is better to wait until you have a project that matches their current grant-making interests than to press ahead with a premature request. Rejections provide little encouragement to fund-raising efforts.

It is equally important not to manufacture a need that matches their interests just to become a grant recipient. Once a grant is received, your organization will be expected to perform according to the stated intent. You might think, *If I can get the seed money on a project that might not have been high on my priority list but is a priority of the foundation, I can use their funds to launch the project and then find funds later on to continue it.* It isn't that easy! Down the road other needs will surface, and it will be difficult, even undesirable, to have to raise funds to continue a project that wasn't essential to your ministry at the start.

In submitting a grant proposal, know what expectations the funding foundation(s) will have. All of them want to see evidence of a realistic fund-raising plan that is likely to achieve success. None want to grant money, or even make a preliminary commitment of funds subject to the achievement of a total goal, if they don't believe the project will be fully funded. Many foundations will also want to know about other projected sources of funds. In some communities the various foundations communicate among themselves, and they often desire to be involved in projects that will also be funded by their fellow foundations. If, in preliminary visits to these foundations, you sense an interest in foundation collaboration and if some synergy can be created by getting one to commit if others will join in the project, that might help to get the snowball rolling. When I did fund-raising for a college in Chicago, I often found this to be true. The executives of a number of foundations worked closely together on projects. They didn't want to be the only one on board, nor did they want to be the one left out.

Knowing the timing philosophy of each foundation can be advantageous. Some like to make an early commitment with an expectation the funding process will be completed by a particular date. A time-limited grant can be a wonderful motivating force to help a fund-raiser get to work and to keep his or her nose to the grindstone; but it can also create a terrible pressure cooker when progress is being made, but the deadline is not likely to be met. It is extremely disappointing when a foundation withdraws a commitment because their deadline was not achievable.

One major midwestern foundation likes to come on board in the middle of a campaign process so that they can make a grant and use it as a matching challenge. They might make a commitment of a certain amount but only if the remaining portion is raised, often double or triple their grant, by a certain date. A Dallas-based foundation likes to be the one that puts the project over the top. That approach is a great motivator if there is assurance their funding will be available near the end. Knowledge of these timing philosophies is necessary to be certain that the request to the foundation is not done in reverse order. Otherwise funds might be denied from all of the foundations approached.

At one time I failed to get a much-needed grant because I approached one foundation too late in the process, causing them to think I did not have enough challenge remaining in our campaign to warrant their commitment. They thought we could complete the campaign without their participation even though I knew I had already picked all the known fruit off the tree and was counting on their involvement.

Guidelines for a Proposal

Dr. N. Edwards, a Seattle-based fund-raising consultant, who also served two noted universities as their vice president for advancement, has provided this outline for a grant proposal in some of his workshops. These are only suggested inclusions, and the actual proposal must always be made to conform to the guidelines provided by each individual foundation.

Introduction or Executive Summary. Provide a brief background about the organization being represented, with enough information that brings credibility and purpose to the organization in a brief format. The proposal should include evidence of the context in which the requested funding will be used.

Problem Statement. Document the problem or the need and define its components and the magnitude of the problem with evidence of how it will be addressed. This is a good place to link proposed actions with the funding interests stated by the foundation. It is advisable to be concise and hit all the high points of the plan.

Project Methodology. Specify activities as well as the personnel who will help to achieve the goals. The identity and experiences of the people involved will help sell the project.

Project Evaluation. How will results be measured against objectives? Will this be reported to the foundation?

Project Budget. Personnel and other costs should be included in the project budget.

Funding the Project. This aspect of the proposal should include evidence of funding progress to date and, if appropriate, a list of others who are expected to support the project. At this point a request is made for a specific amount of funding without being unreasonable in the amount requested. The request should be based on research of the giving patterns of the foundation as well as the size of the project, realizing that they will never give more than the requested amount; however, they can always reduce the amount to their desired level. It is prudent to state plans for recognition of the foundation for its gift and whether there will be naming opportunities.

Supporting Materials. These materials should include tax-exempt letters, audited financial statements, lists of board members, promotional materials, anything to reinforce the request.

Once the written proposal is ready to submit, it should be double-checked against the guidelines of the foundation. Timing is important, and the proposal should be submitted on time, as foundations often have strict schedules. Their boards or review teams have many proposals to read and cannot be expected to take proposals after the announced deadlines. The proposal should be professional in its appearance, and any communication to the foundation should never be handwritten. If possible, someone who has writing and editing expertise should review the proposal for appropriate spelling, grammar, and word usage.

The relationship building that has been previously undertaken becomes most valuable at the time of submitting the proposal. Ideally, it is wise to schedule an appointment for hand delivery of the proposal with time to review it with the foundation officer that is already known to the presenter. I once had a situation that, upon my presentation, the officer stated it would have been better to leave out a particular element and to include a statement that tied it more specifically to one of their strong interest areas. We still had time to make this change and then submit it to them.

This is also the time to contact any member of the foundation's board who is an acquaintance and communicate to that person that a proposal has been submitted. If that person supports your organization, he or she might make a special appeal to the foundation staff to give careful review to the proposal. Additionally, other persons in your sphere of influence, such as members of your governing board, should contact any acquaintances they may have within the foundation structure.

Time to Pray. The next step, though saved almost to the end, is the most important. As a Christian leader, you will want to seek the wisdom and intervention of God in all undertakings. This is most certainly true in fundraising. St. Benedict (AD 480–547), the founder of Western monasticism, made famous the motto, "*Ora et labora,*" pray and work. While I may have failed on a few occasions, I tried to arrive a few minutes before making a personal fund-raising presentation and sat in my car to ask God to bless our efforts. I asked Him to provide insight into what we might do to make our proposal more appealing to the donor, to provide us affirmation of His being the force behind the successful proposal if we were to receive funding, or to provide us with the understanding as to why it might be better that we not receive it. If we were simply mailing in the proposal, it was always a great spiritual team-building time to gather together those responsible for preparing the proposal and have a time of prayer prior to putting it in the envelope to mail.

Many times I would walk out of the meeting amazed at how God guided the conversation in a way I would never have taken it, how He had already prepared the donor to make the gift, and how His provisions were often bigger and better than what I might have hoped to achieve. On the many occasions when we were rejected, and that will happen for numerous reasons, I never looked back with great remorse because I knew we had both worked and prayed, and the outcome was in God's hands.

What's Next?

Follow-up

Immediately after submitting the proposal, send a follow-up letter to the foundation thanking them for the privilege of interacting with them and for the consideration they have given to the proposal. If you spent personal time with the foundation staff, either at the foundation or at your organization, make special reference to that time in the letter. There is no benefit in being defensive if the hearing did not seem to be fair or objective, nor should there be language in the letter that is presumptively optimistic about the outcome.

This letter might include a reminder that, should the funding be granted, the organization will want to be in touch with the foundation leadership regarding the special recognition that would be provided to them in the way of publicity or naming opportunities. The groundwork might be presented for their invitation to the grand opening or dedication ceremonies that will follow the completion of the project. If there are special events on the campus or ministry location, this would be a timely opportunity to invite them to attend. This not only reinforces the relationship that has been built around the specific proposal but also helps to begin to build a bridge for bringing future proposals to their attention.

Persistence

Earlier in my career, when I first engaged in fund-raising, I attended a fund-raising conference to pick up some pointers and to begin making professional contacts. I was told that on average an initial gift from an individual, corporate, or foundation donor came only after a minimum of seven contacts had been made with that entity. This does not assume that all of those contacts are face-to-face encounters, but it does mean that ongoing, persistent cultivation is needed in order to build a relationship that will result in a gift. Even a successful fund-raiser will be turned down more often than he or she receives a donation.

Never take rejection personally or become discouraged by the fact that it takes time and hard work to achieve success. For more than a decade I made an annual visit to a foundation based in Fort Worth to present a proposal. The foundation officer was always warm and gracious and expressed positive feelings toward me, my institution, and my proposal. He always promised to take our proposal to his board that reviewed and made the grants. Each time we received the same letter of rejection. We persisted and finally hit on a project that captured the interest of the foundation's board when we presented a project focused on the development of new and creative programs for training public school teachers through an accelerated program for persons who already had bachelor's degrees. This endeavor met a need for filling the 40,000 teacher vacancies in Texas. The foundation provided generous funding for this program and even came back to fund a follow-up proposal. Persistence is the key! I've been told that one foundation systematically rejects all first-time proposals. Only those who had the staying power to return with another proposal received serious consideration. Winston Churchill's challenge to "never, never, never give up" holds true in work with foundations.

Resources for Further Study

Drucker, Peter. *Managing the Non-Profit Organization.* New York: HarperCollins, 1990.

Foundation Center. *"Glossary."* 1998.

Gayley, Henry T. *How to Write for Development: Bigger Communication Brings Bigger Dollar Results.* Washington, DC: Council for Advancement and Support of Education. 1991.

Glass, Sandra A., ed. *The Changing World of Foundation Fundraising: New Challenges and Opportunities.* San Francisco: Jossey-Bass, 1999.

_____, ed. *Approaching Foundations: Suggestions and Insights for Fundraisers.* San Francisco: Jossey-Bass, 1998. Part of a series entitled New Directions for Philanthropic Fundraising sponsored by The Center on Philanthropy at Indiana University.

Publications and meetings of the National Society of Fundraising Executives, Christian Stewardship Council, Council for Advancement and Support of Education, Christian Management Association.

Questions for Further Reflection

1. What are you doing with intentionality that will increase the quality, credibility, and public knowledge of your organization?

2. Has anyone been identified within your organization that will have leadership over grant writing and foundation relations? Is the leadership of your organization assisting them in their further training?

3. Have several foundations been identified as likely candidates for funding your organization, and how are relationships being developed with those foundations or with their staffs and boards?

Endnotes

[1] See P. Drucker, *Managing the Non-Profit Organization* (New York: HarperCollins, 1990).

[2] Foundation Center, *"Glossary,"* 1998.

[3] S. A. Glass, ed., *The Changing World of Foundation Fundraising: New Challenges and Opportunities* (San Francisco: Jossey-Bass, 1999).

Chapter 9

LEADERSHIP, ORGANIZATIONS, AND EXTERNAL RELATIONS

Carl Zylstra
President, Dordt College

John Donne may have said that no man is an island. Yet it seems that the women and men who hold leadership positions in the not-for-profit world really have a hard time believing that.

Oh, they still go to conventions and seminars, particularly those winter events held in warm-weather locales. Yet spend an hour or two at such a "leadership" gathering, and it soon becomes apparent that pretty much everyone there considers themselves to be leaders, and they don't seem inclined to follow anyone. Instead, most such gatherings appear more to resemble a temporary chicken-house lockup where the first two hours are spent establishing the pecking order. Name tags are quickly scanned to determine who is worth the leader expending his or her social capital in engaging. Or maybe more to the point, which of the folks carry an aura of prestige or credibility such that hanging out with them at the reception or managing to snare an empty chair at their dinner table might spill over onto the aspiring leader some of their evident surplus of credibility.

Yet for all the time and money expended on what often passes for "leadership events" in the present era, that type of social preening hardly seems to carry much payoff for the leader, the institution the leader serves, the profession of which the leader is a part, the social movement of which his

157

or her institution is a component, society at large, and the kingdom of God in particular.

Or maybe that's really what's missing—an awareness that the leadership position does not exist for the sake of the leader but rather the leader carries a divine trust to be exercised on behalf of the institution, his or her profession, the social benefit the leader's institution can provide, and the commonweal—in both the city of God and the city of man. Jeremiah said that his responsibility to God's people is to seek the prosperity of the society in which they are placed. And it's the responsibility of the leader to help them do just that.

No matter how you look at it, solipsism is hardly a positive trait in almost any context; certainly it is a rather counterproductive characteristic of a leader. Indeed, it's probably worth remembering that "individualistic leader" is pretty close to an oxymoron. But if a leader really is going to focus both personal and professional energies on advancing the institution he or she leads in a context that benefits the kingdom of Jesus Christ and the world of which we are a part, then the bottom line is clear: involvement in professional and civic endeavors is intrinsic to authentic calling, not merely an optional add-on to be fit into personal preferences and convenience. In other words, anyone in a leadership position who is not actively involved in ever-widening circles of professional and organizational associations needs to reexamine whether she or he really understands the heart of the leader's calling.

Active involvement in professional and organizational associations is probably one of the best antidotes to self-centeredness in a leader. The besetting sin of leadership is obviously self-seeking. After all, the leader is, of necessity, pretty much always the center of attention within the organization he or she leads. Being continually in the middle of the whirl of organizational effort and impact isn't necessarily a sign of narcissism. Quite the contrary, being at the heart of the organizational impact could well be an indicator of diligent, dedicated effort by an authentic leader. But if the leader never steps outside of the context in which he or she is the center of attention, then self-centeredness is likely to result. A good healthy life within broad professional circles can be a great antidote to the allure of self-focus.

Consider as well the responsibility of the leader to rally internal and external constituencies around the central mission of the organization he or she serves. That's a key task of the leader, but anyone who does nothing in life but gather support for the central mission of their own personal lives is living life on a high wire that will be difficult to maintain with Christ-like authenticity. It reminds me of the popular bumper-sticker slogan of a couple decades past, "Lead, Follow, or Get Out of the Way." Somehow I always have trouble imagining Jesus saying that. Maybe it's because most of the people I encountered repeating that mantra seemed more accurately to be saying, "I'm planning on leading so it's up to you to make sure you either follow me or else get out of my way." To escape that trap, there's probably no better strategy than to plan regular and vigorous interaction in associations and/or affiliations where the task you and your organization share with others takes center stage; but you, as your own organizational leader, most definitely do not.

Individualism is hardly a biblical concept, and so an individualistic approach to leadership is not likely to be blessed either. Yet individuals can flourish in their own particular calling, also as leaders, when nurtured in a context of common and communal goals. Professional associations are a great expression of that biblical principle that upholds the calling of individual leaders on the one hand but demands communal accountability and common effort to flourish on the other.

Here's both a caution and a challenge. In order for such professional associations and contexts to flourish, someone also will have to become a leader within them. Fortunately most professional associations operate on a principle of rotating leadership. The leadership mantle gets passed around the circle. Yet when the mantle comes your way, you'd better be ready to wear it when it's your turn. Catch yourself when tempted to beg off (or duck out unnoticed), pleading the busyness and burden of your own organizational responsibilities. That excuse, unless specifically resulting from a particular convergence of unusual circumstances at that moment, is really one of the most conceited dodges imaginable. To think that your own institutional responsibilities are heavier or more significant than those of your colleagues belies a presumptuousness that is hardly born out of the Spirit of Christ.

For a while I was puzzled a bit that somehow the best examples of institutional leadership within my various professional circles always managed to become leaders in the professional associations as well. I always wondered how year after year the best seemed to take the leadership of my associations. After all, the screening hardly seemed all that rigorous, and sometimes it appeared to be more the luck of the draw that landed some of these colleagues as heads of our associations.

I finally realized it was really the other way around. The reason some of my colleagues were so effective within their own institutional settings was precisely because of the growth experience they had as leaders at the heart of our professional associations and exchanges. The bottom line is that, when the calling to serve the professional associations comes round to you, recognize that far from taking away from your own organizational effectiveness, it is likely to add to it significantly. Yes, it's worth doing simply because "somebody has to do it" and the organization won't be there to serve you in the future if no one will lead it. But it's also worth doing because leadership in an association in which you are not the permanent center of attention will only magnify your own service within that institution of which you truly are the linchpin and permanent leader.

But if the first reason for an expansive vision of leadership is to avoid solipsism in the individual, an equally significant reason is to preclude institutional solipsism as well. If Donne said no man is an island, I'd like to argue that no institution or organization is an island either; and an active, broadly involved leader is going to be the greatest antidote against that tendency.

It's only natural, I suppose, that an excited and dedicated staff and support group will think that their own particular ministry focus is the best there is and that they and the Lord are able on their own to tackle any obstacle in the way. To a certain degree that's an admirable tendency. The problem is, that's not the way God has structured this world.

Sociologist P. Berger popularized and accented the significance of "mediating structures" in a vigorous civil society. Indeed, that's probably at least part of what God Himself had in mind when He split people up at the tower of Babel. It just doesn't work to have one monolithic society. A wide range of subgroups is needed in any society to divide up the tasks and to keep creativity and the creation of new possibilities alive and well.

Our mistake comes when we think we're the only ones doing it—when we forget to look around and discover all the other mediating structures besides our own organization that are engaged in roughly the same task and with parallel, or at least overlapping, missions with ours. Thinking that we are the only ones in the world with a particular vision or commitment to a particular purpose reveals an arrogance that is not only unworthy of people of faith but just isn't an accurate picture of reality either.

Already in the first chapters of Genesis, there's a pretty clear description of the fundamental structure God built into His creation right from the start. He began with the relationship of man and woman and structured that into the institution of marriage. But also right from the start He laid out the blueprint for unfolding and developing those social structures as well when He declared that those new children nurtured within a marriage are responsible eventually to leave that relationship of father and mother and create their new structure as husband and wife, or, to use the old word, "cleave" to each other. The multiplicity and continual multiplying of social structures is clear right from the beginning of time; that's just fundamental to the way the world works best in keeping with God's design standards for his world.

Yet even there at the beginning, it's also evident that those newly created family social structures continue to be linked to one another. Leaving father and mother didn't imply disregarding the family structure of origin. Quite the contrary, at least three of the Ten Commandments deal specifically with respecting the structure from which our new social relationships emerge (honor your father and mother) and also to respect the parallel social structures that are emerging with us (do not commit adultery and do not steal). Yet far too often in the name of institutional mission, even sincere Christians seem to act as if they have no responsibility toward the welfare of parallel organizations with which they share that mission.

So how do we maintain an appropriate focus of energy on our own tasks as an organization while also encouraging and strengthening the common task we share with others? Clearly the leader of each organization will be the point person in that effort as they link themselves together in networks and broad associations that can protect the interests of each member institution that follows parallel purposes.

A classic example is the American system of accreditation in higher education. Traditionally, and in distinction from most of the world, that system has been based on peer accountability rather than on government regulation. The principle that has guided accreditation in American higher education has been the principle that peer institutions can develop common standards for credibility that they then can enforce by peer review of one another's programs.

But that system simply won't work unless presidents and other academic leaders on the individual college and university campuses invest at least some of their time into maintaining those peer review associations and also in being willing to invest time to visit peer institutions to enforce accountability. Intuitively, there is a common social consensus that institutions of higher education have such a critical role to play in the social welfare that they are granted societal benefits such as tax exemptions and either direct or indirect, full or partial funding of the educational enterprise out of the public purse. But with that recognition of social benefit comes also a consensus that such institutions must be accountable to fulfill those social purposes. And if leaders no longer are willing to invest the time and energy to maintain a vigorous system of accountability, the public will soon demand an alternative accountability, namely, the establishment of a government ministry of education that will impose its own system of accountability.

Nor is that the only area in which institutions of higher education need to band themselves together. Commonalities of mission and challenges to that mission are unique to the type of educational institutions, whether state-owned universities, community colleges, or independent colleges. Specific commonalities and challenges are unique to certain geographical areas, both national and state. Issues unique to a band of institutions take seriously a Christian faith perspective. Similarly some issues are unique to particular and specific faith traditions. And overlaps among institutions from all faith traditions need mutual examination and support. As a result, higher education is filled with associations to the degree that eventually a president or other academic leader may be inclined to wash their hands of all of them.

But that is exactly the wrong direction to turn. Certainly no one leader can dedicate equal amounts of time to all such organizations (and we'll consider ways to select among those possibilities later in this chapter). Yet a key and valid calling of any leader is clearly to seek actively the welfare of all colleague institutions whose missions overlap their own. Both in protecting one another ("I've got your back") and in advancing the common mission ("We can only move forward if we move forward together"), the leader needs to dedicate both energy and time beyond the strict boundaries of his or her organization.

It strikes me as a copout to claim that time spent in merely promoting professional growth organizations fulfills that calling. Professional growth organizations that put on seminars and training experiences certainly are critical parts of a leader's portfolio of opportunities and responsibilities. Those organizations won't be able to continue to flourish unless peers invest time in those organizations. So serving as a leader in a professional organization, organizing a seminar, participating in leading a workshop, or even contributing a chapter to a book on leadership is obviously a valid part of the leader's calling.

But it does not exhaust the leader's external responsibility. Those types of sharing insights really amount to little more than one hand washing the other. Investing in organizations that provide personal and professional growth is important, but in the end it merely ensures that those personal and professional growth opportunities will be available in the future for you as well as for others. So while those professional associations are a good start in fulfilling an organizational leader's external obligations, it is just a start. You quickly have to move also to involvement in those broad-based organizations designed to protect and advance your neighbor institution's welfare as well as your own.

Besides, if such organizations express our care and concern for colleague institutions, our own organization is bound to benefit as well. In fact, unless every leader also makes investments in helping lead such external organizations, eventually those organizations will no longer be there to benefit our own institution either.

The great blessing of leadership organizations is that by definition every member of the association or organization is a leader. So when those organizations need their own leadership, every member is eligible and, to one degree or another, extremely capable of stepping forward. Certainly in an organization made up of leaders, no one can duck leadership responsibility by claiming lack of gifts. It's just a matter of if, where, and when those gifts will contribute to the benefit of all.

The health of the particular college I serve as president depends on many critical associations and organizations. So while I certainly cannot and need not serve as a leader in all of them, at least not at the same time, I cannot avoid the obligation to choose at least some of these organizations in which to invest my time and energy.

Boards of trustees, senior administrators, and faculty and staff often wonder what the payoff is for our own organizations. After all, in every instance where I dedicate myself to external organizational leadership, the energy I expend far exceeds the amount of benefit that comes to our college from that specific organization. But the critical point is that the amount of benefit we receive from the sum total of all the professional associations and alliances outweighs the energy I as a particular leader invest in the one or two specific organizations where I am called to help lead.

Any specific leader could just "sit it out" and take the benefits without any investment. There's always room for a freeloader in every crowd. But should any significant number of leaders become focused solely on their own particular organization, soon the alliances and associations that sustain any charitable enterprise will collapse, and ultimately the health of every particular member organization will collapse with it. If an external organization contributes in any way and to any degree, either directly or indirectly, to the health of the particular institution or ministry you lead, then it is worthy of your investment of time and energy; and, as a responsible leader, you have an obligation to provide that investment.

Yet to this point the discussion in this chapter has centered almost exclusively on what's best for the leader's own personal and organizational health. But since this is a book on Christian leadership, it's probably important to include a third argument for external involvement by organizational leadership. That is the recognition that if our organization thinks only of itself as an end in itself, it probably is relatively useless in the ultimate purpose of every Christian organization, namely the advancement of the kingdom of God for the benefit of the society around us and for the glory of the God we serve.

My own conviction is that vigorous participation in external organizations is the best way to guarantee that the leader and the organization she or he leads avoids the trap of institutional idolatry but instead keeps focused on the ultimate goal of strengthening society as a whole and bearing witness to God's universal kingdom in particular.

Every ministry and organization participates in several overlapping circles of common interest. First, everyone who looks hard enough can find at least some other efforts that have almost an identical mission statement as your own. The difference may be only in the constituency whose efforts you embody, but the goal is the same. Relief organizations are just one particularly clear example. Almost every major church or denomination has such an agency. And they all have virtually identical objectives. The only difference is the denomination in the name of whose members the particular relief organization carries out its efforts. For such organizations not to seek one another out, learn from one another, and collaborate to synergize their individual efforts probably would be little more than malfeasance of leadership.

But there will be broader circles as well. The Christian relief agencies, for instance, could well overlap governmental and other secular humanitarian agencies in carrying out their goals. True, the secular organizations will hardly be seeking to advance the kingdom of God, and that difference in goals will also show up in differences of methodology. But surely the secular and Christian organizations will find their relief efforts overlapping in the face of natural disasters to which they respond. And their interests in interacting with government agencies and funding entities cover a wide swath of common ground. For a leader not to interact with such groups in associations and collaborations again leaves badly isolated and exposed to social and political pressures the organization the leader is pledged to lead.

Such circles can be multiplied, depending on the nature of the organization, on national and international stages. Admittedly, higher education is where I contribute most of my energy particularly webbed into overlapping networks. In the first place a college may be part of a network with other universities and colleges across the country based on denominational or theological tradition. There may also be an international network in which that particular national network is intertwined. Parallel to that network are state associations dedicated to defending the rights and privileges of independent colleges and universities against government encroachment of control, on the one hand, and restriction of access to society's resources (tuition grants, loans, and tax exemption, etc.) on the other hand. Then there are foundations that colleges are often associated with on the state, national, and ecclesiastical affinity levels. Moreover there are myriad professional development groups. Then there are national and international associations of far more broadly based Christian colleges and universities than the particular tradition any one college represents. And, to top it all off, in the United States there is also an extensive system of peer accreditation agencies that help ensure academic excellence and serve as gatekeepers to governmental recognition and the benefits that come with that.

My point is that such multiplication of associations ought not to be decried, but indeed associations are a central responsibility of the leader's task of placing her or his organization firmly in the mainstream of the society of which we are a part. I am reminded of Jeremiah's prophecy to his kinsmen who had been removed from their homes in Jerusalem and deported to Babylon, and he said, "Seek the welfare of the city I have deported you to" (Jer 29:7 HCSB). Clearly, if we want to "seek the welfare" of the city in which we are placed, then we must embed our institution deeply within the network of associations who participate in that civic enterprise.

Is that a sellout of our institution's Christ-focused missions? Quite the contrary. Berger's point remains well taken. Without these mediating structures of civil society, we will inevitably find that governmental bureaucracy will absorb all our social efforts and make our tasks their own; and when that occurs, there will be no place for Christ-centered communal action at all. And at that point our Christ-focused missions will be lost. So if we want our organizations to benefit from the protective buffer that civil society offers, then we as leaders will have to dedicate effort toward sustaining the networks that enliven and maintain that civil society.

It might be fair to ask whether the leader has to carry the full burden of participation in all these networks. On one level the answer certainly is no. Such broader organizations and networks will prove their worth largely by the opportunities they offer for multilevel administrative and staff participation in their common activities. Such networks need not be, and probably should not be, simply a series of club memberships for leaders of the individual ministries or organizations.

Yet on the other hand, the chief leader never can delegate institutional direction setting. No matter how collaborative the decision making may be in an organization and no matter how shared the governance structure may actually be, by definition direction setting remains the responsibility of the ultimate leader. And because most of these collaborations and networks are focused on the placement of each organization within the broad social context, that is a task that will have to be retained in the leader's portfolio of responsibilities.

Many leaders protest that they are far too busy with "running their organization" to participate in broader associations. The burden of this chapter is that such an argument is exactly upside down. Management decision making can be delegated, and fund-raising efforts can be carried out by others. But what responsible leaders cannot entrust to others is determining the place and direction of their organizations within civil society and sustaining that direction through personal contributions of insight and effort. The goal is to support the vitality of the networks which maintain that place and direction for their own organizations' efforts in the name of Christ.

To use a military analogy, throughout history the battle leader has always stood on the highest ground. That's because the leader always needs to be able to see farther over the horizon than anyone else in the organization. Moreover, the leader also has to have a wider perspective of the total battlefield so that he or she can ascertain clearly the particular place and context in Christ's worldwide efforts that their particular organization plays. Effective efforts require leaders to leave shining boots to others and instead concentrate on ascertaining the best placement in battle of the troops they lead and then maintaining the network connections with others who share a role in the common battle.

Admittedly, this may sound overwhelming. Contemporary organizational administrators could spend their entire week every week participating in organizations, boards, conferences, and conventions. That would be neither healthy nor necessary. So for those who are convinced of the need for their participation in external organizations, some guidelines based on common sense and biblical grace may be helpful.

First, focus your efforts. You can't do it all, and biblically speaking you don't need to do it all. The apostle Paul reminded us that not everyone in the body has the same role to play. Admittedly, that analogy breaks down somewhat for the purposes of this chapter because leaders are by definition playing a particular and specific role within the body, namely that of leader. Still, the analogy remains *apropos* to the lesson that no one leader has to consider himself or herself to be the entire body.

So, in the case of higher education, not every president has to be active on a leadership level in the accreditation agencies, although all will have to be involved to some extent, and some will have to choose this as their place of leadership. Similarly, not everyone has to be involved in public policy advocacy to protect the rights of independent higher education in general and Christ-centered institutions in particular, although again all should be critically aware and informed, and some will have to dedicate significant time in this area of focus for the benefit of all.

In fact, this can be one of the truly pleasant aspects of a leader's task. Find the area of your greatest motivation, especially if that is where you also find particular insight and gifts. Then from among all the potential opportunities for leadership participation, concentrate your efforts on that particular arena of focus. It will be exciting, motivating, and a blessing not only to your organization but also to all who share in that network with you.

Second, don't hitchhike on rides provided by others. Even in those arenas where you decide not to invest your time on a leadership level, continue to sustain and support those who do. Perhaps you won't do much more than continue to authorize annual dues payments, but that's significant in itself. No one else in the organization understands the need to pay for the support of all these organizations. Taken one by one, it hardly seems that any particular ministry or institution would get its money's worth from any particular association. Only the leader understands that these networks have a collective impact and that they need to be collectively maintained and so can insist that such external dues are a high priority.

In short, use the old universalizing principle learned in introductory ethics courses. Ask yourself, "What would be the result if everyone acted the same way I am?" What if everyone refused to dedicate time and effort to associations in civil society beyond their own? What if everyone refused to pay the dues to this particular organization? What if everyone insisted that the priority of their own internal leadership responsibilities meant that they had to refuse the leadership needs of the broader collaborations? It comes down to this: What if this alliance, association, or collaboration were no longer there? What would be the impact on my ministry or organization if we were in fact cast adrift by ourselves? What will be the impact if civil society collapses in on itself and leaves only the government to run education, social services, health care, community development, and the like? In some cases perhaps you will decide to take a pass on that particular involvement. But if you don't like the prospects of what universalizing your own inactivity would bring, then it probably means you have to be willing to invest in external leadership yourself.

Third, assess your own personal season. There are phases of leadership history in every personal career and every specific organization. Usually the first few years of leadership in a particular organization require the leader to use networks mainly for learning, collaboration, and support. There's probably no faster way to vitalize new leadership in an organization than to tie quickly into existing networks with which that organization is already bound and to look for others who can help speed the forward progress of both your organization and your own personal leadership ability.

But that season doesn't last forever. A successful leader finally comes to the stage in life and career where it's time to pay back. Remember those who were helpful in your beginning and ask, "Now that I have developed my own leadership momentum, how can I help others move forward as well?" And while your organization may be jealous of your time, this is a teachable moment for the rest of your organization as well. Their success depends on others; and in gratitude for support received by others, it is now a duty and a privilege to allow organizational leadership to reach out and sustain others with whom we share our mission and vision.

To summarize, leadership is not a sprint; it's a distance event. More accurately it's a relay in which what we receive from others as we jump into the momentum of our organization's mission needs now in turn to be passed on to others, so that when our time comes to step aside they also will be running well and be prepared to assist the new leader who follows us.

Fourth, stay within the penumbra of your institution's mission. In the biblical sense leadership is not a generic position in society; it is specific to a given task. Even more precisely, individuals are called to leadership in a particular position at a particular time and in a particular place.

So avoid the temptation to think that being a leader of one organization makes you a leader of every civic movement possible. We've all seen the leaders who sign on to every petition and every civic movement that comes along. And it certainly is tempting to put our name on a movement just because of all the other famous folks who are in that movement with us. But that's no longer leadership; that's simply self-aggrandizement.

The simplest filter is to ask whether this associational or collaborative opportunity really falls at least within the shadow of our own institutional mission. Never ask, "Will this opportunity make me look better?" The real question is, "Will it make my organization and my leadership of it more effective, either directly or indirectly?"

No one is called to be leader of everything. However, every authentic leader is called to lead one thing first and then to reach out to share leadership with all those whose mission comes into the purview of the mission to which your organization is dedicated.

Fifth, keep service the goal. Leaders have a tendency to use their own organization as a platform from which to reach a wider stage for their own influence. But that's backwards. We leaders stand underneath our own organizations and hold them up. In effect, we are the platforms on which our organizations stand in order for them to reach the next level of greater effectiveness and impact.

Put simply, leaders exist to serve their organization's needs. Organizations never exist to serve their leader's needs. Just ask, "Will taking this broader opportunity for leadership enable my organization to fulfill its mission more fully?" To be sure, such assistance may be indirect. If not, it's probably time to let that opportunity pass by. Indeed, if stepping out onto a wider stage primarily helps the leader gain greater prestige, such opportunities ought not to be grasped. However, if moving into external leadership helps one's own organization gain greater public position for greater mission effectiveness, then there's nothing wrong with using personal opportunity for the benefit of your organization's greater gain.

Perhaps it comes down to this: anything that makes the individual leader feel important probably is a step into the wider associational world that should be forgone. But anything that will enable the organization to stand tall and true to its mission is an opportunity no leader should shirk. After all what counts is the mission of the institution the leader leads. There is no value in being a recognized "leader," no matter how many personal accolades it brings.

In the end it's always the organization or ministry that counts. A good leader is a necessary condition for organizational mission effectiveness but not a sufficient condition. In carrying out their mission, all institutions require colleague and partner institutions to enhance their effectiveness. As a result, any leader who keeps institutional mission effectiveness as his or her primary goal of leadership will invest as much time and effort as is possible and prudent in the success of those associations and collaborations on which effectiveness of the organization he or she leads so heavily depends.

Resources for Further Study

Scholarly Work

An exploration of the role of "social capital" in communication theory would provide wonderful additional reflection, especially the threefold aspects of bonding, bridging, and linking. An excellent source for beginning further exploration on the topic is the Web site http://www.social-capital research.com updated in February 2010 and originally designed as part of a thesis project: Claridge, T. 2004, "Social Capital and Natural Resource Management," Unpublished Thesis, University of Queensland, Brisbane, Australia.

Leadership Style

An older work by James Fisher, *Power of the Presidency* (New York: Macmillan, 1984), has, in my opinion, been far too quickly dismissed as just another book about the "imperial presidency." Those who disregard his comments on the significance of the president in social and extended networks do so at their own peril.

Contemporary Discussion

The issue of how much time a leader appropriately can give to external activities is an active source of discussion among employees, board members, and external constituencies. Although the particular issue did not involve directly the associations and professional networks discussed in this chapter, a public uproar regarding the president of the University

of California at San Diego illustrates the dynamics involved (http://legacy
.signonsandiego.com/uniontrib/20060128/news_1n28fox.html).

Questions for Further Reflection

1. How should leaders use the organizations/associations in their professional circles to separate themselves from a "bubble" environment where they are the central focus of all activity?

2. How can peer review and active participation in the broader academic community protect and enhance personal and professional development in ways that work to build consensus among systems of higher education accreditation?

3. How can a leader "embed" the institution in its community in such a way that it serves as a Christ-centered community of action and is known as a model of service beyond the needs of its own existence?

Chapter 10

RELATIONSHIPS WITH MULTIPLE AND VARIOUS CONSTITUENCIES

James Edwards
President, Anderson University

P residents have tough jobs in the best of circumstances.

A high-profile president at a nationally acclaimed school made news when he dropped from sight for three or four days, missing appointments and social events. He was located after a few days in a hospital. He simply had an emotional breakdown from the pressures of his impossible schedule. He recovered and reorganized the demands for his time to have a successful tenure. But many asked if the job were truly impossible.

It is not that we should have less demanding expectations for our leaders. It is that we need to organize life around the good and necessary rather than the urgent and relentless.

P. Drucker, prolific writer and international business consultant, writes that the college and university presidency is one of the world's most demanding professions. Similar to a hospital system or a megachurch, a university is a complex organization made even more challenging by the mix, variety, and number of constituencies.[1]

Some traditions within Christian higher education offer a free and open academic culture to students and faculty but then risk offending donors. Community leaders understand that students will be students. But when their activities become noisy and spill out into the rest of the community

172

around social activities or political debates, neighbors become less tolerant and not so generous.

Colleges want to prepare students for the demands of the real world, exposing them to human situations that are often messy. However, in so doing, they inevitably raise questions in the minds of other constituents about faithfulness to long-held beliefs.

Colleges enroll the immature who show great promise but clearly need education. They can make foolish choices that put the school in the news for all the wrong reasons. As one president said to his faculty, "Do not be surprised when ignorance shows up. We invited it."

Most presidents lead with great devotion, love their constituents, love the work and campus life, but lack resources to fund their vision. Their vision often must bend to a donor's dreams that can change priorities institutions may not wish to pursue or sustain. These and other pressures have an impact on the leader's relationship with key constituents.

A leading fund-raising consultant counseled a president planning a comprehensive capital campaign, "If you can just give a little bit of this place away, you will be successful." Presidents feel strong ownership for their universities, and the thought of giving a part of them away to donors may seem like a tall order. Constituents are essential and naturally desire to be far more than tools to be used for the vision of the leader. They have opinions about how great things can be accomplished and at times how the institution should be operated.

Colleges must have students and faculty, parents, caring alumni, town partners, business leaders, government officials, members of the academy, senior staff, colleagues on other campuses, accreditation bodies, financers, donors, bankers, and attorneys; and all play a role in the life of the university.

It is the task of the effective presidential leader to make crucial connections and represent the highest of aspirations and values and the ethos of the mission. The president is a living symbol of the university. An active leader is needed who will do as much as possible to build a relational basis for the success of the institution. Challenges and opportunities may often set the agenda. But long and sustained traditions, renewed and vitalized by fresh strategic thinking and revitalized vision, will serve as a foundation for the future and require insightful leadership from an effective president.

Engagement: Making Connections with
Local, Regional, and National Entities

Two areas of engagement provide a context for thinking about vital constituent relationships: alumni services and community interventions. Both invite our attention.

Alumni are a special constituency because they embody the traditions of the past and have the potential to extend the life of the institution. Keeping the faith of alumni across the years is often challenging. Their support often signals a test of the value graduates place on their education. When alumni engage and are supportive of the university, it is a testament to their regard for the value of the education they received. They also represent a challenge across the generations. At times their expectations are not compatible with current needs of the institution's mission. Their memories are sometimes idealized across the years. However, they have the right to expect an enduring relationship with the school and can bring much to that relationship, given the opportunity.

Alumni support can grow into significant institution-shaping investments across the years. What is in place today may require years of tending before any results are visible. Some of the highest percentages of support come from schools such as service academies and the few "work colleges," such as College of the Ozarks and Berea College, where costly education is offered without charge. For universities where alumni understand and value the gifts of supported education, financial support can improve.

Exemplary alumni programs focus on ways to maintain social connections, reunions, continued services related to placement and continuing education, and recognition for individual achievement through various forms of publications.

In recent years the alumni program at Anderson University has exploded with activity. Concerts by nationally known alumni in gospel music, contemporary secular performances, and opera have provided reasons for alumni to gather and reconnect around the country. Professional sports venues such as AAA baseball games in various regions have welcomed alumni gatherings. Young alumni have been the focus of coffeehouse gatherings. Business faculties have led interested alumni in networking opportunities. Family-friendly gatherings for younger alumni have been hosted in county and state fairs and theme parks. Churches have hosted events to bring young alumni into connection with prospective students with considerable meaning to both groups.

Mentoring programs offer seniors and recent graduates a way to connect with successful alumni in various fields of professional life. Initiated grants support these activities and provide opportunities for placement programs from campus to community.

During a capital campaign the alumni base has been extremely important and is measured by levels of participation. Some of the most significant lead gifts have come from this group. They seem to show up in their own time and sometimes begin with modest early connections.

Serving constituents while also meeting the needs of the university through annual gift support is always a challenge. College leaders flinch at the accusation that they serve alumni only because their financial support is wanted. It is necessary to rise above these concerns to serve and to seek opportunities for meaningful involvement of alumni with their alma mater. Meaningful connections are the goal, and persistent trusted communication pays dividends for the individual and the institution.

Social networking is providing universities a new and relatively low-cost way to serve alumni as we bond with them. Anderson University uses a number of social networks, including those created by the university. Social networking, like any uses of media, appeals to growing numbers of young alumni because it is within the user's experience and choice. As they make use of these networks, give their input, and make decisions about the role these networks will play in their daily lives, an institution can find levels of application that are appropriate to both the individual and the institution.

Currents, a publication of the Council for Advancement and Support of Education (CASE), published these examples of social media used by colleges and universities, cited from a 2008 survey:

73% Facebook
53% LinkedIn
30% YouTube
29% Myspace
26% Google
20% Flickr
16% Wikipedia
15% Yahoo Groups
6% Twitter[2]

A useful source for colleges seeking information about marketing through social media is *Twitter for Dummies*, written by Anderson University alumnus K. Lacy.[3]

Engagement with a city and region may also offer special opportunities, given the particular needs and assets that reside in the university. For Anderson University, impressive work has been done to meet the economic development needs of a Rust Belt region where an old industrial base simply folded and had to be replaced. The result is a unique partnership between the city and the university for the development of a high-tech business incubator.

Historically, Anderson University has provided talent, leadership, and assistance to its local community in traditional academic forms such as the arts, culture, and selected social endeavors. But beginning in the late 1970s, structural changes within global and national automotive markets had a profound impact on the economies of north and east central Indiana, a circumstance that invited a much more active role for Anderson University. From 1975 to 2000, the city of Anderson lost more than 27,000 jobs as General Motors relocated plants elsewhere. For the city the losses were devastating, both in terms of wages and industrial output estimated at $43.5 billion.

Anderson University represented a stability of human capital and worked with community leaders to find new solutions to economic problems that had almost paralyzed the Anderson area. Through economic planning, broad research, and some resources committed by General Motors as they left the community, a subsidiary corporation to Anderson University was created, and a state-of-the-art business incubator was built. Soon after, an educational complex and business planning center was constructed. Other facilities were added to enhance business development. The university's school of business added resources of student interns and consulting expertise to the enterprise.

What resulted, and continues with great strength, was the establishment of more than 50 small businesses and an estimated 1,200 jobs. The complex houses the university's residential MBA program, including education space and student apartments. Purdue University is a partner in the buildings, and other economic development efforts are centered there. It is fair to say that Anderson University and her Falls School of Business are contributing more than jobs and advice. They are giving direction and hope in a time of great need.

Other independent colleges and universities are developing promising engagement projects in their communities. In Wynona Lake, Indiana, Grace College has brought planning and service to industrial efforts, including orthopedic prosthesis corporations. Wilmington College in Ohio is involved in projects at an abandoned international distribution and shipping center, supporting strategic planning, serving displaced workers, and expanding programs that hold promise for educational and economic development. In other regions agricultural and manufactured homes industries have attracted bilingual populations, and colleges are offering education, support services, and language education to support individuals through higher education.

These are but a few examples where colleges and universities have stepped forward to bring significant human capital, economic stability, and quality of life to many with whom they share a common life. Every need provides an effective leader the opportunity to evaluate compatibility with mission and the appropriate way to serve. Service learning, so highly valued as an educational strategy, can provide students with priceless experiences and meaningful connections as they begin a lifetime journey of service.

Internal Constituencies: Winning at Home

Just as a business's customers are often individuals and departments within the company, universities have internal constituents of vital concern for the leader.

Most presidents see little possibility of success without an effective leadership team. Effective teams are more collaborative than competitive in spirit. They often consist of strong individuals. They have strong opinions and see things from a particular perspective. But they know how to be a team. They do not hold back when they have contrarian views. The leadership team at Anderson University wanted to improve their work together so they developed a covenant agreement that has been honored and renewed across the years. It has proven to be helpful in orienting leaders new to the team. The agreement, which is revised when necessary, is built around these nine principles:

1. *Respect:* We will respect our own areas of responsibility and those of our colleagues. We will speak to what is within one's own range of responsibilities and refer other matters to individuals who bear those responsibilities.

2. ***Support:*** We agree to be supportive of each other.

3. ***Trust:*** We will manage information of a confidential nature with absolute confidentiality.

4. ***Protection:*** We will offer appropriate protection to other members of the leadership team.

5. ***Servanthood:*** We will serve with one another in an atmosphere of mutual respect.

6. ***Fidelity:*** We will serve with the highest degree of loyalty and in fidelity to the institutional agenda. We will put the institutional good above self-interest or the narrower interests of any one area of institutional life.

7. ***Help:*** We will do all within our power to be a source of help to every other member of the leadership team.

8. ***Solidarity:*** We will communicate openly, directly, even confrontationally in our private sessions, but publicly, with one voice.

9. ***Accountability:*** We will open ourselves to assessments and evaluations from those whom we serve, and we will consider it an obligation of this covenant to confront one another personally when we feel a colleague has missed the intentions and expectations of this covenant.

Some Principles: 20 Ways to Sharpen Your Leadership with Constituents

Below are some practical ideas and ways of serving that can sharpen the leader's effectiveness with many constituencies.

1. Ask and Listen

The art of building a good relationship with constituents at any level is to build trust. One engages another often not by impressive speech but by the sincere act of asking good questions and active listening. Active listening takes energy, leaning forward to hear, clarifying what is being said, respecting the notion that the other may have only begun to reveal the heart of an idea by first words that are but a prelude to what may come if one is patient and asks follow-up questions that are to the point.

Communication happens not when something is said but when it is heard. A gifted orator will add an immeasurable asset to leadership skills by acquiring the art of listening.

2. Keep Focused on Principles, Values, Virtues, and Ethos

To successfully relate to diverse and changing constituents, it is important to know where to center. A university may represent faculties from one generation, parents from another, and students with generational qualities distinctive from those of the leader. Where is common ground? How does one honor the differences and find personal integrity? Focus on principles, articulate values, develop and promote virtues, and respect the ethos.

Diverse constituents cannot be expected to agree about the many issues that often divide the culture, the church, and the academy; but they can unite around common values, seek to develop common virtues, and celebrate a common ethos. Lift up values and center on virtues that can be embraced without dividing on the basis of narrow political or religious ideologies. When the leader makes principles, relationships, and common virtues the focus, better decisions can be made that will enhance and encourage all concerned.

3. Stay Above Politics

Constituents often have strong political views. They are free to share them and often assume others agree. Little is gained in conducting debates over ideological points. An institutional leader can be a catalyst for principles and gain the support of a diverse constituency, including those with whom he or she may differ on various matters of public, global, and economic or social policy. The only safe territory is to remain principled and above politics. Having a spirit of kindness and hospitality advances these relationships above the controversy, rather than entering into the political debate.

4. Be Personally Generous

Generosity of spirit and deeds can reveal the heart of the leader. Takers rarely become givers, and the frugal are always in danger of becoming keepers. Search committees rarely ask, but it would be well if they did inquire of a prospective leader his or her personal blessing from being a generous person. If the fundamental mission of the university is tied to generosity of spirit, service, and giving, that is an irreplaceable virtue in the university's leader.

The leader is often pulled away from key constituent groups by the demands of the work, leading to a perception of affluence and elitism. Nevertheless, there is still a need to be engaged on a meaningful level with all constituent groups. The president of a college may live in a large, well-maintained home, drive a fine car, dine in a private club on a regular basis, and always appear to have friends in high places. All of this goes with the territory if leaders are expected to garner the goodwill and support of major resourceful friends.

But an effective leader also has the personal habit of generosity. Those who are being asked by a leader to step up to a significant giving level will ask, in their own minds if not aloud, "What does the leader give?" Those who serve in the not-for-profit world, perhaps at lesser compensation, are aware that the leader may receive a larger cash salary and attractive benefits commensurate with the duties of office. When people see the name of the leader high on the published donor list, named on commemorative plaques, and also supporting other major community causes, others will more likely follow such an example.

5. Live Accountably

Accountability is required of both organizations and leaders. If one cannot operate in the most open light of day, suspicion of compromised ethics might be well founded. The leader can create a lifestyle of openness and accountability that includes strong bonds with one's family, one's closest associates, and with all the ways one lives life.

Saint Augustine was known to have said that one should live in such a way that the harshest of criticisms and malicious gossip was unbelievable. This is good advice for the leader today.

The key to being a trustworthy leader is to live accountably. If we practice safe boundaries of marriage and family, open our business practices to audited accounting, and refuse to look the other way when those around us excuse shortcomings, we can practice trustworthy leadership.

Privilege is interesting and sometimes insidious. Those who ascend into a position of accomplishment and leadership can readily feel they have the right to certain conveniences or considerations. Only the privilege of service should be assumed, and other considerations that come in a leader's life should be tested from time to time to see if they add to accomplishment of duty or to one's standing of importance.

The corporation and leader are inseparably linked in the area of accountability. Best practices such as those promoted in public corporations by the Sarbanes-Oxley regulations in financial affairs need to have the attention of not-for-profit organizations as well. And the standard for the leader should be just a bit higher than that which is required by law. It is important to have an audit committee that includes outside and competent experienced members. It has always been the practice of one chief executive officer to make the chief financial officer available to the board even though the president is the sole report.

6. Spend the Leadership Credits

Over the tenure of long service, one begins to add to the credits of one's leadership. Some call them idiosyncratic points one collects across the years of one's life of service. However at some time those points must be spent for the good of others and the mission, or they will become a sign of an inept leader. The leader needs to spend those credits earned across the years with integrity and in a principled way.

Some things can be accomplished only during the early tenure of leadership. We think of this as the honeymoon period. Other things can be accomplished only when one has served long enough to have earned the right to be heard or to point the way. To put it another way, if one has earned the right to be heard, speak up and lead.

7. Mend Fences Personally and Institutionally

Good fences make good neighbors is a well-deserved axiom. And those fences will inevitably need to be mended when we experience failure, make poor choices, or create unintended results. It is amazing how powerful and utterly remarkable a sincere apology sounds in today's culture. "I am truly sorry" are difficult words for many in our society. "If I have offended you . . ." is a qualified apology and falls far short of words like, "I know that I have disappointed and offended you, and I am sorry." "I will work to make things right and hope that you can forgive me." Both parts of an apology—acknowledgment of the offense and commitment to do better—are needed to mend the broken relationship.

8. Nurture Spiritual Bonds and Family Ties

Demonstrate an uncomplicated devotion to faith, to family, to the cause.

It is no imposition to an organization when a leader takes personal delight in the rich life of a wonderful family. In good humor one president was known to say, "When I became a grandfather, I became a kinder, gentler person." Such good messages come from this kind of mature and enriched life and bless the organizations and team members in so many ways.

Some leaders of Christian and faith-based organizations have grown weary with some aspects of religious life and begin to exhibit a waning devotion to the practice of faith. Bible reading and regular worship are less frequent. There are few signs of a rich inner and spiritual development, and the demands of office can leave the leader brittle around the edges where kindness once resided. Relationships suffer. Even the capacity to delight in the disciplines of spiritual life can diminish.

The remedy is to practice the disciplines of the spiritual journey, including those aspects that are public and private. A leader steeped in the literature of an academic discipline can find refreshing transformation in discovering the devotional classics and in sharing the spiritual quest with a group of trusted friends.

Understanding what drives the leader of a faith-based organization should not be difficult. The faithful practice of sincere worship has its inner blessings and outer benefits as others come to understand the ground on which the leader stands in all seasons of life.

9. Rest for the Benefit of All

In one of those honest encounters between board chair and president, one leader was told, "When you are rested, you are really good." Another wrote to a friend in reply to a late night e-mail: "Go to bed. You owe it to your university to be rested." These important messages need to be taken to heart and practiced for the benefit of the organization being served.

The Quaker philosopher D. Elton Trueblood often said, "He who is available all the time is not worth being available when he is available."

In the interest of extending the tenure of a strong and effective president, one board insisted on two or three practices that seem to commend themselves to leaders at almost any stage of tenure. The board asked the president to have an annual executive physical examination and to take a week each quarter for rest, reading, reflecting, and personal renewal. They expected an annual report on both of these assignments. These days of rest were in addition to periodic sabbaticals and annual vacation leaves.

Leaders owe it to their organizations and team members to take personal responsibility for their lives, physically and spiritually, and need to offer fresh, rested minds for such important work.

10. Keep the Company of Trusted Friends

In his book *A Resilient Life*,[4] G. MacDonald writes about the blessings that have come to him and to those he has served through his habits of renewal. He describes how he selected "A Band of Brothers," three friends not from his professional context and with different skills but devoted to one another for the long haul. The four pledged to be there in the critical moments of life and to care for the interests of spouses should death interrupt this committed group. They sustained these relationships by planning time together and helping one another through challenging activities.

As career places one in the vistas of ultimate responsibility, friends find it more difficult to come around as they once did. The results can be an unexpected level of personal loneliness. The leader will have to build abiding relationships that can, over time, sustain that inner relational life that only good friends can meet.

One area available to the CEO that may prove beneficial and is growing in popularity among college presidents is the role of a coach. Coaches who look in on leadership issues are truly beneficial and help leaders see and hear opportunities that may be blurred by the pace of daily issues. They can also meet a need for open candor that may not be assumed by a board chair or one who is in the reporting line. Managing such valued confidentiality within the boundaries of good professional conduct can prove to be enriching when it is invited and respected for all it has to offer.

11. Feed the Inner Life

David Hubbard was the much loved and highly effective president of Fuller Theological Seminary whose devotion to the connections of mind and spirit created a legacy in seminary and church-related education. He loved to see the Dodgers baseball games and could often be found sitting in Dodger Stadium for several innings after a day in his Pasadena office. He was not just a fan. He was a man who took the diversion of great athletics as a means by which to clear his mind and restore his spirit.

Many who love the theater or great music find shows and concerts to be restoring outlets that chase away some of the tension that comes with the office of a busy leader. Such experiences shared in good company are more than a luxury. They are essential nourishment for the soul. The better the orchestra, the more the music lifts the soul.

Bill and Gloria Gaither have brought their love for great poetry and close harmonies to the world. Their body of work, seen across the world on stages, has always been a blend of joyful entertainment and spiritual worship, and they do it openly as their calling and pleasure. Some might be surprised to know that their music of choice in the family room of their home is the great classics performed by some of the world's great orchestras. Both avid readers with graduate degrees in literature, they love the turn of a phrase in a great novel and in the poetry of some young writer who has yet to find an audience.

Since leadership is essentially an art lived out in relationships, it is vital that the leader find a way to bring to all the constituents of the enterprise something of herself or himself that is real and rich with a fresh sense of the wholeness of the person. Only those who have cared for their own inner life will have that consistent well from which to draw as they give of themselves to their calling.

12. Give the Benefit of the Doubt

The benefit of the doubt is a gift that often gets put back on the shelf as leaders are called upon to render judgments and make decisions, the most difficult of which seem to involve people. The relevant facts are rarely all related upon the first hearing of a situation. Giving the benefit of the doubt is often a wise place to begin to find the right answer to some problem.

Good and faithful people do make mistakes that are costly and embarrassing, even life shattering. However, a truly creative environment requires some toleration for mistakes, or it risks being wound so tight that no one will take a chance and try new things. IBM's president T. J. Watson Jr. was famous for receiving a report of a million-dollar mistake made by one of his researchers in the early development of the computer. It came at a high price, including the investment of months of work by many. When asked if the researcher would be fired, Watson's comments assured that he considered the mistake, though costly, a worthy investment in future successes. He said, "Every time we've moved ahead in IBM, it was because someone was willing to take a chance, put his head on the block, and try something new."[5]

Making room for failure is wise. In an inaugural address, one college president said, "I envision a place where failure is not fatal and where forgiveness is both given and received."

13. Show Up

"Ninety percent of success is showing up" is a quote usually attributed to sage Woody Allen. It is what leaders do, and it makes a difference. Constituents want a relationship with the leader. They want contact. The pastor of a large congregation spends all of Sunday morning open and available to those who come to the multiple worship services. The contact, warm and sincere, is pastoral work and builds bonds needed to advance the cause.

When leaders show up unexpectedly, there is an opportunity to build strong relational bonds with constituents. Over time some leaders are simply known as the ones who are sure to be there. One kind, elderly donor said to a busy president of a college, "I just knew you would be here." It was a special occasion for a special couple, and they had learned to expect that leader's timely attention.

All those who write about leadership will not agree with giving availability such high priority or praise. In his work on the effective presidency, James Fisher counsels that one of the tools of an effective leader is to maintain some distance.[6] Wisdom must be applied in balance, and there are benefits to preserving the importance and dignity of the office. Leaders who are just first-name buddies to all in the organization may not be able to cast a vision and a level of expectation that is helpful to the mission. However, on balance, constituents want access. Being known as a leader who shows up is a valuable investment in the moments that count.

14. Write Notes

Rediscover the lost art of handwritten notes. A senior mentor to several college presidents once offered, "If you want a note to be read, word for word, handwrite it." The benefits of this personal touch can hardly be overestimated. One sentence from a familiar hand is like a touch on the shoulder that brings the warm assurance of encouragement.

Some personal organization may be required. One leader has a hand-addressed stack of cards waiting attention first thing in the morning, with a sticky note attached to each stating the note's purpose. This kind of help from an assistant makes the note more personal and strengthens the bond between leader and constituent. In this day when many executives use personal communication devices, sending a quick text can communicate volumes to a key constituent, a trustee, or a colleague. The note may be the first opened and read even by the busiest recipients.

A faculty member once told a president that the little note scribbled on the letter accompanying the annual contract that thanked her for her good work made a memory and was read again and again across the years as a gift of priceless support. Notes are powerful. That president can still quote a note he got from another faculty member in a Christmas card in his early years of leadership. It read, "In almost every way, things are better since you came."

15. Serve the Needs of the Staff

Senior staff members are key constituents for the leader. They are sometimes regarded as extensions of the leader or tools for executive success. In so many ways they reflect the credibility of leadership. No group is more vital. No loyalty is more important. No successful work is more closely tied to the effective service of the leader. They extend the reach of the leader to others needing to be a part of the good work.

If a staff colleague needs the leader to make a call, it would be well to make that call in a timely way. When a staff member has a personal crisis, some encouragement may make all the difference and impart confidence and strength. Boundaries are important. However, respectful care is at the heart of a Christian community and can make a world of difference for the whole organization. It sends a powerful message to all about living out the values and virtues of the organization.

16. Have a Confidant

Leaders are blessed if they have a spouse who understands, is insightful, and knows when to give an opinion and when to refrain from doing so. It is also an enormous benefit to have other confidants—a senior staff person or a colleague who has earned the leader's trust over time. Sometimes the truth is difficult to hear until it is spoken aloud to someone and repeated back.

The wise dean of a school of theology confessed to his students, "I have always had a counselor, a confidant who would honor my confidence and who would be available at my call to help sort out some of the big questions of my life."

It is also important to clarify with such a person the need for confidentiality, for the leader to be heard but not always to step directly into the matter. Those who have the need to fix things are usually not very good at being confidants. Nevertheless, all the risks accounted for, having a confidant is a blessing for the leader, and all leaders need them.

17. Check the Act

A leader new to college presidency relates that he was fortunate to have a visit from an experienced board chair six months into his tenure to see how things were going. After a brief report on a busy beginning, and accounting for all the critical issues on the campus, the new president was surprised to hear the chair say, "That's about half the job."

"What's the other half?" he asked.

The wise chair said, "The other half is theater."

Leadership is also about symbolism, building confidence, touching constituents. That does not mean the leader should lack sincerity. If the leader approaches constituents, wearing a smile, speaking to almost everyone as she or he passes on the campus in the course of the day, the leader is confirming, shares the energy of hope and purpose, and the mission is advanced. When the leader appears to be carrying the weight of the world on his or her shoulders, it can give unintended credence to doubts about the success of the enterprise.

Leaders have many obligations. Among them is to look the part and act in ways that make it a pleasure to be a partner in the work.

18. Humor Can Be a Great Gift

Be careful with humor, but be yourself. Positive humor, the kind that comes naturally and is not used at the expense of others, can provide energy and delight in the midst of important, even difficult moments. Humor comes with some risks when others are not ready to receive these emotions. Experienced pastoral leaders have a way of reading a room and a relationship and will not inject a light spirit when the moment is filled with the heaviness that must be shared with heartfelt empathy. However, in the general discourse of relationships, it is fair to ask, "Am I fun to be with?"

National leaders have won over their opponents on a personal basis when they were just being themselves in sharing humor. President Ronald Reagan was a good example of one gifted in humor. It was a part of his personality, and even his detractors seemed to enjoy his presence. When humor is natural, use it, but with wisdom.

19. Center Your Life in the Words and Ways of Jesus

A global Christian leader once confessed, "I know many who have little regard for Christianity but who are openly curious about Jesus." Some are at times disappointed by the reputation sometimes carried by those who are known to be Christians but express discourteous and even rude behavior. However, followers of Jesus, who have become students of His words and ways, will find welcome and even trust in many places in a contentious world.

The Christian leader who aspires to be like Jesus would do well to become a diligent student of the Gospels, especially the teachings of Jesus in His sermons and prayers. Matthew 5, 6, and 7 can be a prime source for the student of the Master Teacher and Leader. John 17 clarifies much about the heart of Jesus as teacher, model, and guide.

P. Palmer writes eloquently about the need of the leader to "get into what one cannot get out of."[7] It is entirely appropriate to expect the Christian leader to be more knowledgeable about Jesus than any other hero or model of leadership theory and practice. Leadership is the work of both spirit and mind. J. Baker calls it "faith and friendship."[8] Ultimately, leadership is a spiritual matter, and one's devotion to Jesus is a pathway for a lifetime of service, especially for those committed not just to success but also to faithfulness.

20. Take Your Leadership Seriously

An experienced student of the college presidency observed, "Being the president is more of an asset than we might know." Institutions need their leader to use the power of the office to accomplish the mission. Having the common touch is a gift and a blessing. It reveals a measure of attractive and genuine humility. It must also be balanced by the full investment of one's office including the image and persuasive powers of the office.

Some who would not give an appointment to other members of staff will take the call of a college president, even invest their time and resources when it matters to the one with highest authority.

Sacrificing one's leadership for selfish personal pleasures and habits is a costly waste of one's ultimate duties. Using the office with integrity as a tool for leadership is altogether appropriate. Good stewardship calls for a healthy willingness to be the leader. It goes with duty and is an asset. It deserves the highest of consideration.

Concluding Summation

Leaders are effective when they find joy in relating to an array of constituents. They need understanding, energy, and a sense of joy in their work. They will be visionary leaders if they find ways for the vision to come out of those important relationships for the good of the organization they serve. Leadership is mostly relational, and those who love people, who are innately hospitable, and who learn to reach out in meaningful ways will likely succeed.

Presidents of colleges often joke that the best times on the campus are summers when most constituents are absent from the campus. But they do not really mean it. The privilege of serving with promising young people and others who care about the future is an unspeakable joy. Constituent relationships will likely tell the story of ultimate advancement of a university's mission.

Resources for Further Study

Collins, Jim. *Good to Great and the Social Sectors: Why Business Thinking Is Not the Answer*. New York: Harper, 2005.

_____. *Good to Great: Why Some Companies Make the Leap . . . and Others Don't*. New York: HarperCollins, 2001.

Covey, Stephen M. R., and Rebecca R. Merrill. *The Speed of Trust: The One Thing That Changes Everything*. New York: Free Press, 2006.

Crabtree, J. R. *The Fly in the Ointment: Why Denominations Aren't Helping Their Congregations . . . and How They Can*. New York: Church Publishing, 2008.

Currents. October 2009: 7.

Fisher, James L., et al. *The Effective College President*. New York: American Council on Education; Macmillan, 1988.

Gardner, John W. *On Leadership*. New York: Free Press, 1990.

Lacy, Kyle. *Twitter Marketing for Dummies*. Hoboken, NJ: Wiley, 2010.

Lindsay, D. Michael. *Faith in the Halls of Power: How Evangelicals Joined the American Elite*. New York: Oxford University Press, 2007.

MacDonald, Gordon. *A Resilient Life*. Nashville: Thomas Nelson, 2006.

Palmer, Parker J. *Let Your Life Speak: Listening for the Voice of Vocation*. San Francisco: Jossey-Bass, 2000.

Peters, Thomas J., and Robert H. Waterman. *In Search of Excellence: Lessons from America's Best-Run Companies*. New York: Harper & Row, 1982.

Robinson, Bill. *Incarnate Leadership: Five Lessons from the Life of Jesus*. Grand Rapids: Zondervan, 2008.

Wallis, Jim. *Rediscovering Values: On Wall Street, Main Street, and Your Street*. New York: Howard Books, 2010.

Questions for Further Reflection

1. If leaders are developed and not born, how does one take appropriate steps to lead?

2. What attributes are needed in the leader to build healthy bonds with key constituents?

3. Are all constituent groups equal, deserving equal consideration by the leader?

4. What are some perils to good constituent relationships? Can key constituents overstep their privileges? How can leaders impose boundaries for key constituents when they overreach or expect certain privileges?

5. What does the Christ-centered perspective have to say about one's leadership with constituent groups?

6. What should the leader know about various constituents and constituent groups to be the effective relational or servant leader with them?

Endnotes

[1] J. R. Crabtree, *The Fly in the Ointment: Why Denominations Aren't Helping Their Congregations . . . and How They Can* (New York: Church Publishing, 2008).

[2] *Currents* (October 2009), 7.

[3] K. Lacy, *Twitter Marketing for Dummies* (Hoboken, NJ: Wiley, 2010).

[4] G. MacDonald, *A Resilient Life* (Nashville: Thomas Nelson, 2006).

[5] T. J. Peters and Robert H. Waterman, *In Search of Excellence: Lessons from America's Best-Run Companies* (New York: Harper & Row, 1982).

[6] J. L. Fisher et al., *The Effective College President* (New York: American Council on Education; Macmillan, 1988).

[7] P. J. Palmer, *Let Your Life Speak: Listening for the Voice of Vocation* (San Francisco: Jossey-Bass, 2000).

[8] D. M. Lindsay, *Faith in the Halls of Power: How Evangelicals Joined the American Elite* (New York: Oxford University Press, 2007), 32.

Chapter 11

Selecting and Building Leadership Teams

Thom S. Rainer
President, LifeWay Christian Resources

U se your imagination. Your ideas will probably be close to numerous settings and situations.

The setting could be a church, a Christian organization, or a secular organization. And though any illustrations need not be limited to the top leadership group in an organization, let's suppose that is the case in our fictitious examples. Further, so the comparisons are somewhat the same, let's imagine that we are observing each of two leadership groups in the setting of a weekly meeting.

You may see some similarities to some groups of which you have been a part. I call it a tale of two teams.

A Tale of Two Teams: Meeting with Team A

Leadership Team A meets every Monday for two hours. That meeting is truly a microcosm of the relationships and workings of the team throughout the year.

Team A is led by Mike Hoffner. Mike is a charismatic and intelligent person. Indeed he is often seen as an expert in his field, and many outside the organization turn to him for advice and counsel. He regularly affirms the rest of the team in public.

But that's where the good news ends.

Mike is typically the last to arrive at the meeting. From the moment of his arrival, he dominates the conversation. When someone else on the team attempts to speak, he typically interrupts. As one of Mike's direct reports said in a confidential conversation, "It's as if he can't stand the voice of anyone other than his own."

On those rare occasions when a team member has the courage (or foolishness) to challenge something Mike said or did, the tension in the room rises immediately. Mike's face turns red, and within moments he is lecturing the team member on the insanity of that position. The anger is palpable, and Mike's tone is condescending.

Most of the team learned the lesson. To disagree with the leader does not make sense. Nothing constructive ever results.

The weekly meeting is indeed a microcosm of what takes place at Organization A. Mike is a controlling leader. Though the other team members have some authority in their respective areas, that authority is subject to revision or revocation according to the whims of the leader.

Morale is low at Organization A. The problems of the organization are usually masked to the outside world because of the intelligent and charming persona Mike conveys. Still, personnel turnover is high, particularly at the leadership level.

To be fair, the organization is not doing poorly. It is not imploding. Mike is a man of high intelligence. He has made many right decisions. But many who are in the know realize that the potential is much higher. They see an organization that could be doing so much more.

A Tale of Two Teams: Meeting with Team B

Like the previous scenario, Team B meets weekly. Again, this meeting is reflective of what takes place throughout Organization B. The leader of the team, Jerry Reuben, has built a solid leadership team. Some of the team members served with the previous leader, and Jerry has added four others to the team. He made the tough call early in his leadership tenure and removed three members from the team.

Jerry and all of the other team members are punctual to the weekly meeting. Camaraderie among the team members is good. The meetings typically begin with lighthearted conversation and laughter. It is not unusual to hear the members banter with one another about sports, family, or the organization.

Jerry is good about keeping the meeting moving, but he does want team members to enjoy one another's fellowship. The meeting closely follows an agenda. Anyone on the team can add an agenda item each week. In addition to the weekly meeting, the team has a monthly strategic meeting.

The most obvious dynamics of this meeting are the energy in the room and the freedom to speak to important issues. Jerry is clearly the leader of this team, but other team members are vital contributors.

The weekly meeting is a microcosm of the ongoing work of this team. All of the team members are empowered to get the job done in their respective areas. Accountability takes place in the weekly meetings and in regular meetings with Jerry. But the leader truly trusts the team members to lead their areas without his micromanagement. If he sees that a member can't get the job done, he is willing to make the tough call to move the person to another position or to move the person out of the organization.

The team is healthy but not perfect. It has taken a while for newer team members to trust longer-term members. And some on the team wish that Jerry would be more directive and clearer in his vision casting. At least one member has expressed concern that the weekly meetings are more tactical than strategic.

Still the overall morale is good. And all of the team members feel free to express their concerns to Jerry. They say consistently that he is a good listener and that the team is getting healthier every week.

Two Different Teams

Team leadership is in vogue. Volumes have been written on the topic. Secular organizations are implementing it. Churches and other Christian organizations are using it.

But not all teams are healthy.

Team A is dysfunctional. The leader is an autocrat. Those who work under his authority are demoralized. Observers are not surprised each time someone on the leadership team departs. Although the leader is smart and can be charming, his weaknesses are glaring. To his credit he has done well in recruiting quality people for his leadership team. But those who are closest to him are most quickly disillusioned.

Team B is mostly healthy. Relationships among the team leaders are good. Perhaps the most frequent positive comment among them is that they feel empowered and encouraged. Many significant initiatives have developed at the organization because the team works so well together.

Relationships, however, are not perfect. Trust is building among the members, but more progress needs to be made. The leader of Team B is so focused on team leadership that he sometimes fails to be directive. He needs to provide more strategic leadership as well.

Still, the contrasts between the two teams are stark. The future of the organization represented by Team A is limited. The future of Team B's organization is promising. And the morale and emotional health of the leadership members of Team B are good. That team will likely grow into an even more dynamic leadership group. The leadership team of Organization A probably will not even exist in two years. The revolving door of its members will be an ever-present reality.

Defining Team Leadership

Throughout this book you have heard from incredible leaders who have offered unique perspectives on leadership in the Christian world. Several have provided substantive biblical foundations for leadership. In this chapter I presume upon the biblical foundations they have articulated. Do not take the small number of specific biblical references as a lack of dependence on biblical truth for this chapter.

On a similar note this chapter will not argue that team leadership is the only biblical model for leadership. Certainly the entirety of the book of Nehemiah could be used as an apologia for team leadership. And also one can likely see the merits of team leadership as Jethro instructs his son-in-law to build a team to carry out the leadership demands placed upon Moses by the Israelites (Exod 18:13–27).

Still, other models of leadership are evident throughout Scripture. There were times when Moses had to be directive in his leadership of the Israelites. The tone of Paul's letter to the churches in Galatia is almost entirely autocratic. He was dealing with a serious doctrinal problem and had to address the issue quickly and decisively.

Something, however, about the team leadership model is akin to servant leadership. The members of the team submit their own personal interests to the good of the goals of the whole organization. Good team dynamics require an interdependent and even submissive spirit. Led well, team leadership can be an incredible approach to moving an organization to new levels of excellence.

At this point it might be helpful to provide a definition of team leadership. Dennison provides a longer definition for team leadership and team ministry in the church:

> A group of diversely gifted people who complement one another, and who feel called by God to be committed to work together toward an agreed vision, which is otherwise unobtainable. This involves the willingness of the team members first to submit individual accomplishments and personal preferences to achieve the common goal; second to be accountable to and to submit to the appointed leadership of the church.[1]

Though unwieldy, the definition does point to some elements essential to the health and success of team leadership. First, the team must agree about the overarching goal or vision of the organization. Second, members must be willing to submit to the authority of a designated leader. Of course, a corollary to the second element is that a designated leader must be willing and able to lead. We will look at this issue later in the chapter. Third, the definition includes the reality that the team will include people with diverse but complementing gifts and abilities.

We would add to the definition the matter of open and honest communication among team members. Many teams fail because members are reticent to speak openly and honestly, even if the conversation becomes a matter of conflict. Indeed, the team that does not experience some level of conflict is not functioning as a healthy team. Conflict is necessary to work toward the best solutions. Such conflict can be difficult, but it should not harm the overall unity and purpose of the team.

Six Significant Benefits of Team Leadership

As one peruses the plethora of resources on team leadership, he or she often gets the impression that forming a leadership team is the answer to any organization's woes and struggles. To the contrary, healthy leadership teams do not just happen, and they do not happen easily. Shortly, we will look at the four key characteristics of healthy teams. But for now we recognize that team leadership is a challenging process. Indeed, our anecdotal observations are that more unhealthy teams exist than healthy teams.

For those organizations that are successful with team leadership, however, the benefits are significant. Brad Waggoner has done an excellent job of summarizing the benefits from both literary and experiential sources.[2]

We examined Waggoner's sources and others and found six broad categories of benefits, though our list is not exhaustive.

First, good team leadership can have a broad and positive cultural impact. Team members truly feel as if they are an integral and contributing part of the organization. Others in the organization often follow the example of team leaders and cooperate with one another. There is a sense that everyone is on a team with a purpose and that everyone on the team is valued.

Team leadership works well where those with a diversity of gifts and abilities exercise those gifts and abilities for the good of the organization. Morale is enhanced as those in the organization are able to contribute in a way that motivates and excites them.

Second, good team leadership leads to greater efficiencies in the organization. Repeatedly we hear in organizations that "the right hand doesn't know what the left hand is doing." If the team is effective, not only will there be greater knowledge of the activities in the organization, but one area can also make contributions in another area. Silos can be broken. One team member may have a solution set for a problem that another team member has never discovered. Redundancies can be reduced or even eliminated as knowledge about them increases.

This greater awareness of activities in an organization leads to a third important benefit in an effective team leadership model: communication improves. So much of healthy team leadership depends on healthy relationships among the members. As members work together, they develop stronger relationships. Those relationships lead to enhanced communication.

The matter of better communication among team members typically takes place in both formal and informal settings. The formal setting is the regularly scheduled meeting. While not all teams can have the benefit of meetings where everyone is physically present, those that do often see communication improved dramatically among team members.

The irony of my writing about the benefit of regular meetings is my own disdain for meetings in general. Like most, I have sat through some incredibly unproductive meetings, and I have been bored beyond words. The key, of course, is that meetings should have a clear purpose and should therefore be productive.

While a regularly scheduled meeting is helpful in communication among team members, the most helpful communication is often informal. With my own leadership team, we often speak of "hallway talk," where two or three of us begin an impromptu conversation that leads to some meaning-ful decisions. Of course, frequent informal communication will not take place unless relationships are first healthy.

Fourth, healthy team leadership engenders healthy accountability. If all the team members see themselves as valued contributors, and if they know they have the freedom to express their perspectives, they will challenge other team members periodically. Such free exchange leads to healthy conflict and healthy accountability. There is often a mispercep-tion that conflict is unhealthy. To the contrary, the absence of conflict is unhealthy among team members. That conflict should not lead to ongoing tense relationships, but short-term tension can be healthy.

Leaders of teams should give other team members the freedom to chal-lenge them as well. While team members should respect and follow the authority of the leader, they should have a healthy culture that allows them to disagree with him or her.

My current leadership team includes seven vice presidents and me. The team includes high-quality individuals who are leaders in their own rights in their respective fields. Jim Collins, in his seminal work, *Good to Great*, discusses the importance of getting "the right people on the bus, the wrong people off the bus, and the right people in the right seats" and then figur-ing out where to drive the bus.[3] I have little doubt that our leadership team includes the right people in the right seats.

The quality of this team was never more evident than early in my third year of leadership. I presented a specific path down which I was about to lead the organization. Three of the team members spoke quickly and pas-sionately against my idea. They presented their perspective with clarity and conviction. The rest of the team did not weigh in on the matter since they were not as informed as the three contrarians.

Because of my respect for the three team members, I agreed to table my idea for a week to think about their arguments and to do further research. I came to the conclusion that they were right and I was wrong. They stopped me from making a bad decision.

A fifth benefit of team leadership is cross-training. The definition of a team indicates that team members will have a variety of experiences, train-ing, and knowledge. The opportunity to learn from one another is great. I worked with one leadership team that was able to move team members to different seats on the team because they had learned so well from one another. In some cases issues of succession can be handled significantly better since all of the team members have a greater knowledge of one another's work. When vacancies occur, the members are able to offer meaningful input on what the successor's qualities and abilities should be.

Finally, team leadership leads to greater balance in the organization. Some team members are conservative in their business philosophies; others are more aggressive. Some members might be long tenured and able to offer sound historical perspectives on the organization. Others may be relatively new and constantly challenging "the way we've always done it." Teams may have variety in age, gender, ethnic background, and education. And while diversity does not guarantee effectiveness, it can provide healthy balance on a healthy team.

Selecting and Building Healthy Leadership Teams

The pervasive amount of literature on leadership teams is equally matched by suggestions on how to select and build a leadership team. As one would expect, many of the suggestions and characteristics have points in common. The consistency in the research and the application of the principles suggests that we can build healthy leadership teams.

MacMillan, for example, notes six characteristics of healthy teams:[4]

1. Common purpose
2. Crystal clear goals
3. Accepted leadership
4. Effective processes
5. Solid relationships
6. Excellent communication

Hackman notes five conditions that must be met to build a healthy leadership team.[5] Note the similarities to the characteristics articulated above by MacMillan:

1. A real team
2. Compelling direction
3. Enabling structure
4. Supportive context
5. Expert coaching

It should not, therefore, be surprising, that the characteristics noted in this chapter are likewise similar. I am indeed indebted to the works of others that shape my thoughts. But, in addition to the biblical foundation and literary sources, much of my formative work is experiential. Perhaps, for the sake of full disclosure, sharing some of my background in team building will be helpful.

My first venture in team building took place while I was still a 20-something young husband. Due to a variety of reasons, not all of them based on merit, I was promoted to vice president in a large bank holding company. The particular bank where I worked was in a small city about an hour from the bank's corporate headquarters. My responsibilities included all of the bank's commercial loan portfolio and the people who worked in that division.

After I left the corporate world to answer the call to vocational ministry, I had the opportunity to build teams in four different churches. The churches were significantly different in size, community they served, and location. As senior pastor, I dealt with issues of integrating existing ministry staff with new staff I presented to the church.

My next stop was in the world of academia, where I had the unique opportunity of starting a graduate school. That particular entity was a school within the Southern Baptist Theological Seminary, so I was not without resources to begin this venture. Still, I had the exciting task of forming my own leadership team, bringing in a world-class faculty, and hiring administrative support personnel. One of the challenges was the time line. I had only six months to recruit the team, develop a degree program, seek accreditation, and recruit students.

Another team building opportunity I had was starting a consulting company. I took the advice of several mentors in the secular world and kept the company's overhead low. In essence I was the only full-time employee, but I formed leadership teams by contract for each assignment. Over several years I began to use the same 10 to 12 consultants. Though they never became full-time employees of my consulting company, they did become a *de facto* leadership team.

My present leadership role is president and CEO of LifeWay Christian Resources, a $500 million organization with approximately 7,000 full-time and part-time employees. The company includes four major ministry business divisions: a 160-store retail chain, a large book publisher, a large resource company for churches, and Christian retreat centers in North Carolina and New Mexico.

The first-level leadership team includes seven vice presidents and me. Each of the vice presidents leads one of the major ministry business divisions or one of the major support areas of LifeWay. One of my first initiatives when I came to LifeWay in late 2005 was shaping the leadership team.

While leadership assignments I have experienced have great variety, I have seen four common themes emerge from building leadership teams. The four characteristics I have experienced are simple but not simplistic. To the contrary, team building is certainly not an easy process. It takes significant planning, buy-in, and old-fashioned work. Most of the time it takes tough decision making as well, particularly with personnel decisions.

But the rewards of healthy leadership team are enormous. Some of the healthiest organizations today have discovered and implemented these four factors. To them we now turn.

Healthy Leadership Team Factor 1:
A Compelling Purpose

My son, Jess Rainer, and I wrote a book on the millennial generation, those born between the years 1980 and 2000.[6] The foundation for our study was a survey of 1,000 older millennials born between 1980 and 1991. One of the chief traits of this largest generation in America's history is their desire to be part of something bigger than themselves. That compelling purpose drives their vocations, their relationships, their beliefs, and their service to and for others.

Though the millennials may be the first generation to articulate this compulsion, we can say with little doubt that most people want to find purpose and meaning in all they do. Any healthy leadership team must likewise have a compelling purpose, a clear understanding of the direction of the organization.

Christian organizations would seem to have a definitive edge here. A local church clearly has the Great Commission and the Great Commandment as its compelling purposes. A Christian educational institution has the compelling purpose to equip students to have a Christian worldview as they engage the world and its values. A Christian publisher and resource provider has the compelling purpose to provide ministry products that can further the work of God's kingdom.

Thus, one might conclude, leaders in a Christian organization need not worry about having a compelling purpose. It is, after all, inherent in the basis of our existence. Of course, such a presumption is wrong.

While Christian organizations have a clear biblical purpose, that purpose doesn't drive those organizations. Instead, the organization typically drifts from its original mission, and the entity is no longer driven by a compelling purpose. A church thus often exists to keep the staff paid and the programs going. The means becomes the end. A Christian education institution becomes driven by enrollment and elite academic programs rather than by a compelling purpose to equip students with a worldview that can change the world in which they live. And a Christian publisher becomes driven by market share and profits rather than by publishing kingdom-building books.

The organization must first have a compelling purpose that is clear and evident in the actions it takes each day. Of course any leadership team in the organization must likewise be driven by that compelling purpose. Institutional drifting is more common than not. But true leaders want to be part of something that is bigger than themselves. There must be, therefore, a continuous and honest assessment to see if the organization is remaining true to its mission and purpose.

But a leadership team needs not only the *what* of a compelling purpose. They need the *how* as well. Let us return to a local church as an example. We would suppose that most on the leadership team of that church would readily affirm the congregation's commitment to follow the Great Commission and the Great Commandment. Cognitive affirmation of the two great commissions, however, is insufficient.

Some in the church could declare that the weekly check they give is sufficient to follow the congregation's purpose. Others may conclude that having a nice building where people can gather for worship and Bible study is sufficient. Both of these certainly can aid in carrying out the purposes of the church, but they are not the ultimate actions that carry out the purpose.

A Christian college may declare that its purpose is to equip its students with a Christian worldview that will prepare them in the world where they will work and serve. The purpose is certainly noble, but if it is little more than a catchy slogan, it will not be compelling.

A healthy leadership team is drawn to the organization it serves because that organization exists for a greater purpose and because the organization has a clear plan for fulfilling that purpose. Great teams serve great organizations that have compelling purposes.

Healthy Leadership Team Factor 2: A Conducive Culture

Check the conditions in which you would like to work on a leadership team:

- Oppressive environment
- Open communication
- Fun and joyous
- Lack of support
- Tense and hostile
- Good reward system
- Mutual trust
- Micromanaging

OK, the choices are obvious. Of the eight characteristics listed above, we quickly recognize the environment where we would choose to be. It is likely that you readily identified with many, if not all, of the descriptions above. You have been in some healthy cultures, and you have been in some unhealthy cultures. Of course, a leadership team cannot be any healthier than its culture.

As we have worked with leadership teams across America, we have seen a number of characteristics of leadership teams with healthy cultures. Four of these characteristics seem to be the most pervasive.

Trust

Without mutual trust there is no chance of a healthy team. In a church consultation my team conducted several years ago, all of the factors for health seemed to be present. The leadership of the church included some of the most theologically astute people we had ever encountered. The organizational structure of the church was excellent. The church had a strong missional emphasis. The congregation was in the middle of a growing community with many favorable demographics. The senior pastor was one of the best preachers we had heard. His exposition of Scripture was superb, and communication skills were outstanding.

But the church was struggling greatly.

There was dissent in the congregation. Giving was declining. For the first time in nine years worship attendance declined. Morale on the leadership team and the rest of the staff was low. The church's healthy external focus was giving way to an unhealthy internal focus.

After working with church staff and congregational leadership for a few weeks, we were able to pinpoint the source of the problem: lack of trust among the leadership team members. It was really a simple but tragic beginning. One leader made a decision that another team member questioned. But no questions were asked. Instead of confronting his peer, he remained silent and bitter. That attitude soon spread to the rest of the leadership and eventually throughout the congregation.

So much damage was done that it was impossible to get the two members back in a trusting relationship. One voluntarily left the church while the other was eventually asked to leave. The church recovered, but the time of healing took almost two years.

A healthy leadership team exhibits mutual trust among its members. And that trust leads to another major trait of a conducive culture: openness.

Openness

At the beginning of this chapter, we saw a tale of two leadership teams. Though Team B was not perfect, it did have mostly healthy traits. For example, the weekly leadership meeting was an open forum for all who were present. Rarely did someone feel constrained from speaking his or her mind. Even in informal settings team members felt free to express themselves.

An environment of openness presumes the previous characteristic of trust. It also presumes that trust leads to freedom of expression that unleashes new ideas and creativity.

Healthy Conflict Resolution

As leadership team members feel the freedom to express themselves, there will be inevitable times of disagreement. Sometimes the disagreement can become heated, even in healthy cultures.

A common misconception is that conflict is bad for leadership teams. To the contrary, the absence of conflict is always problematic. Any group that works together for an extended time is bound to have differences. Problems occur not because of the differences but because of the absence of resolution to those differences.

I thoroughly enjoy watching our leadership team members interact. The exchange can be interesting and sometimes intense. We have leaders who are conservative and leaders who are aggressive. We have leaders who are careful to stay within historical precedents and others who don't know how to color in any manner except outside the lines. We have both introverts and extroverts.

Differences of opinion occur frequently. Sometimes frustration and anger erupt among members. Ultimately, however, conflicts are resolved, and we move forward as a team. I have been really encouraged to see how our team members balance and complement one another. It has made for a much stronger leadership team and, thus, a much stronger organization.

Empowerment, Support, and Reward

Though these factors are unique unto themselves, they are also interdependent on one another. Empowerment means that team members have both the responsibility and the authority to lead their respective areas. Too often team members are given an assignment with little authority to carry out that assignment.

I once led a division of an organization where I was given a clear assignment to grow that division. The first budget I was given, however, had expense detail with no revenue projections. In other words, even though I had a big responsibility to lead toward growth, in reality I was little more than a cost control manager. I never had direct involvement with the revenue my division generated. It was an extremely frustrating experience. I had responsibility, but I was not empowered.

Closely tied to healthy empowerment is the provision of resources for the leader to get the job done. Does he or she have adequate personnel? Are sufficient opportunities for growth and training available? Are good financial, technological, and other resources available at the disposal of the leader? These needs must be considered in the context of limited budgets and resources.

Rewards are related closely to empowerment as well. Rewards take many forms. They can be simple words or notes of encouragement. They can come in the form of promotions in position and responsibilities. They can be as basic as recognizing someone in the presence of others. Of course, compensation, raises, and other forms of financial remuneration are included in rewards.

In the organization noted above where I had leadership over one key division, I was again frustrated at the financial reward system. Every year the entire organization received across-the-board raises. Everyone received the same percentage raise. I was not empowered to differentiate the level of raises among those who worked in my division. The message we sent to all employees was clear. The most productive and the least productive received the same raises each year. There was no financial reward for superior performance.

Healthy organizational cultures have leaders who empower others. And with that empowerment comes a healthy means of support and rewards.

Joy

Healthy organizations and healthy leadership teams are characterized by a pervasive sense of joy. Leaders and employees simply enjoy working at the organization. Work is fun. Laughter and smiles are commonplace.

It is ironic that many Christian organizations do not reflect a culture of joy. The apostle Paul wrote the Philippian church to "rejoice in the Lord always. I will say it again: Rejoice!" (Phil 4:4 HCSB). We who are believers in Christ have been forgiven of our sins by Christ's death on the cross. Because He conquered death, we conquer death. And we have the promise and hope of His ongoing presence in our lives (Matt 28:20). If we don't have joy for these reasons, then we have failed to grasp the promise we have been given.

A culture conducive to healthy team leadership is a culture of trust, of openness, of healthy conflict resolution, of empowerment, and, of course, of joy. All these factors are interdependent on one another. And the leader of the team influences all of these issues significantly. To that factor we now turn.

Healthy Leadership Team Factor 3:
A 12-Factor Team Leader

Describing an effective team leader is no easy task. Some are extroverts, but a number are introverts. Some are comfortable with details; others prefer to keep things at a higher level. Some tend to make decisions with an abundance of data and objective information. But others, though not ignoring objective information, are more likely to form their decisions instinctively on subjective factors.

While it is overly simplistic to list a set of factors that best describe team leaders, it is still helpful. No single list is either sufficient or exhaustive, but the literature and research do point to 12 factors consistently. And our own work with team leaders across two decades confirms these factors.

Factor 1: High Character. Without this foundation, every other attribute of a team leader fails. Everyone knows a story about a seemingly great leader who fell because of some character failure. A weak character will be exposed in time.

Factor 2: Controlled Ego. This factor could easily be included as a subset of character. But an inflated ego is so pervasive in failed leadership that its opposite is worth mentioning as a category unto itself. Note that the factor does not say lack of ego. We all are sinners who, in the temporal life, will never fully conquer our focus on self. But great team leaders are successful in avoiding self-absorption.

Factor 3: Competent. The team leader has the requisite abilities, disposition, experience, training, and education. This factor presumes that not all people will have the necessary skill set to be team leaders.

Factor 4: Courageous. Good team leadership requires the willingness to make tough decisions. Such leaders often pay a price in the level of criticism they receive when they make such decisions. "It is lonely at the top." The phrase is a cliché but often true.

Factor 5: Decisive. Most of the time a leader can't have every piece of information that he or she would like in order to make a decision. Good leaders move ahead anyway. Delay can often result in disaster.

Factor 6: Consistent. Team members must see a leader who is consistent in his leadership of others, in making decisions, and in providing direction and vision. An inconsistent leader has a confused and directionless team.

Factor 7: Loyal. The leader demonstrates loyalty to the team he serves and to the organization. Team members do not hesitate to turn to the leader because they know they can count on him or her.

Factor 8: Communicative. Team members know what is taking place in the organization because the leader regularly tells them. The culture is one of openness because a great team leader demonstrates that openness by example.

Factor 9: Visionary. The leader can describe the preferred future of the organization. And if he or she is not particularly comfortable in grasping the vision for the organization, the leader has no problem bringing in team members for mutual vision casting and investment.

Factor 10: Strategic. Vision is the destination, the preferred future. Strategy is the road map from the present reality to the preferred future. Team leaders not only know where they want to go; they also know how to get there. Again, the team leader may not know all the components of strategy, but he or she can do well bringing the team together and using the members' collective knowledge and wisdom to build this pathway.

Factor 11: Strong Work Ethic. Leadership takes time and effort. Great team leaders are not lazy. They set the example with their work ethic.

Factor 12: Ability to Build a Great Team. Those who know me are fully aware of my love for Alabama football. I try not to be obnoxious about my team loyalty, but I fear that I'm not always successful. Nick Saban became the Tide's head coach in January 2007. He took a losing team and transformed it into a national champion in only three years.[7] I love what Saban told Alabama's athletic director Mal Moore on the day he was hired. He said his coaching was only as good as the players he recruited. He could not be a good team leader without a good team.

Team building is a subject of great interest today. And though I included it as a major factor in the description of great leaders, it is worthy of a brief discussion as a category unto itself.

Healthy Leadership Team Factor 4:
Team Building Using the Three Cs

Perhaps it is an oversimplification to narrow the major facets of team building to three categories. In our research of team building literature, however, we have found that most, if not all, of the discussion can be included in one of the three Cs. From my perspective, the three Cs fall into a natural order of priority.

The first priority in team building is to be totally confident that the prospective team member has high *character*. Does he embody biblical moral values? Is she a person who keeps her word? Is she able to keep confidences? Does he have a good reputation among those who know him?

Second, does a potential candidate for a team have the right *chemistry* to work well with other team members? Having the right chemistry is not the same as having a team of clones. To the contrary we have demonstrated in this chapter that a variety of perspectives and backgrounds is often healthy for teams. Ultimately, however, team members must be able to get along with one another. They must be respectful of one another, even when they disagree. And they must be committed to the greater purpose of the organization.

The third C is *competency*, the overall skill set. These factors are those most closely associated with a good résumé: education, experience, technical expertise, and training, to name a few. Unfortunately, many attempts at team building focus first on competency and often disregard character and chemistry. Some of the worst teams we have ever seen include some of the most competent people we have known. They passed the third C of team building but failed the first or second.

The Great Cry for Leadership

The theme of this book could not be more timely. The urgency could not be greater. The world needs true leaders. Governments are crying for good leaders. Schools need leaders more than ever. Businesses are often void of leadership. And many churches are desperate for true leadership.

At the risk of redundancy, I will remind you that this chapter on team leadership was not designed to be an apologia for the only way to lead organizations. Certainly other leadership approaches have proven effective over the past decades.

But team leadership has been one of the most useful approaches to leadership for over a quarter of a century. It avoids the extreme of a demoralizing autocratic leadership, but it does require the force of a strong leader. It avoids the inertia of consensus leadership, but it does call for the collective wisdom of many. And it often embodies the best of servant leadership in that the focus is turned away from self to the needs of others.

Team leadership does indeed have much to offer. But don't be fooled. It is one of the most difficult approaches to implement. Many teams exist, but few healthy teams exist. Such teams require a strong leader who has courage and esteem to let others share in the decision making and receive the credit. It requires team members who are some of the most competent persons that can be found but who are willing to put the team and the organization before self. Team leadership will only be successful where there is a compelling purpose and a culture conducive to true teamwork.

Difficult? Yes. Impossible? No.

And the reward of a healthy team is potentially an organization that excels in many areas and, above all, makes a difference in the lives of those it serves.

Resources for Further Study

Collins, Jim. *Good to Great*. New York: Harper Business, 2001.

Dennison, Justin. *Team Ministry: A Blueprint for Christian Leadership*. London: Hodder and Stoughton, 1997.

Hackman, Richard J. *Leading Teams: Setting the Stage for Great Performance*. Boston: Harvard Business School, 2002.

MacMillan, Pat. *The Performance Factor: Unlocking the Secrets of Teamwork*. Nashville: B&H, 2001.

Rainer, Thom S., and Jess W. Rainer. *The Millennials*. Nashville: B&H, 2011.
Waggoner, Brad J. "Effective Team Ministry." Unpublished Presentation, 2004.

Questions for Further Reflection

1. How can leadership teams be formed that will be strong enough to accomplish goals and tasks as well as maintain good morale and emotional health among its members?

2. How can cross-training team members prepare and build the future of the organization? What responsibility does the team leader bear in fostering an atmosphere of cross-training?

3. What safeguards can be put in place to keep the "compelling purpose" of the Christian organization/institution from drifting from its original mission?

4. How can the priorities of the three Cs of team building (character, chemistry, and competence) be nurtured so that all aspects of healthy team building remain balanced?

Endnotes

[1] J. Dennison, *Team Ministry: A Blueprint for Christian Leadership* (London: Hodder and Stoughton, 1997), 15.

[2] B. J. Waggoner, "Effective Team Ministry" (Unpublished Presentation, 2004).

[3] J. Collins, *Good to Great* (New York: HarperBusiness, 2001), 41.

[4] P. MacMillan, *The Performance Factor: Unlocking the Secrets of Teamwork* (Nashville: B&H, 2001), 23.

[5] R. J. Hackman, *Leading Teams: Setting the Stage for Great Performance* (Boston: Harvard Business School, 2002), 37–198.

[6] T. Rainer and J. W. Rainer, The *Millennials* (Nashville: B&H, 2011).

[7] S. Wieberg, "For Alabama, Nick Saban Has Been Worth Every Penny," *USA Today* (January 3, 2010): 1.

Chapter 12

From Peer to Manager

Carla Sanderson
Provost, Union University

The first class of America's 77 million baby boomers turned 65 in 2010, beginning what will be a 20-year demographic shift downward in the professional workforce in the United States. A deep loss of trust in leadership resulted from a decade of scandalous and greedy decision making at the top, causing many to question integrity and trustworthiness at every turn—in business, politics, health care, the church, and even education. The collapse of the banking industry late in the decade left investments, savings, and discretionary spending severely compromised for many individual Americans and the institutions and organizations they financially support.

Across our nation people express concern for the development of future leaders who will be prepared to take on the responsibility of leading institutions and organizations to pursue their purposes and express their core values. These factors lead us to the questions: Where will our leaders come from? Can we trust them? Can we afford the expense of lengthy national searches and competitive compensation packages?

Christian entities in particular are facing these intense challenges. Leadership for these organizations largely comes from the upper range of the baby boomer generation. Some are retiring, but all baby boomers are now somewhat removed from the next generation, young adults who are making life-setting choices about involvement in Christian organizations.

This is a crucial time of change in Christian organizations, a time to act wisely and boldly to avert a crisis in leadership. The purpose of this chapter is to suggest that the leadership needed in our Christian organizations may well be in place in the form of associate ministers, faculty, and staff and, by God's grace and help in selection and development, a generation of future leaders is poised to advance the global work of sharing the gospel through initiatives such as higher education, parachurch ministries, and mission organizations.

Prioritizing the Development of Future Leaders

It has been estimated that developing people comprises up to 40 percent of a leader's time and even more in emotional energy. The work of choosing and developing people well is seen in many successful businesses that are showcased today as models to study and emulate. Top leaders themselves devote serious time and attention to the task, as opposed to delegating leadership development to others.

In *Execution: The Discipline of Getting Things Done,* Bossidy and Charan describe many of the challenges.[1] Finding the right leaders is not about finding comfort zones; knowing, liking, and trusting candidates are important first steps, but finding evidence that someone is the right leader reaches beyond what is comfortable for the leader to what is best for the organization. Executives are wise to give attention to the verb form *execute*, appraising the situation and appointing individuals who have a proven track record of *getting things done.* Rather than getting sidetracked by people who talk a good game, pursue the doers, coming beside them to coach, educate, and train.

P. Drucker's work reinforces the need for time spent on people development. He has found effective executives investing hours of continuous and uninterrupted thought to decisions on people. "People-decisions are time-consuming. . . . People do not come in the proper size and shape for the tasks that have to be done. . . . People are always 'almost fits' at best. Therefore, to get the work done with people (and no other resource is available) requires lots of time, thought, and judgment."[2]

Investing in people for the sake of effective leadership in Christian work and service is a biblical imperative. We work and strive together, focused on the prize, running the race with endurance, iron sharpening iron, bearing one another in love because if we are to take ourselves seriously and advance the pursuit of becoming Christlike, and we must, nothing but excellence will do.

Looking for Leaders from Within

The particular focus of this chapter is to explore implications for tapping strong leadership potential from within our Christian organizations, to suggest what qualities senior leaders must look for in making new leadership appointments, and to offer insight to those transitioning from peer to manager in their effort to lead from within. The chapter is written out of experience with the Council of Christian Colleges and Universities in developing new chairs and deans for academic leadership but has application to others in similar roles in various organizations and entities. The focus is not just on the new leaders but also on his or her predecessor, senior leader, and former peers who will report to them in the new leadership role.

Finding leaders from within our communities is a grace-filled approach to building up the body of Christ and also a key strategy for success. In *Built to Last: Successful Habits of Visionary Companies,* J. Collins demonstrates that visionary companies realize the importance of preserving their core and therefore look inside their own doors to find and develop leaders to a greater degree than comparison companies. Collins attributes continuity in quality leadership, what he calls a "leadership continuity loop," as the distinguishing factor in setting companies apart as visionary.[3] Strong leadership development programs and ongoing succession planning initiatives put the best leaders on the biggest opportunities as opposed to the biggest problems. Even though much of Collins's study focuses on the chief executive officer, it stands to reason that the same benefit of leadership continuity translates to other leaders in the organization.

Specific to Christian institutions, our leaders must be thinking about the challenges of today and the next generation while acknowledging our past and its heritage for the good of alumni and donors. To the extent we can entrench our entities with leaders deeply committed to them, pursuing the age-old purposes and expressing the core values in timely and relevant ways to new people, we can do our part to preserve and strengthen what are beloved, worthy, and highly significant places.

Faculty members have historically served as the source of academic leadership in Christian colleges and by good design. One of ServiceMaster leader W. Pollard's leadership hallmarks is that the most important people in any organization are those closest to the customer.[4] Similarly, it is apropos to think of faculty in one-on-one interaction with students as the heartbeat of colleges and universities. Equipping and empowering faculty for leadership brings frontline knowledge and experience to bear on daily decision making ultimately aimed at the heart of the goal of every Christian college—excellence in Christ-centered teaching-learning-living.

Faculty members are uniquely prepared to lead. As graduate students involved in research, faculty finely hone the abilities to question, doubt, and identify falsehood; to search, test, and find new approaches. The dark side of these skills can result in cynicism and skepticism about the ways things are done in their colleges or universities. If left unchecked, such attitudes can and should impede a transition into leadership. Yet there are opportune times when faculty can be developed to combine their spirit of discovery, bent toward reexamining current wisdom, and keen understanding of student learning to bring strength to university administration.[5]

Serving on committees and *ad hoc* task teams with administrators can help equip faculty to understand better the university's core values, its culture, and the expectations for its future. Tireless service on a committee or project can provide indication to both faculty and administration of interest in and readiness for leadership. The combination of a faculty member's critical eye toward addressing the university's greatest opportunities and his or her deep understanding and appreciation for the university's context makes for an ideal approach to improving *status quo*. J. Maxwell notes in *Developing the Leaders Around You* that discontent with the status quo is often a signal to individuals and their leaders of a willingness to be different and take risks.[6] When a leader gets too comfortable with the *status quo*, it is time for transition; in the same way, when followers become restless with the *status quo*, it is perhaps time for them to consider leadership opportunities.

Leadership Qualities to Look For

A great wealth of research has been collected on what it takes to be a successful leader. J. Collins's work in *Good to Great* has provided a helpful and systematic way of leveling the progression of contribution individuals make from a basic level of productivity for the sake of the common good all the way to building greatness for an organization.[7] The following levels can be applied as a guide when finding leadership at various rungs in the organizational ladder.

Level 1: Highly Capable Individual. Makes productive contributions through talent, knowledge, skills, and good work habits.

Level 2: Contributing Team Member. Contributes individual capabilities to achievement of group objectives and works effectively with others in a group setting.

Level 3: Competent Manager. Organizes people and resources toward the effective and efficient pursuit of predetermined objectives.

Level 4: Effective Leader. Catalyzes commitment to and vigorous pursuit of a clear and compelling vision, simulating higher performance standards.

Level 5: Executive. Builds enduring greatness through a paradoxical blend of personal humility and professional will.

A fresh perspective on leadership capacity has been provided by Bennis and Thomas in *Leading for a Lifetime.* Matters of age, generation, gender, ethnicity, and race are disregarded; and four basic qualities are identified as universal principles for leaders: adaptive capacity, the ability to engage others through shared meaning, a distinctive voice, and unshakable integrity.[8]

Adaptive capacity is prioritized as the essential competence of leaders and is defined as having the critical skills and abilities to "understand context and to recognize and seize opportunities." Leaders are made from people who have experienced and adapted to life, its challenges and hardships, and have made good from their experiences. Their setbacks and difficulties have forced them to apply creativity to finding unconventional solutions to problems and to develop a capacity to thrive in situations of ambiguity and change with an eye on the desired goal. This ability is naturally transferred to other contexts through a process of socialization whereby good can come from difficult experiences not just at an individual level but at an organizational one.

The other three principles, engaging others, speaking with a distinctive voice, and unshakable integrity point to the fact that leadership is public. Effective leaders recruit others to a shared vision. Bennis and Thomas liken leadership to one of the performing arts where the leader is always called upon to project values, purpose, and meaning to followers.

"Stripped to its essentials, leadership involves just three things—a leader, followers, and a common goal."[9] Finding the best leaders within the organization will be finding flexibility, engagement, statesmanship, honesty, and nobility. We must not settle for less when looking to appoint and promote leaders in our Christian organizations. When in doubt, do not hire; keep looking.

On Promoting from Within: Considerations for the Predecessor

Finding a new leader is only the first step; creating the best environment possible for the leader's success comes next and can be greatly facilitated by careful and thoughtful succession planning on the part of the predecessor. When the new leader is making a transition from peer to manager, the predecessor's planning has added implications.

In *The Top Ten Mistakes Leaders Make* H. Finzel speaks boldly about leadership transitions, noting that the ideal is for the outgoing leader to prepare psychologically for the transition long before it happens. The tasks at hand for a healthy transition involve coming to terms with one's own dispensability, committing to have faith in the new leader for the good of the organization's future.[10]

When the outgoing leader has enjoyed a long and successful tenure, it is natural for members of the community to continue to turn to their former administrator for advice and consultation even if he or she is in a non-administrative position or gone from the organization altogether. It can also be the case that "the old guard" works to complicate the leadership transition. Predecessors are best advised politely to forgo petitions from their former colleagues; instead, they should champion a positive transition and then distance themselves, knowing that continued influence can be both intimidating and detrimental for the new leader.

On college campuses it is often the pattern for the predecessor to return to the teaching faculty following his leadership tenure. This will work only to the extent that the predecessor redefines his relationships across the campus community with great care and intentionality. Planning for a low-key first year is wise, where there are no committee assignments, and even physical presence is limited for a time. All too often the transition is not as straightforward as it should be. Transitioning out of leadership is hard work. For some it is the challenge of grieving the loss of personal investment and deep devotion to work and people developed over the course of a long career. Many people are blessed to have loved their work; to others it can be a matter of job security, fear of retirement, resistance to change, or a threat to self-worth.[11] Unfortunately in some situations the challenge comes from a lack of confidence in the successor.

Regardless of the challenges, transitions out of leadership must be deliberate, with the organization's best interest in mind, turning over responsibility and walking away in gracious humility as the final act of strong leadership. Finzel challenges outgoing leaders to see the transition as the ultimate completion of one's leadership, finishing well with a strong faith in the organization's future while acknowledging the future belongs to someone new. With great fanfare, the predecessor should affirm, support, mentor, and launch the successor into his or her new role.

Scripture gives us role models. Moses was a leader who held his position loosely, "in a humble grip."[12] Moses lived with an attitude of his own finitude and dispensability and blessed his successor Joshua, laying his hands on him as an act of affirmation and support. His doing so resulted in the Israelites' acceptance of Joshua as their new leader: "Joshua son of Nun was filled with the spirit of wisdom, because Moses had laid his hands on him. So the Israelites obeyed him and did as the Lord had commanded Moses" (Deut 34:9 HCSB).

Paul's successor was Timothy, whom he mentored and launched into the work of building the early church; Paul even charged Timothy to in turn find his own successors: "And what you have heard from me in the presence of many witnesses, commit to faithful men who will be able to teach others also" (2 Tim 2:2).

Equipping one's successor is perhaps the best way that the Lord can continue the good work He started in us. The work in us will not be completed until the day of Christ's return. We are to commit to those who will faithfully continue the work, knowing that none of us has the potential to complete it.

On Promoting from Within: Considerations for the Senior Leader

J. Collins' concept of people on a bus has quickly become a classic metaphor for how to move institutions forward. Making the right appointment significantly minimizes the problem of how to motivate and manage people. Yet the senior leader's involvement as encourager, facilitator, and coach is critical for the organization to navigate toward its goal. Collins promotes beginning with *who*, and then figuring out the *what* and the *where* as you go along, "getting the right people on the bus (and the wrong people off the bus) before you figure out where to drive it."[13]

Applied to Christian organizations, this concept means making sure you have the right Christ-centered individuals working within their areas of giftedness and then discovering together the specific means for expressing the organization's core values and achieving the mission you are pursuing. Spending time together in regular meetings and occasional retreat settings can bring into being a shared sense of direction for the organization.

Sharing the work and responsibility of leadership can lead to the formation of meaningful friendships, which seems also to be an indicator for success. Collins notes that teams in the most successful companies tended to become and remain friends for life. Experiencing the joy of sharing wins together as well as sharing the hardship that comes from crisis brings team members into friendship. Leaders working on highly effective teams frequently characterized such experiences as the high point of their lives,[14] going beyond mutual respect to lasting comradeship, working hard for the sake of advancing the other, clearly loving what they did because they loved who they did it with. Indeed it takes time for senior leaders to invest in new people on the leadership team, but doing so enlarges their potential and shows publically that you have confidence in them. The greatest gift a senior leader gives a new leader is an invitation to build a friendship that starts with respect and admiration for one another.

On Promoting from Within: Considerations for Moving from Peer to Manager

Making an informed decision to move into a leadership role within one's own organization is an exercise in honest and serious self-reflection wrought by prayer and meditation. Following are questions often raised by individuals encouraged toward leadership along with insights that can guide serious contemplation about moving forward.

Do I have what it takes? When approached about the possibility of considering a leadership appointment, a common first question in self-reflection is about aptitude for leadership. *Why me? What has prompted others to think of me as a leader?* Seeing yourself as others see you is sometimes difficult. What you do best is probably so easy and natural for you that you underestimate its value and the contribution your gifts can make. Leadership ability is acquired by applying natural strengths and working to develop new ones.

A more probing question is, *Am I resilient?* The adaptive capacity mentioned earlier as the prominent principle required for effective leadership is sometimes described as resiliency, the ability to improvise in the face of challenge. Resilient people have a steadfastness that accepts reality and a firm conviction, often buttressed by strongly held values.[15] Resilient leaders take responsibility and own the organization's challenges as their own, and they get other people to do the same. They are realistic people who know they may not always be able to accomplish what is fully required, but they are willing to give it their best effort, aware they may come up short or even experience failure, determined to do better the next time around.

In *The Resilience Factor* K. Reivich and A. Shatte identify traps to becoming a resilient leader, a list that can be helpful in identifying one's own level of resiliency. Nonresilient people jump to conclusions, magnify the negatives and minimize the positives, and see the world with tunnel vision. They are by nature likely to personalize, obsess, blow things out of proportion, or catastrophize where they dwell on adversity to the point of setting off a mental chain of disastrous events.[16] Leaders need to be cool headed, patient, positive, reasonable, and self-aware. Matthew 6:34 says, "Therefore don't worry about tomorrow, because tomorrow will worry about itself. Each day has enough trouble of its own." Resilient individuals have the ability to gain perspective and make decisions accordingly.

Can I do the work? Can I handle the pace? No doubt the pace of the work quickens for the administrator, and the number of tasks and duties becomes more varied. Where perhaps there was time for reflection and solitude before, the leader must transition from one responsibility to another quickly and effectively. In the face of conflict, immediate action is required to manage and minimize compounding variables.

What about crisis? It has been said that true leadership ability is best formed in the coals of adversity. Handling crises requires the leader's best—defining reality, having openness and candor, accepting uncertainty, sustaining confidence in your and others' ability to manage the challenge and lead your followers through. Leadership is both proactive and reactive and requires intense focus for long periods of time using finely honed skills in planning, decision making, communication, shared governance, and preservation of self and personal time.[17]

Most importantly for the Christian, *Do I have what it takes?* is a question about perspective. H. Heie, an academic statesman in Christian higher education, reminds us that we are not called to be successful; we are called to be faithful.[18] The question is not about being successful; the question is, *Can I be faithful?* Good leaders know that effective leadership is hard and that feelings of inadequacy are more frequent than feelings of completion and success. They know that being faithful takes dependence on a strong and powerful God and a commitment to faithfulness, staying the course in pursuit of their responsibilities. J. Iorg says in *The Painful Side of Leadership*, "Feeling inadequate to lead can be healthy if it deepens dependence on God. These feelings are only unhealthy when you use them as an excuse for not leading."[19]

What's so attractive about leadership? Do I even want to be a leader? Some people are reluctant to take on the responsibilities and consequences of leadership. By nature, some people are more comfortable working independently or as part of a team where collaboration and shared decision making are possible on a level playing field. For instance, many find great contentment in academic life in being the teacher in relationship with the learner for the humble and noble sake of advancing truth. By comparison, others feel great reticence toward placing themselves in a position to be criticized or even ridiculed for decisions that must be made and even greater reticence in being placed in what may be perceived as a self-promoting leadership spotlight.

Indeed you can easily find examples of arrogant leaders who abuse power in most unbecoming ways. And to be sure you know of examples of ruthless church or faculty members or others in Christian organizations who constantly question the leader's best judgment. The realities of fallenness are often readily apparent. Yet for some people becoming a leader is the full and proper use of one's talents. Refusing a leadership position in order to disassociate from unattractive examples of prideful leadership or as self-protection from the unpleasant consequences of having to make hard decisions may be an abuse of a different kind. Holding back on one's talents is at least misuse, if not abuse and disobedience.

Some people ask: "*Should I* want *to be a leader? Is wanting leadership prideful?*"

To be a leader isn't antithetical to Christian humility. Humility isn't self-abasement. Humility is appropriate self-appraisal, seeing yourself as God sees you. It's adopting God's perspective on what you are assigned to do. Being humble means you accept God's assignment and submit yourself for his service. If God has made you a leader, obedience requires you to accept the assignment. Doing God's will, God's way, leads to humility, not arrogance. This is true even if God calls you to a prominent leadership role.[20]

Eleanor Roosevelt is often credited with saying, "You gain strength, courage, and confidence by every experience in which you really stop to look fear in the face. You must do the thing you think you cannot do." Portraying a similar message, J. Ortberg authored, *If You Want to Walk on Water, You've Got to Get Out of the Boat.* Like Peter, we are to develop ourselves through faith in a settled conviction that we must step out and do the thing we think we cannot do. And when we do, when we let go of the hold we place on our talents and yield them to God's original design and purpose, we find ourselves at the top of our game, walking in harmony with our Maker, indeed sensing His presence so realistically that we can step out on the water toward Him. The constant grind of leadership may not be attractive, but everything is attractive about using one's talents for the glory of God.

But would a leadership position be good for my family, my friendships, for me personally? A decision to lead is a decision to make sacrifices but not a decision to place work before family and friends. In the ordering of God's design on our lives, God is to be first, relationships second, work third. Time alone with God is a personal responsibility that gives meaning and purpose to everything else; it is our first duty. Marriage and parenting demand our relational best and must be a top priority every day; being in sustaining relationship with family and friends and holding membership in one's church and neighborhood bring joy and enrichment. Each demands our choosing to live an integrated life where home and work are in harmony and at peace in a Christ-centered life. Family must work together, first to consider whether to pursue leadership as an entire family decision and then to make sacrificial decisions for the sake of the call to leadership in our family's life. *Can sacrifice be good for my family?* Living out one's call through stewardship of talent is a good we owe God and an example we can share with others, especially our children.

While the impact of a move into leadership can be a shared family decision that prizes the leadership opportunity and strengthens commitment to one another, the impact can be the opposite on peer relationships at work. J. D. Rockefeller is often credited with saying, "A friendship founded upon business is superior to a business founded upon friendship." Even in grace-filled Christian organizations, significant strain on relationships with friends can form if left untended.

Obviously a shift in the balance of power occurs in relationships where a new leader is now managing former coworkers. Embracing a proper perspective on power is a good place to start when tending to important relationships. Leaders learn that real power is influencing others by supporting their ability to accomplish their work for God, and any other use of power is disingenuous. What all people want, including former coworkers, is a sense that they are valued, a sense of community where they belong to something special, and a sense of personal purpose. When these needs are met, people feel fulfilled in their roles and empowered to join the team and go to work.

Established friendships will necessarily change, and concessions need to be made to create a new leader-follower relationship separate from the existing friendship. In highly significant relationships, start with a conversation about taking the job before it is a done deal, asking the friend to give insights on concessions that will need to be made in the nature of the friendship. The goal is to avoid a double standard and even the appearance of one, separating a relationship of equals as friends from the different relationship that will be required of the two of you when you become the leader. This investment in conversation acknowledges the importance of the friendship that has been built but is faithful to the requirement that friends will be treated the same and held to the same objective standards as everyone else.[21] A true friend will commit to doing his or her part to become someone different in your life. As a tip for friends, this list of do's and don'ts might be helpful when your friend becomes your boss.

Tips for the New Leader's Friends: Do's and Don'ts

When building a strong working relationship on the foundation of an existing friendship:

Don'ts

- Don't expect too much. Things cannot be the same. Your friend faces new pressures, problems, demands, and divisions as leader.
- Don't attempt to tell your coworkers what the boss thinks or what they can expect from him or her.
- Don't let others use you to get their messages across to the boss.

Do's

- Do respect your friend's position. Show appropriate deference in public, refraining from familiar banter between the two of you.
- Do be a good wingman. When in public meetings, offer subtle support by asking questions and inserting comments that help sustain a positive, productive tone.

- Do step up. Show you can handle a greater share of responsibility and leadership in the friendship in spite of new boundaries. Be proactive and take initiative.[22]

Keen attention must be given to public perception about established friendships in light of an appearance of favoritism and unfair treatment of friends, even when none exists. Avoiding the appearance of impropriety will require that the leader curtail connections with friends in the workplace, setting up boundaries such as limits on time spent together during the workday. The goal is to avoid the possibility of assumptions, never having to defend an innocent situation. Perhaps the best assessment is to put yourself in your employees' shoes and ask yourself, "Would this action make me feel uncomfortable or cause me to worry about favoritism?" Acknowledge up front that some friendships will not stay the same, and some may not last.

The threat of impropriety when hiring friends must also be taken into consideration for the same reasons. Acknowledge that it will be difficult to evaluate a friend's true fit for a position because of the threat of bias and forgone assumptions. For instance, one of the goals in an interview is to see if you can establish rapport with the candidate, to determine if you have a shared trust and shared values. When interviewing a friend for a job, trust and positive feelings already exist. You may then overgeneralize his or her suitability for the specific requirements of the job and fit as a member of your team.

At the same time, peer support in the leadership role is essential; having friends in the workplace is a source of encouragement, support, and joy. The time of transition can be unsettling as old friendships change and the search for new ones begins. Prioritize the development of new peer friendships; consider a peer mentor relationship. Find people to share the journey, choosing those who will challenge and push you toward excellence and who will hold you accountable to your family and friend priorities, to taking good care of yourself personally and to reach your ultimate leadership potential. When you find no possibilities for such relationships within your organization, network to find a peer in someone external. You may find peer mentoring programs in several national councils and associations to facilitate networking and friendship building.

Is this opportunity a calling on my life? The definitions of *vocation* (*vocatio*) and *calling* are interchangeable; stated most eloquently *vocatio* is where our greatest passions meet the world's greatest needs. Perhaps you have previously discounted that definition as an overstatement, as Pollyanna thinking. If so, please think again.

God has placed stirrings within us so that we will be moved through His strength and power to take up ministry and serve in building His kingdom. *Are you being moved where you are?* It may be more comfortable to find a groove, fit yourself in it, and sit tight with what you are accustomed to and what you feel you have control over. That may be right for you. But if some people are honest, they are bothered with stirring notions of restlessness from time to time. Their thinking wanders with visions of change and betterment for the organizations where they serve. In these moments the question of calling must be addressed.

Leadership roles are 100 percent guaranteed to provide moving experiences. They are filled with decisions, interactions, and opportunities that are new every morning. They are roles where you can turn restlessness into action aimed at change and betterment. Finding your calling is finding a place and a role where you have a chance to advance what you care about most deeply in relation to the mission and purpose of your place of service.

Some may read that last sentence and determine they have found their proper place, and that may be so. But before saying no to leadership, consider the power of multiplication and the matter of impact. We are all placed on a continuum of influence in our work. A faculty member's influence, for instance, is teaching, listening, nurturing, and understanding. A leader's influence is enlarging, navigating, connecting, empowering, and reproducing. Both the faculty member and the leader share a passion for excellence in teaching; but through the power of multiplication, the leader has the greatest opportunity to make the greatest impact for progress. Leadership is stewardship of one's influence in the lives of others to bring about strength, growth, and excellence.

An obvious next question then is: *Am I called to a life of influence over these people in this place where I am?* J. Collins has found that the most satisfied leaders in retirement were in organizations where they had at the most basic level a strong sense of fit with the organization's values and mission and where they had made a conscious decision to perform really well and develop the skills needed to progress within that same organization over the course of a career.[23] Much can be said for holding membership in community with others over time, experiencing life together, choosing to stay in one place across time. Company loyalty does not have to be a thing of the past. The goal is to be able to look back in retirement on the organization where you served and be proud to say, "That's where I worked."

Also consider whether the senior leader over you will allow you to exercise your call in the organization and help develop you to do your best. Someone once suggested that if you have a choice, always work for either the best or the worst boss, because from the good ones you learn what to do and from the bad ones you learn what not to do. From those who are mediocre, you learn practically nothing. Someone else also once said that association with the best cools affection for the mediocre. It is far better to work for a leader who is the best, one who will bring out the best in you, who will come alongside you as coach to bring out the best for the organization. For that to happen, you need a synergy between the two of you where your skill sets are complementary rather than cookie-cutter. Participating in a deliberate process for determining strengths and patterns is a helpful activity toward this end.

Ultimately, however, the determination of calling may be more about the people who you will influence than those who will influence you. This chapter began with a focus on the importance of the leader's role in people development. When considering a leadership position, we must determine our commitment to others.

The leader is to maintain hopefulness about the institution and lead others to believe in a positive future. Any notions of skepticism must be abandoned and replaced with a commitment to convey the belief that the institution is becoming better and stronger despite the challenges and small setbacks that come. R. Palm observes that "optimism, even undue optimism by administrators, is essential for success." The leader's job is keeping hope alive by sharing possibilities through a positive and optimistic outlook. "To be accused of being a Pollyanna in administration is not all bad."[24] There is nothing Pollyannaish about portraying optimism when the leader then goes to work with a stubborn drive to make good on his or her word. It requires great patience, keen planning, and a tough minded stick-to-itiveness to keep the fires of hope kindled.

A call into leadership is a call to role modeling and talent management, motivating and inspiring others to achieve a higher level of performance over time. Driven by visions of change and betterment, leaders realize that the way to seeing their passions become reality is through the hands-on work of influencing the effectiveness and productivity of others within their sphere of influence.

What would I do to get started? What would be my first steps? The same universal principles applied to finding the best leader can be applied to leading in the best way: maximizing adaptive capacity, engaging others through shared meaning, establishing a distinctive voice, and acting with unshakable integrity.

Maximizing Adaptive Capacity

- Fully and completely adapt to the organization by memorizing the mission statement if you have not already done so, operationalizing the core values into a plan of action for your leadership.
- Focus first on the important and most appropriate priorities that constitute the life and work of the organization and adapt your personal agenda accordingly.
- Adapt to the new pace of administrative life by establishing a system to manage workload priorities.

  For filers: Color-coded paper files or computer-based electronic files.
  For pilers: Designated desktop piles for categories
  Prioritize files or piles: Today/Immediately, ASAP, Capable of Deferment, or Critical, Important, Routine

- Build capacity for stress. Prioritize attention to the objective (reality) and minimize attention to the subjective (what ifs). Your being overwhelmed is not good news.
- Adapt your day when conflict arises. Handle conflict early and decisively.
- Surmount criticism or pointed attacks from others. Don't take it personally and don't retaliate. Never retaliate. Hesitate. Do not push the send button. Sleep on it. You cannot unsay a cruel word.
- Seek forbearance. A stronger word than patience, *forbearance* is a fruit of the Spirit and grows only under duress from prolonged pressure, tension, or difficulty (Gal 5:22). Forbearance comes when you endure and mature.[25]

Engaging Others Through Shared Meaning

- Get to know the people on your team. Ask the fundamental moral questions. Understand personal values and ideas. Seek to interpret their perspective on leadership transition. Construct meaning out of the input given.

• Give context to others. Establish and then share an understanding of the context for your leadership given the context of their meaning.

• Realize that engaging others means taking care of them. Avoid the development of a paternalistic relationship by promoting the development of servanthood. Embrace working for them and not the other way around.

• Share your life as a role model for others. Share your struggles, not just your successes, but take care to share more successes than struggles. (As a matter of integrity, share only your struggles, never anyone else's.)[26]

A Distinctive Voice

• Align your voice with that of the senior leadership of the organization. Be willing to align your priorities so that your voice echoes that of the top administration. Always give deference to the senior leader's voice as the spokesperson for the organization.

• Be the voice of a leader, an energizer, an envoy, an intellectual. Promote and immobilize values by sounding like a leader.

• Choose a worthy cause, distinctive to you, that advances the organization's mission. With distinction promote your cause. Assert and reassert the vision in appropriate settings.

• Voice information, not just vision. Remember this corollary: "In the absence of information, people will make it up." People have a low tolerance for uncertainty. They want to know who, what, when, where, and why.[27]

• Understand that everything you say (and do) will come under close scrutiny. People will remember everything you say long after you will. Leaders are always on display. Strive to be the kind of exemplar who serves your organization well.

• Build broad relationships through which to share your voice. Market your organization wherever you are. Raise funds for it. Put forth positive press. Manage public relations in your area of responsibility.

• Herald good news. No matter how dire circumstances may seem, Christians always have good news. Therefore, always be ready to share the hope you have in Jesus Christ and the work of building His kingdom through your organization.

Unshakable Integrity

- Integrity is established in the small things. It is not determined by circumstances and is not based on credentials. It is about honesty, reliability, and confidentiality. Decide ahead of time that you don't have a price. Do what you should do before doing what you want to do.
- Major on confidentiality. Letting the cat out of the bag is a whole lot easier than putting it back in.
- Ask the fairness question. Treating others equitably is an expectation placed on every leader.
- Stay away from the rumor mill. A leader cannot become tangled up in the affairs of others. Strike a balance between being informed and being overly involved. Maintaining objectivity and foregoing any tendency toward biases is a must.
- Stick to nepotism policies. You cannot with integrity make exceptions for some and not for others. Nothing is more painful than being in the middle of conflict involving family members.
- Claim steadfastness. Acting in a consistent, reliable, and prudent manner through trials and tribulations is an act of integrity. Always be predictable to do the right thing, responding patiently with confidence and poise.
- Display courage and patience. Leadership is about making tough choices through a careful process of fact finding, a process that includes bringing biblical standards to bear on the decision. People will come to respect the process even if they disagree with the decision.
- Trust trumps many things. The sign of a healthy organization is when the leader takes a stand on something and everyone actually believes him or her without any question. A leader must set the conditions of trust.
- Strive to deepen the reverence for your organization. With an eye keenly focused on advancing the organization, work relentlessly to make it look good by always doing good.

Leading our organizations the best way is learning the way of Christ. The ultimate question for consideration about a move toward leadership is, *What does the Lord require?* Our calling has been established; it is to "contend for the faith that was delivered to the saints" (Jude 3 HCSB). Our role model is clearly known. We are to become like Christ.

The opportunity to serve others through a leadership role can develop us toward Christlikeness. As hard as it is to fathom, we are designed with the potential to be like Him. In *The Cost of Discipleship,* Bonhoeffer reminds us that because Christ lives His life in us, we too can "walk even as he walked" (1 John 2:6 KJV), do as He has done (John 13:15), love as He has loved (John 13:34; 15:12; Eph 5:2), forgive as He forgave (Col 3:13), have "this mind, which was also in Christ Jesus" (Phil 2:5 KJV). Ultimately, we are enabled to do the work we are called to do when we model our lives on His.[28]

Resources for Further Study

Bennis, Warren, and Robert Thomas. *Leading for a Lifetime.* Cambridge, MA: Harvard Business School, 2007.

Bossidy, Larry, and Ram Charan. *Execution: The Discipline of Getting Things Done.* New York: Crown, 2002.

Collins, James C., and Jerry I. Porras. *Built to Last: Successful Habits of Visionary Companies.* New York: HarperCollins, 1996.

Drucker, Peter F. *The Effective Executive.* New York: HarperCollins, 1966.

Finzel, Hans. *The Top Ten Mistakes Leaders Make.* Wheaton: Victor, 1994.

Gunn, Robert W., and Betsy R. Gullickson. "When Your Friend Becomes Your Boss." *Strategic Finance,* February 2006.

Iorg, Jeff. *The Painful Side of Leadership.* Nashville: B&H, 2009.

Palm, Risa. "Perspectives from the Dark Side: The Career Transition from Faculty to Administrator." *New Directions for Higher Education Series* 134. Wiley Periodicals. Summer 2006.

Reivich, Karen, and Andrew Shatte. *The Resilience Factor.* New York: Broadway, 2002.

Strathe, Marlene, and Vicki W. Wilson. "Academic Leadership: The Pathway to and From." *New Directions for Higher Education Series* 134. Wiley Periodicals. Summer 2006.

Questions for Further Reflection

1. Moving into leadership is a life-changing decision. What specific steps can you take in discerning your interest in and fit for a new position?

2. What lessons can you draw from pervious life experiences that have taught you adaptive ability? How can you apply those lessons to becoming a good leader?

3. Leadership is about engaging people for change. Think back on individuals in your life who have led you toward growth. What did they do? How did you respond? What can you learn from them about engaging others?

4. Describe the leadership traits of a respected leader who has retired or is near the end of his or her career. Describe the traits of someone who has assumed a leadership position early in his or her career. What lessons can you learn from each that might give shape to the development of your own leadership?

5. Choose a leader you admire who has moved from a peer position to a leadership position within the same organization. What are the top three qualities you admire most in the leader? Relate how these qualities likely contributed to the leader's ability to transition from coworker to leader.

6. Complementary gifts are essential for highly successful teams whereby job responsibilities are aligned with giftedness. How does your leadership team ensure that the right people are doing the job they are most gifted to do?

Endnotes

[1] L. Bossidy and R. Charan, *Execution: The Discipline of Getting Things Done* (New York: Crown, 2002).

[2] P. F. Drucker, *The Effective Executive* (New York: HarperCollins, 1966, 1967).

[3] J. C. Collins and J. I. Porras, *Built to Last: Successful Habits of Visionary Companies* (New York: HarperCollins Publisher, 1994).

[4] W. C. Pollard, *The Soul of the Firm* (New York: HarperCollins, 1996).

[5] R. Palm, "Perspectives from the Dark Side: The Career Transition from Faculty to Administrator," *New Directions for Higher Education* 134, Wiley Periodicals (Summer 2006).

[6] J. C. Maxwell, *Developing the Leaders Around You: How to Help Others Reach Their Full Potential* (Nashville: Thomas Nelson, 1995).

[7] J. Collins, *Good to Great: Why Some Companies Make the Leap . . . and Others Don't* (New York: HarperCollins, 2001).

[8] W. Bennis and R. Thomas, *Leading for a Lifetime* (Cambridge, MA: Harvard Business School Publishing Corporation, 2007).

[9] Ibid.

[10] H. Finzel, *The Top Ten Mistakes Leaders Make* (Wheaton: Victor Books, 1994).

[11] Ibid.

[12] Ibid.

[13] Collins, *Good to Great*.

[14] Ibid.

[15] B. J. Avolio and F. Luthrans, *The High Impact Leader* (New York: McGraw Hill, 2006).

[16] K. Reivich and A. Shatte, *The Resilience Factor* (New York: Broadway Books, 2002).

[17] M. I. Strathe and V. W. Wilson. "Academic Leadership: The Pathway to and From," *New Directions for Higher Education* 134, Wiley Periodicals (Summer 2006).

[18] H. Heie, *Learning to Listen, Ready to Talk* (New York: Universe, 2007).

[19] J. Iorg, *The Painful Side of Leadership: Moving Forward Even When It Hurts* (Nashville: B&H, 2009).

[20] Ibid.

[21] J. Janove, "FOB: Friend of Boss," *HR Magazine* (June 2005).

[22] R. W. Gunn and B. R. Gullickson, "When Your Friend Becomes Your Boss," *Strategic Finance* (February 2006).

[23] See Collins and Porras, *Built to Last.*

[24] R. Palm, "Perspectives from the Dark Side: The Career Transition from Faculty to Administrator," *New Directions for Higher Education* 134, Wiley Periodicals (Summer 2006).

[25] See Iorg, *The Painful Side of Leadership.*

[26] Ibid.

[27] Ibid.

[28] See D. Bonhoeffer, *The Cost of Discipleship* (New York: Simon & Schuster, 1959).

Chapter 13

EMPLOYEE RELATIONS IN A GRACE-FILLED COMMUNITY

Philip W. Eaton
President, Seattle Pacific University

I have this dream that people will look in on my organization, in my case a Christian university, and say, "Wow, those people know how to get along. They seem to work together so well, and they get the job done. They know how to collaborate, cooperate, across the lines of organizational structure. They seem to have less need to protect turf. They get the purpose, identity, and vision for the institution, to be sure; but remarkably they also treat one another with kindness and care and respect as they carry out the goals of the organization." In fact, these imaginary folks might say, "That organization is filled with grace. Those people have shaped a *community of grace*, and it works!"

The Big Dream: Those People Know How to Get Along!

Well, that's my dream. That's what I hope people might say about the organization I lead. Idealistic? To be sure. Doable? I certainly hope so. While we are always falling short of the mark, I think something like this must be the high calling of every Christian leader. *Building communities of grace is at the heart of what Christian leadership is all about.* It is in our DNA. Scripture provides the foundation for such a vision. It is deep in the roots of Christian history, modeled over and over again by Christian leaders throughout time.

And here's my hunch: If our organizations are operating in this way, as communities of grace, I can almost guarantee we will be effective in carrying out the purpose of the organization, fulfilling our mission and reaching our shared goals. And, most importantly, I also believe that people within the organization will flourish, nurturing their individual gifts and investing those gifts in the goals of common vision. Those are two huge goals for any leader, and I have learned out of long experience that the best way, perhaps the only way, to achieve these essential goals is *to imagine our organizations as communities of grace*. That's what I want to talk about in this chapter.

I know all of this may sound a bit softheaded in our day, a bit mushy perhaps, especially given our current climate of leadership. The culture of our day presses us to lead in ways dramatically different from the building of such communities of grace. We are asked to place an emphasis on extreme forms of individualism, for example, where we all try to get what we can: "Get real, people are people, and they are in it for themselves." Community is a thing of the past, we are told, and it has never really been a high value in America. We have come to believe that our organizations actually should foster conflict among individuals, believing this is the best way to get results. Or we are taught to lead with such a fierce focus on the bottom line that sometimes the individual and perhaps the organization itself seem expendable. It's all about results. Who cares what happens to the people or to the organization? I worry about the long-term sustainability of our institutions with cultural forces like these at work.

I am a big believer that people need vision to do their work well in our organizations. Organizations without clarity of vision and direction and purpose are not organizations that place high value on their people. People need vision. People will flounder without vision. They will grow restless and disgruntled if they do not understand the bigger purpose to which they are contributing. People need the chance to gather around a big and worthy idea, a big purpose that gives direction for the organization and thereby gives meaning and purpose to the lives of the people invested in that organization. Leaders must lead with fresh and compelling ideas. They must be constantly at work thinking and reading and reflecting and writing about ideas that matter to the organization. In the end, people respond to good and big ideas about the meaning of their work and the purpose of their organization.

But once that vision is articulated—a vision that is clear and compelling and meaningful—then the organization functions best; indeed the organization will flourish only when people are invited to *gather intentionally in community* around that vision. It is how we *intentionally gather in community around a compelling purpose* that is the work of Christian leaders. How do we pull this off? Are we given the tools as leaders for this essential charge of forming communities of grace? This is what we must foster in our organizations. This is what we must teach our young leaders to accomplish. This is what we must model as we carry out our own responsibilities as leaders. This is where Christian leaders can be right out on the leading edge of effective leadership for a culture that sees too often the damage and disaster of an extreme individualism run amok.

In his provocative book *The State of the University*, Duke Divinity School professor and scholar S. Hauerwas says this about the Christian university: "If Christians are people with an alternative history of judgments about what is true and good they cannot help but produce an alternative university."[1] As we think about Christian leadership for our time, I echo this sentiment heartily. For our purposes we will expand this notion to say something like this: "If Christian leaders embrace an alternative story of what is true and good and beautiful at the heart of our lives and our work, then we will find ourselves leading in profoundly alternative ways. We will build different kinds of organizations." And I am convinced, as we dig into the history of teaching from the Christian movement across time, we will indeed discover an alternative way of leading, and in the end we will find alternative kinds of organizations. And for me the key to building these alternative kinds of organizations is the formation of communities of grace. This is the position I hope to unfold in the pages ahead.

Two Models in My Life of Grace-Filled Leadership

I begin with a personal story that led me to this deep conviction about building communities of grace. When I first began my work as president of Seattle Pacific University, I invited two of the towering figures of leadership in my life to come and speak to my board of trustees during a planning retreat. Oh my, as I look back, how bold and brash of me to be hosting a planning retreat for my board as one of my first acts of leadership. And how presumptuous of me to invite these two great leaders. But I knew that working well with my board was critical to my effectiveness as a leader, and I knew that boards too seldom talk about their own effectiveness or about that crucial relationship between the board and the president.

And so I turned to two men who had worked together exceedingly well for a long time as board chair and president of one of our finest Christian organizations: the great Max De Pree, at that time just retired as CEO of the Fortune 500 company Herman Miller, and longtime chair of the board of trustees at Fuller Theological Seminary; and the amazing David Hubbard, who for 30 years as president of Fuller was one of the most thoughtful, evangelical Christian leaders of the late twentieth century. I was brash, indeed, to assume I could even invite these two giants in my life to join me as I launched my time as a leader. To my surprise, they agreed to come, and they talked with us that day about Christian leadership and the formation of effective Christian organizations. As it turned out, that day was somehow formative for me as a leader.

Before I began my work as president of Seattle Pacific, I had already devoured and underlined and reread De Pree's extraordinary books on leadership. I knew he would put an emphasis on taking care of people in the organization. And of course he did. If we take away anything from De Pree on leadership, it is that people matter; people matter hugely. In his beautiful book *Leadership Is an Art*, for example, De Pree says it is fundamental for leaders to "endorse a concept of persons." As Christians we should understand this well: We are profoundly informed in our lives and our work with a theology of persons. We are made in the image of God—what a radical, foundational notion to shape our commitments as leaders. That's the beginning point, this strong and abiding view of the immense value of people.

We must recognize as leaders that "each of us is needed," De Pree says, that everyone in the organization has something important to offer. We must "think about being abandoned to the strengths of others, of admitting that we cannot *know* or *do* everything."[2] Our job as leaders is to assist people to discover their gifts, their unique contribution to the organization, and to maximize the giving of their gifts. As we enter into this kind of engagement with our people, people have a chance to realize their potential and at the same time make a meaningful contribution to the success of the organization.

"The first responsibility of a leader," De Pree says with such freshness, "is to define reality. The last is to say thank you. In between the two, the leader must become a servant and a debtor."[3] This has been a huge statement for me over time in my work as a leader. Sometimes, in our arrogance, we get the defining-of-reality part right, and too often we think this is our chief and only role as leaders. I believe strongly that a leader must articulate compelling vision for the organization, but we must remember as well that our final task is to say thank you to the people who carry out that vision. We must adopt always a posture of gratitude. We should figure out how to say thank you every day, D. Winter, longtime president of Westmont College and one of my mentors, told me early on, advice I have not always followed faithfully. Christian leaders must never forget that people matter hugely.

But then Hubbard, having just retired as the longtime president of Fuller, brought another dimension into the discussion that day on how to lead effective organizations. Hubbard shared with our board a story about someone who came up to him at one of his retirement events and said, "You know, Dr. Hubbard, what you brought to Fuller was a note of *grace*. It seems as though Fuller has become a community that is full of grace. It was not always easy, I am sure, but it seems you have tried in every way to teach and model grace at Fuller." He then said to me and the board that day that he could imagine nothing more satisfying about his legacy at Fuller. Could it be that perhaps he left a *grace-filled community* for others to carry on into the future?

That comment hit me like a bolt of lightning. That language eventually became part of the mission of my institution: We say that "we seek to model grace-filled community." We must have a high view of the value of the people who serve our organizations, and we must assume a posture of gratitude for the gifts and contributions of our people. But we seek as well to build community, and the communities we build have a chance to be full of grace. People flourish in such communities. People come to understand their gifts better in such communities. Out of such communities organizations realize their purpose and meaning and effectiveness.

This seems so simple and clear and compelling, doesn't it? And yet I have learned through long experience it is not so easy. We have to think hard and work hard to bring grace into our organizations. We have to be intentional about that task. It is not easy because our highly individualized culture does not encourage community. It is not easy because it requires of us as leaders a genuine posture of gratitude and humility. When we think we are the big shots and lose our ability to say thank you, that is when the communities we lead begin to tear apart at the seams. And that is not good for people, and it is not good for the effectiveness of our organizations.

Building Communities of Grace: The Biblical Model for Christian Leaders

How then do we build communities of grace out of the organizations we have been entrusted to lead? And what do we actually mean by *grace*? If the culture draws us in different directions, where do we turn for teaching and encouragement in this alternative way of leading. So many of our organizations, even Christian organizations, even churches, reflect a culture that is highly politicized, polarized, decidedly individualized. It breaks my heart when people look into our Christian organizations and our churches and see nothing different from what they see in the broader culture. Is that the reputation we want? People at one another's throats? People protecting their territories and battling for turf? And when leaders think far too much of themselves, we create and foster an atmosphere of competitiveness and dissension. Is this acceptable? Is this Christian leadership? Is this the best way for our organizations to accomplish their tasks? Is this the biblical alternative to the ways of the culture? Is this the way we want to model the gospel of Jesus, the good news of grace and love and respect and kindness? And so, where do we turn as Christian leaders to learn to build communities of grace?

I propose, first of all, that we turn to our sacred Scriptures. Let's begin with the apostle Paul as he opens his great, first letter to the Corinthian church. We know from the text that Paul is responding to an earlier letter he had received from this scruffy group of Christians. Here they were, trying to discover how to live and do their work Christianly, right out there in the midst of a thriving, secular, pluralistic, sometimes decadent urban center of Corinth. The first thing we note here is that Christians don't get the luxury of forming their organizations separate from the swirl of the surrounding culture that pulls in so many different directions. Separatism is not an option for Christians or for our organizations. Let me say that as emphatically as I can: We've got to do this work in the mix, right out there on the leading edge of culture. We've got to engage that culture when it seeks to pull our organizations in directions that are contrary to the deepest convictions of our alternative tradition.

As we open 1 Corinthians, Paul is teaching, coaching, preaching, and leading this group in just these ways. They had discovered that engaging the culture of this prosperous, pluralist society with the gospel of Jesus Christ was hard work indeed. People were calling their message scandalous. Others thought it utterly foolish. And Paul discovered these Christians were fighting fiercely among themselves. They had become highly politicized, splintered, divided. They questioned authority: So, whose gospel are we following anyway? Why is it, Paul asks, that "each of you is saying, 'I am for Paul,' or 'I am for Apollos; 'I am for Cephas,' or 'I am for Christ'" (see 1 Cor 1:12).

Paul has caught a vision about the Christian movement throughout the world. We actually begin the letter with vision, the place where every leader must begin. From the opening lines we find Paul, as a leader, articulating a big idea, a vision that defines purpose and direction for Christians in the world. After his transforming experience on the road to Damascus, that utterly breathtaking encounter with the risen Lord, Paul woke up to a really big idea. He went through what New Testament scholar R. Hays calls a "conversion of the imagination." If we follow Paul's example of "how to read Scripture faithfully," Hays says, "the church's imagination will be converted to see both Scripture and the world in a radically new way."[4] How exciting. This is vision work. This is in part where the energies of the leader must reside.

And this is what happened to Paul. After the conversion of his heart, his imagination exploded with a big idea that the gospel of Jesus Christ must be shared for all the world. He discovered this amazing news that the gospel is good news for all of God's children everywhere. This is the new vision. We can no longer hoard and squander the promises of God within the ethnic confinements and restrictions we thought were necessary. And if we watch carefully what happens as Paul reads the Scriptures, with these new eyes, we find, Hays believes, "a way of reading that summons the reader to *an epistemological transformation, a conversion of the imagination.*"[5] The Scriptures provide the big ideas for Christians that by embracing God's message we will find vision for our organizations. We as Christian leaders must seek that conversion of the imagination that will spring loose big ideas for our organizations, ideas that can change the world through the power of the gospel.

As Paul opens the first letter to the Corinthians, this is what he is saying: "Catch the vision. Let your imagination be stretched to the limits. Followers of the new way are spreading out all over the world." In the wonderful opening sentence of this great book, Paul stacks clause upon clause into an exhilarating crescendo: We are "called to be his people, *along with all* who invoke the name of our Lord Jesus Christ *wherever they may be*—their Lord as well as ours." I love that. Here is the really big idea of a leader. We are taking this great transforming news all over the world. A movement is going on out there. Enlist yourselves in this grand purpose, this amazing, unfolding drama. You can actually be God's people in this great work. Imagine that! Use your individual gifts to get the job done. Align the purposes of your organizations with this really big idea: The gospel of Jesus Christ is changing the world.

But then, having set up the big vision, Paul launches into some stern scolding for the people of Corinth. Paul says essentially, "You've got to stop fighting with one another!" Don't you see? We've got a world to change. The movement of Christ is spreading everywhere, and you are fighting about whether you are of Paul or Apollos or Cephas or Christ? "Surely Christ has not been divided!" Don't you see? If we are going to be effective in our work of changing the world, "Now I urge you, brothers, in the name of our Lord Jesus Christ, that you all say the same thing, that there be no divisions among you, and that you be united with the same understanding and the same conviction" (1 Cor 1:10 HCSB).

Here is the point for our purposes: Paul clearly sees that the work of the Christian leader is to build communities of grace. It is the grace of our Lord Jesus Christ. This grace holds us together. This grace calls us to "complete unity of mind and thought" (v. 10). This is what it will take to accomplish our mission to reach across the globe. This is the only way we will change the world. We've got to come together intentionally. We've got to do our work in genuine, grace-filled community.

Paul is acutely aware of how much this cuts across the grain of his own culture. The message of the cross, outlined so powerfully later in the first chapter, is the radical notion that sits right at the heart of our communities of grace. This message calls us to gratitude and humility, the only way for communities to form in grace. Paul knows well this message is a scandal to the Jews and sheer foolishness to the Greeks, that the word of the cross is profoundly countercultural.

But Paul is as relentless as he is clear and compelling. We have a vision. We have indeed experienced a conversion of the imagination. We believe we are called to gather together as Christians to bring the good news into the world. That's the big idea. But the only way to accomplish that big vision is to submit ourselves in community of purpose and love and grace. We've got to drop the pretenses of our own individual importance. We've got to "agree among yourselves, and avoid divisions; let there be complete unity of mind and thought." Of course, as we know, there is no shortage in 1 Corinthians on the practical commitments to genuine community. The extraordinary thirteenth chapter contains some of the most profound teaching on love ever written, a kind of love, by the way, that is intended for more than individuals. It is a love we bring to our communities of grace.

We might also turn to Romans 12 as a rich and wonderful text to guide our way as Christian leaders in the formation of grace-filled communities. This chapter includes that familiar passage, of course, that every educator and Christian intellectual loves to quote about the need to "be transformed by the renewing of your minds" (v. 2 NIV). I too love this passage. I have carried it around with me in my travel notebook for years. Don't be conformed and shaped by the culture of this world, Paul says, but *be transformed*. Be utterly changed. Study and read and reflect and write—*renew your minds*.

But Paul then moves immediately, as he always does, from individual transformation into the huge value and importance of Christian community. Such transformation of the individual happens in community and for community. Transformation is not for us as individuals as an end in itself, important as that is. No, we are powerfully impacted by the communities in which we live and do our work, and we are called into the work of shaping those communities. And so Paul moves, after the marvelous notion of renewing our minds, into the language of community; and we get here some of the most important teaching ever written about how we gather together in Christian community, how we shape and build communities of grace where people may flourish.

Romans 12 talks about the model of the church community that brings with it human flourishing. We hear the influence on De Pree when Paul says, "Let us use the different gifts allotted to each of us by God's grace" (v. 6). As Christians using our gifts to serve Christ, we enhance our organizations. We must build our organizations out of an unmovable notion of the high and sacred worth that God gives each individual. Everyone has something to offer. This is where Christian leaders must begin, on this bedrock notion that each person has a gift to offer the organization.

But then we shift into Paul's ringing call to form Christian community. We must recognize the gifts of each individual, but we each are able to use our gifts meaningfully only when we build together supportive, encouraging, enabling, grace-filled communities.

Love must be without hypocrisy. Detest evil; cling to what is good. Show family affection to one another with brotherly love. Outdo one another in showing honor. Do not lack diligence; be fervent in spirit; serve the Lord. Rejoice in hope; be patient in affliction; be persistent in prayer. Share with the saints in their needs; pursue hospitality. Bless those who persecute you; bless and do not curse. Rejoice with those who rejoice; weep with those who weep. Be in agreement with one another. Do not be proud; instead, associate with the humble. Do not be wise in your own estimation. Do not repay anyone evil for evil. Try to do what is honorable in everyone's eyes. If possible, on your part, live at peace with everyone. (Rom 12:9–18 HCSB)

Can we imagine a better text to inform our understanding of the role of the Christian leader? This is the job we must tackle even as we recognize how much this runs against the grain of our own selfish human nature, against the grain of a culture that supports a radically individualized view of life.

What do you mean, Paul, to "esteem others more highly than yourself" (v. 10)? Do you really think that is possible in the world in which we live and build our organizations? What do you mean "rejoice with those who rejoice; weep with those who weep. Live in agreement with one another"? Impossible in the world in which we live, isn't it? Well, no, of course not, if we live our lives as Christians transformed by the renewing of our minds. We are different, from the inside out. But we will not complete Paul's circle until and unless we build Christian communities of grace and love. These are communities of human flourishing. These are communities that can change the world.

It takes hard work to shape such communities. It is radically counterculture, counterintuitive, at least in the terms the culture provides for us. This seems too soft for effective leadership, too mushy for effective organizations. And of course it can be too soft. I have always felt that modeling grace-filled community, as the mission of my university declares, is not simply to roll over in some kind of mushy kumbaya organizational culture. It is the hard and disciplined work of changing our lives, renewing our minds, developing the habits of our heart, looking at the work of the world with different eyes. It is the intentional work of calling people to Christian community formation, sometimes tough and exacting work, but I believe, guided by the scriptural witness, the only way to go about Christian leadership for our organizations.

Communities of Grace: The Christian Movement across Time

Scriptures are clear and emphatic about the call to build communities of grace. We enter those communities with the commitment to be transformed by the renewing of our minds. We pledge that we will develop the habits of the heart that bring us together in love, grace, kindness, and hospitality. This is our modeling for the world about the real way for organizations to operate effectively. As we align the vision of our organizations to the big idea that the gospel of Jesus Christ holds the power to change the world, we understand then that only through communities of grace will our vision be accomplished.

And so the Scriptures are clear on just these points of leadership. But what are the models we discover as we scan the history of our great Christian movement across time and across the globe. We find models of leadership that call for the building of communities of grace. We think here of the great Bonhoeffer in his marvelous reflection *Life Together*. Just as the forces of unspeakable evil press in on Bonhoeffer and his band of Christians in Nazi Germany, he calls on the people to rejoice in the profound gift of community. If we have any chance of resisting this evil, if we have any chance of changing this horrifying world, let us get on our knees and give thanks for Christian community. This is the only way for Christians to live in this complex and threatening world in which we find ourselves.

We might also think much farther back to the amazing work of Saint Benedict in the sixth century. Benedict, like Paul, apparently went through a powerful conversion experience; and with the new eyes of a transformed imagination, he looked out on a disintegrating Roman civilization. He saw all kinds of decadent and destructive behavior. He saw chaos and looming destruction. He was appalled and frightened. The barbarians had attacked and sacked Rome in 410 and again in 455, and Benedict decided the only hope was to withdraw from Roman society. The questions he asks in his extraordinary work *The Rule* are these: With chaos and confusion swirling all around, is it possible to imagine a community of order and health and grace that might counter the forces of disintegration? Is it possible to build a community that is life-giving, steady, and stable, withdrawn but reaching out to all the learning of the world? Is it possible that from this community of grace, centered so emphatically on Holy Scripture, that the world could become a better place?

Well, essentially, this is what happened. "Without a doubt," says J. Leclercq, one of the really fine scholars of monastic culture and theology, "the monasteries had at times exerted such great influence that all Christian society lived, more or less, in the light they diffused."[6] Imagine that out of what we perceive as such closed communities, seemingly separatist communities, such marginalized and powerless communities— imagine that enormous world-changing influence did indeed emerge. This is the power we find throughout history of these communities of grace.

If we look back at the seventeenth century, as some 700 Puritans landed on the ragged and fierce shores of New England in 1630, we find another model of Christian leadership in the figure of John Winthrop. What in the world was this venture all about? How in the world would this scruffy band accomplish the task for which they risked their lives? What was their vision? And what were the keys to accomplishing that vision?

As Winthrop began to articulate a vision for his people, a vision of economic opportunity, a vision of beginning again in fresh new ways, a vision of release from the grips of religious persecution, the stakes for Christian community formation were clearly high for this group of visionaries and settlers. Their success, their survival, depended on coming together in Christian community, each of them bringing their individual skills to the task but joining together in mutual appreciation and application of those individual gifts.

Look to the history of the church "in all ages," Winthrop said to his followers. What we find when the Christian movement is succeeding is "the sweet sympathy of affections which was in the members of this body one towards another." Winthrop was immensely concerned to "avoid shipwreck," but in order to do so he felt so strongly that

> we must entertain each other in brotherly affection, we must be willing to abridge ourselves of our superfluities, for the supply of other's necessities. We must uphold a familiar commerce together in all meekness, gentleness, patience, and liberality. We must delight in each other, make other's conditions our own, rejoice together, mourn together, labor and suffer together.

In other words, our mission depends on forming genuine communities of grace.

This is going to take some serious work on our part, Winthrop reminded his people often. How is it that we can make love a "habit in the soul"? We will only succeed "by framing these affections of love in the heart."

We are thinking boldly, no question about it. We are launching out on a hugely idealistic vision of settling a new land. We are trying to change the world. Can we do it? Will we succeed? What will it take to keep us on track? Only by committing ourselves to the arduous task, modeled throughout Christian history, modeled and mandated in the Scriptures we hold dear, of Christian community formation. Only by making grace-filled community the "habit in the soul," only by "framing these affections of love in the heart" will we succeed.

If we succeed, Winthrop concludes, "the Lord will be our God, and delight to dwell among us as His own people, and will command a blessing upon us in all our ways." If we do the hard work of forming such a community of love and grace, "He shall make us a praise and glory that men and women shall say of succeeding plantations, 'the Lord make it like that of New England.'" Others will look in on our experiment and see that it works. Others will look in and say, "Wow, those people know how to get along. They understand something special about how to live in a grace-filled community. Those people just might have a chance to change the world."

But then Winthrop also sees the consequences of failure: "For we must consider that *we shall be a city upon a hill*. The eyes of all people are upon us." If we fail to adopt such love and civility and kindness for one another; if we fail at our aspiration to model grace-filled community; if we fail to let the Scriptures transform the way we live and work and learn together, well, then, "we shall be made a story and by-word through the world."[7]

Indeed, Christian community is among the deepest of our commitments and aspirations as leaders. Of course with hindsight, we wish that Winthrop's imagination had included the native settlers of this land within the circle of his community, but at least he knew, without community, the new settlers would not succeed. To be sure, the world is watching. Community matters.

Conclusion: Let Us Be Radiant over the Goodness of the Lord

If I were to gather out of all we have said various practical principles that might guide our work as Christian leaders, our list might include at least these things: Christian leaders must lead with compelling vision. We must recognize the dignity and worth of our people. We must learn to say thank you every day. We must lead with utmost attention to integrity and honesty. We must create cultures of trust within our organizations. And though we have not focused on the really practical commitments, I say here we must pay our people fairly and generously, even as we establish orderly organizations. We could, of course, spend a great deal of time on each one of these practical principles. These are the things on which we must work daily. These are some of the practical principles on which communities of grace are built.

But finally, as is always the case, we turn to the poet to imagine and express what it is like to live and work in communities of grace. We bring in the poet because, as the great Old Testament scholar W. Brueggemann says, there is no other way "to speak about this *alternative life* wrought by God." We know surely what is required of us in practical terms, "but we do not know concretely enough to issue memos and blueprints. We know only enough to sing songs and speak poems. That, however, is enough. We stake our lives on such poems."[8]

If we ask what are the foundations, the basic premises, that anchor our communities of grace, it just may be that the poet has compelling answers. What are the promises, the expectations, for living and working in such communities? What must we pay attention to, as leaders, as we seek to build for our organizations these communities of grace? Perhaps the poet can speak with new language some final answers to these questions.

And so as we draw to conclusion these reflections on Christian leadership and the essential task of building communities of grace, let us turn to the great biblical poet Jeremiah. As we are well aware, Jeremiah was writing out of a cultural and historical context not promising at all for the people of God. The people faced exile, persecution, and a deep-seated hopelessness. Culture antithetical to the ways of God was intensely pressing in on the people. Jeremiah sternly called the people of God back to the path laid out for them, back to the old covenant that had shaped their lives and their identity. They had strayed from that path miserably, and the poet called them to renewed and reoriented commitment.

As Jeremiah spoke into this context, he called for a profoundly new recognition of God's ancient promise to make all things right in the end. This again is the vision work for the leader. The poet says clearly that we must do our work in the present in the light of a better, transformed, and flourishing future. Our job is to roll up our sleeves and make the world a better place in light of this promise. And where does this promise come from? This was God's promise to Abraham, of course. This is the promise fulfilled, and yet to be fulfilled supremely in Jesus Christ. We have hope that justice and reconciliation and comfort and human flourishing are on the way. "The glow that suffuses everything here is the dawn of an expected new day," says the great theologian of hope J. Moltmann.[9] We can see glimpses of that hope all around us, but clearly work is yet to be done.

But what does this hope and this promise look like? What does it feel like when we have come closer to realizing the promise of God for all of His children? Listen to the poet as he imagines such a vision.

> They will come and shout for joy on the heights of Zion;
> they will be radiant with joy because of the LORD's goodness,
> because of the grain, the new wine, the fresh oil,
> and because of the young of the flocks and herds.
> Their life will be like an irrigated garden,
> and they will no longer grow weak from hunger.
> Then the [young woman] will rejoice with dancing,
> while young and old men rejoice together.
> I will turn their mourning into joy, give them consolation,
> and bring happiness out of grief. (Jer 31:12–13 HCSB)

We can't help but "sing aloud" the joy that can be ours as we live and do our work in communities of grace. We cannot help ourselves. Our whole vision for such communities is grounded on a fundamental premise: The "goodness of the Lord" supports everything. We can count on the goodness of the Lord to make things right. We can lean on that promise, that assumption, the presupposition about the ways things are. We accept that presupposition on faith. We read the promises of God trustingly. We look at the world attentively, and we see there evidence of the "goodness of the Lord" cropping out. This is the source of our joy. This is what allows us to live lives of radiance. As Christians we are called to be "radiant over the goodness of the Lord." How exhilarating.

But notice this: This promise, this radiance, is not for us alone as individuals. As Brueggemann says, texts such as these do not only "concern our relationship with God, decisive as that is." This is not just about the promise for an individual life of comfort, rescue, and prosperity, though it is that as well. In presupposing the "goodness of the Lord," we declare that relationship to be strong and real and vibrant. And we must be reminded, over and over, in worship and prayer and study, of the goodness of the Lord.

But the vision of the biblical imagination is also about community. It is profoundly about communities of grace. Brueggemann notes that in texts such as these we find an

> anticipation of the restoration of public life, safe cities, caring communities, and secure streets. . . . There is anticipation of the restoration of personal and interpersonal life, happy families, domestic well-being and joy, shared food and delighted relation-ships. Both public and interpersonal life depend on the self-giving action of God who makes newness possible.[10]

This is where we get our vision as Christian leaders. These are the kinds of organizations we want to build. This is a vision of human flourishing, but it is a vision of life lived fully and exuberantly in community. We shall be radiant in community. In community we will find comfort and gladness and joy instead of mourning and sorrow.

This is God's promise. And this is why we are Christian leaders. We have the opportunity to participate in this promise. We have the chance to build these communities of grace and radiance and joy so that all of God's children might flourish. I find here the source, the foundation, for the high calling of Christian leadership. We are called indeed to the notion that people matter immensely in God's eyes. But we are called to the grand vision that people flourish best in communities of grace. Cutting against the grain of our culture of extreme individualism, we have a chance to model a different way, an alternative that is based on our Christian under-standing of what is true and good and beautiful. We have the chance to be out there on the cutting edge of what organizations are all about, how those organizations can most effectively fulfill their charge, how indeed people may flourish best. We have a chance, indeed, to lead in ways that are fresh, exciting, and effective by building for our organizations these communi-ties of grace. That's the high calling for the Christian leader.

Resources for Further Study

Bonhoeffer, Dietrich. *Life Together*. San Francisco: Harper, 1954.
Brueggemann, Walter. *Finally Comes the Poet*. Minneapolis: Fortress, 1989.
De Pree, Max. *Leadership Is an Art*. New York: Doubleday, 2004.
Dockery, David S. *Renewing Minds*. Nashville: B&H, 2008 (see chap. 7).
Hays, Richard. *The Conversion of the Imagination*. Grand Rapids: Eerdmans, 2005.

Questions for Further Reflection

1. What intentional ways can leaders develop communities of grace that stand in contrast to a culture that is "highly politicized, polarized, and decidedly individualized"?

2. How does the gospel radically change the vision of an entire institution to reflect the grace of God given to individuals and their relationship with one another?

3. How can a grace-filled community be built without compromising excellence and efficiency?

Endnotes

[1] See S. Hauerwas, *The State of the University: Academic Knowledges and the Knowledge of God* (Malden, MA: Wiley-Blackwell, 2007).

[2] M. De Pree, *Leadership Is an Art* (New York: Doubleday, 2004), 9.

[3] Ibid., 11.

[4] R. Hays, *The Conversion of the Imagination* (Grand Rapids: Eerdmans, 2005), viii.

[5] Ibid., x.

[6] J. Leclercq, *The Love of Learning and the Desire for God* (New York: Fordham University Press, 1982), 256.

[7] J. Winthrop, "A Model of Christian Charity," *Norton Anthology,* vol. 1, 23–24.

[8] W. Brueggemann, *Finally Comes the Poet* (Minneapolis: Fortress, 1989), 41.

[9] J. Moltmann, *The Theology of Hope*, trans. J. W. Leitch (London: SCM, revised 2002).

[10] Brueggemann, *Finally Comes the Poet*, 41.

Chapter 14

Engaging the Culture

Barry H. Corey
President, Biola University

M any good thinkers have written a good many words on the engagement of the Christian faith in the world, so much so that Christian leaders will not struggle to find ample resources to give the big picture of understanding the times through a thoroughly Christian framework. I am not one of those authors. Neither a theological scholar nor a cultural critic by training, I try to pay attention to thinkers wiser than I who deeply ponder worldview from a biblical perspective and make me aware of the intersection of Christian faith and culture. Most of these thinkers are engaged in the life of the university, the place of my vocational home.

Outside of the academy, there were those who taught me to understand the times through a thoroughly Christian framework, even if they could not articulate that framework, and whose worldview shaped my thinking. My father, a modestly educated Canadian cleric who followed Jesus intimately, taught me about the role of love in winning over the skeptic. The poor, with whom I lived during a "find myself" year in Bangladesh, helped me hone the discipline of living out my faith in the crucible of suffering. The fiery preachers with big voices under whose spell I sat as a boy, with their big Bibles and commanding voices, convinced me of their belief when they said, "Thus saith the Lord." There were others, too. Neighbors. Our children. Thoughtful friends. Sunday school teachers. Over the decades, I observed many extraordinary people—the notable and the not so—who helped me form my thoughts about the place of thinking Christianly and living Christianly. And I continue to watch and to learn to be Christian in my life as I relate to the public square of ideas or as I relate to my children's friends.

For those reading this book without the intellectual advantage of an advanced degree in systematic theology or the social sciences, welcome to the club. What I will attempt in these pages is to unpack how I, a guy who works in an office and is a follower of Christ, process Christian convictions in a broken world in a way that leads to courageous faith.

Theological and cultural engagement is not merely an academic exercise. For the follower of Christ, this is our reality. It is how Christians in the trenches of life are meant to think and act born out of their most fundamental beliefs. It comes down to simply this: When we see the world as a broken place God wants to redeem, we need to have the convictions to tether us to the ancient and timeless Christian truths and to stir in us the courage to act as voices of redemption.

Conviction without courage is hardly conviction. When I, a bit of a cynical undergraduate, was in college a long time ago, one of the young, hip philosophy professors was waxing eloquent on the theories of social altruism and public responsibility. A young coed who spent summers in the Bowery serving the indigent raised her hand. "You know where you're missing the point, Professor," she said. "You get the ideas, but you've never wiped the nose of a homeless man." Perhaps the professor *was* a courageous man. I don't know. But for a moment he got quiet. The class got quiet. For the rest of the hour, attention diverted from the professor's musings, and students sat convicted by a classmate who understood obedience to Christ far more than most. Convictions lead to courage and not just conversation.

A colleague of mine recently shared with me about the contemporary Christian philosopher, Paul Moser, who distinguishes between "two modes of being human," the discussion mode and the obedience mode. "An obedience mode responds to an authority by submission of the will to the authority's commands. A discussion mode responds with talk about questions, options, claims, and arguments." It causes me to wonder if many of us as Christians crave the discussion mode like an intellectual narcotic that keeps us happy and safe. Why are we not instead treading into the messy and more dangerous world of the obedience mode? Says Moser, "We undermine the authority of Jesus when we respond to him just with a discussion mode that does not include an obedience mode. We then treat him as something less than the Lord of heaven and earth. We reduce him to a philosophical interlocutor."[1]

Where I have been guilty beyond a reasonable doubt, like the lesson of that philosophy class, is in allowing the academy to shape only my worldview rather than also shape my actions. When asked to submit a chapter in this book, *Christian Leadership Essentials* and its importance in theological and cultural engagement, my own conscience was pricked as I thought about engagement, a word far more active than passive. Engagement presumes more than mulling over ideas or processing concepts, something I like to do. It implies activism, doing something that matters from a unifying worldview. Engagement means engaging.

To move from the discussion mode to the obedience mode takes more than the bravado of saying, "Just do it." Rather, I would say three important dimensions are essential to a Christian's healthy understanding of graciously engaging the challenges of the world from a theological core. The first dimension is grasping the reality and the scope of cultural brokenness and fragmentation. The second dimension is the importance of theological foundations and confessional commitments as our personal and collective moorings amid the cultural vertigo that follows brokenness. The third dimension is born out of our Christ-centered convictions, and that is to become so grasped by the world's brokenness that we are compelled out of courage to act. Context. Grounding. Action. These are the three dimensions Christian leaders need to understand as they develop a sustainable practice of engaging the culture Christianly.

Like a three-legged stool, things will tip absent one of these legs. If we understand the cultural brokenness and consider our theological foundations to address the challenge yet fail on the practice, we risk living in a bubble. If we never fully understand the cultural brokenness and yet grasp a mature biblical framework and go about being "doers of the word," we risk being irrelevant. If we grasp the cultural brokenness and then grasp at practical ways of addressing the challenge without building a biblical framework, we risk doing good for humanity's sake rather than the sake of glorifying God and drawing others to His redemptive love.

Grasping the World's Brokenness

I remember cuddling with my 10-year-old son, watching him watch *The Incredibles* one more time. At the movie's outset the superhero of superheroes, Mr. Incredible, comments on what is theologically true about a broken world: "No matter how many times you save the world, it always manages to get back in jeopardy again. Sometimes I just want it to stay saved, you know? For a little bit. I feel like the maid. 'I just cleaned up this mess. Can we keep it clean for ten minutes?'"

As generations pass, is the world becoming less of a broken place, or is it what one existential author calls a "cruel infinity loop, consist[ing] of dark highways stretching to the horizon"?[2] The so-called "Christian century" just completed was the most violent, exploitive, materialistic, and permissive century in history. Mr. Incredible had it right. "No matter how many times you save the world, it always manages to get back in jeopardy again."

The brokenness, however, is not limited to above-the-fold headlines in the *International Herald Tribune* or the *Los Angeles Times*. A few clicks on an Internet browser, and brokenness is there, tantalizing the Web surfer to gamble away money or ogle away purity. Brokenness is found in the drunk driver devastating a family or the public official paid off to approve a lucrative contract. Brokenness is found in the media pushing the limits of debauchery as the norm without regard for its effect on a susceptible culture. Brokenness is found among those who scoff at honesty by cheating on income tax returns or plagiarizing somebody else's content for sermons or term papers.

Brokenness is found when reconciliation is bypassed between racial groups, and we don't give a rip about the world of "the other." Brokenness is found in fragmented marriages, overworked husbands, and uncherished wives. It rears its head in cynicism. It skirts our awareness through ignorance. It numbs us with its ubiquitous presence. We don't have to look hard to find the broken dimensions of what God designed for good—like money, sex, food, art, music, words, leisure, marriage, family, vocation, and imagination.

If brokenness is perpetual and if we're no better today despite advancements in science and human understanding, why bother doing anything about it? This was the question the fundamentalists asked in the past century as they argued from a posture of separationism. "All we do to become involved and make a difference is nothing more than rearranging the deck chairs on the *Titanic*," they would say. If Jesus is coming at any moment and the wages of sin are irreversible, shouldn't our main concern be winning the lost and not involving ourselves in cultural redemption?

But others believed something *could* be done. The twentieth-century Evangelicals thought that perhaps, unlike their fundamentalist brothers and sisters, they should *refuse* to separate and instead roll up their sleeves and work to redeem the culture. This was the approach of many Evangelicals in the 1940s and 1950s, when walls of separation among Christian groups began to come down and Christian leaders recognized that their influence in the world would be greater together despite their theological or denominational differences. Harold John Ockenga, one of the prominent evangelical voices of the 1900s, together with many of his colleagues, abandoned the propensity to withdraw from the culture and its institutions, committing instead to the principle of infiltration. Ockenga was convinced that the reason for adopting such a strategy was to reform society, renew the church, return to intellectual respectability, and spread the gospel around the globe.[3]

The twenty-first century didn't start off much better than the twentieth, with 9/11 and its ensuing wars and bloodshed, with a greed-crippled economy, and with crazed entrepreneurs of human sex trafficking tearing the dignity from women and girls. So let's ask that question again. Why in the world should followers of Christ engage Christianly these challenges of the day when goodness doesn't seem to be gaining much traction? Is not the impact of brokenness too broad and deep, too big to conquer in our lifetime, or too diffused to get our hands around?

Christians are still asking, "Do we give up, or do we take over?" Rather than choosing between giving up or taking over based on our eschatology, we need to be the voices of hope as pilgrims, strangers, aliens, sojourners, or exiles—whatever biblical image works for you. The remnant of God's people in Babylon from Jeremiah 29 were called to "seek the shalom of the city and pray." So should we, as resident aliens called to be voices and activists of redemption, influencing the world for the cause of Christ.

Demolishing and tearing down the causes of brokenness, what the apostle Paul calls "strongholds," is incomplete unless there is also a building up and restoring of that which is broken. The good news is that the early Genesis story is filled with God responding to His creation at every stage by saying it was "good." Our world and our cultures are filled with that which is either good or once was. There *is* good, lots of it. A God of truth, beauty, goodness, and peace calls us to preserve and restore truth, beauty, goodness, and peace. Like Isaiah reminding God's people to be voices of redemption and hope, we are called to preserve the foundations that God established and to be repairers of those dimensions of His creation that are broken. "Some of you will rebuild the ancient ruins; you will restore the foundations laid long ago; you will be called the repairer of broken walls, the restorer of streets where people live" (Isa 58:12 HCSB).

Christians at their best recognize brokenness when they see it and then raise up the age-old foundations and restore the broken walls. One timeless indictment on God's people is found in the words of Jeremiah when he confronts prophets and priests alike for their cavalier attitudes about the problems of the day, in the culture and even in the church. Jeremiah confronts God's people for ignoring brokenness when he says:

> For from the least to the greatest of them,
> everyone is gaining profit unjustly.
> From prophet to priest,
> everyone deals falsely.
> They have treated My people's brokenness superficially,
> claiming: Peace, peace,
> when there is no peace. (Jer 6:13–14 HCSB)

Jeremiah comes down hard in these verses on those who are greedy for gain (read: narcissism) and say "Peace, Peace" when there is no peace. They say that everything is all right—shalom, all is well—when it's not. Culturally the moral, spiritual, family, and community lives of Jeremiah's audience were unraveling, but even the prophets and priests were saying, "Shalom. Don't worry. Forget about what Jeremiah is saying. He's an alarmist. What you are doing is culturally appropriate."

So Jeremiah says to the leaders among God's people, "Why aren't you speaking out against sin? Why are you saying, 'Shalom, God's peace dwells among us,' when there is no shalom? Don't you see the breakdown of moral law and families and the wholesale disregard for God's power and creation? Why have you stopped believing in the absolutes of God's law? Why do you shrug at God's authority and have a jaundiced view of the covenant and Scripture? Do you not see what's happening to yourselves? In a broken culture, you've become smug."

These are blunt, harsh words from the crying prophet. He's calling God's people, then and now, to be awakened and not numbed to the brokenness of the day. This means we aspire to restore and preserve all that God created as good, those age-old foundations: the arts and literature, the preservation of morality and decency, the protection of family and the nurturing of children, the stewarding of natural beauty and the acknowledgment that truth exists and that it is knowable. At the same time Christians need to be aware of the searing of conscience when they get to the place where they "no longer know how to blush" (Jer 8:12). Instead, obedience means we are convicted and blush at brokenness, in turn acting as restorers and preservers of that which is broken.

If we look at the problems as either too large to fix or too long to reverse, we'll be irresponsible by not doing what God expects of His followers. Even a cursory look at the people of God in the Old Testament is a stark reminder of the gradual atrophy that happens when the righteous do not step in and intervene with thoughtful solutions and muscular faith, undergirded by the work of the Holy Spirit. The people began to do what was right in their own eyes. As the ancient societies began to decay from selfishness gone rampant, God raised up holy kings who walked with integrity to remind a culture of its leisurely trends toward waywardness. God used the jeremiads of prophets to startle and spiritually revive a community that, over stretches of time, had lost its sense of decency by doing what was right in its own eyes.

The first dimension of cultural and theological engagement is becoming so aware of the world's brokenness and so convinced of the redeeming hope of the gospel that we individually and collectively resolve to fulfill our biblical mandate to preserve and restore that which is good. We do so because God is a God who created and called His creation good. When we are alarmed at cultural brokenness, it is best to know that full redemption will not be realized until the kingdom of God is fulfilled in Christ's coming. In the meantime, redeem the broken walls and raise up age-old foundations.

Understanding the context of brokenness is the starting point for Christians who need to be theologically engaged with the cultural issues of our day. And as we understand this context as women and men, colleges and universities, churches and organizations, it will drive us even deeper into grounding ourselves in a theological foundation.

The way forward, Timothy Keller explains, is to "discern the idols of our hearts and our culture." But he goes on to say that there must be more than that. "The only way to free ourselves from the destructive influence of counterfeit gods is to turn back to the true one. The living God, who revealed himself both at Mount Sinai and on the Cross, is the only Lord who, if you find him, can truly fulfill you, and, if you fail him, can truly forgive you."[4]

The Convictions of a Theological Core

When we recognize brokenness, our response should be to think about it in terms of knowing and being known by the living God and grasping His cosmic plan: God's good creation fell because of willful sin, and through the grace of redemption, God called us to restore that which is broken and to raise up age-old foundations. To do so, we need to understand the importance of timeless theological foundations and confessional commitments of our Christian faith. In *The Book of Common Prayer*, we pray God would grant us "even now, while we are placed among things that are passing away, to hold fast to those that shall endure." By nurturing our theological core and Christian worldview, our convictions will deepen and our efforts at repairing and restoring will be guided by a defining center. For the Christian the concept that our faith is an all-encompassing faith informs and affects all dimensions of our life. This faith-life integrative understanding is grounded in the Bible's claim that through Jesus "all things have been created through Him and for Him" (Col 1:16 HCSB).

In the Christian life the role of theology is to call and enable us to think from the center of all knowledge—to *know* that God is the Author of all truth. Followers of Christ are wise to begin asking the question, "How then should I live in a way that honors Christ and brings glory to God in the world of finance or law, medicine or politics, art or the media, the family or in nonprofit volunteering?" Do I have a center that informs all I do?

Harry Lewis, a former dean at Harvard University, asks hard questions of his university in his book *Excellence Without a Soul*. In it he discusses faculty turf wars and a lack of consensus on what constitutes an ideal Harvard graduate—factors he believes lead to a soulless academy. Lewis covers a wide range of what he perceives to be his university's shortcomings. Ultimately, he points his finger at the lack of a unifying ideal for Harvard, adrift from what was once a university with a soul. He worries about the state of the American university, lamenting that "universities have lost their sense of how to fit their problems into an encompassing educational mission."[5] The result is a curriculum with little coherent meaning, for the designers cannot agree on what an ideal graduate looks like.

Dean Lewis's point—that the university must have a common understanding of what it is about—is well taken and widely applicable beyond the university. What does it mean when we lack an all-encompassing mission, a soul that informs our motives, and an ideological core? Or for us as Christians, what happens if we lack a comprehensive Christ-centered worldview and an orthodox grasp of biblical doctrine?

My former boss at a seminary where I served for 16 years in New England was the inimitable Old Testament scholar Walter Kaiser. He would often reflect with concern about the undoing that happens when people and communities lose a conviction for a common understanding of Scripture's authority. Proverbs 29:18 is the pad from which he would often launch his compelling point. The writer of this proverb wrote, "Where there is no vision, the people are unrestrained, but happy is he who keeps the law" (NASB). The first part of this verse we happily print on annual report covers or strategic planning documents, since vision is so central to motivating a community forward. But the context of this verse, Professor Kaiser reminded me time and again, is not strategic planning but biblical fidelity. In essence, where there is no revelatory input of God's Word, the people come undone. They become unrestrained, unraveled. And if that is true, then the inverse ought also to be true. Where there *is* an input of God's Word, there is a coming together, a coherence and unifying understanding.

Fuller Seminary's Richard Mouw discusses how Carl F. H. Henry, one of the twentieth century's leading evangelical theologians and provocateurs (in the highest sense of the word), minced no words in his conviction that "the Bible is critically relevant to the whole of modern life and culture—the social-political arena included."[6] Biblical faithfulness is a nonnegotiable for Christians, and is one of the core characteristics of the evangelical tradition as it pertains to all of our lives. But biblical faithfulness does not mean getting sidetracked by the nonessentials of the faith, even when they are a precious dimension of a particular strand of Christianity.

Christians need to build a theological framework and embrace unifying confessional commitments as a foundation to implementing an action plan to address the brokenness of our world, be it hunger or the environment, illiteracy or disease, injustice or ignoring the marginalized. Most of all, Christians need a biblical framework to take on the greatest challenge of all: the spiritual blindness so many have to the truth that Jesus saves.

The cornerstone of the Evangelical movement from its starting point was an ineradicable belief in the authority of the Bible and a call for radical religious reform by going "back to the Bible" with contextual interpretations of the Old and New Testaments. The great challenge today for Christians is remaining authentically biblical in a culture that is increasingly uninterested in the Bible. A commitment to biblical fidelity is a virtue vital to the preservation of the Christian community.

Biblical interpretation, therefore, should not be delegated to those who believe the Bible speaks relatively to a culture and subjectively to its readers. This hermeneutic is dangerous for a Christian to embrace or even entertain. If there's one thing that never changes, it is the truth of God. Now more than ever, Christians need the staying power of deeply held biblical principles to shape them into godly and global leaders to impact the world for Christ.

In an increasingly pluralistic world, where brokenness abounds, we need the unifying and sense-making grounding of Scripture at our core. If we are to be thoughtful leaders in the places God calls us to serve, if we are to be equipped for good works empowered with a Christlike spirit of bringing the gospel to bear on all of life and culture, then we need a robust grounding in the Bible and its doctrinal truths. "All Scripture is God-breathed and is useful for teaching, rebuking, correcting and training in righteousness, so that the man of God may be thoroughly equipped for every good work" (2 Tim 3:16–17 NIV).

To get to the "every good work" part, Christians need to set aside time to study God's Word and to ask the question, "How does the Bible inform how I live my life and perceive others?" It means we grapple with the great truths of the Christian tradition and immerse ourselves in the writings of courageous thinkers over the centuries. We cannot be ahistorical, ignoring the great writers of the ages. Our orientation should be to reflect on the implications of Christian perspectives historically and contemporarily, for such reflection is more than just impacting moral judgments. It is about the spiritual discipline of glorifying God in all things. At our theological center we are a people and community marked by a belief in God as the source of all truth. If we get wobbly on the doctrine of Scripture, core underpinnings get knocked loose, and loosened convictions on biblical truth will be the early steps toward drift. Every kind of heterodoxy starts with recklessness on the subject of Scripture and a mischievous hermeneutic of the Bible. This takes an active discipline on our part, stirring us from a passive grasp of God's Word and toward its real-world implications on our daily lives.

Among many in today's rising generation, I see a return to the depths of wanting to know Scripture. So what if students are sitting on the floor with torn jeans, wild hair, and pierced noses? What gives me hope is when I see young Christians today who don't play fast and loose with Scripture, and they work hard to understand how God's Word is relevant to their culture. As Christians in the West, we are not alone. Young Christians around the world are taking the Bible more seriously. These believers—in places like the Sudan and Indonesia, Brazil and China—are standing resolutely on God's Word without equivocation, nor picking and choosing which parts to believe.

At this point my argument might be well served by an actual story from the Bible. In John 11, Lazarus, the one Jesus loves, dies. By the time Jesus arrives at the grave, Lazarus has been dead for four days. When Lazarus's sister Martha meets Jesus, He assures her, "I am the resurrection and the life. He who believes in me will live, even though he dies. . . . Do you believe this?" (v. 25). Martha answers saying all the right things. "I believe that you are the Christ, the Son of God, who was to come into the world" (v. 27 NIV). Martha responds with conviction in a creedlike confession that was theologically accurate and foundationally sound. Martha believes with conviction in the objective truths of Christ. But is that enough? Is *believing* the truth of God's Word enough? I don't think so.

Living the Practice of Courageous Action

Perhaps a few minutes later Jesus comes to Lazarus's tomb, a cave with a stone laid across the entrance. He says, "Take away the stone." "Lord," Martha responds, "there's a bad odor in there. He's been there four days." Then comes the signature statement of John 11 in verse 40, when Jesus says to Martha, "Didn't I tell you that if you believed you would see the glory of God?" (HCSB). Martha had just declared her *convictions* in the words of Christ, but He is now asking her to act on her *courage* in the power of Christ.

Jesus is not merely calling His listeners to believe with conviction that what He says is true. He is asking them to act with courage in ways that took them out of their zones of the familiar. It's one thing to state the propositional truth that Jesus is the resurrection and the life. It's another to move a stone entombing a dead man. We believe with conviction on that which is true. And we act with courage for that which we have yet to see. John 11:40 calls us to believe with conviction *and* to act with courage. Martha says all the right things, doesn't she? "I believe you are the son of God, the Messiah, the one who has come into the world."

When Jesus tells the people to "roll away the stone," calling on those around him to become people of action, she wasn't so quick to respond.

"But Lord," she says. "It's been four days. Lazarus's body is gonna smell!" Jesus is communicating to Martha that He is far more than a creedal concept to be understood or a theological thought to be mulled over. He wants to see His followers' convictions mobilized into courage, even if it pushes them outside their comfort zones.

And this is precisely what those around the tomb listening to Jesus do. Not sure what is going to happen, they obey and roll away the stone. Then when the dead man staggers out, they take off his grave clothes and let him go.

Jesus doesn't do this alone. He calls His followers to action as a community beyond their current frame of reference, and their actions take them into a place they never anticipated, even in their highest moments of faith. A.W. Tozer wrote, "The dynamic periods were those heroic times when God's people stirred themselves to do the Lord's bidding and went out fearlessly to carry His witness to the world. . . . The miracle of God went when and where His people went; it stayed when His people stopped." From the strength of our convictions, we are called to move forward in courage.

So here *we* are. We understand the context of our culture and that we are to be preservers and restorers of that which is good. We grapple with our biblical framework and confessional nonnegotiables and how to think Christianly about the major issues of our day. But this is nothing if we have not taken our faith to the next level and become activists for those virtues that deeply convict us. In this sense our idealism leads to activism.

We've come a long way toward this activism as Evangelicals over the past century. Christians are in positions of public leadership at the highest levels, unapologetic about their faith. God is renewing the church by raising up leaders who are committed to His Word, who welcome the empowering work of the Holy Spirit and who are winsome in their witness. Evangelicals continue to emerge as thought leaders and as scholars, winning the widest academic respectability. And the gospel is raging like wildfire in the global south, where the epicenter of Christianity is now moving.

So why is it, then, that there remains a growing negative perception of Christianity, as David Kinnaman argues in his book, *unChristian*?[7] I believe this perception remains because many Christian voices remain shrill and uncaring, communicating convictions in tones that are hard, edgy, and loveless.

Not long after I joined the team at Biola University, a pastor stopped me after a speaking engagement and spoke one sentence to me on the way out the door. "Spend more time as president focusing on what you are for than what you are against." That line nagged me, so I tracked him down days later and asked him to unpack those words. He wrote me and shared that those outside the church are not being won over by Evangelical lobs at one another or at the culture at large. The good pastor gave me some examples of noted leaders who gained renown with a polemic of attacking rather than by attracting. He believed, and I agree, that it's a new day for a winsome Christian witness without a diluted gospel message.

From our deep-seated convictions steeped in a theological foundation and confessional beliefs, we approach the brokenness of the world with neither defensiveness, aloofness, nor anger. To be responsible citizens and leaders of the communities God calls us to, we are neither elitist nor combative, more what we are for than against. Loving our enemies implies two realities. First, enemies are out to upend us. Second, we are to love them. Loving does not mean we're coy and hesitant about our beliefs lest we offend another. There is a battle for the soul and an enemy that wants nothing less than to take us down.

But the battle need not be violent.

When called to action before the burning bush, Moses unstrapped his laces and stood barefoot before the presence of God. Likewise, may we learn to take off our shoes and understand that leadership and servanthood are about going barefoot, not putting on steel-toed boots to kick the heresy out of our brother or Jesus into our culture. Going barefoot, with openness to "the other" is the position Jesus' disciples took as He washed their feet and taught them about being servants. We are called to engage the culture with a deep conviction in truth but in a way that is meek, loving, graceful, and with an attractive fragrance. We need a firm center and soft edges. No saber rattling. No fist shaking. No scowled conversations. No voice raising.

We engage the culture with temperate tones by serving alongside rather than throwing stones from pedestals. It's the "gentleness and respect" language the disciple Peter used about defending our faith through conversations with the others God places in our lives: "But set apart the Messiah as Lord in your hearts, and always be ready to give a defense to anyone who asks you for a reason for the hope that is in you. However, do this with gentleness and respect, keeping your conscience clear, so that when you are accused, those who denounce your Christian life will be put to shame" (1 Pet 3:15–16 HCSB).

For centuries Christians addressed the world's brokenness with a Christ-like love, and only in recent decades the approach of some Evangelicals turned acidic and angry. But just as some want to pick a fight, others err by leaving their convictions at the conversational door for the sake of niceness. The indictment goes both ways. Not long ago I made note of a Christian leader I heard discussing the Lutheran scholar Martin Marty who wrote in one of his books: "People today who are civil often don't have very strong convictions. And people who have strong convictions often are not often very civil." We need both.

I spend my days within an educational community where thousands of students have committed themselves to following Christ and making a difference in their world for the cause of the common good and to bearing witness to the redeeming love of Jesus, the only hope of the world. Not long ago I was having lunch with several students, including a sophomore named April. I asked her what typifies today's students at our university. She responded by telling me about a heist movie in which the characters are planning a big job in a casino vault and someone says, "It's a crazy idea. It will never work. When do we start?" April's insight embodied the beauty of today's idealism in the rising generation of Christian students who may see the world's greatest challenges as so unconquerable that people tell them: "Don't bother. It's a crazy idea. It'll never work." But these students are climbing onto our shoulders as future leaders asking, "When do we start?"

The future of Evangelicalism will look a lot different 10 and 20 years down the road. With a world that is more accessible, with a nation that is more ethnically diverse, with the interreligious dialogue more at our doorstep than ever, cultural complexities and global realities are part of our daily lives, whether we like it or not. In this messiness we need to relax, relate, and *not* let go of our deepest convictions that God so loved the world that He gave His one and only Son that whoever believes in Him will have everlasting life. We demonstrate the love of Jesus Christ without sacrificing our deepest convictions but in ways that recognize all of our brokenness. It means creating safe places in our lives for conversations with the other.

The face of Evangelicalism is changing, and what concerns the younger generation is not necessarily what concerns the older generation. In a conversation with a mature Christian leader, he reflected on the way in which the rising generation is seeing the world. As he looks at the church, he has concluded that "there is a new generation of passionate Christ-followers who have set their sights on different issues that are less about morality and politics, and more about Jesus and the world." He went on to say that "if we're going to effectively communicate to them, we have to understand their mindset and passions and, even more, realize that God may be speaking truth into the culture through their voice in more ways than we realize."

The Christian leaders of our past century, none perfect, tried to live lives faithful to their calling as gospel witnesses. This same zeal is embodying the emerging leaders who are creative and relational, entrepreneurial and global, winsome and gracious. May they also be deeply convicted by the authority of Scripture and make decisions radically tethered to the Word of God and the unfolding story of redemption through the blood of Christ that washes away all sin.

Conclusion

To impact the world for the cause of Christ is to recognize the problem of brokenness, to develop deep theological convictions which become our moorings, and then to live a life of gracious activism by restoring broken walls and raising up age-old foundations.

My father taught me that gracious activism should spring forth out of deep theological convictions. One otherwise uneventful conversation with him stands out in my life as a "lightbulb moment" of illumination. This is how I remember it.

It was January 1991, and I went for a walk with my father. The streets of Dhaka, Bangladesh, that morning were still quiet. We had walked together many different times in many different countries. But that morning, that walk, ignited in me something transformational as he wove into the fabric of my being a part of his life. I did not fully understand then, and am only beginning to grasp today, the full meaning of the early morning walk through the streets of Bangladesh.

I had been studying in that country for several months of my yearlong assignment when he and my mother paid me a visit. Each morning before breakfast he and I would walk together, catching up on all that was happening in each other's lives.

This particular morning was different. As our walk began, he started to share with me that in the 53 years since he began his pilgrimage with Jesus, much remained that he did not know about his faith. My father held no seminary degree. He never completed college. But as we walked, my father began to share with me what his life in Christ had taught him.

"And he that taketh not his cross, and followeth after me," he continued, recounting with me the words of Christ, "is not worthy of me. He that findeth his life shall lose it; and he that loseth his life for my sake shall find it. He that receiveth you receiveth me, and he that receiveth me receiveth him that sent me" (Matt 10:38–40 KJV).

Then he stopped talking for a few minutes, and I replayed the words of Christ he had just spoken. "He who receives you receives me, and he who receives me receives the one who sent me."

Knowing I was the student at that moment, I waited for the teacher to continue. My father said, "Barry, I don't fully understand what Jesus meant when He said, 'He who receives you receives Me, and he who receives Me receives the one who sent Me.' But this I do know: In everything I do I must make myself receivable to the people God places in my life. If the lives God intersects with mine lack the opportunity to receive me, how will they ever know the infinite love the Father has for them? I must live my life in a way that strangers, friends, aching, lonely, family . . . they receive me and receive through me the amazing love God alone authored."

We finished our walk in silence. Although he wanted only to share his heart with me as he had done so many times before and since, this thought was different. Maybe it was different because I had not heard his voice for many months. Maybe it was different because I was trying to make sense of my life in Christ while I lived among some of the world's poorest people. Maybe it was just different because I was ready to hear what he had to say.

As I have recalled that walk many times over these past years, I understand that moment as one ordained by God when I would receive a priceless gift. On the fetid streets of Bangladesh, the bedrock of his faith was being passed on to me, his son. It was as if he had traveled halfway around the world to find me and grant a truth to me about being receivable. Over the decades, I watched my father put himself in the position of being receivable by "the other," giving of himself without any need for recognition.

I remember when he hugged an Islamic man who serviced his car at a gas station. He asked an Eastern Orthodox cobbler to pray for him across the counter of his little store, and they clutched hands and prayed. He looked a Jewish furniture merchant in the eyes and told him, "I love you." Scores more stories like these I know I'll never hear. But the lesson I learned is that we, as followers of Christ—as universities, as scholars and as neighbors, as journeymen and as citizens—will be living biblically as we live receivably, making ourselves receivable to those who don't know the redeeming love of Christ.

The alchemy we need as Christians to impact the world for the cause of Christ is to recognize the problem of brokenness, develop within ourselves deep theological convictions which become our moorings, and live lives of gracious activism by raising up the age-old foundations by being restorers of broken walls.

"The anxiety and the defensiveness of the evangelical has begun to quiet down," Nicholas Wolterstorff writes, exhorting Christians in their activism. "So let us move on into the uncertainties of that most certain future of working for the coming of our Lord's kingdom of justice and peace and love."[8]

The world needs a generation of Christians with servants' hearts, who live lives of hope by seeing the world as a place God wants to redeem. The world needs a generation of Christians who believe it is a noble endeavor to live a life of bold faith, taking on challenges that demonstrate their commitment to a cause greater than themselves. May there be more Christians who speak courageously, compassionately, and humbly about the truth of God's Word to an increasingly skeptical generation.

May more Christians than ever understand the Word of God as the Bread of Life so they might clearly and passionately proclaim not only that there is truth but that Jesus Christ *is* the Truth. May there be those whose lives are led from a position of biblical strength and not from one of fear or intimidation. May we grasp what the apostle Paul means when he exhorts us, to "prepare . . . for works of service, so that the body of Christ may be built up" (Eph 4:12 NIV). And may we together make ourselves receivable as we take the gospel and proclaim it and teach it and live it and pray it toward the great spiritual renewal our world so desperately needs.

Resources for Further Study

Briner, Bob. *Roaring Lambs: A Gentle Plan to Radically Change Your World.* Grand Rapids: Zondervan, 2000.

Keller, Timothy. *Counterfeit Gods.* New York: Penguin, 2009.

Kinnaman, David, and Gabe Lyons. *unChristian: What a New Generation Really Thinks About Christianity . . . and Why It Matters.* Grand Rapids: Baker, 2007.

Kullberg, Kelly Monroe, and Lael Arrington. *A Faith and Culture Devotional: Daily Readings in Art, Science, and Life.* Grand Rapids: Zondervan, 2008.

Moreland, J. P. *The Kingdom Triangle: Recover the Christian Mind, Renovate the Soul, Restore the Spirit's Power.* Grand Rapids: Zondervan, 2007.

Stackhouse, John G., Jr. *Evangelical Landscapes: Facing Critical Issues of the Day.* Grand Rapids: Baker, 2002.

Turner, James. *Without God, Without Creed: The Origins of Unbelief in America.* Baltimore: Johns Hopkins University Press, 1985.

Willard, Dallas. *Knowing Christ Today.* New York: Harper Collins, 2009.

Wright, N. T. *Surprised by Hope: Rethinking Heaven, the Resurrection, and the Mission of the Church.* New York: Harper One, 2008.

Questions for Further Reflection

1. What are some of the areas of brokenness you see in your daily world, and how might you be a voice of redemption into that brokenness?

2. How does the Bible inform the way you live your life and make your decisions of leadership, and where can you point to a time when biblical truth made a difference in your leadership?

3. In which areas do you need to shift from being against something to being for something?

4. Where do you see yourself or the organization you serve as becoming more receivable as a reflection of Christ's love?

5. What do you envision as the coming decade's trends of evangelical Christianity, and how can you adjust your leadership in heart and mind to prepare for these changes?

Endnotes

[1] P. K. Moser, "Jesus and Philosophy: On the Questions We Ask," *Faith and Philosophy*, vol. 22, no. 3 (July 2005): 273.

[2] "The Journeyman," *New York Times Book Review* (January 17, 2010): 1.

[3] G. Rosell, *The Surprising Work of God: Harold John Ockenga, Billy Graham, and the Rebirth of Evangelicalism* (Grand Rapids: Baker Academic, 2008).

[4] See T. Keller, *Counterfeit Gods: The Empty Promises of Money, Sex, and Power, and the Only Hope that Matters* (New York: Penguin, 2009).

[5] H. Lewis, *Excellence Without a Soul: Does Liberal Education Have a Future?* (New York: Public Affairs, 2006).

[6] R. J. Mouw, "Carl Henry Was Right," *Christianity Today* (January 2010).

[7] D. Kinnaman, *unChristian: What a New Generation Thinks About Christianity . . . and Why It Matters* (Grand Rapids: Baker, 2007).

[8] N. Wolterstorff, "The Mission of the Christian College at the End of the 20th Century," *The Reformed Journal* (June 1983): 18.

Chapter 15

CRISIS MANAGEMENT

Kimberly Thornbury
Vice president for student life, Union University

"An institution reveals its soul during a crisis."
Arthur Sandeen, former vice president for student affairs at
the University of Florida, offered that assessment to his colleagues in
the National Association of Student Personnel Administrators. Sandeen
articulates what leaders in higher education must know: when a Christian
organization reaches a moment of truth in its history, you will quickly
discover how well the mission of your institution is understood and
practiced by your colleagues.[1] Christ-centered institutions which walk
through a crisis have a tremendous opportunity to bear witness for Christ
as the world looks into the heart of an organization in need. The art and
science of crisis management reveal the true colors of leadership and can
thus provide a unique platform for gospel-centered witness.

Unfortunately, leaders in the field of higher education and parachurch
organizations may be less technically prepared for crisis than their secular counterparts. Research shows that institutions of higher education are
playing catch-up to corporate cultures who have more long-standing and
defined plans for a day of reckoning. Ironically, there can also be a sense
in which the theology of some well-meaning Christian institutions may
inadvertently leave them unprepared for crisis. Efforts tend to be focused
on the mission, and the responsibility to think about crisis management is
too often neglected, leaving crisis situations "up to God."

A leader's work is endless, and the best leaders are relentlessly focused on their mission. Although busy organizations may value crisis management, in reality, leaders may unconsciously think that their organization will never be faced with a crisis situation. Even if they realize the need to plan and prepare in case something does happen, this work always seems to fall into the "not urgent/not important" category. It is not as though one thinks of oneself or one's organization as invincible; it's just that the everyday business of life (sharing vision with others, goal setting, personnel issues, relationship building, event planning) already take 12-plus hours of a leader's day.

The degree of support for crisis management (usually defined as the amount of perceived financial, political, and institutional backing) ranks lowest among concerns in higher education, behind key tasks such as undergraduate teaching, fund-raising, facilities improvements, trustee and community relations, research, athletics, etc.[2] While this fact might not be surprising, one cannot discount the need for and positive results that can come from effective crisis management.

The Case for Crisis Management

A "mismanaged crisis can damage [one's] reputation," the *Financial Times* observes. It can "cost significant amounts of money and much worse—lead to criminal charges. During an emergency incident, poorly prepared executives can make very bad decisions. Out of their comfort zone, they may panic, make strategically incorrect decisions and compromise their company's reputation."[3] Despite this potential for damage, "most colleges and universities are poorly prepared to efficiently address and manage crisis."[4]

Even in the wake of significant natural and man-made disasters, Katrina and 9/11 serving as two well-known examples, many organizational divisions are yet to be convinced of the need for planning or are unsure how practically to implement such planning. Other organizations have written a lengthy, technical handbook for crisis management that is unread by anyone outside the security office. But having a plan that is unread, lengthy, and not understood is like not having a plan at all. In a time of crisis, few will reach to their shelves and pull out their red "crisis management binder."

Similarly, many institutions have crisis teams in "name only." According to research data conducted by SimpsonScarborough, a higher education consulting firm, 71 percent of respondents said the crisis teams at their institutions did not meet regularly.[5] It is understandable if colleges and universities do not have perfected plans or do not fully understand how best to use such committees. Research shows that the field of crisis management is only 20-plus years old, which may contribute to a sense of not knowing exactly what to do and a feeling that the task may be too large.[6] These factors—coupled with the common Christian perception that if we work hard and trust God, everything will be OK—may cause Christian institutions to neglect the hard work of crisis management. This attitude is not only bad theology but also dangerous ethics. If a school fails to react in a timely and competent fashion to a watershed moment, not only can people get hurt, but constituencies may develop a crisis of confidence in the aftermath that can permanently damage the college's ability to continue its mission.

This chapter provides examples of varied crises organizations have faced. Each short example can be used by leaders as a case study to help guide their thinking. For example: What was involved in that organization's comprehensive response? What would we have done? Who within our organization would be responsible for different solutions? Despite the varied nature of each crisis, the leader will see how successful organizations and top leaders respond in similar ways. And, like an army, this type of strategic thinking is best done before one goes into battle, especially before one experiences an unannounced attack. Though different crises arise, organizations do not have to reinvent the wheel. Macro principles for effective crisis management and successful leadership emerge regardless of the trial.

Following the case studies, the chapter provides a framework for an institutional crisis plan. Every university, seminary, or parachurch organization's crisis plan must be accessible, understandable, and realistic at every level. Good leaders have a plan and have the ability to execute that plan simply in the midst of a seemingly complex situation. This chapter outlines good systems, procedures, and practical advice that work for all organizations. Specific action steps a good leader and organization must do before a crisis, during a crisis, and following a crisis are included. Finally, the chapter coaches the leader on the emotional toll and spiritual benefits of leading an organization through a crisis. Even the best-made plans cannot buffet the effects of seeing one's organization suffer and the amount of plain hard work it takes to rebuild. Advice is given on how the leader can best refocus an organization to have the mind of Christ in all things in the days, weeks, and months following an institutional crisis.

Examples of Institutional Crisis

Businesses generally look to the Tylenol Scare of 1982 as the gold standard for organizations dealing with a crisis and excellent response. The following postcrisis steps capture what Tylenol did right after seven people died after ingesting the pain reliever laced with cyanide and provide an excellent model for organizational crisis response.

1. Tell the public what happened. In the case of system or ethical failure, be honest about bad news. G. Grabowski, head of crisis and litigation practice at Levick Strategic Communications, explained that a slow drip of bad news is the worst thing that can happen. "Better to rip off the Band-aid all at once."[7]
2. Apologize and/or show sincere empathy early.
3. Tell them what you are going to do about it.
4. Do it. Follow through on what you say you are going to do.

Examples follow of some classic and/or recent examples of unexpected disasters organizations have faced. Crisis teams or executive leadership can use these case studies as roundtable discussion exercises. Teams can ask themselves how well each organization handled the four questions above. Going further, executive teams should ask themselves, "What would we have done?"

Recent findings indicate that "colleges and universities were generally prepared only for those crises that they had already experienced."[8] By continually looking at a variety of case studies, leaders can have stronger confidence in their ability to handle unexpected and diverse challenges.

Weather Emergencies

Hurricane Katrina, the Iowa floods, and mid-South tornados are just a few examples of natural disasters that created devastating damage to institutions. As chief student affairs officer at Union University in Jackson, Tennessee, I personally witnessed the aftermath and recovery from the F-4 tornado that ripped through the heart of our campus on February 5, 2008, at 7:02 p.m. In less than a minute, the tornado left behind more than $47 million worth of damage. The storm destroyed or damaged 31 of the 41 buildings on Union's main campus, including the destruction of some 75 percent of residence life complexes. The university was five days into the spring semester. Students were bleeding and hurt, and all residential students needed immediate shelter, not just those who had their bedrooms blown away. Fifty-one students were seriously injured, including 13 students trapped under building rubble or in a collapsed bathroom. Even hours after the tornado, questions of life and death hung in the balance. President David Dockery was faced with questions including:

- Will injured students survive?
- How are our students faring? Where will they sleep?
- How do we begin the technical assessment of a destroyed campus?
- Can we continue this semester?

Almost immediately after the devastation, local emergency management took President Dockery to a safe, basement location downtown where he could communicate with all emergency services at once. He was able to connect with trustee and senior leadership by cell phone, hampered by sporadic signal strength and overloaded systems. Dockery returned to the campus at 2:00 a.m. and identified a location for leaders to gather the next morning and returned at 5:00 a.m. to handle media. At 7:00 a.m. senior administrators met at a campus sorority house. Dockery began our first meeting with a time of extended prayer where he asked God for strength, wisdom, and protection. He then outlined a five-step plan for senior leadership and key administrators, who served as the crisis team.

1. Our 48-hour response
2. A focus on students beginning from day one and beyond
3. Recovery plans beginning from day one
4. Restarting the spring semester within two weeks from the impact of the tornado
5. Issues relating to the fall semester and beyond

God's grace sustained the campus and leadership. He provided the resources necessary to arrange alternative housing for the now homeless students at a church-owned hotel complex and provided the university with the ability to complete its promise and restart the academic semester after only two weeks. Additionally, the university was able with divine help to build 769 bedrooms within a six-month period (816 total bedrooms within nine months), just in time for students to move in before the fall semester began.

Fire

Fire is a common disaster for organizations. In 2008 Westmont College in California experienced the terrifying, fast-moving destruction of wildfires. In 2009 Point Loma's office building burned. In May 2008 fire destroyed a University of Michigan frat house. Fires are common and devastating, and recent data show that many plans account for this type of common disaster.[9]

Crimes or Ethical Breaches of Leaders or Students

Expecting or preparing for ethical breaches in the context of Christian organizations is difficult. The effects of negative publicity damage internal morale of an organization and stain the external reputation of faith-based institutions more than their secular counterparts. Studies have shown that "there are several important types of crises that were frequently experienced but not prepared for. These tended to be the softer areas such as reputation and ethics, as well as other non-physical crises such as data loss and sabotage."[10]

Social Media Crisis

Images, falsehoods, or rumors posted or tweeted on social media sites are perhaps the most recent potential crisis for which an organization must prepare. Recent technology has only increased ways to spotlight employee missteps. Consider the PR nightmare Domino's dealt with after a YouTube video showed an employee doing "gross things" to a sub sandwich he was making. The video was viewed more than 555,000 times in less than three days.[11] As Domino's spokesman T. McIntyre explained: "Nothing is local anymore. That's the challenge of the Web world. Any two idiots with a video camera and a dumb idea can damage the reputation of a 50-year-old-brand."[12] Eventually over a million people viewed a Domino's employee adding bodily fluids to a Domino's product.[13]

In an effort to stay ahead of the curve, the athletic departments of universities such as the University of Mississippi have contracted with an outside firm that "scans social network profiles of its athletes for over 500 keyword references to drugs, alcohol, sex, violence, racial slurs and profanity."[14] The fact that there is a market for such "external eyes" underscores the level of damage certain messages can cause.

Technology Compromises

Computer hacking by students, grade tampering, social security number thefts, and loss or alteration of data create crises and leadership stress, especially when the technical solutions are outside the realm of most senior administrators familiar knowledge base. Consider Oregon University's computer hacking nightmare in June 2009 that posted anti-Obama and racial slurs on the university Web site. Computer systems have some deficiencies, but the organization needs to know where the weaknesses are and prioritize protection measures.

Lawsuits

Whether the charge is well founded or not, just the allegation of a crime can cause an organization to be tried early in the eyes of public opinion. Even more difficult is the institution's inability to respond to rumor or criticism before a trial due to other legal restraints. Not being able to tell "the full story" is frustrating and can be difficult at best. The lawsuits following the Texas A&M bonfire collapse, which killed 12 students, lasted just under nine years.

Pandemic Flu or Other Outbreaks

Mass education about hygiene makes hand sanitizers and even the use of masks understandable practices. Despite such precautions, an outbreak can cause financial, emotional, and logistical challenges to an institution, especially those with residential campuses.

Other outbreaks such as the fall 2008 lice crisis at Eastern Nazarene College (which had at least 46 confirmed cases) and recent bedbug infestations in the tri-state area in the fall 2009 have also caused widespread panic. In addition to the outbreak being contained, campus leadership needed to deal with campus emotions targeted toward students and others identified as having brought the lice, bugs, or sickness to their campuses.

Business Interruption Because of Crisis and/or Revenue Issues

Unexpected or continual declines in revenue are a reality for institutions facing a serious predicament, but the pain of working through a recovery plan is difficult even with warning. Finding solutions to financial challenges is sobering and can affect morale. Lower enrollments or higher attrition decrease the amount of tuition dollars, the greatest source of income for most private schools. Economic collapse or even market downturns can significantly affect a school's endowment and donations. Many challenges, such as Union's tornado crisis, can energize a community's esprit de corps. However financial challenges and commensurate layoffs can result in a demoralizing and ongoing somber climate.

Active Shooters/Terrorism

Bomb threats require building evacuations, and deranged individuals with guns terrorize communities. The senseless violence makes regular headlines. The unprecedented 32 deaths at Virginia Tech in April 2008 and the five students killed during a shooting in a lecture hall at Northern Illinois University in February 2008 make college campuses seem increasingly vulnerable. While the active shooter profile is males aged 15–24, the middle-aged female professor who shot and killed two faculty and wounded others at the University of Alabama Huntsville in February 2010 makes it more difficult to stereotype killers and scenarios.

Suicide/Student Deaths

Suicide is the second leading cause of death among college students.[15] According to a 2007 study, the five types of crisis institutions reported most frequently included student death, fire, infectious disease, suicide, and evacuation of buildings.[16] Fraternity hazing at worst can result in the death of a student, such as the death of an 18-year-old freshman during a Phi Kappa Tau initiation ritual at Rider University. One of the aftermaths of a crisis can be the lengthy reporting of the incident in the media as it moves through a lawsuit phase over a period of years.

Transportation Accidents

Transportation accidents are also common and can cause additional complications due to distances from the campus at the time of the accident. Consider the Bluffton University (Ohio) bus accident in March 2007 in Atlanta, Georgia. The 5:30 a.m. bus accident killed seven, including the driver, his wife, and five baseball players traveling from the university.

Taylor University walked through a devastating crisis in spring 2006 when four students and one staff member were killed in an automobile accident. The crisis also included understandable mistaken identity, as five weeks later, facts emerged that one of the female students waking from her coma was in fact a student who had been pronounced dead from the crash.

The List Continues

The sorts of catastrophes that confront institutions are seemingly endless. Often they are the stuff of national headlines, such as the November 1999 Texas A&M bonfire collapse which killed 12 students and injured 27 others. The sudden loss of key executives within an organization or celebratory riots that get out of hand add to an endless list of possible crises an institution could face.

Before the Crisis

Leadership Actions and Lessons

Any top leader will tell you that it takes the efforts of a diverse team to keep an organization humming and future-directed. Organizational presidents will not be involved in every technical aspect of crisis preparation, but they must ensure that someone within the organization is attending to the details. When a crisis is happening, the president needs to be able to talk to the media and senior-level officials in government, as well as corporate and sister institutions. They must be given space for macro planning in finances, new physical needs, and next steps. Swift and people-focused responses by the team will enable good talking points for the president and allow the top leader time to place valuable calls to senior government and educational and denominational leaders.

Proper planning before a crisis event begins will save an institution time, money, and possibly lives. Several practical "before" steps are listed below that must be addressed in one's crisis plan. However, the first four points deserve a senior leader's special attention.

1. Before a crisis, a leader must have the ability to develop ongoing relationships and generate goodwill with a variety of constituents. Without friends you can't manage a crisis. Top leaders build strong relationships with their organizations, with trustees, with local business leaders, with government officials, with sister institutions, and with other key influencers. Building such a diverse pool of friendships allows you to call needed people with a particular skill set during times of crisis. Remembering names, having key phone numbers in your cell phone, and making goodwill deposits through the years will result in finding yourself surrounded by a strong community when you need support at an unexpected hour.

People view institutions suffering as a result of a natural disaster with sympathy. The photos are often heart wrenching and elicit immediate concern and support. Other crises such as key leadership transitions or the effects of disgruntled employees have the most potential for being misunderstood by an outside world. Often in lawsuits, institutions are not legally allowed to comment or provide a framework for the situation, thus creating unique communications challenges for public relations. In other instances financial challenges call for big, often unpopular risks or cut-backs. At those times the strength of your relationships both internally and externally will be tested. There must be a deep emotional bank account from which you can draw, both internally and externally. Governmental officials have learned this lesson the hard way. Columnist P. Noonan explains it best.

> In politics you must tend to the garden. The garden is the constituency. . . . No great endeavor is possible without its backing. In a modern presidency especially you have to know this, because there will be times when history throws you a crisis, and to address it you may have to do an unpopular thing. A president in those circumstances must use all the goodwill he's built up over the months and years to get through that moment and survive doing what he thinks is right.

Noonan goes on to explain that presidents have to build up popularity to use on a rainy day.[17]

2. Before a crisis, a leader must develop a working crisis team. Crisis teams are important because "the literature suggests that even if an organization cannot prevent all possible crises from occurring, it nonetheless can recover substantially faster and at much less cost if it has a well-trained, inter-departmental crisis-management team in place."[18]

Even if the president is not on the crisis management team, he or she needs to champion the team. Presidential support of a crisis team includes creating a team, listening to or reading executive summaries, dedicating at least one senior leadership meeting a year to reviewing checklists of who is responsible for what specific actions in times of a crisis, reviewing key relationships and contact information, and finally, discussing classic or recent case studies if time permits.

3. Before a crisis, the institution must have a strict policy for media communication. Response to a crisis must be done quickly and only by a spokesperson designated by the president. This is critical to set the emotional tone for the organization's response, to establish credibility, and to identify a key spokesperson as the source of timely and accurate information. Without a key spokesperson, the added layers of rumors, misinformation, and confusion will complicate an already difficult situation. Timely organizational spokesperson response is especially important in cases of ethical breeches or leadership transitions. Rumors develop quickly, and organizations always want to appear proactive, not reactive.

In addition to the tone that is set up through quick organizational response, it is important that the organization's Web site be accurate, short, clear, and timely. The director of news services for the University of Iowa stressed the importance of their accurate Web blog following the Iowa river flooding in June 2008. "I think it absolutely became the Rosetta Stone of information for campus."[19]

Spokespeople and Web information must also find the right balance between legal liabilities and compassion in certain situations. Christians should err on the side of compassion but be wise about legal implications.[20] When in doubt, leaders should always ask, "What is the right thing to do?"

When talking to the media, the spokesperson should also continually underscore the mission and vision of the institution, even in times of crisis. Using talking points that are layered throughout the organization help frame an institutional message. Try to inform internal constituents before the media, if possible. In a Twitter age internal communication may take place only minutes before general news, but it can establish goodwill from those within the organization.

Treat the media with respect. Understanding mutual deadlines and listening to what they need helps build a mutual working relationship. In addition, the president or spokesperson may consider establishing scheduled times to talk to the media (e.g., on the hour) even if the statement is "no statement." These agreed-upon times can provide helpful clarity by letting news reporters know exactly when news will come.

4. Before a crisis, a leader must give thought to a continuity of business plan/continuity of instruction plan. Nonprofit leaders generally run an organization on thin financial margins. There is little room for error even in the best of climates. If there is not a sophisticated plan for recovery, crisis can cause financial ruin. Decisions such as physical relocation options and/or Web-based/distance delivery of services and communication, cash-flow access, and replacement and/or business interruption insurance coverage are key precrisis questions.

Alternatives for how essential functions will continue (housing, transportation, food services) as well as a business continuity plan must be developed. For example, answers to questions such as, What systems are needed to conduct all administrative functions, including payroll and computer and telephone services? must be identified.

The president and key leaders must identify sources of funding. Help from donors and constituents, insurance payments, denominational support, and bank relationships can release funds immediately for both immediate and long-term cash-flow needs. Big-picture financial questions and solutions are solved at the highest levels of organizational leadership.

Attention to Details

Many responses to crisis will have unique action steps and benefit from slightly different preparation. However, a top leader must ensure that several key aspects are in place. These include communication strategies, alternate instructional or business delivery options, care for internal constituents, organizational advancement work, and safety and security protocols. Leaders ensure the organization both adopts and understands the crisis plan.

Communication Strategies. Perhaps of greatest importance, develop a chain of command for decisions. While utmost flexibility needs to be shown during a crisis, major decisions still need the approval of senior leadership. There does, however, need to be a short communication loop from the crisis fact finder, president, spokesperson, and emergency alert person. Stated differently, it shouldn't take a committee to send out a text that says: "Possible active shooter on campus. Remain inside, lock doors, turn off lights, and stay down."

The senior leadership team should know one another's alternate e-mail address (from gmail, Yahoo, etc.). Alternative e-mails can keep leaders in communication if the organization's server is down, especially with a message longer than a text or tweet. Text messaging is currently one of the best ways to communicate after a crisis. (That is, if you have taken time to enter key numbers in your cell phone.) Also think about technological solutions that have impact and affect the way you manage communications. Simple text-messaging emergency alert systems are inexpensive. Allow other key stakeholders like trustees, parents, or spouses to sign up for such alerts. Swift, accurate communication has the potential to make all stakeholders into the strongest ambassadors for the institution.

Have a system for getting the message out. Once the president decides or approves messages, senior leaders should know who can access the organizational Web site, Twitter, Facebook and YouTube accounts, send mass organizational e-mails and update organizational blogs remotely. Several staff should have the technical knowledge and passwords to update the Web site, as this is one of the most critical ways to send unified facts about the crisis. Contact information for the authors of key or popular blogs is helpful to have on hand. Key administrators should understand and/or be registered with Skype or other Web-based distance meeting options (e.g., gotomeeting.com) or phone conference options with access codes and pin numbers. These options are good both for meetings that cannot happen in person or for a call-in meeting by organizational members, parents, or other constituents.

An alternate Web site (e.g., organizationalnameRESPONSE.org with low graphics so the site doesn't crash if it receives heavy volume) should be registered in advance in case the organization's server goes down. A moment of crisis is not the right time to be registering an alternative domain name.

A new shared Facebook or Twitter logo can allow the organization and supporters to come together in unity. For example, following the tornado a popular Facebook symbol for Union University included hands in prayer as a sign of solidarity with the school. Following the Virginia Tech shootings, a popular profile picture listed the school's logo in front of a black ribbon. A leader should not discount the positive effects of these images.

The Importance of Personal Communication in Times of Crisis

One cannot overemphasize the importance of technology (e-mail, Web, media) in mass communication. Technology can also help students/ organizational members connect with their families in case of an emergency. For example, after the Virginia Tech shootings, a Facebook page entitled "I'm OK at VT" allowed over 3,000 students to let people know they were safe, find others, and eventually list the victims.[21]

Most of the public will judge an institutional response by these public statements. However, one cannot discount the role of personal communication in times of crisis. Examples of personal communication include trained live switchboard operators to handle incoming questions and a team to proactively place calls to affected organizational members. A phone tree is also important because certain news, like a suicide or emotional crisis, is best delivered in person and not via e-mail.

After the tornado at Union University, volunteers and staff began calling every student within 48 hours of the crisis to ensure they were OK and to discuss long-term housing options. While the president or senior leader

will be involved in the communication to family members who are seriously ill or lost life, a follow-up team must be identified to address family
details such as transportation, food, housing, hospital care, and funeral
arrangements. Local alumni chapters or churches can also assist in ongoing care for families far from campus.

Instruction/Delivery

Who has the authority to seek out alternate space for business/class functioning? If your place of leadership is in higher education, how quickly can
your organization move to an online learning platform? Other organizations may have formal or informal agreements to share space. Any business depends on the delivery of the product.

General Security Measures

Because many institutions have multiple buildings and security may be
busy elsewhere during a crisis, faculty or staff volunteers may serve as
building or floor leaders. These area leaders will be trained to ensure compliance and will remind people of what to do should a crisis occur. The
general campus may not remember action steps in a crisis. Having a calm,
trained presence in each location will ensure the safety of all in the building and help the building protocols and procedures such as a "shelter in
place," lockdown, or evacuation.

Taking specific care to identify provisions for vulnerable populations is
the right thing to do during a crisis. An organization that does not have in
place someone to respond to the needs of those with physical disabilities,
language barriers, those who are far from home or emotionally at risk can
become a target for criticism.

How to Share the Plan in a Short, Easy-to-Understand Way

- Desktop guides with short "what to do in case of . . ." bullet
  points.
- A short "responsibility centered" crisis plan that is available on
  the Web or in hard copy. This means that specific responsibilities
  are identified by name.
- Annual training (or at least awareness) with employees as to
  their specific responsibilities during a time of crisis. Include
  expectations of the use of social media during new employee
  orientation as well as crisis training.

- Market text-message sign-ups or buy software that pulls student/ employee cell phone numbers from your computer database.
- Allow parents and spouses to sign up for text-message alerts.

Each of these steps for disseminating information about your institution's plan will demonstrate to constituencies that those tasked with the organization's governance are taking their leadership roles seriously. These measures set the tone for personnel or students, faculty, and staff while simultaneously reassuring them that the decisions being made are borne out of reliable facts and record keeping.

During a Crisis

Leadership and Setting the Tone

Leadership response to a crisis sets the framework for the recovery and rebuilding phase. Those first media interviews will be played over and over again. In a state of shock, the organization mirrors the tone and words of a leader. Within 12 hours of the devastating tornado at Union University, President Dockery used uplifting phrases such as, "We pray God will bring renewal out of this rubble," and verses such as, "We do not lose heart" taken from 2 Cor 4:1. These words brought strength and hope to our community.

The leader should show empathy early and often. Images of the president walking around a destroyed residential complex or a picture of a weary leader with hands folded in heartfelt prayer are important and meaningful.

Good leaders during a crisis are calm and encouraging. They are symbols of hope and continually point others toward Christ. During the 2008 tornados at Union, President Dockery organized the first senior leadership meeting less than 12 hours after the impact of the storm. The meetings were held in a campus sorority lodge, which had two main rooms. One large room served as a station center where hundreds of employees were assigned to dozens of rebuilding tasks. The other room, connected by a short, dark hall, was smaller and would serve as the "cabinet war room." During our first meeting there, he began with an extended time of prayer. As 10 minutes became 20 and then 30, I could hear the growing din in the room next door. Hundreds of people were lined up with pressing questions or wanting to know exactly how they could help. Officials were calling in or en route. Cell phones were buzzing, and one could see from the windows that people were literally circling the room.

No sense of urgency could stop our leader from "putting first things first." We knew without God's help we were helpless to complete the task before us in our own strength. It is easy for a leader to get caught up in the urgency of the moment. Good leaders set the tone with prayer and a Christ-centered focus. The burden of leadership dictates that people will follow the tone and tack of the president. If he is gloomy and negative, those who follow him will be as well. A leader cannot change the past, but if he is future-directed in the wake of a calamity, his words will bring cheer and courage to those preserving the institution as it seeks to move forward.

Fact Finding as a Leadership Challenge

As a leader, your decisions are only as good as the facts on which they are based. In times of crisis your team needs to feed you accurate information or qualify information if they are not certain the information is correct.

Factual answers to questions such as: Who is hurt? What is damaged? are essential to establish the credibility of the president or spokesperson.

Keeping Accurate Records of Those Who Helped

During a crisis flurries of people reach out to assist with monetary, emotional, and physical support. Good leaders thank those who helped both during and after. The speed at which needs are identified and help comes in is incredible. It may be helpful to have a trusted staff or volunteer shadow senior leadership for days to record to-dos and capture names and addresses of people who have helped. There is little time for daily reflection in the days and weeks following a crisis, so on-the-spot record keeping is invaluable.

Advancement teams will need to coordinate accepting supplies and receipting gifts and gift-in-kind. Leaders will appreciate the details of those who helped with money, services, and gifts.

Caring for Your Spiritual and Physical Health

The Lord grows His believers by the practice of spiritual disciplines and through crisis. Though leaders who have experienced a crisis would not wish their experiences on anyone else, many reflect on that period as a time of blessing and accelerated spiritual growth. Leaders, who sometimes can flirt with the sin of pride and self-sufficiency when looking at a their well-run and effective organization, are completely emptied of self in times of crisis. Faith is tested; faith is sustained. However, many leaders face times of quiet desperation as they are still before God. A common acronym for sin triggers is HALT. When a leader is *hungry, angry, lonely,* or *tired,* our spiritual defenses can be down.

In light of these realities, one cannot afford to avoid practicing the spiritual disciplines before a disaster occurs. Spiritual maturity cannot be developed in a hurry-up, post-facto manner. Rather, it is the result of habitual attention to the care and nourishment of one's soul. The fruit of attention to God's Word, repentance from one's sins, and the cultivation of a life of prayer is the rare jewel of courage. As C. S. Lewis observed in *The Screwtape Letters*:

> This, indeed, is probably one of the Enemy's motives for creating a dangerous world—a world in which moral issues really come to the point. He sees as well as you do that courage is not simply one of the virtues, but the form of every virtue at the testing point, which means at the point of highest reality. A chastity or honesty, or mercy, which yields to danger, will be chaste or honest or merciful only on conditions. Pilate was merciful till it became risky.[22]

Caring for Your Health and Family

A crisis can leave a leader bereft of time or an appetite to eat. Rest is often elusive for top leaders before a crisis and becomes almost nonexistent during storms. A leader and his or her team must rest (if only lying on the bed in prayer) and eat to sustain energy. Attempts at rest, eating, and time for personal devotion will decrease anxiety as the days and weeks prolong.

The care of a supportive family (who may not see you for days or weeks) and the kindness of others to keep you fed (and in clean clothes) cannot be discounted. Bills need to be paid, dishwashers need to be emptied, and toothpaste needs to be purchased. Thank your spouse for his or her support in encouraging and supporting you.

Often top executives can focus so entirely on their organization as the years go by that they can neglect to nurture nonwork-related relationships. During a crisis relationships outside of one's organization or field can provide both care and needed perspective.

Leadership After a Crisis

"What Mean These Stones?"

"College and universities, if not necessarily their leaders, generally survive everything from earthquakes to grade scandals."[23] Leading well cannot only help the college, university, or ministry to survive and thrive; but it can also help personally demonstrate the faithfulness of God through the God-given gifts of excellent leadership.

Following a crisis, good leadership always provides time for ongoing affirmations and anniversary celebrations for how the Lord has brought you through. This crucial practice ensures continued *esprit de corps*. After the darkest days are over, it may be a sin of omission to fail to thank those around you who helped the organization survive. Formal days of remembrance combined with ongoing acts of service to the communities that sustained you will demonstrate that you have not forgotten those who sacrificed themselves over significant periods of time to achieve the common good.

Throughout the Bible we see that proper ceremony is a function of leaders. When the people of God crossed over the river Jordan on dry ground, Joshua instructed representatives from the 12 tribes of Israel to construct a stone memorial as a permanent reminder to the nation of what the Lord had done for them (Josh 4:6). Consequently, anniversary celebrations, key worship services, and plaques serve in important respects as modern-day altars. Even secular institutions model such observances, from which Christian institutions can learn a great deal. For example, Northern Illinois University plans to build a memorial garden near the site of the tragedy where a gunman opened fire during a lecture hall and killed five people before taking his own life.[24] Union placed bricks from the destroyed residence complex into the corner of each new residence life building and used other rubble in creating a new coffeeshop that opened three weeks following the storm. The president's office led a worship service at 7:02 p.m. two weeks after the storm on the eve of classes restarting. Top leadership plans such services, honors those who have helped, and reminds the community of God's sustaining grace.

Senior leaders understand various crises their organization could face. They prepare plans to enable good crisis management beforehand and exhibit Christ-centered leadership during a crisis. Finally, top leaders honor others following a crisis. Such behaviors model biblical leadership

and allow Christian organizations to shine for Him even in the darkest
hours.

Resources for Further Study

CNN.com. "Texas A&M Students Killed, Trapped in Collapse of Bonfire Logs."
November 18, 1999. (Web posted.)

Curtis, T. "Educational Program Emergency Planning." *Radiologic Technology.*
80:6. July/August 2009.

Dolan, T. G. "Few Schools Are Ready to Manage a Crisis." www.eddigest.com,
October 2006.

Holland, J. "How Colleges Are Dodging Facebook Embarrassment."
HigherEdMorning.com. As posted in "In this week's e-newsletter," Latest
News and Views, Tech News. February 15, 2010.

Horovitz, B. "Domino's Nightmare Holds Lessons for Marketers; Companies
Have to Learn How to Handle Social-Media Attacks." *USA Today.* April 16,
2009.

June, A. W. "Crisis-Management Plans Are Untested, Survey Says." October 19,
2007.

Kennedy, M. "Rebounding from Tragedy." *American School and University.*
April 2009, 81.

Klockentager, D., and C. Klockentager. "Voice of the Parents" in K. S. Harper,
B. G. Paterson, and E. L. Zdziarski, eds. *Crisis Management: Responding
from the Heart.* Washington, DC: National Association of Student Personnel
Administrators, 2006.

Lewis, C. S. *The Screwtape Letters.* London: Fontana Books, 1955.

Mastrodicasa, J. "Technology Use in Campus Crisis." *New Directions in Student
Services.* No. 124. Winter 2008.

Merriman, L. S. "Managing Parent Involvement During Crisis." *New Directions
in Student Services.* No. 122. Summer 2008.

Mitroff, I. I. "Why Some Companies Emerge Stronger and Better from Crisis: 7
Essential Lessons for Surviving Disaster." AMACOM, New York. 2005.

Mitroff, I. I., M. A. Diamond, and C. M. Alpaslan. "How Prepared Are
America's Colleges and Universities for Major Crisis?" *Change.* January/
February 2006, 60–67.

Noonan, P. "God Is Back." *Wall Street Journal.* September 28, 2005.

———. *Wall Street Journal.* January 6, 2010.

O'Leary, N. *"Toyota: A Battered Giant."* February 8, 2010.

Phillips, M. "Toyota's Tylenol Moment." *Newsweek.* February 15, 2010.

"Planning for a Crisis." *Financial Times.* May 7, 2009.

Pykett, E. "Debate & Opinion: News Review: The Secret of Taking the Drama
Out of a Crisis." 2009.

Sandeen, A. "Voice of the Vice President," in K. S. Harper, B. G. Paterson,
and E. L. Zdziarski, eds. *Crisis Management: Responding from the Heart.*

Washington, DC: National Association of Student Personnel Administrators, 2006.

Slevin, P., and A. Chatman. WashingtonPost.com. "Six Killed as College Athletes' Bus Crashes." March 3, 2007.

Zdziarski, E., N. W. Dunkel, J. M. Rollo, and associates. *Campus Crisis Management: A Comprehensive Guide to Planning, Prevention, Response, and Recovery.* San Francisco: Jossey-Bass, 2007.

Questions for Further Reflection

1. Have you experienced a personal or organizational crisis? Despite the tragedy, what went well? What would you have done differently?

2. What traits should a leader exhibit following a tragedy? What institutional leaders have exhibited these characteristics?

3. What systems or policies can be implemented within organizations to minimize potential crisis?

4. When crisis arises, leaders need a deep spiritual and relational well from which to draw. How are you as a leader personally making daily deposits into these areas?

5. What critical relationships might need to be nurtured that are essential in times of crisis?

Endnotes

[1] See A. Sandeen, "Voice of the Vice President" in K. S. Harper, B. G. Paterson, and E. L. Zdziarski, eds., *Crisis Management: Responding from the Heart* (Washington, D.C.: National Association of Student Personnel Administrators, 2006).

[2] See I. I. Mitroff, M. A. Diamond, C. M. Alpaslan, "How Prepared Are America's Colleges and Universities for Major Crisis?" *Change* (January/February 2006): 60–67.

[3] See "Planning for a Crisis," *Financial Times* (May 7, 2009): 1.

[4] See T. G. Dolan, "Few Schools Are Ready to Manage a Crisis" (October 2006), www.eddigest.com.

[5] See A. W. June, "Crisis-Management Plans Are Untested, Survey Says" (October 19, 2007).

[6] Mitroff, Diamond, Alpaslan, "How Prepared Are America's Colleges and Universities for Major Crisis?", 61.

[7] See M. Phillips, "Toyota's Tylenol Moment," *Newsweek*, 155:7 (February 15, 2010): 12.

[8] Mitroff, Diamond, Alpaslan, "How Prepared Are America's Colleges and Universities for Major Crisis?", 65.

[9] Ibid.

[10] Ibid.

[11] See B. Horovitz, "Domino's Nightmare Holds Lessons for Marketers; Companies Have to Learn How to Handle Social-Media Attacks," *USA Today* (April 16, 2009).

[12] Ibid.

[13] "Planning for a Crisis," *Financial Times*.

[14] J. Holland, "How Colleges Are Dodging Facebook Embarrassment." HigherEdMorning.com, http://www.higheredmorning.com/how-these-colleges-are-dodging-facebook-embarrassment.

[15] www.suicide.org.

[16] See E. L. Zdziarski, ed., *Campus Crisis Management: A Comprehensive Guide to Planning, Prevention, Response and Recovery* (San Francisco: Jossey-Bass, 2007).

[17] See P. Noonan, "God Is Back," *Wall Street Journal* (January 6, 2010).

[18] See Mitroff, Diamond, Alpaslan, "How Prepared Are America's Colleges and Universities for Major Crisis?", 64.

[19] See M. Kennedy, "Rebounding from Tragedy," *American School and University* (April 2009): 18.

[20] See D. Klockentager and C. Klockentager, "Voice of the Parents," in Harper, Paterson, and Zdziarski, *Crisis Management: Responding from the Heart*, 64.

[21] J. Mastrodicasa, "Technology Use in Campus Crisis," *New Directions in Student Services* (Winter 2008), 46.

[22] C. S. Lewis, *The Screwtape Letters* (London: Fontana Books, 1955), 148–49.

[23] Mitroff, Diamond, Alpaslan, "How Prepared Are America's Colleges and Universities for Major Crisis?", 60–67.

[24] Kennedy, "Rebounding from Tragedy," 81.

Chapter 16

THE LEADER AS MENTOR AND PASTOR

Randall O'Brien
President, Carson-Newman College

L eadership is a sacred calling, a divine commission, which fell upon the First Couple (Gen 1:27–28) and extended to God's representatives throughout Scripture, then forward in time. Patriarchs, judges, kings, prophets, priests, sages, warriors, family heads, and other specially chosen persons in biblical times led Israel with the blessing of God. Moses (Exod 3:10), Jesus (Matt 4:19; Mark 9:7; John 1:1–18;), the disciples (Matt 4:19; 28:19–20), government officials (Rom 13:1–5), Paul (1 Corinthians 9), and those in Christian households (Eph 5:21–6:9), to name but a few, stand out in receiving leadership charges in the Bible.

Surprisingly, the term leader is mentioned only six times in the King James Version of the Bible, while the term servant is mentioned more than nine hundred times.[1] History's leader nonpareil taught, "Whoever wants to be first among you must be a slave. . . . For even the Son of Man did not come not to be served, but to serve, and to give His life—a ransom for many" (Mark 10:44–45 HCSB). Conversations regarding leadership models among followers of Christ necessarily privilege the servant-leader model endorsed and embodied by Jesus.

287

Who Is a Leader?

"At last count, there are more than 10,000 books in print that have 'leadership' in the title."[2] We might only imagine just how many books are circulating with words in the title such as *leader, lead, leading*; or *CEO, coach, president, pastor, mentor*; or *trust, vision,* or *business*—all of which pertain to the task of leading. Amazingly, no clear, universally accepted definition of a leader has surfaced. Leonard Sweet notes, "After nearly 200 pages and 7,500 citations on leadership one report concluded that it found no clear and unequivocal understanding of what distinguishes leaders from non-leaders, effective leaders from ineffective leaders."[3] He goes on to say, "Another study of the congested analysis of leadership, having compiled one hundred and ten different definitions, concludes that 'attempts to define leadership have been confusing, varied, disorganized, idiosyncratic, muddled, and according to conventional wisdom, quite unrewarding.'"[4]

An old leadership proverb advises, "He who thinks he leads, but has no followers, is only taking a walk." Seen in this light the simplest definition of a leader is, "one whom others follow," or "anyone who has someone following him." This definition implies that each one of us is likely a leader. If so leadership does not depend on a title but on influence upon another person. Leadership so understood is found in the home with spouses, parents, grandparents, aunts, uncles, brothers, sisters, and cousins and extends to friends and neighbors; fellow employees in the workplace; fellow church, school, club, and team members; government, business, academy, and military personnel; and to all other relationships throughout society.

Christian leaders naturally embody a leadership model that differs radically from many of their secular counterparts. Jesus outlined the difference between the world's way and His way for James and John as they sought status over service (Mark 10:35–45). "If we want to lead like Jesus, we have to become like Jesus," K. Blanchard reminds us.[5] Not all Christian leaders "get it." B. Robinson, former president of Whitworth University, laments, "Perhaps our desire to be good leaders has elbowed its way in front of our desire to be imitators of Christ."[6] Robinson notes, "From the manger to the cross, Jesus sacrificed," pointing out that Satan tempted Christ by taking Him "up" to the heights of the temple, and "up" to the top of the mountain, whereas God points us "down" to lowly stations of life and to the "least of these" in our midst.[7]

When Jesus was born, He was placed in a livestock feed trough. He nailed boards together for a living, helped the needy, associated with sinners, rode a donkey into Jerusalem, washed dirty feet, and died a criminal's death between thieves outside of town, offering a radically different leadership model for believers. Servant leadership says no to self-promotion, self-indulgence, and self-exaltation; instead, it says yes to self-denial, self-surrender, and self-sacrifice (Luke 9:23). "Service above self" characterizes the Christian leader. As leadership guru J. Maxwell rightly notes, "Leaders are meant to help others become the people God created them to be."[8]

Putting others before self serves as the distinguishing mark of a servant-leader (Mark 10:45). Our standard is Christ. Framing, alliteratively, the life and work of the Christian leader highlights the following components:

- Character
- Competence
- Care
- Commitment
- Communication
- Community building
- Collaboration
- Cooperation
- Calling
- Consensus building
- Cabinet leadership
- Complaint management
- Conflict management
- Crisis management
- Critique management
- Change management
- Capital management
- Casting the vision
- Constituent relations
- Compliment giver
- Cheerleader in chief
- Company, college, clan, or communal rules steward
- Confidentiality
- Christlikeness

Some of these areas of leadership may not apply to all leadership roles, but most will.

Who Is a Mentor?

A mentor is one who shares wisdom with another, preferably but not always in a one-to-one relationship. The term comes from Greek mythology where Odysseus asks Mentor, a wise and respected teacher, to assume responsibility for his son, Telemachus, while Odysseus is away from home on a long voyage. Mentor consents and provides love, nurture, protection, encouragement, instruction, guidance, and support for Telemachus in the absence of the boy's father. Today one who guides the development of another through the sharing of wisdom and the giving of care is called a mentor.

The opportunity to learn from the experience and wisdom of a respected model provides an avenue for development of our full potential. In the mentor-mentoree relationship our confidence and self-esteem grow. Guided experience in a safe environment allows us to erase self-doubt and ease into responsibility. Examples of mentor-mentoree relationships include:

• Teacher	Student
• Politician	Aide
• Manager	Employee
• Coach	Athlete
• Head coach	Assistant coach
• Professor	Graduate student
• Senior professor	Junior instructor
• Military or police officer	Junior officer
• President	Vice president
• Parent	Child
• Older sibling	Younger sibling
• Editor	Author
• Senior clergy	Junior clergy
• Maestro	Musician
• Artist	Apprentice
• Actor	Understudy
• Supreme Court justice	Law clerk
• Electrician/bricklayer/plumber	Apprentice
• Physician	Medical student/intern/ doctor in residency

- Experienced worker   Trainee
- Any other relationship where wisdom, experience, and guidance are shared with one seeking to learn from the more accomplished one.

Examples of mentors in the Bible include:

- Jethro   Moses
- Moses   Joshua
- Eli   Samuel
- Elijah   Elisha
- Naomi   Ruth
- Gamaliel   Saul
- Barnabas   Paul
- Lois   Eunice
- Eunice   Timothy
- Paul   Timothy
- Jesus   Disciples

Almost everyone is both a mentor and a mentoree. That is, each of us learns from another, and in turn, influences others. Naturally, as with all other areas of human performance, levels of accomplishment vary. The best mentors, however, are first the best mentorees. Leaders are learners. Lifelong learners both receive help and give it. They embrace teaching and learning, being mentored and mentoring. A. Toffler argues that "the illiterate of the 21st century will not be those who cannot read and write, but those who cannot learn, unlearn, and relearn."[9]

Mentors and mentorees define each other. Neither can exist without the other. Both become aware of the gaps in their knowledge as they assume their respective roles and benefit from the relationship. As we all know, experience remains the best teacher. There is simply no substitute for learning by doing. Mentors allow mentorees to do the work but then critique, encourage, listen, question, affirm, and capitalize upon the teachable moment. At the same time the mentor never fully realizes the gaps in his or her own knowledge until assuming the role of teacher. So the mentor and mentoree help each other fill in the gaps of their learning.

Based on informal polls conducted during his leadership seminars, J. Maxwell estimates that 85 percent of leaders surveyed became leaders because of the influence of another leader.[10] Paul (with Silvanus and Timothy) reminds the Thessalonian believers that "you became imitators of us and . . . became an example to all the believers in Macedonia and Achaia" (1 Thess 1:6–7 HCSB). Mentoring works that way, creating incoming and outgoing lines of influence.

Because of individual differences, mentorees may learn from their mentors but may also amend or reject some of their ideas. This is natural and understandable. Since the mentor is neither perfect nor identical to the mentoree, it is logical to expect the mentoree occasionally to adapt, rather than adopt, the ways of the mentor. Such expression of personality and individuality by the mentoree is blessed, not cursed, by the mature mentor. Mentorees need a degree of freedom to express their own creativity. When characterized by inspiration, not domination or oppression, mentoring liberates rather than stifles or enslaves. The need of mentorees is not to be dominated or controlled but to be taught, cared for, encouraged, and blessed. The essence of mentoring may be beautifully summarized in the words breathed by the French physicist and mathematician, B. Pascal, "I bring you the gift of these four words: I believe in you."

Who Is a Pastor?

The traditional, technical view of the role of pastor reserves the office for an ordained minister in a Christian Protestant church. The position corresponds to the work of the priest in the Catholic Church and the rabbi in the synagogue. A pastor is one who "shepherds a flock," or more specifically, one who guides and cares for an organized community of followers of Christ. This task of shepherding a Christian congregation is understood by church, pastor, and believers at large as a call from God. Secular society also recognizes the office of pastor as a religious office with an important function in community life.

Any leader or mentor, however, may fill a pastoral role in the life of an individual or organization by assuming pastoral responsibilities normally associated with the office of a pastor. The primary role of a pastor, which corresponds to pastoral possibilities for nonordained leaders, is caregiver.

How Is the Leader a Mentor?

The leader is a mentor when he or she shares wisdom with others verbally and behaviorally in a caring, influential manner, thereby becoming a respected model to emulate. Jesus was a mentor to His disciples in the first century AD, and remains the unparalleled leader-mentor for believers today.

The evangelist Matthew preserves the record of the temptations of Jesus following His baptism just prior to the beginning of His ministry in Galilee (Matt 4:1–11). Repeatedly, the devil takes Jesus "up"—to the pinnacle of the temple and to a high mountain—and tempts Him to "dazzle the world." The tease to elevate self over service fails. Temptations of pride and power, of sensuousness or intoxicating lust, and of materialism vividly contrast the way of the crown with the way of the cross. Jesus chooses the path of self-denial over self-interest. For Him God's works trump Satan's perks. Later He illumines the path He modeled, saying, "If anyone wants to come with Me, he must deny himself, take up his cross, and follow Me" (Matt 16:24 HCSB). A Christian leader is called to lead like Christ, embracing self-surrender, self-denial, and self-sacrifice. The alternative way—self-indulgence, self-promotion, and self-interest—represents the tempting path of the tempter.

The leader serves as a mentor when she or he teaches, guides, nurtures, and equips another to thrive. The Christian leader is called to lead and mentor like Christ in the following critical areas.

The Character of the Leader

As the Sermon on the Mount draws to a close, Matthew reports, "The crowds were astonished at His teaching, because He was teaching them as one who had authority, and not like their scribes" (Matt 7:28–29 HCSB). The Greek word that translates "astonished" means "to strike with astonishment." The term appears in the Greek imperfect tense, which indicates a past event that continues to the present. Why did the people so respond to Jesus? "Because He was teaching them as one who had authority." The Greek term employed here for "authority" is *exousia,* a word formed by adding the prefix, *ex,* meaning "out of," to the term, *ousia,* meaning "being," to form the new word *exousia,*which renders "out of his being." The crowds left Jesus amazed at His teaching and literally "awe struck" because He taught with authority, which came "out of His being."

Matthew uses bookend stories to communicate a powerful spiritual message. Prior to the beginning of Jesus' public ministry, Jesus underwent temptations in the desert. He did not sin. With the temptations of Christ appearing in Matthew 4 (front bookend story), the Sermon on the Mount appearing in Matthew 5–7, and the astonished crowd reference (bookend story two) falling at the close of the Sermon on the Mount, these bookend stories—Jesus' temptation and the crowd's reaction to His teaching—offer a theological lesson of their own: spiritual power and purity go hand in hand. The secret of Jesus' astonishing teaching power lies in His being.

Effective Christian leadership and exemplary character go hand in glove. Is there any wonder Jesus astounded others? The sinlessness of Jesus is equally impressive, perhaps more, than any miracle He performed.

Heraclitus noted, "Character is destiny." General N. Schwartzkopf (United States Army, retired) once remarked, "Leadership is a potent combination of strategy and character. But, if you must be without one, be without strategy." One survey of a sample population seeking to identify characteristics most admired in leaders found honesty named by nearly 90 percent of the respondents, or 13 percent more frequently than the second-leading trait, which pertained to vision.[11]

The Bible provides an unlimited resource for instruction in leadership training and character building. First, as Jesus told Nicodemus, "You must be born again" (John 3:7 HCSB). Life must be reoriented from self-centeredness to God-centeredness and neighbor-centeredness, since love of God and neighbor and service to them characterize the life of the Christian leader (Matt 22:37–40).

The blueprint for living like Christ appears in the Sermon on the Mount (Matthew 5–7). Other unforgettable biblical pictures of a model life come from the servant-leader Christ, who with basin and towel washes the feet of the disciples, routinely spends time with the lowly, and forgives from the cross. His is the life of love Paul describes in the "love" chapter of the Bible (1 Corinthians 13). The apostle taught, "Love is patient; love is kind. Love does not envy; is not boastful; is not conceited; does not act improperly; is not selfish; is not provoked; does not keep a record of wrongs; finds no joy in unrighteousness, but rejoices in the truth; bears all things, believes all things, hopes all things, endures all things" (1 Cor 13:4–7 HCSB). The great apostle confessed, "If I . . . do not have love, I am a sounding gong or a clanging cymbal," and then again, "If I . . . do not have love, I am nothing" (1 Cor 13:1–2 HCSB). On another occasion Paul wrote to the believers in Galatia, "The entire law is fulfilled in one statement: Love your neighbor as yourself" (Gal 5:14 HCSB)." "If we live by the Spirit, we must also follow the Spirit" (Gal 5:25 HCSB), he encouraged, noting, "The fruit of the Spirit is love, joy, peace, patience, kindness, goodness, faith, gentleness, self-control" (Gal 5:22–23 HCSB). This is the way of Jesus. As Jesus lived, loving and serving others, so should the Christian leader live, love, and serve.

The appropriate course for leaders and all other believers is summarized by the prophet Micah when he said, "He has told you men what is good and what it is the LORD requires of you: Only to act justly, to love faithfulness, and to walk humbly with your God" (Mic 6:8 HCSB). Jeremiah delivers a similar word from the Lord, saying: "The wise must not boast in his wisdom; the mighty must not boast in his might; the rich must not boast in his riches. But the one who boasts should boast in this, that he understands and knows Me—that I am the LORD, showing faithful love, justice, and righteousness on the earth, for I delight in these things" (Jer 9:23–24).

The simplest charge for Christ-centered leadership-living comes from Jesus: "Whatever you want others to do for you, do also the same for them" (Matt 7:12). God's standard is the gold standard for Christian leaders.

In the Area of Service

The Christian leader models servant leadership just as Christ lived. Jesus did first whatever He expected others to do: trust God, love God, obey God, revere and study Scripture, pray, help the needy, love others, treat others right, evangelize, disciple, pray, serve, wash feet, forgive, deny self, lead the cross life. Jesus left no doubt that He came to serve, rather than to be served, and that the believer's call is also to serve (Matt 10:35–45). Christian mentoring teaches the way of Christ. To believe in Christ is to serve; to lead is to serve; to mentor is to serve; to love is to serve; to find purpose, meaning, and joy in life is to serve. Christian leaders are servant leaders.

When Criticism Comes

Leadership is not easy. Mentors should provide mentorees a realistic road map into the future. Leadership brings with it hardship. Even so, optimism is a far superior leadership trait than either pessimism or fatalism, both of which tend to become self-fulfilling prophecies. As Colin Powell, former chairman of the Joint Chiefs of Staff, and former U.S. Secretary of State, likes to say, optimism is a "force multiplier." Optimism inspires. Still, realism is imperative. Facts should be confronted squarely and then faced optimistically.

"So here's the hard truth: if you're a leader, you're in the battle of your life."[12] Nationally acclaimed lay leader H. E. Butt Jr. warns leaders of the dangerous JOAP Factor where JOAP stands for Judas, Oedipus, Adam, and Pharisee. Leaders face betrayal, envy, rebellion, and judgment.[13] D. Allender, founder and president of Mars Hill Graduate School near Seattle, cracks, "If we didn't have to deal with people or problems, leadership would be a piece of cake."[14]

Leaders can bank on this truth: you will be criticized. It is impossible to lead without opposition. At times the opposition gives way to hostility and personal attack. In the Bible, Moses was opposed by Korah, Dathan, Abiram, and On, and by Jannes and Jambres (Numbers 16). David's life was sought by Saul and Absalom (2 Tim 3:8). Elijah's enemies included King Ahab and Queen Jezebel (1 Samuel 18; 2 Samuel 15). The prophet Micaiah ben Imlah was despised by King Ahab and the false prophet Zedekiah (1 Kings 19, 22). Nehemiah, who led Israel to rebuild Jerusalem's walls after the exile, met strong opposition from Sanballat, Tobiah, and Geshaem (Nehemiah 2, 6). Mordecai was hated by Haman (Esther 3). Job was targeted by Satan and accused by his friends Eliphaz, Zophar, Bildad, and Elihu (with friends like these who needs enemies?). The psalmist knew countless unnamed enemies. Jeremiah's life was threatened by priests, prophets, and people (Jeremiah 26); he was beaten by Pashur the priest (Jeremiah 20) and violently opposed by Hananiah the false prophet (Jeremiah 28). Daniel, Shadrach, Meshach, and Abednego were targets of King Nebuchadnezzar (see the book of Daniel). Hosea's wife, Gomer, deserted him. Amos was criticized and chastised by Amaziah, the priest of Bethel (Amos 7). Paul was opposed by Alexander the coppersmith (Acts 19:33; 2 Tim 4:14) and countless others until he was finally beheaded. John met opposition from Diotrephes (3 John 9). The disciples were martyred, and Jesus was consistently criticized and violently opposed by Pharisees, Sadducees, scribes, and Romans, leading to His crucifixion.

The two greatest leaders in the history of Israel, Moses and the Messiah, met with severe resistance to their leadership. Murmurings and near mutinies against Moses broke out on at least 16 occasions (Exodus 14–Numbers 25). He did not make it to the promised land. Jesus was mocked, threatened, beaten, and crucified. What does it say about human nature that Jesus entered Jerusalem to shouts of "Hosanna, hosanna," from the throngs on Sunday, only to hear by Friday shouts of "Crucify Him. Crucify Him"?

Three of America's most revered leaders—Abraham Lincoln, John Fitzgerald Kennedy, and Martin Luther King Jr.—were assassinated. Prospective leaders should steel themselves for the hardship of leadership. Mentors should prepare others for life in the real world.

Is the call to Christian leadership a call to dazzle the saints or a call to die to self? Jesus' temptations from the devil were in part an attempted seduction to dazzle: (1) Turn these stones into bread—dazzle us! (2) Jump from this temple—dazzle us! (3) Rule all these kingdoms—dazzle us! (4) Choose crown, not cross—dazzle us!

Jesus' life response to the allure of self-indulgence, self-interest, and self-promotion rings loudly in His own words, "If anyone wants to come with Me, he must deny himself, take up his cross daily, and follow Me. For whoever wants to save his life will lose it, but whoever loses his life because of Me will save it" (Luke 9:23–24). But Jesus' loudest sermon was the cross.

Inevitable issues of criticism, conflict, and crisis, which a leader must face, when framed positively rather than negatively, lead to a healthier response and resolution than otherwise might occur. Obstacles viewed positively as opportunities for individual and communal growth in problem solving provide valuable occasions for team building. Challenges met head-on with calmness by the leader are more confidently met by the unit than they would be otherwise and are more readily resolved. Negative framing of issues only magnifies systemic stress. A positive approach to issues understands that teams are built around challenges. Challenges constitute the call to serve, a call to community, a call to grow and to achieve.

When leaders and their communities view issues of disagreement between themselves or within the group as battles to be fought, division occurs. Lines of engagement are drawn, opponents square off, unity is broken, a win-lose construct is established, and dysfunction in the system results. On the other hand, when those same issues are viewed as problems to be solved together, teamwork happens. The unified group puts the problem in front of them and works together as a team to solve the problem that threatens group harmony and well-being. Viewing one another as friends and allies working together for the welfare of the whole, as opposed to seeing others in the group as enemies who oppose the common good, generates incredible energy and problem-solving intelligence. Communities are always healthier, happier, stronger, and more productive when unified than when divided.

In the face of challenges, optimism remains possible for the leader whenever God's voice whispers, "I am sending you; I will be with you." Moses, Joshua, Jeremiah, Isaiah, Amos, Mary Magdalene, and others beyond number, in biblical times and in modern times, have found reassurance in the call and presence of God. The question has been asked, "Does

God call the equipped or equip the called?" Either way, the results are the same. For as Paul puts it, "I am able to do all things through Him who strengthens me" (Phil 4:13).

Within Relationships

There can be no leadership apart from relationship. Nothing, absolutely nothing, exists independent of its relationships. The interrelatedness of all matter lies at the center of creation and holds together the universe. Interpersonal relationships allow us to accomplish objectives we could never accomplish alone. Political races, military battles, legislation navigation, symphony performance, athletic team contests, city council government, governing board operation, jury work, church ministry—all these and more depend on relationships. The key to effective leadership is healthy relationships.

Leadership is primarily about three things: relationships, rules, and results. Every game has rules that govern its play; every organization has rules or policies; every society, community, or state has laws. Life cannot be lived apart from expectations or limits. Effective leaders communicate expectations and rules. However, systems characterized by healthy relationships as opposed to an oppressive focus on rules experience greater morale and much less apathy and rebellion among their members.

Basically, only one rule applies to all: do right! The "right" is generally determined by action as it relates to the welfare of the group. Words, attitudes, and deeds that harm the team, family, company, or community are "wrong." Immorality, evil, lawlessness, and unacceptable behavior are generally associated with individuals whose person and presence undermine the welfare of the whole. Exceptions certainly exist, but as a rule, "The team comes first."

Healthy relationships yield good results within the operation of a system. The four domains of leading like Jesus are head, heart, hands, and habits.[15] Heroes within the group are those who benefit the group by excelling within these four areas. Results matter; without positive results no leader is considered "a good leader."

Leaders must be trustworthy; teammates must trust one another. Joe Paterno, head football coach at Penn State, who has won more football games than anyone in the history of the game, says, "Whether you're on a sports team, in an office, or a member of a family, if you can't trust another there's going to be trouble."[16] Building trust on any team is the top priority of the leader.

One important way for the leader to build trust is to be vulnerable. When leaders are transparent, confessional, and vulnerable, rather than prideful and self-exalting, they generate respect from their also human troops. Confidence is important in leaders, but confidence and conceit are not synonyms. Humility does not impede the pursuit of excellence. The journey "to the top" is simply a shared mission with mutual demands on leader and troops rather than a "summons to my mountain or pedestal of perfection."

Team building requires molding diversity into unity. Unity is not uniformity. The apostle Paul describes the diversity of spiritual gifts in his letters to the Romans and Corinthians (Romans 12; 1 Corinthians 12). Athletic teams consist of players with different strengths suitable for particular positions. College cabinets include vice presidents with expertise in various areas. Church ministerial staffs benefit from the skill sets of ministers educated and trained in music, preaching, counseling, finances, children and youth ministry, and other areas. Teams are built on diversity. But unless diversity is turned into unity, any hope for a dream team will go unrealized.

Shared goals, visions, dreams, strategies, and sacrifice help build team unity. Listening, talking, working together, playing together, and eating together bring teams closer together. Character, competence, commitment, communication, and care inspire confidence and create cohesiveness. Trust is the foundation of team building; respect is the cornerstone. As love, trust, and respect for team members grow, so grows unity.

Even the best leaders will have critics and opponents. Paradoxically, leaders need critics, even enemies. Frequently, critics of the leader or of the team help mold team unity. Equally important is the gift of learning from criticism. Dissent deserves respect. An enemy may prove to be a valuable teacher. Critics and enemies help us with our humility needs. Pride creates defensiveness and deafness; humility improves hearing. Jesus said, "Love your enemies." Learning from them is important too.

Leadership is not first and foremost how we handle other people but how we handle ourselves. Gandhi advised, "Be the change in the world you want to see." The leader is a part of a relational system that comprises an emotional unit. Since humans are imperfect and systems—families, churches, schools, companies, and governments—are all composed of humans, no system is perfect, nor will it ever be. Nor will an emotional unit comprised of human beings operate without interpersonal conflict.

Family systems theory teaches that it takes only one person to change a relationship pattern. Moreover, our own part in the relationship is the only part we have the power to change. To work on a relationship is to work on our self. Neither treatment nor change need be focused on the symptomatic person, that is, the one exhibiting dysfunction in the relationship or group. We can change an unhealthy relationship pattern by changing the way we respond to dysfunction. When one person changes, the whole pattern of relating changes. Therefore, a determined focus on our own deportment in relationships is important. Emotional calm is huge![17] Family systems theory is a valuable tool in a leader's toolbox.

A mentor will help others understand effective ways to respond to challenges. Tests of character and competence come from adversity, but tests also spring from prosperity and power. The adage correctly claims, "Power corrupts, and absolute power corrupts absolutely." A prosperous and powerful leader will be tempted by pride and self-sufficiency. The Bible warns, "When pride comes, disgrace follows." Then, "Everyone with a proud heart is detestable to the LORD; be assured, he will not go unpunished." And then again, "Pride comes before destruction, and an arrogant spirit before a fall" (Prov 11:2; 16:5,18 HCSB).

In the Realm of Power

Psychologist M. Madden warns, "Evil . . . resides near to the centers of power."[18] History offers a thousand proofs that Madden is correct. Yet power is a battery awaiting its charge. Power may be exercised positively or negatively. Power used to help others is constructive; power used to oppress or otherwise hurt others is destructive. Power may be used altruistically or narcissistically. Power exercised for the welfare of the group is considered good. When used to the detriment of the group or for self-serving immoral purposes, power is abused and considered evil.

Psychologist R. May defines *power* as "the ability to cause or prevent change."[19] So understood, power is influence. Leaders are especially influential persons. May identifies five levels of power common to all persons:

1. The power to be
2. Self-affirmation (cry for recognition)
3. Self-assertion
4. Aggression
5. Violence

Each person possesses the power to exist, needs recognition, and will assert himself in some manner if not recognized. When self-assertion fails, aggression results, followed by hostility or violence. Mentors of future leaders would do well to instruct their less experienced associates of the need to respect, affirm, and recognize others. *Value, voice,* and *vote* are three good words for leaders to remember. All persons want to be valued, given voice, and allowed to participate in decision making that affects them.

Most can recite the adage, "Power corrupts." Far fewer understand that powerlessness corrupts also and that, like absolute power, absolute powerlessness corrupts absolutely, as well. Violence is born from powerlessness. When we feel powerless, hopelessness, apathy, and rebellion (sometimes passive, sometimes active) set in. Boundaries within relationships are important, to be sure. Excessive control, however, exercised by "control freaks" leaves others feeling oppressed and demoralized. Human levels of self-esteem vary radically, correlating positively with feelings of power/powerlessness.

"Power is always interpersonal."[20] So are its effects. The blessing and its effects are also interpersonal. In fact, "blessing is the gift of power."[21] To love and accept another, to enjoy him, to believe in him, is to bless him, empower him, and forecast his destiny. To reject someone on the other hand, or not to believe in him, is to curse him. In the Bible, Jacob was a blessed child; Esau was not (Gen 27:38). The gift of blessing is the gift of one's self and trust to another. Leaders are called to bless.

Listening

"Leadership is an acoustical art."[22] We lead best with our ears. Appearing to Solomon in a dream, God said, "Ask. What I shall give you?" Revered as one of the wisest leaders in Israel's history, King Solomon asked the Lord for a listening heart. Solomon's request pleased the Lord immensely. "Because you have requested this and did not ask for long life or riches for yourself, or the death of your enemies, but you asked discernment for yourself to understand justice, I will therefore do what you have asked" (1 Kgs 3:5–13 HCSB). Wise leaders listen. Leaders who listen please God in that regard. Although some translations of Solomon's response render his request as one for an "understanding heart" rather than a "listening heart," the original language reveals that Solomon prayed the Hebrew word which means "to listen" or "to hear." His primary concern was to listen. A secondary definition of the term he used means "understanding." Therefore the usage of the term in the Hebrew language and the selection of the word by Solomon deliver a plain message: in order to understand, we must *first* listen and not only listen but hear.

Voltaire said, "The road to the heart is the ear." Folk wisdom adds, "They won't care what you know until they know you care." Leaders care about their followers. They care what their teammates have to say. Wise leaders care and they listen. In his highly acclaimed book *Good to Great,* J. Collins encourages leaders to "lead with questions, not answers."[23] He writes, "Leading from good to great does not mean coming up with the answers and then motivating everyone to follow your messianic vision. It means having the humility to grasp the fact that you do not yet understand enough to have the answers and then to ask the questions that will lead to the best possible insights."[24]

Leadership experts distinguish between overfunctioning leaders (low-level leaders) and high-level leaders in several ways, one of which is the willingness to listen. Low-level leaders are more dictatorial, listening poorly or not at all, to input from others. High-level leaders, on the other hand, function well and listen carefully. High-level leaders are "relationship masters." Relationship masters listen.[25] Effective leaders are listeners.

Vision

According to a survey published in *The Leadership Challenge,* after honesty the most frequently named characteristic of admired leaders is "forward-looking." Following close behind is "inspiring."[26] Leaders are visionaries. They dream dreams and see visions. Leaders ask: "Where are we? Where do we want to go? How do we get from here to there?"

People want to know where they are going. In Lewis Carroll's classic tale *Alice in Wonderland,* the Cheshire cat tells Alice, "If you do not know where you going, any which way will do." Vision provides a road map from the present into the future. Or as Victor Hugo put it in *Les Misérables,* "There is nothing like a dream to create the future." Every team or organization needs a clear set of challenges. One leadership challenge, as Hugo correctly observes, is determining how much future to introduce into the present.

Leading people is like tuning a stringed instrument: the tension must be just right—not too little, not too much. Leadership is the art of change management. Change creates stress. Sensitivity to the pace of change is important for the well-being of the system. The familiar proverb states, "Where there is no vision, the people perish" (Prov 29:18 KJV). True, but without a job the leader may perish. Pace is critical for both people and leader.

Effective leaders set direction, cast vision, and create appropriate strategies in order to accomplish the team goals. It is not enough to have a dream. One must also have a plan. Leaders learn that process is as important as the product when it comes to establishing plans. Involving team members in goal setting, strategic planning, and action plans promotes ownership of the vision and commitment to it. The old iron-fisted, top-down, dictatorial style of leadership has given way to the contemporary preference for dialogue, cooperation, collaboration, consensus building, and teamwork. Listening and communication matter.

Management differs from leadership in that the former maintains order in an organization through planning, budgeting, operating daily, problem solving, personnel supervision, crisis management, decision making, and other such functions. By contrast, vision, direction, and strategies for change characterize an important part of a leader's work.[27] The leader must also inspire, motivate, implement, evaluate, and communicate. Often, however, the lines of distinction between managers and leaders are blurred as the leader also manages.

"Vision arises out of our burden to know the will of God, to become whatever it is God wants us to become."[28] Unless the vision conforms to the will of God for the group, it is a bad vision. The Christian leader should ask, "Is our vision God-given or man-made?" Is our corporate prayer, "Thy will be done," or "My will be done"?

Acclaimed conductor R. Nierenberg writes, "The most important thing a conductor brings to the orchestra is a vision of the music that the musicians will want to bring to life with their playing."[29] Leadership guru J. Maxwell focuses on the character of the one casting the vision when he shares, "When I teach leadership seminars . . . invariably someone will . . . ask me, 'Do you think my people will buy into my vision?' My response is always the same: 'First tell me this. Do your people buy into you?'"[30] He concludes, "People buy into the leader first, then the leader's vision."[31]

Other Important Areas of Mentoring by Leaders

The leader will want to serve as mentor in many other areas of professional and personal living. Two of these areas include time management, which is essentially managing one's self, and a balanced life, which includes work, rest, leisure, exercise, worship, prayer, family time, devotional life, eating properly, recreation, and service. Effective time management makes possible a balanced life. Time with God, family, and self require desire, planning, and commitment. Mentors have a responsibility to model and teach the disciplined, balanced life.

In relation to others, Jesus both treated and retreated.

How Is the Leader a Pastor?

A leader need not be an ordained minister overseeing a Christian congregation in order to fulfill a pastoral role among his people. Whereas a pastor of a church teaches, preaches, leads worship, and officiates ritual ceremonies in the life of the community, pastoral duties reach far into other areas of service as well. A pastor also counsels, visits the sick, helps the needy, affirms and encourages the members of the congregation, attends important events in the lives of the people, knows their names, writes notes of congratulations and condolences on significant occasions, loves and prays for the church and the people, and models a Christlike life.

A leader serves in a pastoral manner when performing pastoral duties. Since caregiving, or care living, summarizes a defining part of pastoral ministry, a leader who cares for his people and shows it by fulfilling traditional pastoral functions serves as a pastor. A pastoral leader attends weddings and funerals related to the families of his organization. Funeral attendance is mandatory for a leader, and wedding attendance should be. People remember when the leader is present and when he is not. Hospital visitation, when possible, delivers the message that people matter and that the leader cares for his people. Attendance at ball games, concerts, recitals, lectures, and other significant occasions in the lives of his flock build tremendous goodwill and morale. Letters, notes, and cards written on birthdays and anniversaries express care and value to the recipient. Gifts at childbirth express love and shared celebration. Knowing the names of everyone in the organization is an important goal for the leader. Persons feel valued when their name is called in a courteous, respectful manner.

A leader is a pastor when he is a caregiver during a crisis. Illness, surgery, death, bereavement, divorce, substance abuse, drug addiction, emotional, verbal, physical, or sexual abuse, marital separation, unwanted pregnancy, problem pregnancy, foreclosure, bankruptcy, accident or crime victimization—all these and more represent crises which may strike members of the leader's community. Love and concern shown during times of crisis serve as golden threads to knit souls together.

A pastor listens. Listening means not doing the talking. Leaders serve as pastors when they listen. What more need be said?

Most Christian leaders know the Ten Commandments, or at least know of them and could recite some, if not most, of them. Leaders who would serve as pastor would be well served to know the eleventh commandment. What is it? Jesus delivered a farewell discourse in which he said, "I give you a new commandment: love one another. . . . By this all people will know that you are My disciples, if you have love for one another" (John 13:34–35 HCSB). To serve as a model of Christlike living and to serve as a pastor of the group one oversees, love of the flock is nonnegotiable. Jesus gave us an eleventh commandment: "Love one another."

Pastors serve in many roles, including administrative ones. Along with "shepherding the flock" in commonly understood ways, pastors also manage the church's day-to-day operation. Ethical business practices and respectful interactions with others in the exercise of managerial duties signify commitment to Christ in word and deed in the pastor's life. Purity in all areas of one's life characterizes the Christian leader-pastor.

In a survey of 12,000 persons in 47 denominations, including both laity and clergy, respondents were asked to name or select "characteristics expected of a Christian pastor." The most frequently listed characteristic was an "open, affirming style," meaning, "handling stressful situations by remaining calm under pressure while continuing to affirm persons."[32]

A pastor is "different." The biblical words which translate *holy* mean "to be set apart," or "to be different." A pastor is holy or different by being set apart *from* the world and *to* the service of the Lord. When a leader feels called by God away *from* the ways of the world, *to* the ways of God in living the Christian life and in giving Christian care to others, he is different. The leader has become a pastor and a mentor.

Resources for Further Study

Allender, D. *Leading with a Limp.* Colorado Springs: WaterBrook, 2006.

Blanchard, K., and P. Hodges. *Lead Like Jesus.* Nashville: W Publishing Group, 2005.

Covey, S. R. *Principle-Centered Leadership.* New York: Fireside/Simon & Schuster, 1990.

Dale, R. D. *Ministers as Leaders.* Nashville: Broadman, 1984.

Gilbert, R. M. *Extraordinary Leadership.* Falls Church: Leading Systems Press, 2006.

Kouzes, J., and B. Posner. *The Leadership Challenge.* San Francisco: Jossey-Bass, 1995.

Maxwell, J. *The 21 Irrefutable Laws of Leadership.* Nashville: Thomas Nelson, 1998.

Oates, W. *The Christian Pastor.* Philadelphia: Westminster, 1982.

Robinson, B. *Incarnate Leadership.* Grand Rapids: Zondervan, 2009.

Questions for Further Reflection

1. How is the effective Christian leader like any other effective leader?
2. How is the Christian leader different from other leaders?
3. Who has served as an important mentor in your life, and in what ways?
4. To whom might you more intentionally serve as mentor?
5. How might God use you to show His pastoral care toward others in your sphere of influence?

Endnotes

[1] K. Blanchard and P. Hodges, *Lead Like Jesus* (Nashville: W Publishing Group, 2005), 47.

[2] L. Sweet, *Summoned to Lead* (Grand Rapids: Zondervan, 2004), 16.

[3] Ibid., 17–18.

[4] Ibid., 18.

[5] Blanchard, *Lead Like Jesus,* 154.

[6] B. Robinson, *Incarnate Leadership* (Grand Rapids: Zondervan, 2009), 19.

[7] Ibid., 20.

[8] J. Maxwell, *Leadership Promises for Every Day* (Nashville: J. Countryman, 2003), back cover.

[9] S. Covey, *The Speed of Trust* (New York: Free Press, 2006), 177.

[10] J. Maxwell, *The 21 Irrefutable Laws of Leadership* (Nashville: Thomas Nelson, 1998), 133.

[11] J. Kouzes and B. Posner, *The Leadership Challenge* (San Francisco: Jossey-Bass Publishers, 1995), 21.

[12] D. Allender, *Leading with a Limp* (Colorado Springs: WaterBrook, 2006), 1.

[13] J. E. Butt Jr., *Who Can You Trust?* (Colorado Springs: WaterBrook, 2004), 49.

[14] Allender, *Leading with a Limp,* 29.

[15] Blanchard, *Lead Like Jesus,* 31.

[16] Covey, *The Speed of Trust,* 11.

[17] See R. M. Gilbert, *Extraordinary Relationships* (San Francisco: Wiley, 1992), 34.

[18] M. C. Madden, *Blessing: Giving the Gift of Power* (Nashville: Broadman, 1988), 58.

[19] R. May, *Power and Innocence* (New York: W. W. Norton, 1972), 99.

[20] Ibid., 35.

[21] Madden, *Blessing: Giving the Gift of Power,* 19.

[22] Sweet, *Summoned to Lead,* 17.

[23] J. Collins, *Good to Great* (New York: HarperCollins, 2001), 74.

[24] Ibid., 75.

[25] R. M. Gilbert, *Extraordinary Leadership* (Falls Church: Leading Systems Press, 2006), 94–99.

[26] Kouzes and Posner, *The Leadership Challenge,* 21.

[27] J. Kotter, "What Leaders Really Do," *Harvard Business Review on Leadership* (Boston: Harvard Business School Publishing, 1998), 41–42.

[28] E. Fullam, "Grasping the Vision," *Leaders,* ed. H. Myra (Waco: Word, 1987), 98.

[29] See R. Nierenberg, *Maestro* (New York: Penguin, 2009), 22.

[30] Maxwell, *The 21 Irrefutable Laws of Leadership*, 145.

[31] Ibid.

[32] W. Oates, *The Christian Pastor* (Philadelphia: Westminster, 1982), 17.

Chapter 17

LEADERSHIP FOR A
GLOBAL WORLD

Charles A. Fowler
Senior Pastor, Germantown Baptist Church,
Germantown, Tennessee

Changing World

O ne cannot help but observe that the world around us is changing in unprecedented ways. Change seems to be a constant in almost every sector of life, both here and abroad.

Economically we are seeing tremendous shifts and growing uncertainties. Just a few years ago it would have been unimaginable that the troubled economies in our world would be primarily Western. Today debt and deficits are strangling the economies of Greece, Italy, Hungary, the United Kingdom, Ireland, Spain, and even the USA.[1] To look for growing economies, we must turn to Argentina, Brazil, China, India, and Australia. While the U.S. economy is still the world's largest,[2] its influence is most definitely lessening on the world stage with the vibrancy of some of the new and emerging markets around the world.

There is a monumental shift, worldwide, of people's abandoning rural communities and choosing to live in urban areas. This trend is growing across every continent. Cities with over 10 million inhabitants are known as megacities. Scholars predict that by the year 2015, 23 megacities will exist.[3]

The long-term impacts of these trends are impossible to measure. It will certainly offer benefits of concentrated living, but it will also present some of the greatest challenges in human history. This migration to megacities will create a sudden and unprecedented demand for services. Currently, 70 percent of India's 1.2 billion residents live in rural areas. Internal migrations are transforming it into a country with 25 of the world's 100 fastest growing cities.[4] Virtually every country is experiencing some degree of impact from these population shifts.

This overall trend toward megacities becomes more pronounced when we realize that just 60 years ago New York and Tokyo were the only two megacities in the world.

Currently Dhaka, Bangladesh, is the fastest growing megacity in the world. It is rapidly becoming the picture of the new megacity. Contrary to traditional images of megacities focused on wealth and opportunity, many of the new megacities are known for poverty, political unrest, and hopelessness. Dhaka is not immune to any of these challenges. It doubled in size from 1990 to 2005.[5] It is overcrowded, polluted, poor, and experiencing significant shortages of energy and water. The number of people migrating to Dhaka continues to climb in spite of these challenges. The trend will likely continue.

The growth of new megacities presents interesting and compelling opportunities for Christian organizations. Among the needs are humanitarian relief, education, research, sustainable energy supplies, fresh water, and many more. Christian organizations have an incredible opportunity to serve these populations by meeting real human needs and, through intensive research, helping organizations and governments understand these population trends and providing some intervention for future generations. Perhaps through serving these peoples, doors can be opened not only to hear the gospel but also to see it expressed through the love and service of volunteers mobilized through the work of thoughtful Christian organizations.

In addition, the needs are so broad that the opportunities are not limited to just churches, Christian colleges and universities, and humanitarian relief organizations but extend to the full spectrum of faith-based organizations.

Closer to home, Mexico City exemplifies the transition impacting megacities. For each of the last 10 years, over 270,000 people have moved into Mexico City from rural areas.[6] This movement has made it one of the largest cities in the world, and the rapid growth continues. Mexico City, like the other megacities developing in Asia, Africa, and Latin America, experiences the same as Dhaka and the other new megacities. Each of them will likely struggle with food production, energy issues, education, political unrest, and poverty.

By the year 2030, experts anticipate that 80 percent of the world's population will live in urban centers.[7] Many, if not most, of Christian organizations in America are located in rural areas with little or no urban engagement. These population trends provide both challenge and opportunity to these organizations. With bold and wise leadership that develops strategic initiatives to prepare for meaningful urban engagement, Christian organizations can position themselves for sustainable viability and success for the foreseeable future. Developing new markets, new approaches, new competencies, and new opportunities will strengthen institutions. To do so will require a new paradigm of leadership.

In addition to the impact of urbanization, the growth of social technologies is changing how people relate to one another in every sector of our global society. People interact with friends and colleagues around the world with the same ease as they have always done with neighbors. The sobering reality is that now the interactions with neighbors and colleagues around the world are done in the same way—technologically. Users of these technologies are increasingly using them not only to nurture friendships but also to conduct business. Social media create a perceived openness in every society that is exciting to many and deeply concerning for others.

There are many examples of the power of social media and how it is changing the face of business, education, and health care. For instance, a young Canadian musician named Dave Carroll had an unforgettable impact on United Airlines via social media. On a trip in 2009, Mr. Carroll boarded his United Airlines flight and prepared for takeoff. He looked out of the window and noticed baggage handlers tossing suitcases on the tarmac at Chicago's O'Hare airport. Among those tossed bags, many of which were dropped on the ground, was a guitar case of particular interest to him. So he called the flight attendant over and asked that she look at the scene outside of the window and intervene. She told him she could do nothing and that he needed to report the situation to the gate attendant when they reached their destination.

Mr. Carroll did just that and was informed that complaints regarding luggage handling had to go to the corporate offices. To his dismay, when he retrieved his luggage, he discovered that the tossed guitar case was indeed his. Unfortunately, he discovered in baggage claim that his guitar was damaged. Being a professional musician with performances to give, this created quite a problem. After repairing the instrument and giving three days of performances, he finally had the time to contact United's corporate office. Once again, disappointing news came. They told him that there was a three-day window for reporting damaged luggage; and, therefore, his $1,200 claim would not be covered. Mr. Carroll pressed his case for months to no avail.

In frustration, he wrote a song entitled "United Breaks Guitars" and posted it on YouTube on July 7, 2009. Within three days more than a million people had viewed the video. After just a few more months and more than seven million viewings of the video that in turn prompted hundreds of news stories worldwide, United's senior vice president decided to give Mr. Carroll a phone call to see what United could do to satisfy his claim.[8]

In our increasingly open society, it takes only one person to replace a well-established corporate brand with a song like "United Breaks Guitars," and a multinational, multibillion-dollar company must yield to a professional musician from Canada. This is just one vivid example of the power of social media, and this is increasingly where and how our world connects.

What does this story have to do with the work of Christian organizations? At a minimum it reminds us of the power of social media and the growing influence of technological platforms where people connect and build community. Wise observers understand that there is a global shift in how people relate, communicate, interact, do business, and engage with society at large. Recognizing this fact should encourage us to position ourselves strategically to remain viable in the face of an avalanche of change.

Technology is already a source of some degree of stress for most Christian organizations. With all of the benefits it provides, it is accelerating change in organizations in ways that can be alarming. It is changing communication patterns. It is changing how community is developed. It is changing where and how people think about career options. It is changing how people shop, take college courses, and manage their money. It is making the world a different place at a mind-numbing pace. All of these changes not only hold implications for how we work and relate, but they also come at a significant cost when financial resources are hard to acquire. Christian organizations seem always to be lacking a clear vision for the best and most prudent use of these limited resources when it comes to technology. It can be one of the most complicated and perplexing aspects of leading a Christian organization due to costs, uncertain benefits, and the rapid procession of new generations of technologies that seem never ending and unavoidable.

The upgrading of technologies can be overwhelming as a factor itself. Often new generations drive down pricing and create different entry points into the technology race for countries, companies, and Christian organizations. Like organizations, some countries place technology research and development at a higher priority than some Western countries who have historically been leaders in the technology world. By so doing, technology is integrated into their cultural fabric in fresh and creative ways. This can result in an uneven playing field. It is also a new dynamic that America is no longer leading the way in technology development. We remain a primary consumer but no longer the dominant leader in development in this field. This reality creates uncertainties and challenges regarding the future for all of us.

The new reality is that more people are online worldwide than ever before. According to http://www.internetworldstats.com, 1.9 billion people globally are active on the Internet. Regular usage by continent ranges from 10.9 percent in Africa to 21.5 percent in Asia to 77.4 percent in North America.[9] Our world truly is wired.

Not only is use of the Internet worldwide, but use of interactive and social Web sites is accelerating. In September 2006, only 32 percent of all active Internet users in the world had watched a video clip online. By March 2009, this number had grown to 83 percent. In the same time period, global online users of social Web sites jumped from 27 percent to 63 percent of all users.[10] People are now spending more time online, and they are spending more time viewing content they created themselves. This is a revolutionary change in communication and culture.

Not only do these trends indicate increased usage of the Internet and social media, but they are also creating a new electronic "culture of sharing."[11] Until just a few years ago, sharing personal information required a fax, an e-mail, a letter, a landline phone, or some other traditional means of communication. Today users share personal information, family photos, and anecdotes online, worldwide, instantly, and with relative ease.

For the first time in history, when hot spots occur around the world, news media seem to turn first to social media sites to get video footage and stories from "on the ground" eyewitnesses who share practically live videos and real-time blog postings. Anyone with a mobile phone has the ability to communicate worldwide instantly. Truly communication has already shifted so much that individuals think no more of connecting with friends on other continents than they do coworkers in adjoining offices.

These trends are upon us, and their impact is felt both personally and professionally. Even if we choose not to participate in social media outlets, the world around us is radically different. Our students, customers, stakeholders, partners, and coworkers no longer even think in traditional communication or community-building patterns. The world has become smaller and more connected than most are able to realize. The implications of this new reality are profound.

Like urbanization and countless other global population trends impacting culture and work, social media and broader technology developments exert enormous influence on the thought patterns and lifestyle choices of an increasing number of people. The changes that loom in the near future are hard to predict, but with certainty one can say that the pace of the change and the influence on culture will likely only grow.

Vast changes are taking place in almost every sector of our society and the world. This era of our history may be remembered more for the speed and comprehensiveness of change than for the outcome of the changes themselves. The result of changes provides a new baseline for the next wave of change to come.

This limited overview should cause us to pause and reflect on the impact of these extraordinary global changes on the leadership and international work of Christian organizations whose identity and mission lead them to serve with an overarching purpose designed to transform culture and renew minds through service. In this day of global change, to accomplish this high calling, Christian organizations must understand the new and changing world where those they serve live and work. This reality could allow organizations with a Christ-honoring mission to experience increased effectiveness by using the opportunities provided through technology and understanding of cultural shifts to speak with a compelling voice into an increasingly urban world.

These are weighty matters. When considering them and attempting to formulate a response, the dynamic of personal and organizational leadership is a construct through which a proactive approach to change can be facilitated rather than merely waiting to respond with a reactive approach. The breadth and depth of current societal changes heighten the challenges inherent in any organizational leadership model. The change is unprecedented, the challenges are daunting, but the potential is immeasurable with a commitment to wise leadership centered around a strong mission.

A rowing team has been used as an illustration in many contexts to understand leadership. A rowing team could be described as "eight people going backwards as fast as they can, without speaking to each other, steered by the one person who can't row." That is a rather clever description. Peter Drucker illustrated a leadership dynamic with this example one day and discovered that he had an oarsman in his audience.

Following the presentation, the oarsman came forward to correct Dr. Drucker's apparent misunderstanding of rowing. The oarsman said, "How do you think that we could go backward so fast, without communicating, if we were not completely confident in each other's competence, committed to the same goal, and determined to do our best to reach it? It's the perfect description of a team."[12]

Drucker had to agree but asked, "Who is the leader of this team?" The oarsman replied:

> That depends. During the race it is the little person in the back of the boat, the one who can't row, who is in charge. He or she is often the task leader. But there is also the Stroke, who sets the pace and the standard we all must follow. Off the river, however, the leader is the captain of the boat. He or she is responsible for choosing the crew, for our discipline, and for the mood and motivation of the group; but on the river the captain is just another member of the crew. Finally, there is the coach who is responsible for our training and development. There is no doubt who the leader is when the coach is around. We don't have one leader, nor do we give anyone that title. The role shifts around depending on the stage we are at.[13]

This model is certainly one perspective through which we can consider the process of leadership. Some refer to this as "leadership from the middle" while others give it the more academic label of distributive leadership.[14]

Whatever label we give it, the role of those at the top of traditional organizations must change. In this model the leader's role shifts from a traditional, authoritative model to one that provides the adhesive that holds a virtual community together. *Virtuality* refers to managing people you cannot see and cannot control in the traditional sense.[15] It is a style that is congruent with the ever-increasing knowledge base, mobility, technological capacity, openness, and inclusive atmosphere of twenty-first-century culture. This is our new virtual reality. It is a call for open leadership which is "having the confidence and humility to give up the need to be in control while inspiring commitment from people to accomplish goals."[16]

A distributed model of leadership in virtual community instills a new paradigm for the organizational leader. This new role requires leaders to build a shared vision across their organization by leading their staff to embrace a unified sense of identity, purpose, and urgency.[17]

We now live in a world that is seldom disconnected from the rest of world. Via the Web we increasingly live in an open and sharing environment. People who are not even officially connected with our organizations are invited to speak into our organizations and by doing so influence our ability to achieve institutional goals. It is a different world, and this new world requires a fresh paradigm of leadership. For Christian organizations seeking to build a sustainable presence and ministry, virtuality and the growing need for distributive approaches to leadership are profound.

Changing Leadership

Against this background, let me offer a few suggestions for your fresh leadership approaches. First, the role of Christian organizations which connect with an increasingly international constituency and which are challenged with limited financial and personnel resources with increased expectations and opportunities must shift toward becoming a *catalyst and consultant* rather than manager. Attempting to manage projects and partnerships scattered around the U.S. and the world in a traditional sense is an unmanageable task. The necessity of leading those you cannot see and cannot control (the necessity of virtuality) determines the leadership approach.

Christian organizations must consider how they can further embrace a role of catalyst for new opportunities and consultant for the ongoing demands of the programs it facilitates. Organizations can strategically position themselves for greater expansion and more effective approaches. In doing so, they leverage organizational networks and empower constituents to "own" the programs and thereby become the drivers of relationships and ultimately the success of the programs, ministries, and services. Obviously those leading Christian organizations cannot completely withdraw from involvement in any programs but must learn to lead through fresh paradigms that understand the changing landscape of culture. This ownership model that empowers constituents and embraces a distributive leadership model will position leaders to be fruitful for the foreseeable future and hopefully measureably advance organizational mission.

Second, Christian organizations possess a heritage, core values, and committed constituent base that make them distinctive. These organizations generally mobilize individuals who serve as a personal extension of institutional priorities and mission. They commit themselves to serving faithfully within the context of the mission of the organization with which they affiliate.

Organizational culture has become so complex and so closely intertwined with partner institutions and a myriad of stakeholders that it can be easy for institutional mission and expectations to lose priority focus amid so many competing demands and worthwhile work. The urgent can often trump the essentials. In the current economic environment with financial and legal challenges always lurking, leaders of Christian organizations must not lessen their commitment to mission. A Christ-honoring mission must always be the "tip of the spear" for our organizations that leads us forward.

Much has been written about Christian organizations that diluted their mission by employing those who did not personally embrace it or by becoming so distracted by the challenges of existence or operational minutia that they lost sight of core motivation for existing and working, their mission. The core essential for leading Christian organizations is a commitment to mission that permeates every level of our organizations.

Once again a distributive leadership model serves well here. Leaders of complex organizations are called to a role similar to a teacher. They must travel around to inform and educate members and stakeholders of the organization's mission and purpose and ensure that they have the information needed to succeed in their respective roles. To translate this into the world of Christian organizations, it would be to ask leaders to commit themselves to touching base with employees, constituents, partners, and stakeholders to remind them of the mission and to encourage and empower them with necessary resources to thrive. It is a liberating approach to leadership. It allows all constituents and stakeholders to leverage their shared wisdom, professional networks, and experience.

This call is an attempt to articulate a preferred future understanding of some of the challenges and opportunities that lie ahead. The current and past successes of our organizations are to be celebrated. That is important because with each new success a new baseline is established, and the entire organization is lifted. This is a call to invite meaningful and honest input and conversation designed for the purpose of evaluating the philosophical framework for leadership necessary to lead Christian organizations effectively and proactively toward a preferred future.

In conclusion, if the future for Christian organizations is built on a rich and distinguished past and anchored in historic core values that must never be compromised, then there is cause for great hopefulness. Upon this foundation we should embrace the reality of a changing world and position ourselves strategically to remain not only relevant but to thrive. Christian organizations have the means and motivation to lead the way as an example of effectiveness, commitment to mission, and strategic advance in the world, rather than settling for an anemic existence and ineffective service.

No organizational missions are more important than a Christ-honoring mission. There is no better context from which to pursue Christ-honoring excellence, no motivation more compelling, no platform more strategic in the world for Christian organizations. May we embrace the realities of change and be a leader in our communities, nation, and the world.

Many may share my deep appreciation for leadership and have as much passion for seeing Christian organizations and those who lead them to position themselves strategically for sustainable success. My hope is that these thoughts will prompt meaningful dialogue in the days to come. Hopefully, we can find ways to embrace a "rowing team" model of leadership in a new virtual world for the good of the organizations we lead and then ultimately for the glory of God.

We live in a new and perpetually changing world with different demands and more profound cultural shifts than we have ever encountered in the past. It is exciting to consider the unprecedented number of new opportunities that will become available to Christian leaders and Christian organizations who plan for a hopeful future filled with missional advance in spite of the challenges presented by a more global, urban, and technologically dependent culture. The world around us is getting smaller. The need and opportunity for our organizations to thrive is growing. Now is the time to embrace fresh paradigms and release the comfortable and traditional models of leadership upon which our organizations were built if those models are positioning us for irrelevance and increasing ineffectiveness in the future. Viable options require bold and convictional leadership that empowers others, lifts our organizations, and advances mission in strategic ways.

Resources for Further Study

Barone, Michael. *Hard America, Soft America: Competition vs. Coddling and the Battle for the Nation's Future*. New York: Crown Forum, 2004.

Bennis, Warren, and Philip Slater. *The Temporary Society: What Is Happening to the Business and Family Life in America Under the Impact of Accelerating Change*. San Francisco: Jossey-Bass, 1998.

Bossidy, Larry, and Ram Charan. *Execution: The Discipline of Getting Things Done*. New York: Crown Business Publishing, 2002.

Hamel, Gary. *The Future of Management*. Cambridge, MA: Harvard Business School Press, 2007.

Hesselbein, Frances, Marshall Goldsmith, and Richard Beckhard. *The Leader of the Future*. San Francisco: The Drucker Foundation, Jossey-Bass, 1996.

Hunt, Johnny M. *Get Connected: Mobilizing Your Church for God's Mission*. Richmond: International Mission Board of the Southern Baptist Convention, 2010.

James, Jennifer. *Thinking in the Future Tense: Leadership Skills for a New Age*. New York: Simon & Schuster, 1996.

Kim, W. Chan, and Renée Mauborgne. *Blue Ocean Strategy: How to Create Uncontested Market Space and Make the Competition Irrelevant*. Boston: Harvard Business School, 2005.

Kouzes, James M., and Barry Z. Posner. *The Leadership Challenge: How to Keep Getting Extraordinary Things Done in Organizations*. San Francisco: Jossey-Bass, 1995.

Li, Charlene. *Open Leadership: How Social Technology Can Transform the Way You Lead*. San Francisco: Jossey-Bass, 2010.

Pippert, Wesley G. *The Hand of the Mighty: Right and Wrong Uses of Our Power*. Grand Rapids: Baker Book House, 1991.

Sanders, Oswald J. *Spiritual Leadership: Principles of Excellence for Every Believer*. Chicago: Moody Press, 1994.

Sjogren, Bob, and Bill and Amy Stearns. *Run with the Vision: A Remarkable Global Plan for the 21st Century*. Minneapolis: Bethany House, 1995.

Stackhouse, Max L., Tim Dearborn, and Scott Paeth. *The Local Church in a Global Era: Reflections for a New Century*. Grand Rapids: Eerdmans, 2000.

Questions for Further Reflection

1. How should the reality of global change presented in this chapter affect organizations who are not multinational or do not have international stakeholders?

2. Should the scope and pace of change within Christian organizations be determined primarily by internal priorities or external factors such as urbanization and technological change?

3. How should an unchanging gospel influence organizational priorities and leadership style in the midst of a sea of change?

4. Discuss how a more open style of leadership as viewed through the lenses of virtuality and distributive leadership might strengthen Christian organizations.

5. Would serving as both a catalyst and consultant create points of tension or conflict in your current work environment?

Endnotes

[1] "The World's Largest Economies," Economic Statistics, http://www.economywatch.com/economies-in-top/, accessed September 29, 2010.

[2] Ibid.

[3] H. Bruinius, "Megacities of the World: A Glimpse of How We'll Live Tomorrow," http://www.csmonitor.com/layout/set/print/content/view/print 298332, accessed September 12, 2010.

[4] Ibid.

[5] E. German, "Dhaka: Fastest Growing Megacity in the World," http://www.globalpost.com/print/5582295, accessed September 12, 2010.

[6] Ibid.

[7] Bruinius, "Megacities of the World."

[8] D. Carroll, "United (Airlines) Breaks Guitars," July 7, 2009, http://blog.myspace.com/index.cfm?fuseaction=blog.view&friendId-306453459&blogID, accessed September 29, 2010.

[9] "Internet World Stats," http://www.internetworldstats.com/stats.htm, accessed September 29, 2010.

[10] C. Li, *Open Leadership: How Social Technology Can Transform the Way You Lead* (San Francisco: Jossey-Bass, 2010), 5.

[11] Ibid., 6.

[12] The Drucker Foundation, *The Leader of the Future*, ed. F. Hesselbein, M. Goldsmith, and R. Beckhard (San Francisco: Jossey-Bass, 1996), 7.

[13] Ibid.

[14] Ibid., 6.

[15] Ibid.

[16] Ibid., 14.

[17] A. Henley, "What Is Distributive Leadership?" http://www.hrvoice.org/story.aspx?storyid=1526&issueid=688&pagemode=displaystory&..., accessed September 28, 2010.

Chapter 18

LEADERSHIP TRANSITIONS
AND THE SEARCH PROCESS

Tommy Thomas
Partner, SIMA International

When considering leadership transitions in ministries, the following questions should be addressed.

- How will a change in leadership impact the ministry?
- What is the ministry's state of readiness for a change in leadership?
- What mistakes do boards make in selecting the new chief executive?
- Why should you beware of the dollar/year chief executive?
- Should you consider an internal candidate?
- How do you form and evaluate a pool of candidates?
- What if you make a mistake?

How Will a Change in Leadership Impact the Ministry?

In an ideal world the transition from one ministry CEO to the next would be seamless. The outgoing leader would give the board several months' notice of his anticipated departure. He would agree to stay with the ministry until his successor has been selected—a process that, on average, takes four to six months—and then would participate in a planned and orderly transition process.[1]

One of the smoothest transitions I have ever been a part of was when Steve Hayner notified the board of InterVarsity Christian Fellowship that he felt he had made his contribution to the ministry of InterVarsity and it was time for him to step down. He told the board that he would like to leave within a year but was open to staying as long as 15 months if necessary. The search for his successor was completed in 10 months, and Steve remained on the job for a couple of months to aid in the transition. As a result InterVarsity was able to have a smooth transition between chief executive officers.

Although most ministries are not ready for a transition in leadership, this ultimately happens in every ministry. A point comes in every chief executive's life when it is time to leave or retire. Ideally this is scheduled and the transition is orderly.

Many reasons influence a chief executive to retire or depart unexpectedly.

- People have unexpected family situations that require their undivided attention.
- The incumbent gets an offer from another organization. In some cases he or she will give the board ample notice of his or her anticipated departure, but in many cases the leader will give a standard notice (often 30 days) and immediately begin the new transition.
- Sometimes the incumbent isn't getting the job done, and the board chooses to let the person go.
- Tragically, sometimes the incumbent unexpectedly dies or incurs a debilitating disease while in office.

Regardless of the reason, a leadership transition leads to these questions:
- How ready is the ministry for this change in leadership?
- What level of thought and planning has gone into the inevitability that at some time in the tenure of any ministry leader, someone will need to take his place?
- How will a change in leadership impact the ministry?
- What will it do to the morale of the staff?
- How will it impact the donors and their confidence in the ministry?

What Is the Ministry's State of Readiness for a Change in Leadership?

Ministry boards should develop in advance a chief executive succession board policy that details what should happen when the time comes to search for a new chief executive officer. Once this policy is determined, it can be filed and implemented when needed.

By creating this document, the board can prevent hasty and perhaps premature actions or other rash decisions that often occur when unprepared for the inevitable—selecting a new chief executive officer.

Although this policy can be amended for unusual situations, boards should consider these key issues when creating their particular policy.

The Acting Chief Executive Officer

- If the CEO vacancy occurs immediately, as a surprise, who should be named acting CEO the next day?
- Should this person, usually a senior staff person, be paid the same as the CEO was paid?
- Assuming there are reasons to look for someone to serve for up to a year or two as interim, is it appropriate to make that decision now?

The Interim Chief Executive Officer

- If needed, how is the interim chief executive officer to be selected?
- How long should the leader be expected to serve?
- Will the interim chief executive officer be eligible as a candidate for the permanent position?
- How will the interim chief executive officer be compensated?

The Search and Selection Committee

- Will you have a search committee and a selection committee, or will one committee handle both functions?
- How many people will serve on the search committee?
- What groups of constituents (other than board members) should be represented on the search committee?
- Who will appoint the nonboard members?
- Who will chair the search committee?
- Will a search consultant be retained, and if so by whom?
- What is the best way to use the services of a search consultant?

- What is the board's charge to the search committee? To bring their top candidate, or the top two or three, rank ordered?
- What will be the budget for the search?

Staff Support for the Search

- Will someone on staff serve as a liaison to the search committee?
- If so, how much time should this person be expected to spend on search-related activities?
- How will the confidential issues and areas of the search be kept confidential?

Transition Issues of Concern to the Board

- What length of time, if any, should the outgoing chief executive officer overlap with the incoming chief executive officer, if that's even possible?
- If appropriate, will the outgoing chief executive officer receive emeritus status?
- Should you appoint a transition committee to oversee the transition from one CEO to the next?

Baselining the New Chief Executive Officer's Compensation Package

- What correlation should there be between the outgoing chief executive officer's compensation and the incoming chief executive officer's compensation?

Fair Treatment of the Outgoing Chief Executive Officer

- Should the outgoing chief executive officer remain on the board of directors or trustees? If not, what role or relationship should the former leader have with the board?
- What are the pros and cons of the board's retaining the outgoing chief executive officer for limited paid roles?
- Should you appoint a committee to handle the transition from one chief executive officer to the next?

Some of the above questions seem obvious. The others are certainly not rocket science, yet too many ministries find themselves unprepared when facing the many issues involved in changing leadership.

What Mistakes Do Boards Make in Selecting the New Chief Executive?

Beware of the Pendulum Swing

Tom was in many respects a good chief executive officer for the ministry. He certainly loved being able to promote the cause and speak at big conventions. He was always on the podium at key events where the organization wanted a presence. When you met him, he made you feel special. He made you feel important. He seemed to be interested in you. And his writing certainly helped keep the organization in the public eye. So in many respects he filled the bill as a great public persona for the organization.

The fact that he wasn't really interested in running the show was a problem. All sorts of ill will festered in the organization; all sorts of issues were constantly brewing. The board even had a delegation from the staff at one point asking for everyone to address the problem of morale in the organization. The board liked the public profile the organization got and put some of the internal discontent down as a nasty and subversive form of jealousy.

After a few years, Tom was recruited away by a larger and more prestigious organization. The board thought they would address the management issue squarely by going for a candidate with all the right management experience. They quickly decided that the best control would come from an accountant. From flair (and even flamboyance) they moved to safety and control.

The accountant lasted less than a year. New donations to the organization took a nosedive. The accountant was fair at conserving what was already there but dreadful at finding any new sources of income. He reinstituted great controls . . . but of diminishing resources and uninspired staff. The board's flip-flop approach didn't work!

Three of the major mistakes boards make during the selection of a new leader are:

1. Poor selection process
2. Not taking the time and applying the resources to get it right
3. Unarticulated and thus unmet expectations

Poor Selection Process

If you have served on many boards, you have probably observed a wide variety of poor selection-process habits. This list is not exhaustive, but some of the main poor selection processes are these.

- Rushing through the selection process. All too often the board rushes into the selection process. If the board doesn't have a chief executive succession board policy, the tendency is to panic. This is not the time to get in a hurry.
- Promoting the senior person with the longest time of service. Why? Because he has been loyal to the organization and there would be little disruption during the transition. Loyal to the ministry and disruption aside, the larger question centers around the overall leadership needs of the ministry at this time in its life cycle.
- Hiring a relative of one of the board members or a board member who volunteers to take over for little salary or hiring one of the large donors to the organization. Any of these individuals might make an excellent chief executive, and if that is the case, they will rise to the top of the pool during an orderly and thorough search process.

Not Taking the Time and Applying the Resources to Get It Right

Many mistakes in the hiring process happen because adequate time is not given to thinking through the kind of leader the organization needs at that moment in the organization's life cycle and being able to recognize the person who has what it takes to meet the ministry's needs.

- As a result of rushing through the selection process, search committees often do not take the time to assess thoroughly and adequately the needs of the organization.
- One of the biggest mistakes search committees often make comes toward the end of the search. People often want to rush through the interviews. Schedules get crowded, and they are tempted to rush through the interviews. This is not the time to get in a hurry. This is the time to take adequate time to get to know the candidates. This is the time to dig deep into the candidates' skills and experience, a time to check what their references have been saying against what the candidate says.

Unarticulated and Thus Unmet Expectations

Successful hiring is all about meeting expectations. Every board member has expectations of what success will look like for the next chief executive. All too often these expectations are not articulated up front. They are not spelled out to the search committee and thus the incoming chief executive may not be aware of all of the expectations.

Two main breakdowns occur in not articulating expectations. The first is not speaking up about how some aspect of the job should be done. Sometimes those expectations remain unspoken precisely because board members aren't even aware they hold them, or else they just don't think of them. The worst case, of course, is the job for which a board does not have a written, clear job description. That may seem incredible to imagine, but it's actually not uncommon. In fact, some decision makers take the view that "we'll hire the best available person, and he or she can mold the job to fit who they are." That's a recipe for disaster.

Another example is to imagine a board just assuming, but never articulating, its conviction that all royalties from books written by the CEO in connection with the ministry's primary purpose or cause will be shared with the ministry. Needless to say, that could lead to some nasty surprises later on.

Or another case is a board's assumption that it will be involved with the CEO in making all major hires. You'd like to think that both the board and a candidate for the CEO position would spell out something like that before the hire. But that's the point: such expectations aren't always clarified because no one thinks to articulate them. Yet those unspoken assumptions can give rise to some of the worst problems later on.

The other source of confused expectations comes from using generic language to describe the position and assuming that "we all understand what we mean." Even terms like *lead, manage, oversee, team player,* or *collaborate* can be misunderstood. Yet those are exactly the kinds of terms that almost always appear in CEO job descriptions.

The better course would be to have some lengthy dialogue as a board about what exactly you mean by a term like *lead*. For example:

- In our mind's eye, what exactly do we see the prospective CEO doing that would qualify in our mind as "leading"?
- What behaviors are associated with leading?
- What are some examples or scenarios that would indicate the CEO is leading in the manner we expect?

If a board can get beyond generic language to describe the role in terms of specific behaviors any observer can easily see, they will have a much better chance of finding and hiring a person who is gifted to the task of naturally exhibiting those behaviors—thereby fulfilling the expectations of the board.

Should You Beware of the Dollar/Year Chief Executive?

The baby boomer generation is one of the first to have had the luxury of considering leaving their jobs early in life in order to go to work for a nonprofit or charity. One of the biggest influencers toward this way of thinking has been the book *Halftime* by Bob Buford. In *Halftime*, a book about midlife career transitions, Buford focuses on the possibilities at this stage for revitalization, for catching new vision for living the second, most rewarding half of life. His premise is that the second half of life can be better than the first. Many executives and others who are at this point in their lives have taken Buford's challenge to heart. One of the results has been that more of these people are investigating a second career in the not-for-profit sector.

While a large group of people with incredible business and organizational skills fit this model, a word of caution is in order. Make sure that, if you bring one of these people into the organization, he is willing to work as hard as he will have to work to be an effective ministry leader. Often this is not the case.

I have had two significant experiences with dollar-a-year executives. One was good for the client. The other wasn't as successful.

First, the good news. We were conducting a CEO search for a large international organization. The pool of candidates had been strong, so strong that the search committee initially interviewed six candidates. They narrowed the pool to the top two candidates. One of these was an individual who had recently taken his company public and then sold to a competitor. As is the case in most of these situations, the man realized a significant profit from the sale.

The search committee asked me to talk with the individual about how serious he was about the position. My approach to him was direct. I remember asking him if he was up to the challenge of working as hard as he would have to work to lead this organization. I encouraged him to think back on how hard he had to work to take his company public. I asked him if he really wanted to work that hard or harder again. My final challenge to him was, "Wouldn't you rather sit on this organization's board and make a significant financial contribution to them each year than to be their CEO?" He responded that no one had ever been that direct with him about his future. He asked for a few days to think about it. After a week or so he came back and told me that if he was offered the position, he would accept it and work as hard for the organization as he had worked in the private sector. He was offered the job and gave good leadership to the ministry for six years.

Another situation didn't turn out as well as this one. The executive had been fortunate enough to make a small fortune in the IPO of the brokerage house where he worked. He retired from the brokerage house at age 47 and decided that he wanted to work for a ministry. Through a series of events, I introduced him to the CEO of one of my client organizations. After meeting with the CEO, he moved his family and began working for a dollar per year. About 18 months into the job, he realized he had retired from a demanding job that paid him well only to be working 70-plus hours a week for a dollar per year.

Money wasn't the issue but rather the fact that one of the reasons he had retired was to spend more time with his wife and kids. He was putting in as many and often more hours with the ministry than he had been at the brokerage house. In the end he decided that it was in the best interest of the ministry and his family for him to remain on the board but leave his job and be intentional about spending more time at home.

Certainly his intentions in accepting the job with the nonprofit were good. The organization needed someone with his experience. The glitch was that, in the grand scheme of things, he wasn't willing or able to work the demanding hours that most ministry leadership positions require.

Since then in several instances, I have had strong interest in a particular chief executive officer position from people who have enjoyed successful and financially rewarding careers in the private sector and are considering a second career as a ministry chief executive officer. If I believe someone like this is a serious contender for a given position, I have frank discussions about the realities of moving into this role. These discussions usually center on the following issues:

- Given what the particular ministry needs at this time in its life cycle, do you think you have what it will take to move them forward?

- Have you taken the time to look at their particular needs and evaluate them against the skills and natural talent that made you so successful with your previous company?
- Are you sure you want to work as hard in this position as you worked to make your last company as successful as it was?

This is in no way trying to dissuade the person from the job, but I do believe I am doing both the person and my client a big favor by helping the candidate deal with this matter. You would be surprised at the number of people who thank me for asking them that question. During these discussions I usually learn that the person is involved with a small number of his or her favorite ministries. This involvement is usually financial as well as advisory. Many people in this group really enjoy this advisory role and would not like to relinquish it if they took on a 50- to 60-hour-per-week, full-time leadership position with another ministry.

Understand that I have no bias against businessmen or women having a second career in not-for-profit leadership. Quite the contrary! However, the point I make with them is to look seriously at their life and make sure they really want to sign up for another tour of duty where the hours are as long and the work is as hard as it can be in ministry leadership.

Should You Consider an Internal Candidate?

Often current employees or board members of the ministry will surface as internal candidates for the available chief executive officer position. One school of thought says, "All other things being equal, the internal candidate is the best choice." The reasoning is that you have a better idea of the internal candidate's weaknesses, so you can plan for them. With the outside candidate, you probably aren't as confident that you know his weaknesses. In the words of F. Mueller-Maerki, a partner with Egon Zehnder International, "A known risk is a smaller risk than an unknown one because it is manageable."

Some Realities about Internal Candidates

Many people inside the ministry will have seen the internal candidate in a number of situations over a period of years. These circumstances will vary—formal, informal, making presentations, dealing with critics, gaining consensus, and so on. This can make the consideration and evaluation of the internal candidate *seem* easier to members of the search committee.

If the ministry has a fairly traditional culture, it will most likely be difficult not to choose the internal candidate. Unless the other candidates are unbelievably strong or bring something to the ministry for which there is currently a severe deficiency, a vote for an outside candidate is rare, even if the call is for change and new ideas.

If the internal candidate has been doing a good job in his current position and, for the most part, is well liked and respected, many people will have a difficult time selecting someone from the outside over this person, as they will feel that hiring the outside candidate is a vote against the internal one. And some people may go so far as to think that since the internal candidate has been loyal to the ministry and has been doing a good job in his present position, he has earned the right to be the next chief executive officer of the ministry. Occasionally resistance will arise from significant donors and other stakeholders. These people might have strong ties to the internal candidates, or they may think that the ministry's time and money (if you have retained a search firm) are being wasted by even considering external candidates.

Fast Track to the Short List

In some searches the board will say that they would like certain people automatically to make the short list. In this case the members of the search committee must listen carefully and even "read between the lines" of what is really being said.

What the board may be saying is that at this time the internal candidate will be hired unless they can be convinced otherwise. If this is the case, it becomes the task of the search committee to come up with candidates whose credentials, experience, etc., make them as good or better choices than the internal candidate.

The board could be saying that it would be political suicide not to have the internal candidates on the short list. There may be a real or perceived danger of losing these people as employees if they are not elevated to the top position or at least given serious consideration. Another message they may be sending is that certain key financial contributors to the ministry want the internal candidates on the short list. This can be a sticky area and needs to be handled with care.

A way to give the search process credibility is to put internal candidates into the sourcing funnel and through the same rigor as external candidates. If, over time, they compete with others, end up on the short list, and one is then selected as the new leader, his or her leadership will be much more legitimate.

The Internal Candidate and the Interview Process

There are at least two different types of internal candidates:

- Employees of the ministry (such as the executive vice president or other senior leaders)
- Board members of the ministry

In most cases the internal candidate has an advantage in the interview process. Search committee members probably know the person or are at least somewhat familiar with her work. She has made a significant impact or contribution to the ministry, or she would not be on the short list in the first place.

Also, because the internal candidate is obviously more familiar with the ministry, she will be better prepared for the interview, and the illustrations and stories she tells during the interview will appear to be more relevant. In this situation committee members may have a tendency to elevate the candidate because she is perceived to know more about the ministry. The truth is, she does know more about the ministry; she works there every day!

To give credibility to the process, the search committee must work hard initially to evaluate the internal candidates against the standard of what a person must possess to excel in the position. Only after that evaluation and assessment has been made should the candidates be evaluated against one another.

Is the External Candidate Being Used as Fodder?

Searches that include internal candidates almost always inspire the outside candidates to ask at some point during the sourcing process, "Am I cannon fodder in this search?" Organizations must be careful not to get the reputation of using external candidates merely to validate the internal candidate. If this happens too often, the observing public will get wise to this, and over time it will become increasingly more difficult for the ministry to attract good talent from the outside. Potential candidates will check out the ministry as diligently as the search committee members are probing the backgrounds of the candidates. They will talk to their contacts that have knowledge of the ministry; and the reputation, good or bad, of how the ministry has handled searches in the past, will spread. Every effort should be made to ensure that the search is conducted in a manner that is above reproach.

How Will Internal Candidates Impact the Quality of the Pool?

Having internal candidates can definitely impact the quality of the pool.

- How strong is the internal candidate?
- How well is this person known outside the ministry?

If the ministry has a strong internal candidate and this person has a good reputation outside the ministry, attracting other strong external candidates could be difficult. More often than not, if people perceive the ministry has a strong internal candidate, many outside candidates feel that the internal candidate is going to get the job and that the search is just window dressing by the board to give the impression that they are conducting a national search. It is often difficult to convince them otherwise.

Promoting from within can be a good decision as long as that person rises to the top of the pool on a level playing field. However, if the ministry has a strong internal candidate and this is known to external candidates, the pool of external candidates is not likely to be as strong as it might have otherwise been.

How Do You Form and Evaluate a Pool of Candidates?

Before anyone makes it to the final pool or short list for the leadership of a ministry, someone has to ask the tough question:

Are There Any Skeletons in the Candidate's Closet?

A more delicate way to ask this question is, "Is there anything in your background that would bring embarrassment to the ministry if it were known?" This is the best time to get these kinds of things out in the open, and this is the time to let the candidates know that you are going to conduct a thorough screening.

If a candidate knows you are going to be talking to a number of people from a cross-section of his career history, he is more likely to come clean on things you should know. Part of the purpose in doing this is to let the candidate know just how comprehensive your screening process will be and that, if and when he makes the short list, you will know more about him than almost anyone else does.

If the candidate would rather not reveal some past items from his or her background, it is best to eliminate that person from consideration early in the process. If something potentially negative is revealed, however, it should not necessarily disqualify a candidate, depending on the situation; it is just best that everything be known up front. The last thing the search committee wants is this type of surprise.

When you are convinced that you have settled on the small group or pool of candidates you wish to interview, you need to be methodical and thorough when you evaluate what you know about each candidate. As I have stated before, this is not the time to get in a hurry. Take your time and do it right.

Beware of the "Smile Factor"

For the most part the people who make the short list will have a good interview. Chances are they will be rather persuasive. This is to be expected because the strong candidates would not have gotten this far in their careers without having reasonably strong influencing and persuading skills.

Much has been written about the importance of making a good impression. We tend to equate coming across as a bright, articulate, sensitive, likable, aggressive, energetic, participative communicator with "a good interview." Committee members may feel that "wow, this person would make a great chief executive for our ministry." Here is where you need to stop and check yourself. Competency to do a job and the ability to sell oneself are not the same thing.

Unfortunately, when it comes to making hiring decisions, the individuals doing the interviewing and hiring frequently fail to make this distinction. The result? The two are often confused. The person with more polish than substance is often hired, and the selection process fails to find the best person for the job. Many candidate evaluations are contaminated by the "smile factor," and people who make good impressions but who are neither leaders nor managers are selected.

Evaluating the Data

When evaluating candidates, search committee members should look for consistency in the patterns or trends in the data they are collecting on each candidate. The primary areas of consideration are:

- Professional and technical skills
- Style
- Consistency in references

Résumé and Application Package

Require all of the applicants to submit an application package. This includes their résumé, a list of references, and their written responses to a set of essay questions designed to provide information about the candidate far beyond what you are likely to learn from the candidate's résumé. You might be surprised what you can learn about candidates by thoroughly reviewing their application packages.

From the résumé and application package you want to determine the extent of each candidate's experience as it relates to the background the ideal candidate should have. These questions might prove helpful in determining this.

- Has the candidate paid his dues? Has he risen through the ranks and had enough varied experience to learn the profession?
- Does she have the skills and experience necessary to do the job?
- Does he know his stuff? Is his experience superficial, or does he really know the field?

Interview Data

Obviously you will be interested in how the candidate performs in the interview. These questions will help you formulate a more solid opinion:

- What kind of impression did she make?
- Did his interview performance line up with his application package?
- Did she come across as competent?
- What did you learn from the interview about his oral communication skills?

Style

Another area to evaluate is how the person puts his or her technical/ functional experience to use; in a word, what is his style. Skills, experience, and technical competency are fairly easy to observe and evaluate. And people rarely fail in a job because of inadequate skills or a lack of technical or functional competency. The individual's style is far more difficult to determine. As mentioned earlier, good hiring is all about expectations. Failure in job fit is almost always a result of one's style—not doing the job in a manner that pleases the board.

Here are some important questions that need to be addressed.

- Is the ministry accustomed to a style of leadership that involves many people giving input before the CEO makes a decision? Or is the ministry used to a more autocratic style in which the chief executive officer makes all the decisions with little or no input and then expects those decisions to be implemented without question?
- Is the ministry in need of radical change, and how widely accepted is this proposition? Any time I have a client who selects a candidate that I know is a real change agent, I always ask, "Are you sure you are ready for this level of change?"
- What is the board's preferred manner of interacting with the chief executive? If the board is used to providing a high degree of guidance and direction to the previous chief executive officer but ends up selecting a "lone wolf" who operates independently, this can present significant challenges. On the other hand, hiring a person who expects and depends on that level of direction from the board in an organization used to having its chief executive officer operate with a high degree of autonomy can also present great difficulty.
- Does the culture of the organization match the executive's approach to decision making and interaction? For example, some executives prefer a clearly hierarchical culture where all levels of employees and managers recognize the importance of "going through channels" for every discussion and/or decision. Other executives will insist on a more participative culture that encourages all employees to resolve matters in the most efficient way possible, and every manager has an open door for easy access.
- How important are off-the-job social relationships between board members and the chief executive? If your board is highly relational and tends to seek nonwork relationships involving sports or social activities, explore your candidate's avocational interests and club memberships to check out this important aspect of executive style. If the board expects the executive to initiate and develop nonwork relationships, then this is a selection criterion not to be overlooked.
- Is the board noted for its political acumen and strategy? Then you will want to make sure the chosen candidate has demonstrated these motivations in previous positions. Candidates who are

primarily focused on goal and/or purpose outcomes can view political savvy as scheming machination if it is not an important aspect of his or her operational style.

Depending on what the board wants in these areas, a particular individual's style may or may not be a good fit for the ministry's top position. Thus, when interviewing finalist candidates, be sure to ask specific questions that will reveal the details of the candidate's action so that you can assess the evidence for the presence or absence of the appropriate style consideration.

Consistency of References

Consider the level of consistency of information you get from checking a candidate's references. What you hope to see here is a trend or pattern of generally similar data.

You can do two things to help in this area:

1. Check several references. The best reference data comes from checking several references. Let candidates know that if they make the short list, you will be checking several references. The candidates need to know that you will be going far beyond the references they provide.
2. Have search committee members check references. You get better data on reference checking if the members of the search committee check the majority of the references. This seems to work best when the person checking the reference is a vocational peer with the person giving the reference. For example:

    *   If the candidate lists a trustee or board member of his current employer as a reference, I ask one of the trustees or board members of the search committee to check this reference.
    *   If the vice president of advancement is on the search committee, have him/her speak with the vice president of advancement/development at previous places where the candidate worked.
    *   If the chief financial officer is on the search committee, have him/her call the chief financial officer in places of the candidate's current or previous employment.
    *   If the search is for a president of a Christian college or headmaster of a Christian school and the candidate lists a faculty

member at his current school as a reference, ask a faculty member on the search committee to check this reference.

Peer reference checking tends to uncover a lot more information than someone who is one step removed from the ministry can get.

Personal Chemistry

In addition to the candidate's technical abilities, you want to ensure that he will work well with the board and others in the organization. The following questions address issues of chemistry:

- Did you like the person?
- As a board member, would you be comfortable serving the organization during this person's time of leadership?
- How well do you think the candidate would relate with your donor base?
- What did you learn about his interpersonal relationship skills?
- How does the chairman of the board feel about the chemistry? After all, she will be the one spending the most time with your new CEO.

What Is the Recommended Process for Making the Decision?

As the search committee closes in on making their decision, you should be looking for positive alignment or congruence between all they have learned about the candidate from his résumé and application package, interview data, and reference data. When this happens, the search committee can have more confidence in their decision. Once you think you have found congruence between skills, style, and substance, it's time to take a vote! Here are several ways you can go about that.

Secret Ballot

Each search committee will vary on how to vote. Many committees believe it is best to vote by secret ballot. The primary reason is that this gives each person on the search committee the opportunity to vote his or her conscience without the possibility of being intimidated by another member. You would like to think, after working together for many months on this important decision, that the committee would be past this possibility. However, some people still might feel intimidated, and the secret ballot will expedite the decision-making process.

Eliminate Candidates First

When dealing with a large number of candidates (five or six), in the early stages of voting, most search committees find it easier to eliminate candidates than to make strong statements for candidates. Under this scenario ask members of the search committee to list the names of two candidates they want to eliminate or not move forward. The votes are counted, and often it will be obvious which two people drop off. If there isn't consensus about which candidates do not move forward, this provides the opening for discussion either in favor of or against certain people. After a few iterations a decision can usually be reached.

Straw Ballot to See if the Committee Has a Clear Choice

If the number of candidates is small and the chairperson feels you have a clear leader, encourage the committee to take a straw (nonbinding) ballot to see if the choice is clear.

How Long Does It Take?

Sometimes committees vote unanimously on the first round of ballots, and occasionally the committee works for several hours as they debate and discuss the merits of each candidate until they reach a decision. This is not the time to hurry. Let the process work.

What If You Make a Mistake?

Usually the days surrounding the hiring of the new chief executive officer are a happy time. A well-written, bubbly press release marks the beginning of a new chapter in the life of the organization. The great majority of the stakeholders are willing to give the new leader time to make his mark on the organization. Only when the "new" chief executive officer is fired or resigns under a cloud of suspicion do donors and other stakeholders get up in arms.

P. R. Lochner Jr., in his article "Hiring, Firing, and CEO Succession Planning: The Board's Toughest Assignment," correctly sums up this situation:

> Hiring the right person for any task is an enormously difficult proposition. It is difficult to hire clerks and assembly line workers, much less CEOs. The important difference between hiring a clerk and hiring a CEO isn't that one job is easier to do than the other and that one is paid more than the other. It is that the cost of

making the wrong decision is so much higher in one case than in the other.[2]

Lochner makes a good point. The cost of making a mistake at the executive level is high. This increases the criticality of the way you handle a mistake at this level.

In the rare occasion when the results of the search do not bring the desired results, the best thing for the board to do is to admit the mistake, cut its losses, and move to find a new chief executive officer. One of the main issues the board must consider at a time like this is the organization's reputation. The way a mistake at this level is handled can have a big and possibly negative impact. The board needs to come together and reach a strategic consensus on how it will handle the resignation of the chief executive officer and how to communicate this to the ministry's internal and external publics.

As painful as this unexpected change of leadership may be, the key point to remember is that the organization is larger than the office or title of chief executive officer. Making a mistake in this area is not the end of the world. The ministry will move past this and continue its mission.

At this point the board will have to decide how to move forward. If the search process was long and draining, the members of the search committee may be emotionally and physically exhausted and not up to the challenge of conducting another search. In this case a new search committee will have to be formed. The board may reason that the previous search committee did not do a good job with the previous hire, so why should they be given the responsibility for a second time, and thus they appoint a new search committee.

This is not the time to take sides and argue over what happened. It is the time for patience, wisdom, and discernment to prevail. Be patient and keep moving forward. The responsibility to hire and support (and fire if necessary) is the most important decision the board of any organization has to make. Hopefully, the guidelines in this chapter will provide guidance in that process. Moreover, the contributions in this volume will provide an informative resource for both the board and the candidates in the important search process.

Resources for Further Study

Board Source. *The Nonprofit Board Answer Book.* San Francisco: Jossey-Bass, 2007.

Laughlin, Frederic L., and Robert C. Andringa. *Good Governance for Nonprofits.* New York: Amazon, 2007.

Thomas, Tommy. *The Perfect Search: What Every Nonprofit Board Member Needs to Know About Hiring Their Next CEO.* Grand Rapids: Credo, 2008.

Questions for Further Reflection

1. How transparent should the CEO be regarding his/her eminent departure from the organization/institution?

2. How can the type of leader required be appropriately identified across all constituencies of the institution? What are the essential qualities and skills the next CEO must possess?

3. What safeguards should be put in place to protect the search committee from the "smile factor"?

4. How does an organization determine that it made a mistake in hiring the current CEO? What processes should be in place to evaluate if and when a transition should take place?

Endnotes

[1] See *HR Magazine* 39:9 (September 1994): 54–55.

[2] P. R. Lochner Jr., "Hiring, Firing, and CEO Succession: The Board's Toughest Assignment," *Directorship* 25:11 (December 1999): 4–5.

Some Closing Thoughts

David S. Dockery
President, Union University

L eadership has numerous responsibilities and challenges, many of which have been spelled out in this volume. It is unlikely that any one person has the ability or giftedness to carry out all these things in a quality manner. Yet, in order to lead a Christian organization well for any period of length, certain commonalities and expectations are grounded in Holy Scripture. Many topics addressed in the previous chapters are applicable for leaders in non-Christian contexts. We are thankful that this is the case and trust that the book will find wide application in all kinds of organizational contexts. Yet, by design and purpose, the book is primarily intended to provide guidance for Christian organizations. The title of the book in this regard, reveals this purpose: *Christian Leadership Essentials: A Handbook for Managing Christian Organizations.* Thus, these concluding words focus on two distinctive aspects of Christian leadership essentials, which can be categorized as character and confession, conduct and creed, or behavior and belief. To these matters we turn as we conclude this volume.

In Paul's letter to Titus, we find guidelines that can help us think carefully about the kind of leaders needed to lead Christian organizations and institutions. The main responsibility of these leaders is to care for God's people. Leadership, as has been pointed out elsewhere in this volume, includes demonstration of public leadership as well as leadership by personal example. Both assume basic convictional commitments as well as character qualities.

Blameless in Character

Leaders are entrusted with God's work (Titus 1:7). Leaders are selected based on character qualities, matters that are to be taken seriously (Titus 1:5–9). The numerous qualities found in this text can be summarized by the words "blameless" or "above reproach" (Titus 1:6–7). Commentators have noted this descriptive term does not mean without blemish but without blame. Leaders are to be people of integrity and irreproachable character. They are to be marred by no public disgrace; they should have no loophole for criticism.[1]

Leaders of Christian organizations are not required to be perfect, for that would eliminate everyone other than our Lord Jesus Christ. It is a call for faithfulness in character, conduct, and relational commitments, particularly the family and home. One could say that before accepting a wider sphere of influence, leaders must demonstrate faithfulness in smaller spheres of responsibility (Titus 1:6). Such teaching seems consistent with the overall biblical principle that faithfulness in smaller spheres of responsibility helps prepare us for opportunities of greater significance.[2]

In Titus 1:6–8, the apostle intermingled 11 Greek words to emphasize that leaders are to lead disciplined lives, characterized by the fruit of the Spirit (Gal 5:22–23).[3] This kind of lifestyle comes only by the enablement of the Holy Spirit, which means that leaders must evidence the fruit of regeneration, filled with and controlled by God's Spirit.

Leaders are particularly tempted by pride and ambition. They must demonstrate that their fallen passions are under control. Leaders of twenty-first-century Christian organizations must be characterized by self-control and humility in all areas. J. Stott has insightfully observed that leaders must be able to lead families and manage themselves before exercising leadership in broader contexts.[4]

Leaders often bring opportunities and privileges to exert influence. Biblical models of leadership urge against using these opportunities for one's own benefit. In doing so, leaders are tempted toward autocratic models of leadership, which may produce short-term effectiveness but rarely long-term health for communities of faith.

Leaders are called to humility, honesty, and integrity. We need a new commitment to treat others with respect, even those with whom we differ.

A thoroughly biblical anthropology recognizes the importance of treating brothers and sisters, created in the image of God, with much dignity, respect, and care.

Biblical leaders will be motivated by opportunities to serve. In Titus 1, the apostle Paul describes such motivation under the categories of "hospitable" and "loving what is good." Likewise leaders are to be blameless in character and disciplined in conduct.

Convictional Confessionalism

Convictional leaders, who are formed by the Word of God and whose convictions are influenced by the great Christian intellectual tradition, are needed in twenty-first-century Christian organizations. We learn from Titus 1 that leaders are to build their lives and their ministries on the "trustworthy message" of Holy Scripture (Titus 1:2,9). Leaders have the privilege and responsibility to invest themselves in others in a manner that follows Paul's pattern with Titus and Timothy (2 Tim 2:2). What Timothy and Titus had heard from Paul, they were to pass along to faithful leaders who could teach others also.

Christian leaders have been entrusted with the Christian faith, the body of truth "once for all delivered to the saints" (Titus 1:3; Jude 3). The Christian faith is not just faith in faith—some subjective, amorphous feeling—but is, in an objective sense, a body of truth. In the Pastoral Epistles, it is called the teaching, the deposit, the faith, and the truth; and this truth is now available to us in the New Testament.[5]

Certainly the Bible maintains that faith is the means by which we receive and appropriate the salvation purchased for us by the work of our Lord Jesus Christ on the cross (Gal 2:1–6; Eph 2:8–9). Faith includes a full commitment of the whole person to the Lord Jesus, a commitment that involves knowledge, trust, and obedience. Faith is not merely an intellectual assent or an emotional response but a complete, inward spiritual change confirmed to us by the Holy Spirit. Though faith is more than doctrinal assent, it must include adherence to doctrine.[6]

Leaders need a convictional faith. This book has described the many roles and responsibilities of leadership; leaders cannot neglect the high calling to pass along the apostolic teaching in a faithful manner for the next generation. Communication of the truth made known in the New Testament is to be prized and prioritized.

Some may suggest as we reach a conclusion in this book that to prioritize convictional and confessional commitments are the backbone of Christian organizations. Without healthy theological commitments, our organizations and institutions will be tossed back and forth by waves and blown here and there by every wind of teaching (Eph 4:14).

A healthy understanding of our biblical and confessional heritage can help mature both heart and head, enabling believing communities to move forward toward spiritual depth resulting in the praise and exaltation of God. We must acknowledge that some unduly complicate the Christian faith and distract us from aspects of faithful living. We should not, however, conclude that such confessional commitments are in themselves divisive or distracting. Rightly understood, our theological commitments strengthen the foundation of our service. Moreover, these foundational commitments can lead us to an awareness of the grandeur and greatness and goodness of the one, true, and wise God whom we worship.

The renewal of these commitments can also enable organizations or institutions to recover a true understanding of life and the greatness of the soul. We can recover the sense that God is more important than we are, that the future life is more important than this one, and that a right view of God gives significance and security to our lives; and leaders often need these reminders. With this right focus we will understand that happiness is the promise of heaven and holiness is our high calling in this world. Recognizing these things, leaders are responsible for shaping their work on the whole counsel of God (Acts 20:7). Without the foundation of solid biblical and confessional convictions, our organizations will have no long-term faithful Christian leadership and no effective collaborative efforts.

A shared commitment to our confessional heritage can help keep us from confusing what is merely a contemporary expression or challenge with what is enduringly relevant. This heritage will help us gain valuable insights for our ongoing leadership journey, lessons and warnings that are both positive and negative. Knowledge of continuities and discontinuities in our past will enable us to focus on primary theological commitments, those areas of truth that are truly timeless and enduring. Simultaneously, we believe that such historical and theological awareness will encourage genuine humility before God and in our relationships with one another, resulting in a greater dependence on God's Spirit and a hunger for authentic community in our work and service.

While acknowledging denominational distinctives and diversity representatives among us, which means some will want to say more than what follows, we all agree that what is needed is a steadfast belief in a triune God: in one mediator between God and humanity, the man Christ Jesus who came to this earth as God incarnate; it represents a belief in a fully authoritative Bible, and the message of salvation by grace through faith made known therein. Such commitments will inform, form, and strengthen the life of our communities and our growth in Christ.

Conclusion

Our vision for confessional and convictional leadership must be grounded in the gospel that is not enslaved to rationalism or denatured by an alien individualism, experientialism, or postmodernism. The pressures from a rapidly changing culture will only continue to create significant challenges in our efforts to create healthy and faithful Christian communities.

Our various organizations and institutions often reflect considerable diversity. While we are not calling for doctrinal uniformity as a goal, we do call for renewed commitments to the great Christian intellectual tradition. Our communities must take seriously the biblical exhortations and invitations to unity (John 17; Eph 4:1–6), expressed side by side with a clarion call to biblical truth. This unity in truth and truth in unity will be possible as we demonstrate humility, gentleness, patience, and forbearance with one another in love. It will require a diligence to preserve the unity of the Spirit in the bond of peace (Eph 4:2–3).

Leaders need a spirit of mutual respect and humility to serve together with those with whom we have differences of conviction and opinion. It is possible to hold hands and serve together with brothers and sisters who disagree on secondary and tertiary matters of theology and work together toward a common good to extend our shared work around the world and advance the kingdom of God. We can relate to one another in love and humility, bringing about true fellowship and community not only in orthodoxy but orthopraxy before a watching world. Let us pray that God will raise up a new generation of faithful, convictional, and compassionate leaders who are prepared for the ever-changing and ever-expanding challenges of the twenty-first century. Our hope is that the chapters of this book provide helpful guidance for many others for years to come.

Resources for Further Study

Blackaby, Henry. *Spiritual Leadership*. Nashville: B&H, 2007.

Charan, Ram. *Leaders at All Levels*. San Francisco: Jossey-Bass, 2008.

Collins, Jim. *How the Mighty Fall*. New York: HarperCollins, 2009.

_____. *Good to Great*. New York: Harper, 2001.

Collins, Jim, and Jerry Porras. *Built to Last*. New York: Harper, 1994.

Drucker, Peter. *Managing the Nonprofit Organization*. New York: Harper Collins, 1990.

_____. *The Effective Executive*. New York: Harper, 1966.

Finzel, Hans. *The Top Ten Mistakes Leaders Make*. Wheaton: Victor, 1994.

Havard, Alexandre. *Virtuous Leadership*. New York: Scepter, 2007.

Hendricks, Howard, and William Hendricks. *As Iron Sharpens Iron*. Chicago: Moody, 1995.

Iorg, Jeff. *The Painful Side of Leadership*. Nashville: B&H, 2009.

Johnson, Dwight, comp. *The Transparent Leader*. Eugene, OR: Harvest House, 2001.

Kraft, Dave. *Leaders Who Last*. Wheaton: Crossway, 2010.

Larson, Robert C. *The Best of Ted Engstrom on Personal Excellence and Leadership*. San Bernardino, CA: Here's Life, 1988.

Long, Jimmy. *The Leadership Jump*. Downers Grove: InterVarsity, 2009.

McKenna, David. *Leader's Legacy*. Newberg, OR: Barclay, 2006.

Myra, Harold, and Marshall Shelley. *The Leadership Secrets of Billy Graham*. Grand Rapids: Zondervan, 2005.

Olford, David. *Find Us Faithful*. Nashville: B&H, 2009.

Roberts, Randal. *Lessons in Leadership*. Grand Rapids: Kregel, 1999.

Rothschild, William. *Risktaker, Caretaker, Surgeon, Undertaker: The Four Faces of Strategic Leadership*. Hoboken, NJ: John Wiley, 1993.

Smith, Fred. *Leading with Integrity*. Minneapolis: Bethany, 1999.

Stott, John. *Basic Christian Leadership*. Downers Grove: InterVarsity, 2002.

_____. *Guard the Truth: The Message of 1 Timothy and Titus*. Downers Grove: InterVarsity, 1996.

Thrall, Bill, Bruce McNicol, and Ken McElrath. *The Ascent of a Leader*. San Francisco: Jossey-Bass, 1999.

Questions for Further Reflection

1. How can biblical character be measured so as to ensure that the leader is spiritually and emotionally capable of leadership in the institution?

2. How does embracing a confessional heritage enable a leader to engage in their duties of leadership?

Endnotes

[1] See R. Van Neste, "The Message of Titus: An Overview," *The Southern Baptist Journal of Theology* 7:3 (Fall 2003): 18–30; N. N. D. Kelly, *The Pastoral Epistles* (Peabody, MA: Hendrickson, 1993), 231; D. Guthrie, *Pastoral Epistles*, 2nd ed. (Grand Rapids: Eerdmans, 1990), 195; J. R. W. Stott, *Guard the Truth: The Message of 1 Timothy and Titus* (Downers Grove: InterVarsity, 1996), 173–79; and G. W. Knight, *The Pastoral Epistles* (Grand Rapids: Eerdmans, 1992).

[2] See D. S. Dockery, *Southern Baptist Consensus and Renewal* (Nashville: B&H, 2008), 201–18.

[3] See Stott, *Guard the Truth*; also D. S. Dockery, "Fruit of the Spirit," in *Dictionary of Paul and His Letters*, ed. G. Hawthorne, R. P. Martin, and D. G. Reid (Downers Grove: InterVarsity, 1993), 316–19.

[4] Stott, *Guard the Truth*; see also T. D. Lea and H. P. Griffin, *1, 2 Timothy, Titus* (Nashville: B&H, 1992).

[5] See D. S. Dockery, *Renewing Minds* (Nashville: B&H, 2008), 52–70; I. H. Marshall and P. H. Towner, *The Pastoral Epistles* (Edinburgh: T&T Clark, 2004); L. T. Johnson, *The First and Second Letters to Timothy* (New York: Anchor, 2001); T. Oden, *First and Second Timothy and Titus* (Louisville: Westminster/John Knox, 1989).

[6] See T. George, "The Pattern of Christian Truth," *First Things* 154 (2005): 21–25.

Name Index

Scripture Index